A Mirror of the Jewish Religion: A Critical Edition and Translation of Christian Petter Löwe's *Speculum Religionis Judaicæ* (1732)

Religious Minorities in the North: History, Politics, and Culture

Edited by
Jonathan Adams
Cordelia Heß
Christhard Hoffmann

Volume 6

A Mirror of the Jewish Religion: A Critical Edition and Translation of Christian Petter Löwe's *Speculum Religionis Judaicæ* (1732)

Edited by
Jonathan Adams

DE GRUYTER

The publication of this book has been funded by Vetenskapsrådet / The Swedish Research Council (project no. 2019-03669: Antisemitismens arkiv i Skandinavien: Kunskapsproduktion och stereotyper i ett långt historiskt perspektiv).

ISBN 978-3-11-099841-2
e-ISBN (PDF) 978-3-11-098693-8
ISSN 2627-440X
DOI https://doi.org/10.1515/9783110986938

Library of Congress Control Number: 2023950721

Bibliographic information published by the Deutsche Nationalbibliothek
The Deutsche Nationalbibliothek lists this publication in the Deutsche Nationalbibliografie; detailed bibliographic data are available on the internet at http://dnb.dnb.de.

Cover image: The kapparot atonement ritual from Friedrich Albrecht Christiani, D*er Jüden Glaube aber Aberglaube* (Leipzig, 1713), 102. The same ritual is described by Christian Petter Löwe in his *Speculum Religionis Judaicæ*, chapter 21. Photo: Jonathan Adams.
Printing and binding: CPI books GmbH, Leck

www.degruyter.com

*Dla Ewy. Dziękuję za wszystkie lata przyjaźni,
towarzystwa, pomocy i miłości. Dzięki, że jesteś.*

Acknowledgements

This book springs from my long-standing research interest in Christian ethnographical writings about Jews and Jewish customs and is one of the results of the project "The Archives of Antisemitism in Scandinavia: Knowledge Production and Stereotyping in a Long-Term Historical Perspective," generously funded by the Swedish Research Council (Vetenskapsrådet) at the University of Gothenburg (2016–19).

Various people have contributed ideas and information. In particular, I would like to thank Yaacov Deutsch of the David Yellin College of Education (המכללה האקדמית לחינוך ע״ש דוד ילין) in Jerusalem, Maria Diemling of Canterbury Christ Church University, Stefan Gąsiorowski of the Jagiellonian University (Uniwersytet Jagielloński) in Kraków, Cordelia Heß of the University of Greifswald (Universität Greifswald), and Peter Zeeberg of the Danish Society for Language and Literature (Det Danske Sprog- og Litteraturselskab) in Copenhagen. My sincere thanks also go to the three anonymous peer-reviewers who read the book manuscript so carefully and provided positive feedback with insightful comments and necessary corrections. Any remaining errors are, of course, my own.

I am grateful to the Department of Historical Studies at the University of Gothenburg for their assistance and financial support that enabled me to write and publish this book. Finally, my thanks go to the wonderful staff at De Gruyter who helped in the production and publication of this book, especially to Eva Locher, Dominika Herbst, Laura Burlon, Robert Forke, Florian Ruppenstein, and Jakob Brassel.

Copenhagen, September 2023

https://doi.org/10.1515/9783110986938-201

Acknowledgements

Contents

Edition

Appendices

Abbreviations

Arab.	Arabic
Aram.	Aramaic
Fr.	French
Ger.	German
Gk.	Greek
Heb.	Hebrew
Lat.	Latin
lit.	literally, literal translation
OSw.	Old Swedish
Spec. (Sthlm, 1732)	Christian Petter Löwe, *Speculum Religionis Judaicae* (Stockholm: Johan Laurentius Horrn, 1732)
Spec. (Gbg, 1732)	Christian Petter Löwe, *Speculum Religionis Judaicae* (Gothenburg: Lars Unge, 1732)
Spec. (Sthlm, 1735)	Christian Petter Löwe, *Speculum Religionis Judaicae* (Stockholm: Frantz Philip Paulssen, 1732)
Swed.	Swedish
WA	Weimarer Ausgabe – Weimar edition of Martin Luther's works: *D. Martin Luthers Werke*, 120 vols (Weimar, 1883–2009)
Yidd.	Yiddish

https://doi.org/10.1515/9783110986938-202

Illustrations

https://doi.org/10.1515/9783110986938-203

Introduction

In 1732, a most unusual book was published in Swedish: *Speculum Religionis Judaicæ*, “A Mirror of the Jewish Religion.” This short volume, written by the converted Jew Christian Petter Löwe, describes the religious ceremonies and traditions of Jews from cradle to grave and is the first such publication in Swedish. It covers both life-cycle events, such as circumcisions, bnei mitzvah, weddings, and funerals, and holidays of the religious calendar, such as Passover, Rosh Hashanah, Yom Kippur, and Sukkot. Many of the accounts of ceremonies are rather detailed and include biblical and rabbinical references and quotations as well as descriptions of clothing, food, and drink. This is the first time such a depiction of Jewish life became available in Swedish. Yet within a broader European context there was nothing particularly unusual about the book. Löwe's *Speculum* is one of a large number of works that can be classified as Christian ethnographic writing about Jews which first appeared in Western Europe around the beginning of the sixteenth century and remained popular until the end of the eighteenth century. This genre comprises works that contain largely accurate descriptions of Jewish ceremonies and customs but focus on details that portray such praxis as superstitious, ridiculous, and dangerous to Christians. The relatively late arrival of the genre to Sweden in the eighteenth century can perhaps be explained by the absence of a resident Jewish community in the country, although it is noteworthy that the publication of *Speculum Religionis Judaicæ* happened when the question of admitting Jews to Sweden was routinely being debated in the Swedish parliament.

This book aims to make this unique Swedish source available to an international audience for the first time. It includes background information on the history of and attitudes towards Jews in Sweden until the 1730s and on the genre of Christian ethnographical writing about Jews. The text of *Speculum Religionis Judaicæ* has been edited and translated into English, and the edition appears with a commentary that explains technical and foreign (particularly Hebrew) words. Other relevant works, such as Christophorus Bezelius' *Die Herrlichkeit des Christenthums* (1684) and Christian Gottlieb Seeligmann's *Jüdischer Ceremonien* (1725) appear in the appendices either as excerpts or in full with English translations. It is my hope that *A Mirror of the Jewish Religion* will be of interest to both students and researchers of Swedish social history, the history of religions, the history of antisemitism, and the study of Jewish-Christian relations.

https://doi.org/10.1515/9783110986938-001

Jews in Sweden before 1730

The Middle Ages

Jews were not permitted to settle in Sweden until towards the end of the eighteenth century. Nevertheless, they already appear several centuries earlier as characters in medieval Swedish and Latin chronicles, romances, stories based on the Bible, miracle tales, prayers, religious treatises, papal encyclicals, and sermons. This arrival on manuscript parchment as well as in the sculptures, altarpieces, and wall paintings that adorned many church interiors was of course part and parcel of the Christianization of Sweden, a gradual process that took a couple of hundred years before finishing during the twelfth century.[1] It is evidence of just one way in which Swedish culture was incorporated into the broader written and religious culture of Western Europe. The Jews in these medieval works are portrayed largely as elsewhere in Europe: honourable figures from the Old Testament are presented neutrally or even positively, whereas the vast majority of Jews from the time of Jesus Christ onwards are portrayed as deicides, as desecrators of hosts, crucifixes, and icons, as dishonest, extorting usurers, as foul, filthy, and violent beast-like creatures, and as a despised, homeless people punished by God for rejecting and killing his son.[2] These stereotypes were daily fare throughout the lands of Western Christianity and the Swedish material is on the whole rather typical. Nonetheless, there is some evidence of specifically German influence on how Jews are portrayed in medieval Sweden. For example, the *Judensau*, an image originating from and typically found in German churches of Jews suckling a sow, can still be seen today in a corbel sculpture in Uppsala Cathedral (fourteenth century) and in church wall-paintings in Husby-Sjutolft and Härkeberga (both from 1480s).[3] Similarly, the

---

1 On the Christianization of Sweden, see Nils Blomkvist, Stefan Brink, and Thomas Lindkvist, "The Kingdom of Sweden," in *Christianization and the Rise of Christian Monarchy: Scandinavia, Central Europe and Rus' c. 900–1200*, ed. Nora Berend (New York: Cambridge University Press, 2007), 167–213.

2 On the image of the Jew in medieval Swedish works, see Jonathan Adams, *Jews in East Norse Literature: A Study of Othering in Medieval Denmark and Sweden*, vol. 1: *A Cultural Investigation*, vol. 2 *Texts and Bibliography*, Religious Minorities in the North: History, Politics, and Culture, vol. 4 (Berlin/Boston: De Gruyter, 2023). On medieval Latin works from Sweden, see Cordelia Heß, "The Medieval Roots of Antisemitism in Sweden: Old Swedish and Latin Manuscript Traditions," *Nordisk judaistik · Scandinavian Jewish Studies* 34, no. 1 (2023): 6–22.

3 Of the nearly fifty extant *Judensau* images today, only ten are found outside of modern-day Germany, of which three are in Uppland, Sweden; the remainder are located in Austria, Belgium, France, Poland, and Switzerland. On the *Judensau*, see Isaiah Shachar, *The Judensau: A Medieval Anti-Jewish Motif and its History*, Warburg Institute Surveys, vol. 5 (London: Warburg Institute, 1974);

term “Red Jews,” the legendary nation of Jews enclosed behind the Caucasus mountains and primed to invade Europe at the End of Days, is found only in German vernacular works and as “the rødha iudha” in the Old Swedish romance *Konung Alexander* (composed *c.* 1380).[4] Sweden was, of course, under strong German cultural, religious, and economic influence for much of the medieval and modern periods, and with the arrival of the Protestant Reformation in Sweden from 1527, religious teachings there came to be aligned with German Lutheranism.

Martin Luther

Martin Luther’s (1483–1546) changing attitudes to Jews and Judaism are notorious and, especially since the Second World War, much researched.[5] In brief, Luther was

---

Judith Vogt, *Jødens ukristelige image: et studie i katolsk billedmageri* (Copenhagen: C. A. Reitzel, 1996), 44–47; Heinz Schreckenberg, *Die Juden in der Kunst Europas: Ein historischer Bildatlas* (Göttingen: Vandenhoeck & Ruprecht, 1996), 343–49; Claudine Fabre-Vassas, *The Singular Beast: Jews, Christians, and the Pig*, trans. Carl Volk [*La bête singulière: Les juifs, les chrétiens et les cochons*], European Perspectives: A Series in Social Thought and Cultural Criticism (New York: Columbia University Press, 1997); Erika Holm, “Bilden av hat,” *Judiska krönika* 65, no. 4 (1997): 16–18; Birgit Wiedl, “Laughing at the Beast: The *Judensau*: Anti-Jewish Propaganda and Humor from the Middle Ages,” in *Laughter in the Middle Ages and Early Modern Times: Epistomology of a Fundamental Human Behavior, its Meaning, and Consequences*, ed. Albrecht Classen, Fundamentals of Medieval and Early Modern Culture, vol. 5 (Berlin/Boston: De Gruyter, 2010), 325–64. On the *Judensau* motif in Sweden, including the wall paintings in Härkeberga and Husby-Sjutolft churches, see also Anna Nilsén, *Program och funktion i senmedeltida kalkmåleri: kyrkmålningar i Mälarlandskapen och Finland 1400–1534* (Stockholm: Kungl. Vitterhets Historie och Antikvitets Akademien, 1986), 151–55; Viktoria Munck af Rosenschöld, *Främlingsbilder: Om judar och judendom i medeltida danskt och svenskt kalkmåleri* (Master’s dissertation, Lunds universitet, 2007), 22–25; Herman Bengtsson, “Samtida mode eller antisemitism? Demonisering och rasistiska tendenser i medeltidens bildkonst,” *Iconographisk post: Nordisk tidskrift för bildtolkning · Nordic Review of Iconography* 3, no. 4 (2016): 8–12; Anders Andrén, “The *Judensau* in Uppsala,” in *Myth, Magic, and Memory in Early Scandinavian Narrative Culture: Studies in Honour of Stephen A. Mitchell*, ed. Jürg Glauser and Pernille Hermann, Acta Scandinavia, vol. 11 (Turnhout: Brepols, 2021), 351–70; Adams, *Jews in East Norse Literature*, 206–12.

4 On the Red Jews in *Konung Alexander*, see Adams, *Jews in East Norse Literature*, 518–44. Two important studies of the origins and history of the myth of the Enclosed Nations are Andrew Colin Gow, *The Red Jews: Antisemitism in an Apocalyptic Age 1200–1600* (Leiden: Brill, 1995) and Rebecca Voß, *Disputed Messiahs: Jewish and Christian Messianism in the Ashkenazic World during the Reformation*, trans. John Crutchfield [*Umstrittene Erlöser: Politik, Ideologie und jüdisch-christlicher Messianismus in Deutschland, 1500–1600*] (Detroit: Wayne State University Press, 2021).

5 See Thomas Kaufmann, “Luther and the Jews,” in *Jews, Judaism, and the Reformation in Sixteenth-Century Germany*, ed. Dean Phillip Bell and Stephen G. Burnett (Leiden: Brill, 2006), 69–104;

initially hopeful of the mass conversion of Jews in response to his religious reforms and he condemned their ill-treatment at the hands of Christians. For example, in *Das Jhesus Christus eyn geborner Jude sey* [That Jesus Christ Was Born a Jew] from 1523, he writes:

> Und wenn ich eyn Jude gewesen were und hette solche tolpell und knebel gesehen den Christen glauben regirn und leren, so were ich ehe eyn saw worden denn eyn Christen. Denn sie haben mit den Juden gehandelt als weren es hunde und nicht menschen, haben nichts mehr kund thun denn die schelten und yhr gutt nehmen, wenn man sie getaufft hat, keyn Christlich lere noch leben hat man yhn beweyset, sondern nur der Bepsterey unnd muncherey untherworffen [...] Ich hoff, wenn man mit den Juden freuntlich handelt und aus der heyligen schrifft sie seuberlich unterweyßet, es sollten yhr viel rechte Christen werden [...] Wenn die Apostel, die auch Juden waren, also hetten mit uns heyden gehandelt, wie wyr heyden mit den Juden, es were nie keyn Christen unter den heyden worden. [...] Und wenn wyr gleych hoch und rhumen, so sind wyr dennoch heyden und die Juden von dem geblutt Christi, wyr sind schweger und frembdling, sie sind blut freund, vettern und bruder unsers hern. Darumb wenn man sich des bluts und fleyschs rhumen solt, so gehoren yhe die Juden Christo neher tzu denn wyr. [...] Will man yhn helfen, so mus man nicht des Bapsts, sonder Christlicher liebe gesetz an yhn uben und sie freuntlich annehmen, mit lassen werben und erbeytten, da mit sie ursach und raum gewynnen, bey und umb uns tzu seyn, unser Christlich lere und leben tzu horen und sehen. Ob ettliche hallstarrig sind, was ligt dran? sind wyr doch auch nicht gute Christen.[6]
>
> [If I had been a Jew and had seen such fools and halfwits governing and teaching the Christian faith, I would sooner have become a sow than a Christian, because they have dealt with the Jews as if they were dogs rather than human beings; because they have done nothing other than deride them and seize their belongings. When they baptize them, they show them no Christian doctrine or life, but subject them to Popery and monkishness. (...) I hope that if the Jews are dealt with in a kind manner and are taught accurately using the Holy Scriptures, then many of them will become true Christians. (...) If the apostles, who were also Jews, had dealt with us Gentiles as we Gentiles deal with the Jews, there would never have been a Christian among the Gentiles (...) And while we boast about our high status, we are but Gentiles, and the Jews are of the lineage of Christ; we are brothers-in-law and strangers, they are blood relatives, cousins, and brothers of our Lord. Therefore, if one should boast about flesh and blood, the Jews actually belong closer to Christ than we do (...) If we really want to help them, then we must not practise the law of the Pope, but that of Christian love, and receive them kindly, and permit them to trade and work, so that they have a reason and opportunity to associate

---

Thomas Kaufmann, *Luther's Jews: A Journey into Anti-Semitism* (Oxford: Oxford University Press, 2017) with its comprehensive bibliography. More generally on antisemitism during the Reformation, see Heiko A. Oberman, *The Roots of Anti-Semitism in the Age of Renaissance and Reformation*, trans. James I. Porter [*Wurzeln des Antisemitismus: Christenangst und Judenplage im Zeitalter von Humanismus und Reformation*] (Philadelphia: Fortress Press, 1984).

6 WA 11: 314–15, 336.

with us, hear and see our Christian teaching and life. If some of them are stiff-necked, what of it? After all, we ourselves are not good Christians either.]

However, over time Luther became disillusioned and when there was no sign of a mass conversion of Jews, his tone hardened. He became critical of Judaism and filled with hatred towards its followers. His conciliatory approach came to be replaced by calls for destructive persecution and lethal pogroms against Jews. In his most well-known antisemitic work, *Von den Jüden vnd jren Lügen* [On the Jews and their Lies] from 1543, Luther writes about Jews and reveals their alleged secrets and hostile intentions. Jews, he asserts, are walking devils: "So, when you see a real Jew, you may with good conscience cross yourself and confidently say, 'There goes a devil incarnate.'"[7] Towards the end of the work, he lays out his plan for dealing with Jews, who now, in direct contradiction to his words in *Das Jhesus Christus eyn geborner Jude sey*, are "the evil, whoring people, that is, no people of God, and their boasting of lineage, circumcision, and law must be considered excrement."[8] He calls for their synagogues and homes to be burnt down, their prayerbooks to be confiscated, their legal protection to be removed, their rabbis to be forbidden to preach, their means of making a living by lending money to be prohibited, their wealth to be confiscated, and their young to be forced into manual labour:

> Was wollen wir Christen nu thun mit diesem verworffen, verdampten Volck der Juden? [...] Erstlich, das man jre Synagoga oder Schule mit feur anstecke und, was nicht verbrennen wil, mit erden uber heusse und beschütte, das kein Mensch ein stein oder schlocke davon sehe ewiglich. [...] Zum andern, das man auch jre Heuser des gleichen zebreche und zerstöre. [...] Zum dritten, das man jnen neme alle jre Betbüchlin und Thalmudisten, darin solche Abgötterey lügen, fluch und lesterung geleret wird. [...] Zum vierten, das man jren Rabinen bey leib und leben verbiete, hinfurt zu leren [...] Zum fünften, das man den Jüden das Geleid und Straffe gantz und gar auffhebe, Denn sie haben nichts auff dem Lande zu schaffen, [...] Sie sollen da heime bleiben. [...] Zum sechsten, das man jnen den Wucher verbiete und neme jnen alle barschafft und Kleinot an silber und Gold, und lege es bereit zu verwaren. [...] Sölch Geld solt man dazu brauchen (und nichts anders), wo ein Jüde sich ernstlich bekeret, das man jm davon fur die Hand gebe hundert, zwey, drey flo. nach gelegenheit der Person [...] Zum siebenden, das man den jungen starcken Jüden und Jüdin in die hand gebe flegel, axt, karst, spaten, rocken, spindel und lasse sie jr brot verdienen im schweis der nasen, wie Adams kindern auffgelegt ist, Gene.3. Denn es taug nicht, das sie uns verfluchten Goijim wolten lassen im schweis unsers angesichts erbeiten, und sie, die heiligen Leute, woltens hinter dem Ofen mit faulen tagen, feisten und pompen verzeren, Und drauff rhümen lesterlich, da sie der Christen

7 WA 53: 479: "Darumb, wo du einen rechten Jüden sihest, magstu mit gutem gewissen ein Creutz fur dich schlahen, und frey sicher sprechen: Da gehet ein leibhafftiger Teufel."

8 WA 53: 442: "das böse hürisch Volck, das ist kein Volck Gottes sein, Und jr Rhum vom Geblüt, Beschneittung und Gesetz mus ein kot sein."

> herrn weren von unserm schweis, Sondern man müste jnen das faule schelmen bein aus dem rücken vertreiben.[9]
>
> [What will we Christians do with these rejected, damned Jewish people? (...) First, we should set fire to their synagogue or school, and whatever will not burn, cover over and conceal with earth so that no person will ever see a stone or cinder of it. (...) Second, we should also raze and destroy the houses of these same people (...) Third, we should take all their prayerbooks and Talmudic books from them, in which is taught such idolatry, lies, cursing, and blasphemy (...) Fourth, we should forbid their rabbis to teach on pain of loss of life or limb (...) Fifth, we should completely abolish safe conduct and protection for Jews as they have no business in the countryside, (...) they should stay at home. (...) Sixth, we should prohibit usury to them and take from them all their cash and silver and gold valuables and put them aside for the time being (...) We should use such money (and nothing else) when a Jew sincerely converts, so that we hand him 100, 200, 300 florins from it according to his personal circumstances (...) Seventh, we should put a flail, an axe, a hoe, a spade, a distaff, a spindle into the hands of young, strong Jews and Jewesses and let them earn their bread in the sweat of their noses, as was imposed on the children of Adam, Gen. 3:(19). For it is not right that they let us accursed Goyim toil in the sweat of our faces, and they, the holy people, laze away behind the oven, farting and showing off, and moreover blasphemously boasting that through our sweat they are the lords over the Christians. Rather, we have to throw these lazy rogues out by the seat of their pants.]

With the words "So, we are also at fault [...] in not slaying them," he seems to be excusing, if not, in fact, directly calling for, the murder of Jews who "are surely possessed by all devils."[10]

In many ways, Luther's antisemitism echoes that of his medieval predecessors and uses the same polemical arguments:[11] Jews rejected and killed Jesus, and today they are still rejecting Christianity and threatening its followers. As so often in the chronological development of antisemitism, the core message is the same, but the packaging is a little different:[12] there is, for example, no mention of saints who

9 WA 53: 522–26.

10 WA 53: 522: "So ists auch unser schuld, das wir [...] sie nicht todschlahen"; WA 53: 552: "gewislich mit allen Teufeln besessen sind."

11 Jeremy Cohen, "Traditional Prejudice and Religious Reform: The Theological and Historical Foundations of Luther's Anti-Judaism," in *Anti-Semitism in Times of Crisis*, ed. Sander L. Gilman and Steven T. Katz (New York: New York University Press, 1991), 81–102.

12 On the ongoing debate about continuity and change in the development and expression of antisemitism, see Salo W. Baron, "Newer Emphases in Jewish History," *Jewish Social Studies* 25, no. 4 (1963): 235–48; David Engel, "Away from a Definition of Antisemitism: An Essay on the Semantics of Historical Description," in *Rethinking European Jewish History*, ed. Jeremy Cohen and Moshe Rosman (Liverpool: Liverpool University Press, 2008), 30–53; David Nirenberg, *Anti-Judaism: The Western Tradition* (New York: W. W. Norton, 2013); Jonathan Adams and Cordelia Heß, eds, *The Medieval Roots of Antisemitism: Continuities and Discontinuities from the Middle Ages to the Present Day* (New York/London: Routledge, 2018); Dan Michman, "Anti-semit-ism: When and Why was

miraculously intercede to punish a Jew or accusations of Jews blaspheming the Virgin Mary – the kinds of *topoi* that are widespread in medieval Swedish texts about Jews. Furthermore, in his criticisms of Judaism, Luther made use of the Jewish convert Antonius Margaritha's *Der gantz Jüdisch glaub* [The Whole Jewish Faith], a polemical work ridiculing Jewish ceremonies that dates from 1530/31.[13] This enabled him to criticize (alleged) contemporary Jewish practices and traditions, and not just to make theological arguments against Judaism. As in earlier medieval works by other writers, the language in *Von den Jüden vnd jren Lügen* is ugly and shrill and he largely fails to recognize Jews' humanity, but it is perhaps Luther's "solutions" that demonstrate the greatest difference to medieval works. Like other writers in the sixteenth century, such as Poul Ræff in 1516, he looks to secular leaders and city authorities to bring about change through persecution, expulsion, and even murder.[14]

Perhaps it was because his refutation of Judaism very much concerned "real, living" Jews, but Luther's later antisemitism is not picked up by Swedish Lutheran theologians, who, having no "real" Jews at hand in Sweden, focus instead on the Jews of the Bible. For example, the collected works of the reformer Olaus Petri (1493–1552) do not throw up any examples of discussions about contemporary Jews in his writings.[15] Rather, Petri focuses on the people, events, laws, and holidays of

the Term Coined and Embraced and is it Still Useful?," Keynote lecture for the conference *Global Perspectives of Antisemitism*, Bar Ilan University, 12 June 2023/23 Sivan 5783.

13 See Peter von der Osten-Sacken, *Martin Luther und die Juden: Neu untersucht anhand von Anton Margarithas "Der gantz Jüdisch glaub" (1530/31)* (Stuttgart: Kohlhammer, 2002); Stephen G. Burnett, "Luther's Chief Witness: Anthonius Margaritha's *Der gantz Jüdisch glaub* (1530/1531)," in *Revealing the Secrets of the Jews: Johannes Pfefferkorn and Christian Writings about Jewish Life and Literature in Early Modern Europe*, ed. Jonathan Adams and Cordelia Heß (Berlin/Boston: De Gruyter, 2017), 183–200.

14 Chapter 5 in *Libellus de Judaica Confessione* is "en paamyndelsæ til herrer/ Førsther. Prelater. Købstædher oc alle andræ cristnæ mennisckæ" [an admonition to lords, princes, prelates, market-towns, and all other Christian people]. He directly addresses his intended audience again when he writes: "Herrer Førsther Prelater Frigbornæ mend Borg mestheræ Raad Meenæ almwghæ vti cristhenhedhen/ huar som heltz och vndher huess herredømæ Iøder the æræ oc boo. Myn ydmyghe oc gudhelighe bøn er til ether alle/ [...]" [Lords, princes, prelates, freeborn men, mayors, councils and common people in Christendom, wherever you may be and under whose dominion the Jews exist and live: my humble and devout request to you all is (...)]. Johannes Pfefferkorn, *Nouiter in lucem data: iudeorum secreta*, trans. Poul Ræff [*Libellus de Judaica Confessione*] (Copenhagen: Poul Ræff, 1516), 25 [f. c1r]. See Jonathan Adams, *Lessons in Contempt: Poul Ræff's Translation and Publication in 1516 of Johannes Pfefferkorn's* The Confession of the Jews, Universitets-Jubilæets danske Samfund, vol. 581 (Odense: University Press of Southern Denmark, 2013), 162–63, 250, 251, 294.

15 Olaus Petri, *Samlade skrifter af Olavus Petri*, ed. Bengt Hesselman, 4 vols (Uppsala: Sveriges kristliga studentrörelse, 1914–17).

the Old Testament which are all considered prefigurations of those in the New Testament: Judah Maccabee, Shavuot and Pentecost, the correct day for the Sabbath, circumcision, and so on. He describes two types of faith – a dead one and a living one:

> troon är tweggiahanda, Then ena är en döödh troo, then andra är en leffuande tro [...] Här aff fölger nw, ath när wij göra någhra gerninga effter wort sinne, thå äro the icke christeliga ty the skee vtan troona, Fölgher ytermera ath alla sådana gerninga äro synd och äro judhiska gerninga[16]
>
> [There are two kinds of faith: the one is a dead faith, the other is a living faith (...) From this it follows that when we perform deeds according to our minds, then these are not Christian as they take place without faith. Moreover, it follows that all such deeds are sins and are Jewsih deeds.]

He describes the Jews of the New Testament as responsible for the death of Jesus and as enemies of the early Christians, but unlike Luther, he does not repeat medieval libels, such as ritual murder, nor does he call for the persecution and murder of Jews. In the writings of the Swedish reformers, biblical Jews were largely used as a tool to show that Swedish Lutherans understood the word of God better than his (formerly) chosen people, the Jews.[17]

Nonetheless, as Sweden continued to draw spiritual and worldly inspiration from Germany, Luther's hatred of Jews did leave its mark on the Swedish Church and Swedish society at large. Of course, there were many other elements of Luther's teachings that shaped Swedish religious, political, and social life, but antisemitism was an integral component to his personality and theology,[18] and his warnings about Jews, calls to expel them, and concerns about them contaminating Christian society were nonetheless echoed through the following centuries' political debates about admitting Jews to settle in Sweden.

---

16 Petri, *Samlade skrifter*, vol 1: *En skön och nyttig undervisning*, 144–45; cited in Kajsa Brilkman, *Undersåten som förstod: Den svenska reformatoriska samtalsordningen och den tidigmoderna integrationsprocessen* (Skellefteå: Artos, 2013), 216.

17 See Brilkman, *Undersåten som förstod*, 211–17.

18 Kaufmann, *Luther's Jews*, 156. Luther's *Von den Jüden vnd jren Lügen* was not translated into Swedish until 1934 (and again in 1943 – both times by Nazi publishers): Martin Luther, *Om judarna och deras lögner* (Gothenburg: Ernst Hansson, 1934 / Stockholm: Svea rike, 1943).

Calls for the admission of Jews

The first Jew mentioned in Swedish sources before the end of the sixteenth century is Gustav Vasa's doctor Philippus Wulf. A letter dated 9 October 1557 (Västerås) describes a conflict between "these doctors of ours, doctor [Johann] Copp and that Jew [Philippus Wulf]"[19] – apparently Wulf had accused Copp of ineptitude and dubious conduct.[20] As a Jew resident in Sweden, Wulf seems to have been something of an exception as there are very few records of Jews in the country before 1685. Indeed, the lack of legislation prohibiting Jews from settling in Sweden until towards the end of the seventeenth century suggests that Jews were not arriving in numbers that required particular control or regulation.[21] However, whenever requests were made for Jews to be admitted to Sweden, they were usually turned down, but there were exceptions. For example, in 1774, Aron Isak (1730–1816), a Jew from Swedish Pomerania, sought permission to settle in Stockholm, without having to convert to Christianity.[22] In 1775, he and two other Jews (Markus Isak and Abraham Aron) were permitted to settle and work as seal engravers and gemstone cutters.[23] The following year Aron Isak was allowed to summon enough male Jews to Stockholm to form a *minyan* (a quorum of ten adult males required for religious obligation such as communal prayer). Then, in 1776, he was able to purchase a plot of land for use as a cemetery.

---

19 Hugo Valentin, *Judarnas historia i Sverige* (Stockholm: Bonniers, 1924), 8: "desse våre medicos, doktor Kop och den juden"; Hugo Valentin, *Judarna i Sverige* (Stockholm: Bonniers, 1964), 13; Carl Henrik Carlsson, *Judarnas historia i Sverige* (Stockholm: Natur & Kultur, 2021), 19.

20 Ingvar Svanberg and Mattias Tydén, *Tusen år av invandring: en svensk kulturhistoria* (Stockholm: Gidlund, 1992), 61; Bo S. Lindberg, *Inte vid helt sunda vätskor: Gustav Vasa och hans söner ur ett medicinhistoriskt perspektiv* (Uppsala: Uppsala universitet. Medicinhistoriska museet, 2017), 71.

21 The Church Act [*Kyrkolag*] of 1686 was the first law to state clearly that Jews (as well as Muslims, Blackamoors, and pagans) were not welcome within the Swedish realm unless they converted to Christianity (see below).

22 Carlsson, *Judarnas historia i Sverige*, 34–35.

23 After being given permission to remain in Sweden, the newspapers published many antisemitic articles about Isak creating a menacing atmosphere that left him fearing for his life; as he writes in his memoires: "Aber was kriegte ich alle Tage in das Wochenblatt vor schlechtes Schreiben gegen mich, was dachten sie nicht auf vor gemein Sachen gegen Juden, dass die gemeine Leut hinter mir nach schrien. Ich liess mir wohl in 14 Tagen nicht sehen auf der Strass" [But what terrible writings against me did I get in the press! What mean things against Jews did they not think up! Things that mean people behind me then shouted after me. I did not show myself on the street for a good fortnight]; [Aron Isak,] *Aron Isaks Sjelfbiografi efter författarens handskrift*, ed. Josef Seligmann (Stockholm: Israelitiska Litteratur-Sällskapet, 1897), 39; [Aron Isak,] *Denkwürdigkeiten des Aron Isak 1730–1817*, ed. Z. Holm (Berlin: Der Heine-Bund, 1930), 92.

At the beginning of 1779, the Assembly of Estates (*Ståndsriksdagen*) proposed to allow non-Lutheran Christians to settle in Sweden, and in 1781 King Gustav III passed the Edict of Tolerance (*Toleransediktet*) which guaranteed freedom of religion and citizen rights for all Christians in Sweden. On 27 May 1782, the law was passed that regulated the immigration and rights of Jews, the so-called *Judereglementet* [Jewish Regulations] or *Reglemente för them af Judeska Nationen, som wilja hit i Riket inflytta och sig här nedsätta* [Regulations for those of the Jewish nation who wish to immigrate to the kingdom and settle here]. Jews were finally permitted to settle in Sweden, practise their religion, and become Swedish citizens – on the condition they had minimum capital of two thousand riksdaler.[24] They were forbidden to marry or employ non-Jews, buy land, or form craft guilds, while synagogues could only be built in the few cities they were permitted to settle in: Stockholm, Gothenburg, Norrköping, and from 1785 Karlskrona.

Before the *judereglementet*, during the era of Swedish Empire (*stormaktstiden*, 1611–1721) and the Age of Liberty (*frihetstiden*, 1721–72), several calls were made for Jewish immigration as part of the plan for Swedish global trade with its base in the new port city of Gothenburg that had been founded in 1621 by Gustav II Adolf (r. 1611–32). Bringing Jewish traders in from abroad to increase commerce was a successful model that had already been tested elsewhere in Europe. Both Amsterdam and Hamburg had invited Sephardi Jews to settle and both cities had subsequently experienced a boost to their trade, not least thanks to the Jews' mercantile and trading networks. For example, shortly after Gothenburg was founded, Christian IV of Denmark (r. 1588–1648) invited the Sephardi Jews of Amsterdam to settle in Glückstadt and the city likewise blossomed. Furthermore, the integration of Altona into the Danish realm in 1664 and for the next two centuries, saw this city as the foremost site of Jewish life in Scandinavia. Meanwhile, across the North Sea, Oliver Cromwell (r. 1652–58) was holding talks with the leadership of the Jewish community in Amsterdam on permitting Jews to (re-)settle in England with the aim of bolstering the economy; permission was granted in 1655.

It is in connection with plans for mercantile expansion, that the first call to settle Jews in Sweden was made in the 1620s. According to the statesman Magnus Gabriel De la Gardie's (1622–86) account from 1667 of a meeting of the Swedish Privy Council (*riksrådet*) many years earlier, a proposal had been made shortly after the founding of Gothenburg that "the Jews, who are a wealthy people, should be drawn

---

24 The text of the regulations with its 33 paragraphs is reproduced in Hugo Valentin, *Urkunder till judarnas historia i Sverige* (Stockholm: Bonniers, 1924), 18–25; see also Svanberg and Tydén, *Tusen år av invandring*, 184–87.

thither and left there to pursue their trade".[25] The proposal was not successful, and in describing the most vociferous opposition, De la Gardie quotes the reaction of Axel Oxenstierna (1583–1654) who was Chancellor of the Realm and thus the most powerful person in all Sweden:

> Så kärt det vore honom, att en ort, som Gud och naturen synas rätt enkannerligen hava formerat till Sveriges gagn och fördel, måtte tilltaga och förkovra sig uti kommercier och handel, så okärt vore det honom, att han genom Kristi namns hätske förföljare skulle hava något uppsteg, och ville hellre önska, att han evinnerligen måtte bliva en ringa och föraktad torparkoja, än på det sättet förvärva sig namn av en rik och florerande handelsplats.[26]
>
> [As dear as it would be to him that a place, which God and nature seem to have certainly rightly formed for Sweden's benefit and advantage, should increase and become involved in commerce and trade, so disagreeable would it be to him that through the hateful persecutors of Christ's name it should have some success, and he would rather wish that it might forever become a mean and despised crofter's hut than acquire the name of a rich and flourishing place of trade in that way.]

De la Gardie also reports that the Jews of Hamburg approached Queen Kristina of Sweden (r. 1632–54) and offered to pay a sum of money in return for being allowed to settle in Gothenburg and, crucially, to practise their religion in the city. It seems likely that the request was presented to the queen by Axel Oxenstierna's opponent Johan Adler Salvius (1590–1652) who was on good terms with the Jewish leadership in Hamburg. However, once again, and in spite of the queen's generally favourable view of Jews (see below), the request was denied.[27]

Thus, at a time when other north-western European cities and countries, such as Amsterdam and Hamburg (from 1500s) and Denmark (1623), were creating laws to allow Jews, particularly Portuguese Jews, to settle, Sweden refused.[28] This

25 Valentin, *Judarnas historia i Sverige*, 23: "judarne, som ett rikt folk är, måtte dragas dit och dem efterlåtas där att hava sin handel"; Valentin, *Judarna i Sverige*, 21; Carlsson, *Judarnas historia i Sverige*, 20.

26 Valentin, *Judarnas historia i Sverige*, 23; Valentin, *Judarna i Sverige*, 21.

27 Valentin, *Judarnas historia i Sverige*, 24; Valentin, *Judarna i Sverige*, 22.

28 After Isabela and Ferdinand II's 1492 edict of expulsion, the so-called Alhambra Decree, many Spanish Jews fled across the border into Portugal. By the end of the decade, Jews in Portugal were also having to choose between converting or leaving the country. Fearing a brain-drain, the king closed the ports, and most Jews in Portugal were forced to convert. When the possibility arose, many of the descendants of these "crypto-Jews" (also known as *conversos* ["converts"], as *novos cristãos* ["new Christians"], or pejoratively as *marranos* ["swine"]) moved abroad to countries with more religious freedom, such as the Dutch Republic and Brazil, where they again practised Judaism publicly. On mercantilism and Jews in early modern Europe, see Jonathan I. Israel, *European Jewry in the Age of Mercantilism, 1550–1750*, 2nd edn (Oxford: Clarendon Press, 1989).

seems to have been due to the concerted efforts of certain statesmen and Christian religious leaders during the seventeenth century. Furthermore, Axel Oxenstierna's death in 1654 was followed by a period of religious orthodoxy in Sweden in which the alliance between powerful bishops and the Crown made any chance of Jews immigrating to Sweden unlikely. The higher clergy's argumentation for a mono-religious Sweden persisted in the parliamentary debates of the early eighteenth century. They even referred to Sweden's role as a guarantee state for the Peace of Westphalia (1648) as a reason why they should not be obliged to give up their "blessed" mono-religious, Lutheran condition.[29] Nonetheless, a small community of Ashkenazi Jews established itself on the quiet in Stockholm, presumably in the hope that their existence in the capital would be seen as an irreversible *fait accompli* that the government would be unwilling or unable to reverse. However, this proved not to be the case, and when the priest Johannes Vultejus (1639–1700) alerted Stockholm's Consistory to the fact that non-baptized Jews had come to the city and were practising their religion and that more were expected to arrive, King Karl XI (r. 1660–97) issued a stern reminder to the city's officials that banned Jews from residing anywhere in the realm and ordered their removal:

> Såsom Consistorium här uti Stockholm Oss i underdånighet tilkänna gifwit, huru såsom någre Judar skola uppehålla sig här i Staden, och icke allenast de understå sig här att föröfwa deras Judiske Religion, utan ock ännu flere wara hit förwäntandes med hustror och barn, till den ända sig här att nedsättia, hwarutaf lätteligen kan följja förargelse och wara att befrukta, det ett och annat missbruk uti Wår rätta Evangeliska Religion däraf kunna insmyga; Och Wi sådant hafwe tagit betänckiande, och för den Konungsliga ifwer Wi alltid drage för Wår rena obesmittade lära, och på det alt tillfälle må förekommas, hwarigenom den kan råka uti någon fara, hafwe funnit för godt, det inge Judar, såsom Christi Namns och Församlings försmädare, må tillåtas här i Staden eller annorstädes i wåra provincier att wistas; Altfördensskull är härmed till Eder Wår nådige willje och befallning, att I straxt låten ansäja alle här uti Stadens befindtelige Judar, det de, inom 14 dagars förlopp, sig hädan utur Staden och landet förfoga, och wid högsta straff, icke understå sig öfwer den föresatte termin här att förblifwa.[30]

29 See Johannes Ljungberg, "Det respekterade samvetet och den riskabla samvetsfriheten: Perspektiv från det tidiga 1700-talets riksdagsdebatter och statliga utredningar," in *Samvete i Sverige: Om frihet och lydnad från medeltiden till idag*, ed. Linde Lindkvist and Johannes Ljungberg (Lund: Nordic Academic Press, 2021), 88.

30 Stockholm City Archives, 3 December 1685, SE/SSA/0018/Överståthållarämbetets Äldre kansli/E1a:7; reproduced in Valentin, *Urkunder till judarnas historia*, 9. Cf. also the king's letter sent to the Stockholm officials just over three weeks later on 29 December 1685: "Såsom Wi hafwe förnummit, at några Judar sig ännu här i Staden uppehålla skola, hwilka Wi ingen längre härwist wele förunna; Ty är härmed till Eder Wår nådige villje och befallning, att I sådane Judar tillsäja låten, att de ofördröjeligen packa sig utur landet." [We have heard that some Jews are still staying here in the city, to whom we no longer wish to grant residence here; therefore, our gracious will and command

> [The Consistory here in Stockholm has humbly informed us how some Jews are residing here in the city, and not only do they dare to practise their Jewish religion here, but even more of them are expected (to come) here with wives and children with the aim of settling here, which can easily cause anger and fear that some abuse (i. e., false belief or practice) can creep into our correct evangelical religion from this. And we have taken this into consideration, and on account of the royal zeal that we always have for our pure untainted teachings (i. e., Lutheranism) and for any circumstance that might occur whereby it can come into danger, we think it best that no Jews, being blasphemers of Christ's name and assembly, be permitted to stay here in the city or anywhere else in our provinces. For this reason, our gracious will and commandment to you is that you immediately inform all the Jews that are to be found in the city, that they leave the city and the country within fourteen days, and at risk of the greatest punishment do not dare to stay beyond the stated deadline.]

The following year, a new Church Act was introduced with a paragraph that required non-Christians to be taught about Christianity:[31]

> Judar, Turckar, Morianer och Hedningar, som här i Rijket inkomma, skola undervijsas om vår rätta Lära, och befordras til Doop och Christendom; försuma the thetta som böra sig härom vårda låta, tå skola the therföre tiltalas[32]

> [Jews, Muslims (lit. Turks), Blackamoors and Pagans who enter this kingdom shall be taught our correct faith and be encouraged towards baptism and Christianity. If those who are to take care of this are negligent, they will be prosecuted.]

It should be noted that these restrictions were placed on Jews settling in Sweden, not on Jews travelling to or residing for short periods in the country, so foreign Jews who found themselves in Sweden temporarily were not obliged to convert to Christianity. In spite of ongoing disagreements between statesmen about the advantages and disadvantages of Jewish immigration and a continued ban on immigration, Swedes in the seventeenth and the early eighteenth centuries were generally coming into ever greater contact with Jews who were becoming less "fictional" and more "real." Within the religious sphere, the growth of Christian Hebraism and interest in the language of the Old Testament led to a deeper awareness in learned circles of post-biblical literature and traditions, while during the wars waged by Kings Karl X Gustav (r. 1654–60) and Karl XII (r. 1697–1718) in Central and Eastern

---

to you is that you have such Jews told that they are immediately to get out of the country], Valentin, *Urkunder till judarnas historia*, 9.

31 The Church Act [*Kyrkolag*] of 3 September 1686, ch. 2 § 10. It should be mentioned that the new act did not only require non-Christians to be taught about Christianity, but it also introduced a broad educational policy for Swedish Lutherans by means of regular teaching of the catechism.

32 Valentin, *Urkunder till judarnas historia*, 10.

Europe, the Swedish army was present in countries with large Jewish populations, particularly in Poland-Lithuania. Consequently, many Swedes were brought into physical contact with Jewish communities on a much larger scale than had been the case previously, and both Swedish kings took a pragmatic approach towards these non-Christians. According to the historian Hugo Valentin, contemporary sources, the majority in Hebrew, paint a picture of Jews in Poland being treated with a humanity that stood in stark contrast to their treatment by Poles. For example, in 1655 after the Swedish army captured Kazimierz, the Jewish quarter in Kraków, rather than allowing his army to pillage the Jews' property, Karl X Gustav issued an edict placing them under his protection.[33] However, as Carlsson points out "The officers and soldiers were forbidden to attack them and should respect their religion, culture, and rights, even though this was not always adhered to."[34] I would go further and suggest that the reality was certainly not as rosy as Valentin seems to be suggesting. There is little evidence that the Swedes did anything other than oppress everyone in Kraków and Kazimierz, including the Jews. We know, for example, that the Swedes robbed Mojżesz Izakowicz, a Jew in Kazimierz, of goods worth 700,000 Polish złoty. Although Jews and some townspeople were accused of collaborating with the enemy, for example in helping to plunder churches and monasteries, there do not appear to be any extant Hebrew sources that support Valentin's claim.[35]

During the Swedes' wars, Jews proved invaluable as army suppliers, sutlers, and camp followers and by acting as currency exchangers and interpreters. After his five-year stay in Bessarabia in the Ottoman Empire, Karl XII returned to Sweden in 1714 and took with him several Muslim and Jewish allies who had helped him during his time abroad as creditors.[36] They were to remain in Sweden until the king had repaid them his loans, and consequently many of these Jews stayed in Sweden for some time – one of them for more than twenty years – and some of them settled in Karlskrona. In 1718, the king issued a letter that allowed the Jews and Muslims in Karlskrona to practise their religion – the first time that Jewish religious services were officially recognized as divine worship rather than blasphemy:

---

33 Valentin, *Judarna i Sverige*, 25.

34 Carlsson, *Judarnas historia i Sverige*, 21: "Officerarna och soldaterna förbjöds att förgripa sig på dem och skulle respektera deras religion, kultur och rättigheter, även om detta inte alltid efterlevdes."

35 My thanks to Prof. Stefan Gąsiorowski (Instytut Judaistyki at Uniwersytet Jagielloński and Instytut Historii at Polska Akademia Nauk), who has worked extensively on Jewish–Christian relations in Kazimierz (Kraków) between the sixteenth and eighteenth centuries and who kindly looked into Valentin's claims for me and provided me with this information (pers. comm.).

36 Theodor Westrin, "Anteckningar om Karl XII:s orientaliska kreditorer," *Historisk tidskrift* (1900): 1–56.

Utaf Consistorii til mig aflåtne Skrifwelse dat. d. 23. sidstl. December har jag inhämtat, huruledes, i anledning af Kyrko-Lagen, Consistorium blifwit föranlåtit at sig förfråga, huruwida de ifrån Turkiet hit i landet komne Judar och Turkar må tillåtas at öfwa deras Gudstjenst, samt de förre sådane Ceremonier, som de wid omskärelsen förmena sig obehindrat kunna bruka. Hwaröfwer som högsta Ombudsmannen sig har utlåtit, det honom wore obekant uti hwad afseende desse Judar äro uti Riket inkomne eller här wistas; ty har Consistorium min utlåtelse deröfwer begärt, jämväl ock om deras begrafningar, der någon af dem med döden skulle afgå. Och länder fördenskull Consistorio deruppå til wänligit Swar, det har jag detta ärende Hans Maj:t i underdånighet berättat och förnummit Hans Kongl. Maj:ts nådiga mening och wilja wara, det berörde Judar och Turkar fuller intet bör betagas inom lyckta dörar at öfwa deras Gudstjenst, jämväl Judarne at låta omskära sina barn inom lyckta dörar, emedan de icke, som undersåtare, utan som främmande sig här i landet uppehålla, hwarföre dem ock bör efterlåtas på någon tjenlig plats utom Staden at begrafwa deras döda, enär någon af dem skulle igenom döden afgå. Dock om Prästerskapet kunde med goda skäl öfwertala någon af dem at antaga den Christna läran, eller at låta Barnen döpas och i den rätta läran upfostras; så wore det både Gud och Konungen behageligit.[37]

[From the letter of 23 December given to me by the Consistory, I have learnt how, on account of the Church Act, it was necessary for the Consistory to enquire whether those Jews and Turks who have arrived in the country from Turkey may be permitted to practise their worship and the previous ceremonies, such as circumcision, that they think they are able to perform. About which the most supreme ombudsman has expressed that he does not know in what way these Jews have entered the country or are resident here. For this reason, the Consistory has requested my statement on the matter, and furthermore concerning the burial of those of them who might die. And in order to give the Consistory a friendly reply to this, I have humbly told his Majesty about this matter and heard what his Majesty's gracious opinion and will are: nothing should hinder the Jews and Turks in question from practising their religion behind closed doors, equally for Jews from having their children circumcised behind closed doors, as long as they do not reside in the country as subjects but as foreigners, and therefore they should also be provided with some serviceable place outside the city to bury their dead, whenever one of them dies. However, if the clergy could with good reason convince any of them to receive Christian teaching or have their children baptized and raised in the correct faith, it would be pleasing to both God and the king.]

Queen Kristina (1626–89, r. 1632/1644–54)

One of the most learned women of the seventeenth century, Queen Kristina was also one of the few leaders in Sweden who to all appearances did not harbour anti-Jewish sentiments, although it ought to be added that from the beginning that Kristina's involvement with Jews was as a private person rather than as Sweden's

37 Valentin, *Urkunder till judarnas historia*, 10; Svanberg and Tydén, *Tusen år av invandring*, 158.

monarch.[38] In 1645, the physician Benedictus de Castro (Baruch Namias, 1597–1684) was called from Hamburg to the court in Stockholm to see to Kristina's health. The son of the Portuguese *converso* author and doctor Rodrigo de Castro (David Namias, *c.* 1550–1627), Benedictus was a well-known doctor who had been practising in Hamburg since 1622. In 1646, when Benedictus was back in Hamburg, Kristina appointed him her private physician. The following year he dedicated his book on fevers *Monomachia sive certamen medicum* [Monomachy or the Medical Struggle] to her.[39] He returned to Stockholm in 1651 and stayed there for one year.

Kristina had an avid interest in books, paintings, sculpture, and the sciences. She is said to have studied Hebrew and enjoyed learning about "Oriental" literature and culture.[40] From 1651, her supplier of Jewish books and manuscripts was none other than the Amsterdam-based Menasseh ben Israel (Manoel Dias Soeiro, 1604–57), rabbi, author, and printer, perhaps best known for his endeavours for the readmission of Jews to England under Cromwell. Another Jew whom Kristina drew into her most trusted circle was Diego Teixeira Sampayo (Abraham Senior Teixeira, *c.* 1581–1666), a *converso* originally from Portugal but resident in Hamburg from the mid-1640s.[41] Diego acted as Kristina's financier and banker from around the time of her abdication in 1654 onwards. In 1655, she appointed him her *homme d'affaires* and diplomatic representative in Hamburg. After his death, the position went to his son Manoel (Isak Chaim, 1631–1705), who remained her most trusted financier until her death in 1689.[42]

After leaving Sweden for Antwerp in 1654, Kristina stayed *en route* at the home of the Sephardi merchant and diplomat Jacob Curiel (1587–1664) in Neustadt, Hamburg. During a later stay in Hamburg in 1661–62, she lived in the Teixeira home, and in 1667 she stayed in the city in the home of one of Diego Teixeira's relatives,

---

38 Valentin, *Judarnas historia i Sverige*, 39–58; Valentin, *Judarna i Sverige*, 27–33; Carlsson, *Judarnas historia i Sverige*, 20.

39 Benedicti à Castro Lusitani, *Serenissimæ ac Potentissime Principis ac Dominæ Dn. Christinæ, Suecrum, Gothorum, Vandalorumque Reginæ, &c. Medici Monomachia sive certamen medicum: Quô verus in febre synocho putrida cum cruris inflammatione medendi usus per venæ sectionem in brachio demonstratur, præposterus autem ejus abusus per sanguinis missionem in pede, tanquam perniciosus improbatur* (Hamburg: Jacobus Rebenlinus, 1647).

40 Valentin, *Judarnas historia i Sverige*, 44; Valentin, *Judarna i Sverige*, 30.

41 Coming from a *converso* background, Teixeira publicly practised Catholicism until 1647. However, from Easter / Passover of that year, he began following Judaism, and both he and his two sons were circumcised. He took the Hebrew name Abraham.

42 On Queen Kristina and her Jewish bankers, see Bertil Maler, "Drottning Kristina, Abraham Teixeira, Daniel de Prado och greve Bernardino de Rebelledo," *Nordisk judaistik · Scandinavian Jewish Studies* 2, no. 1 (1977): 22–26.

Emanuel Nunes da Costa.[43] However, Kristina did not only have personal dealings with Jewish acquaintances, but she was also interested in the welfare of Jewish communities beyond her private sphere. For example, she tried, albeit unsuccessfully, to intervene with the Holy Roman Emperor Leopold I (r. 1658–1705) when he ordered the expulsion of Vienna's Jewish community across the Danube.[44] During her later years in Rome, Kristina also tried to have the city's Jews placed under her special protection.[45]

Baptisms

Although it is difficult to ascertain precise numbers, no small number of Jews in Western Europe – either individually or with their families – converted to Christianity during the medieval and early modern period.[46] The reasons were many, including a personal, spiritual decision concerning one's relationship to God, an attempt to avoid punishment within the Jewish or Christian community, a way to be able to settle in a certain country or territory, and a means to receive financial support and improved social status. The conversion of Jews held an important place in Christian eschatology as it was considered an important prelude to the End of Days and the Day of Judgement: "For I would not, brethren, that ye should be ignorant of this mystery, lest ye should be wise in your own conceits; that blindness in part is happened to Israel, until the fulness of the Gentiles be come in. And so all Israel shall be saved: as it is written, There shall come out of Sion the Deliverer, and shall turn away ungodliness from Jacob." (Romans 11:25–26) Thus, it was imperative for the Church to convert as many Jews as possible, either by persuasion or force.

The Reformation and subsequent split of the Western Church into Protestantism and Catholicism brought with it a renewed interest in proselytizing among Jews because in the "competition" between Christian confessions their conversion carried with it great symbolic weight.[47] Lutherans compared themselves to the apostles and evangelists of the Bible, and their critique of Catholicism led to their placing new

43 Lebrecht Dreves, *Geschichte der katholischen Gemeinden zu Hamburg und Altona: Ein Beitrag zur Geschichte der nordischen Missionen* (Schaffhausen: Verlag der Huter'schen Buchhandlung, 1850), 73.
44 As a thanksgiving for the expulsion, the former Jewish quarter "Im Werd" was renamed "Leopoldstadt" by the Viennese in honour of the emperor.
45 Valentin, *Judarnas historia i Sverige*, 57–58; Valentin, *Judarna i Sverige*, 30; Carlsson, *Judarnas historia i Sverige*, 20.
46 The most extensive study of the subject is Elisheva Carlebach, *Divided Souls: Converts from Judaism in Germany, 1500–1750* (New Haven/London: Yale University Press, 2001).
47 Carlebach, *Divided Souls*, 56.

emphasis on gaining converts. Furthermore, the apocalyptic atmosphere that accompanied the first years of Protestantism only heightened the call to convert Jews.[48]

Baptized Jews who had moved to Sweden first appear registered in sources from the end of the 1670s: Samuel Kristian (from Amsterdam) in Linköping and Kristoffer Isak Zebulon (from Lübeck) in Oulu (Uleåborg).[49] Baptisms of Jews to Lutheranism that took place in Sweden are first mentioned in an extant source from 1681, when two Jewish families from the Netherlands were baptized in the German Church in Stockholm. They had left all their possessions behind on their departure so that their co-religionists would not be able to put any obstacles in the way of their conversion, and once in Stockholm, the two families, unable to speak Swedish, turned to St Gertrude's, the German Church, for help. They brought with them certificates from two priests in The Hague and a recommendation to the archbishop of their good intentions from the Swedish *envoyé* in the Netherlands. The baptism ceremony was orchestrated as an impressive, theatrical event; in addition to the families and the church's priest Christophorus Bezelius,[50] the bishops

---

48 There are no detailed studies of the conversions in Sweden in the first half of the eighteenth century. However, there are numerous studies of the following periods, all by Per Hammarström: Per Hammarström, "Omvändelseberättelser, judemission och svensk lågkyrklighet runt sekelskiftet 1900," in *Från legofolk till stadsfolk: Festskrift till Börje Harnesk*, ed. Erik Nydahl and Magnus Perlestam, Skrifter från Institutionen för Humaniora (Härnösand: Institutionen för Humaniora, 2012), 137–53; Per Hammarström, "I sällskap med judar: Association, assimilation och konversion i Stockholm 1809–1838," in *Nationen så in i Norden: En festskrift till Torkel Jansson*, ed. Urban Claesson, Henrik Edgren, Bo G. Hall, and Lars M. Andersson, (Skellefteå: Artos & Norma bokförlag, 2013), 157–68; Per Hammarström, "Israels omvändelse som jordens fulländning: Antijudiskhet och antisemitism i Missionstidning för Israel 1874–1885," in *Makt, myter och historiebruk : Historiska problem i belysning*, ed. Stefan Dalin, Skrifter i Humaniora vid Mittuniversitetet (Sundsvall: Mittuniversitetet, 2014), 123–42; Per Hammarström, "Judiska konvertiter till kristendomen i Stockholm 1775–1870," *Historisk tidskrift* 140, no. 1 (2020): 31–65; Per Hammarström, "Luthersk kyrkotidning vs. Sanningsökaren: 'Judefrågan' i kristen offentlig debatt i Sverige under 1870- och 1880-talen," in *Moderniteten som framgång och tragedi: En vänbok till Lars M. Andersson om ett föränderligt 1900-tal*, ed. Mattias Hessérus, Karin Kvist Geverts, Pontus Rudberg, and Malin Thor Tureby (Lund: Nordic Academic Press, 2021), 239–48. The following article focuses on the baptism of Muslims, but the arguments are largely the same regarding Jewish converts: Martin Berntson, "Myten om tvångsdöpta turkar i Stockholm under 1600-talet," *Historisk tidskrift* 142, no. 1 (2022): 3–28.

49 Valentin, *Judarnas historia i Sverige*, 69; Valentin, *Judarna i Sverige*, 34.

50 Son of a printer, Christophorus Bezelius was born in Magdeburg in 1626 and studied in Wittenberg and Helmstadt. In 1650, he was a military chaplain in the Swedish army, and subsequently he became court preacher and father confessor for the queen dowager Maria Eleonora. He became chaplain in the German Church (Tyska kyrkan) in Stockholm in 1655, assisting pastor in 1666, and principal pastor in 1677. He died in in Stockholm in 1689 and lies buried in the cathedral (Storkyrkan) in Stockholm. Gunnar Hellström, *Stockholms stads herdaminne från reformationen intill tillkomsten av Stockholms stift: Biografisk matrikel* (Stockholm: Stockholms kommunalförvaltning, 1951), 564.

of Västerås and Vyborg (Viborg), the superintendents of Karlstad and Narva, two professors from Uppsala, a provost, three pastors, and a consistorial notary all took part in the procession in the presence of King Karl XI, Queen Ulrika Eleonora, and the queen dowager Hedvig Eleonora. On the same day, all the city's churches held collections to raise money for the two families. A few years after the baptism in 1684, Bezelius published his description of the event and an expanded version of his sermon as *Die Herrlichkeit des Christenthums* [The Glory of Christianity].[51] In addition to explaining how best to preach to and convert Jews, the book deals with rather typical topics in early modern Jewish–Christian debates that reveal much about the priest's view of Jews:

- how Jewish circumcision displeases God[52]
- Jews who convert but really remain Jews[53]
- the dangers of consulting Jewish doctors[54]
- the dangers of usury[55]
- the Jews' martyring of Christian children[56]
- the advantages and disadvantages of burning the Talmud[57]
- the punishment of the Jews for rejecting Jesus[58]
- whether or not Jews drink the blood of Christians[59]

Bezelius refers to his sources in marginal notes that include several early Christian ethnographers of Jews and Judaism, such as Antonius Margaritha (b. c. 1500),

51 Christophorus [Christopher] Bezelius, *Die Herrlichkeit des Christenthums/ Welche GOtt/ nach seiner überschwenglichen Barmhertzigkeit und Liebe/ Unter der Vorsorge Sr. Königl. Maytt. zu Schweden/ Zween Jüdischen Männern/ Israel Mandel und Moses Jacob/ Nebst ihren Weibern und Kindern im Jahr Christi 1681. kund gethan hat/ Bey deren Tauffe/ Am Fest-Tage Michaelis geprediget und mit einer Zugabe warhafftiger Begebnissen auch gründlicher Erörterung der Frage; Ob eine allgemeine Bekehrung der Jüden zu hoffen sey?* (Stockholm: Heinrich Käyser, [1684]). The work makes interesting reading when seen in the context of arguments for and against Jewish immigration to Sweden towards the end of the seventeenth century. See Appendix 5 for some excerpts with translations.

52 Bezelius, *Die Herrlichkeit des Christenthums*, under "Die Gnade unders HErrn JEsu Christi…," 40. The book is divided into sections, some of which re-start pagination and some of which do not, which is why "under…" is included in the references.

53 Bezelius, *Die Herrlichkeit des Christenthums*, under "Historische Zugabe," 226, 229.

54 Bezelius, *Die Herrlichkeit des Christenthums*, under "Historische Zugabe," 215: "Die Jüden gute Fleischer/ aber böse Ärtzte" [The Jews (are) good butchers, but bad doctors.]

55 Bezelius, *Die Herrlichkeit des Christenthums*, under "Die Gnade unders HErrn JEsu Christi…," 69–70; under "Historische Zugabe," 249 ff.

56 Bezelius, *Die Herrlichkeit des Christenthums*, under "Historische Zugabe," 218–19.

57 Bezelius, *Die Herrlichkeit des Christenthums*, under "Historische Zugabe," 238–42.

58 Bezelius, *Die Herrlichkeit des Christenthums*, under "Die Gnade unders HErrn JEsu Christi…," 15.

59 Bezelius, *Die Herrlichkeit des Christenthums*, under "Historische Zugabe," 217–18.

Fig. 1: The first baptism of Jews in Sweden. The German Church (Tyska kyrkan), Stockholm, 29 September 1681. A reproduction (1924) of the copperplate used in Christophorus Bezelius, *Die Herrlichkeit des Christenthums* (1684), between pp. 152–53. Source: Wikimedia Commons (Public domain).

Johannes Buxtorf (1564–1629), Christianus Gerson (1569–1627), Johannes Müller (1626–72), and Johann Christoph Wagenseil (1633–1705), and he describes the feud between Johann Reuchlin (1469–1521) and Johannes Pfefferkorn (1455–1522). Drawing on these sources, it is possible that Bezelius' work reflects "learned" opinions about Jews and Judaism rather than the "less learned" views current in the wider society. Nonetheless, it provides us with a valuable insight into what Jewish-related material was available in Sweden during the seventeenth century and how contemporary Judaism was understood.

The baptism in 1681 was the first of about 25 baptisms that took place in Stockholm (not to mention elsewhere in the country) during the century before the *Judereglementet* in 1782. These baptisms seem to have all occurred with much spectacle and solemnity. In addition to the wider social advantages that becoming Christian offered, converted Jews also reaped the benefits of special collections to help them economically; similar financial assistance was not given to converts from the Cath-

olic or Reformed (Calvinist) Churches.[60] Many converts seem to have belonged to the poorer layer of society and the maintenance they received during their Christian education would have been much needed. The money given to converts upon conversion either constituted their main source of income or acted as start capital for a small business. For example, there are letters from the wife of one of the first converts requesting financial support from the state. There were, of course, exceptions with converts taking more important positions in society with better prospects for making a decent living. Some of the men in the 1681 converted families joined the military achieving the ranks of war commissary and officer. Johan Gustaf Renat (1682–1744), the son of one of the first converts, became a famous cartographer whose maps were later "discovered" and used by August Strindberg.[61] Adolf Lewin, baptized in 1754, became one of the country's leading financiers. A rather specific field that was open to converted Jews was that of "Oriental language specialists." The growing interest in Christian Hebraism made them of particular interest to scholars who could draw upon their knowledge of Hebrew, Aramaic, the Bible, rabbinical and Karaite writings, as well as Jewish views on subjects such as heresy and Sabbateanism. Some converts were employed as "masters of languages" and taught classes on Hebrew and rabbinics. Three such former Jews were employed in a row as masters of Oriental languages to teach courses at Uppsala University: Johan Kemper (1700–16),[62] Simon Rosenbom (1716–27), and Christian Petter Löwe (1727–39).[63]

---

60 On some of these earlier baptisms, see Valentin, *Judarnas historia i Sverige*, 76–83; Carlsson, *Judarnas historia i Sverige*, 26–27.

61 Carlsson, *Judarnas historia i Sverige*, 26.

62 Johan Kemper, by far the most significant of these three, was born Moses ben Aaron in Kraków. He converted to Christianity after the date, predicted by the Sabbatian preacher Zadok of Grodno when Sabbatai Zvi was to return as the messiah in 1695, passed without event. On Kemper, see Hans-Joachim Schoeps, "'Rabbi' Johan Kemper in Uppsala: Ein Beitrag zur Geschichte und Theologie der Sabbatianer," *Kyrkohistorisk tidskrift* 45 (1945): 146–77; Mats Eskhult, "Svensk stormakt och levande hebreiska: exemplet Joh. Kemper," in *Den nordiska mosaiken: Språk- och kulturmöten i gammal tid och våra dagar*, ed. Rut Boström Andersson (Uppsala: Studentbokhandeln, 1997), 97–103; Mats Eskhult, "'Rabbi' Johan Kempers skrifttolkning – en maktpåliggande frihet," in *Ordets makt och tankens frihet: Om språket som maktfaktor*, ed. Rut Boström Andersson (Uppsala: Studentbokhandeln, 1999), 159–67; Bo Isaksson, Mats Eskhult, and Gail Ramsay, eds, *The Professorship of Semitic Languages at Uppsala University 400 Years: Jubilee Volume from a Symposium Held at the University Hall, 21–23 September 2005*, Studia Semitica Upsaliensia, vol. 24 (Uppsala: Acta Universitatis Upsaliensis, 2007); Josef Eskhult, "Andreas Norrelius' Latin Translation of Johan Kemper's Hebrew Commentary on Matthew" (Uppsala University, PhD thesis, 2008).

63 On the early history of Oriental languages and their teachers at Uppsala, see Claes Annerstedt, *Upsala universitets historia*, vol. 2: *1655–1718 – Senare afdelningen: Universitetets organisation och verksamhet* (Uppsala: Almqvist & Wiksell, 1914), 290–97; Claes Annerstedt, *Upsala universitets his-*

Ethnographic writing about Jews and Judaism in early modern Europe

From the beginning of the sixteenth century a new genre of literature appeared in Christian Europe in which the rituals of Jews "as currently practised" were described, sometimes in astounding detail. Works included aspects of ritual law and customs as well as local traditions and folklore. This marked an innovation in Jewish–Christian polemic: the (classical and) medieval focus on the theological issues that separated Judaism and Christianity was replaced by a discourse that focused on the ethnicity and cultural foreignness of Jews. Indeed, this new corpus of texts that aimed to describe Jewish praxis contributed to the earliest development – if not, indeed, the actual foundation – of ethnography as the study of the behaviours of participants in a different cultural and social situation.

The first such books to appear were Johannes Pfefferkorn's *Der Joeden Spiegel* [The Jews' Mirror], Victor von Carben's *Opus aureum ac nouum et a doctis vivis diu exspectatum* [A Golden and New Work Long-Awaited by Living Scholars], and François Tissard's *De Judeorum ritibus compendium* [A Compendium of the Jews' Rites], and works in this genre continued to be published until the end of the eighteenth century.[64] In addition to Pfefferkorn (1469–1521), von Carben (1422–1515), and Tissard (*c.* 1460–1508), some of the more important writers of the genre include Antonius Margaritha (1492–1542), Ernst Ferdinand Heß (fl. end of sixteenth century), Johannes Buxtorf (1564–1629), and Johann Jacob Schudt (1664–1722), whose contributions made a huge impact on the development of the genre. In all, there are about eighty works on Jewish rituals, traditions, and liturgy, and they vary widely in size: from short texts of twenty pages or so to multivolume

toria, vol. 3: *1719–1792 – Senare afdelningen: Universitetets organisation och verksamhet* (Uppsala: Almqvist & Wiksell, 1914), 390–405 (esp. 390–93); Johann F. A. de le Roi, *Die evangelische Christenheit und die Juden in der Zeit der Herrschaft christlicher Lebensanschauungen unter den Völkern*, vol. 1: *Von der Reformation zur Mitte des 18. Jahrhunderts* (Karlsruhe/Leipzig: H. Reuther, 1884), 431–33.

64 Johannes Pfefferkorn, *Der Joeden Spiegel* [The Jews' Mirror] (Cologne: Johannes Landen, 1507). The work was reprinted at least six times in Low German, High German, and Latin. Victor von Carben, *Opus aureum ac nouum et a doctis vivis diu exspectatum* (Cologne: Heinrich von Neuss, 1508). A short while later published in German as *Dem durchleuchtigsten/ hochbegorenen fursten und herren* (Cologne: [Heinrich Quentell Erben], 1508/1509). François Tissard, *De Judeorum ritibus compendium* (Paris: Egidius Gourmontius [Gilles de Gourmont], 1508). The work was printed together with several other compositions by the author, including a study of the Hebrew alphabet, under the title *Dialogus Προθυμοπάτρις καὶ Φρόνιμος. Et Prothumopatris et Phronimus* [A Dialogue between Prothumopatris and Phronimus].

works of several thousand.[65] Many of these works appeared in multiple editions and reprints. For example, whereas his other works were printed just once, Margaritha's *Der gantz Jüdisch glaub* [The Whole Jewish Faith] from 1530 had thirteen print runs, and of all of Buxtorf's works, only his *Epitome Grammaticæ Hebrææ* [The Epitome of Hebrew grammar] from 1613 had more editions than his *Synagoga Judaica* [The Jewish Synagogue] from 1603.[66] Furthermore, writers often edited or copied, sometimes verbatim, the works of others and republished them under their own name. For example, in 1717, Wilhelm Friedrich Reich published his *Tractätgen von denen Jüdischen Fabeln und Aberglauben* [A Small Treatise on Jewish Fables and Superstitions], which was subsequently copied and redistributed by Magnus Christian (1718) and Franciscus Xavier (1720).[67] Two years later, he published *Das andere Tractätlein von denen Jüdischen Fabeln und Aberglauben* [The Second Small Treatise on Jewish Fables and Superstitions] and this book too was subject to copying: it was "republished" by Franciscus Xavier (1719), Johann Christoph Lewien (1722), Carl Gottlieb Willig (1736), and Christian Gottlieb Seeligmann (1740).[68]

---

65 Yaacov Deutsch, *Judaism in Christian Eyes: Ethnographic Descriptions of Jews and Judaism in Early Modern Europe*, trans. Avi Aronsky [יהדות בעיניים נוצריות] (Oxford: Oxford University Press, 2012), 49.

66 Deutsch, *Judaism in Christian Eyes*, 45.

67 Wilhelm Friedrich Reich, *Tractätgen von denen Jüdischen Fabeln und Aberglauben, So sie haben von ihrer Kranckheit an, bis zum Tode, Begräbniß und Trauer, Was sie dabey vor Ceremonien und Aberglauben brauchen Und Wie dieser Aberglauben widerleget wird; Bestehen in Achtezehn Puncten Anberglauben, und so viel Widerlegungen oder Gegentheilen* (Gotha: s.n., 1717); Magnus Christian, *Tractätgen von denen Jüdischen Fabeln und Aberglauben, So sie haben von ihrer Kranckheit an, bis zum Tode, Begräbniß und Trauer, Was sie dabey vor Ceremonien und Aberglauben brauchen Und Wie dieser Aberglauben widerleget wird; Bestehend in Achtezehen Puncten Aberglauben, Und eben so viel Widerlegungen oder Gegentheilen* (S.l.: s.n., 1718); Franciscus Xavier, *Über die abergläubischen Gebräuche der Juden in der Zeit von dem Sterben bis zum Begraben* (Hamburg: s.n., 1720).

68 Wilhelm Friedrich Reich, *Das andere Tractätlein von denen Jüdischen Fabeln und Aberglauben, So sie haben von ihrer Geburt an, bis zur Beschneidung und Kirchgang, Was sie dabey vor Ceremonien und Aberglauben brauchen, Und Wie dieser Abergleuben widerlegt wird; Bestehend in fünff Puncten Aberglauben, Und eben so viel Widerlegungen oder Gegentheile* (Gotha: s.n., 1719); Franciscus Xavier, *Tractatus de fabulis et superstitione Judaeorum inde a nativitate usque ad circumcisionem. Darin wird die Blutbeschuldigung gegen die Juden widerlegt* (Hamburg: s.n., 1719); Johann Christoph Lewien, *Ein Tractätlein von denen jüdischen Fabeln und Aberglauben so sie haben von ihrer Geburth an biss zur Beschneidung und Kirch-Gang, was sie dabey vor Ceremonien und Aberglauben, gebrauchen und wie diese Aberglauben wiederleget werden: bestehend in fünff Puncten Aberglauben und eben so viel Wiederlegungen und Gegentheile* (s.l.: s.n., 1722); Carl Gottlieb Willig, *Ein Tractätlein, von den jüdischen Fabeln und Aberglauben, so sie haben von ihrer Geburth an, biss zur Beschneidung und Kirchen-Gang, was sie dabey vor Ceremonien und Aberglauben, gebrauchen, und wie diese Aberglauben wiederlegt werden,bestehend: in fünff Puncten Aberglauben, und eben so viel Wiederlegungen und Gegentheile aufgesetzet* (Stockholm: s.n., 1736); Christian Gottlieb Seeligmann,

By the time Löwe wrote his *Speculum*, there had already been over thirty publications on Jewish life and customs in German, Latin, English, Italian, and Dutch, although there had been just one in a Scandinavian language: Poul Ræff's 1516 Danish translation of Johannes Pfefferkorn's *Libellus de Judaica Confessione* [Little Book of Jewish Confession].[69] Despite the fact that the large number of works that came to be written and published clearly demonstrate the genre's popularity, this original corpus has only been subject to scholarly research during the last few decades.[70]

In these Christian works that set out to denigrate Judaism and Jews, the descriptions of Jewish customs and practices are largely correct: their polemical nature is evidenced by the type of information that the author chooses to include or leave

---

Ein Tractätlein von denen jüdischen Fabeln, und Aberglauben, so sie haben, von ihrer Geburth an, bis zur Beschneidung und Kirchen-Gang, was sie dabey vor Ceremonien gebrauchen, und wie diese Aberglauben widerleget werden; bestehend in: fünff Puncten Aberglauben, und eben so viel Wiederlegungen und Gegentheile, aufgesetzt (Lund: Ludovig Decreaux, 1740). The information is taken from Deutsch, *Judaism in Christian Eyes*, 65–73.

69 A survey of the ethnographic accounts about Jews can be found in Deutsch, *Judaism in Christian Eyes*, 34–76. On Poul Ræff's translation of Pfefferkorn's book, see Adams, *Lessons in Contempt*.

70 Winfried Frey, "'Der Juden Spiegel': Johannes Pfefferkorn und die Volksfrömmigkeit," in *Volksreligion im hohen und späten Mittelalter*, ed. Peter Dinzelbacher and Dieter R. Bauer (Paderborn: Schöningh, 1990), 177–93; Stephen G. Burnett, "Distorted Mirrors: Antonius Margaritha, Johann Buxtorf and Christian Ethnographies of Jews," *Sixteenth-Century Journal* 25 (1994): 275–87; Ronnie Po-Chia Hsia, "Christian Ethnographies of Jews in Early Modern Europe," in *The Expulsion of the Jews: 1492 and After*, ed. Raymond B. Waddington and A. H. Williamson (New York: Garland, 1994), 223–35; Ellen Martin, *Die deutschen Schriften des Johannes Pfefferkorn: Zum Problem des Judenhasses und der Intoleranz in der Zeit der Vorreformation* (Göppingen: Kümmerle, 1994); Stephen G. Burnett, *From Christian Hebraism to Jewish Studies: Johannes Buxtorf (1564–1629) and Hebrew Learning in the Seventeenth Century* (Leiden: Brill, 1996); Elisheva Carlebach, "Attribution of Secrecy and Perceptions of Jewry," *Jewish Social Studies* 2, no. 3 (1996): 115–36; Johannes Graf, ed., *Judæus Conversus: Christlich-jüdische Konvertitenautobiographien des 18. Jahrhunderts* (Frankfurt am Main: Peter Lang, 1997); Maria Diemling, *"Christliche Ethnographien" über Juden und Judentum in der Frühen Neuzeit: Die Konvertiten Victor von Carben und Anthonius Margaritha und ihre Darstellung jüdischen Lebens und jüdischer Religion* (University of Vienna, Diss. Phil., 1999); Carlebach, *Divided Souls*, 170–99; Allison P. Coudert and Jeffrey S. Shoulson, eds, *Hebraica Veritas? Christian Hebraists and the Study of Judaism in Early Modern Europe* (Philadelphia: University of Pennsylvania Press, 2004); Dean Phillip Bell and Stephen G. Burnett, eds, *Jews, Judaism, and the Reformation in Sixteenth-Century Germany* (Leiden: Brill, 2006); Maria Diemling, "Anthonius Margaritha on the 'Whole Jewish Faith': A Sixteenth-Century Convert from Judaism and his Depiction of the Jewish Religion," in *Jews, Judaism, and the Reformation in Sixteenth-Century Germany*, ed. Dean Phillip Bell and Stephen G. Burnett (Leiden: Brill, 2006), 303–33; Aya Elyada, "Protestant Scholars and Yiddish Studies in Early Modern Europe," *Past and Present* 203 (2009): 69–98; Deutsch, *Judaism in Christian Eyes*; Adams, *Lessons in Contempt*; Adams and Heß, eds, *Revealing the Secrets of the Jews*.

out, how these customs and practices are "dressed" (e.g., as anti-Christian, absurd, menacing, and so on), and to what extent certain aspects are exaggerated or played down. The polemics of the genre centre on showing that: 1) Judaism is an anti-Christian religion, and its adherents are thus inimical towards Christians; 2) Judaism is a faith of superstitions; 3) Jewish customs deviate from biblical law.[71] However, as the genre developed the polemical impetus weakened and by the eighteenth century the focus was very much on Jewish praxis.

The leitmotif that ran through the polemics of the genre was the discontinuity between Jews past and Jews present. The Talmud was used to demonstrate that the Judaism practised in the Old Testament and that practised by contemporary Jews in Europe were completely different, and these differences had to be exposed. Writers strove to show that Jews no longer adhered to the law of the Bible but instead favoured the teachings of the Talmud and later rabbinical writings. Judaism, they claimed, was no longer a real religion but rather an artificial, counterfeit one, a superstition.[72] This of course meant that contemporary Jews – false Jews – could not claim to be God's chosen people or to be considered anything other than infidels at best. In order to highlight the inanity of Jewish rituals, discrepancies between religious regulations and their mode of fulfilment by Jews were mocked, while the Protestant belief in salvation through grace was contrasted with the importance placed by Jews on the performance of mitzvot. Jewish ceremonies were described in ways to present them as primitive, dark, and superstitious, and in need of being drawn into the light. Prayers and rituals were presented as containing dark secrets and hidden (or, just as often, blatant) anti-Christian content. The lifting of this "veil of secrecy" proved to be a double-edged sword: on the one hand it led in the long term to "a better understanding of Judaism and more favourable views about the Jews," but on the other by focusing on difference it "reconfirmed and underscored their status as aliens."[73]

An important factor that characterizes a great many of these works is that they are written by converted Jews. Indeed, two thirds of the writers of these ethnographical works about Jews and Judaism were Jewish converts to Christianity. From the Middle Ages on, converts had played a key role in Jewish–Christian debate, acting both as initiators of disputations and as sources of information about the "secrets of the Jews" through their knowledge of texts and rituals. The principal sources that writers drew upon in their descriptions of Jewish ceremonial life were Jewish texts (especially the Talmud, other rabbinical commentaries, and

71 Deutsch, *Judaism in Christian Eyes*, 2.
72 Carlebach, *Divided Souls*, 198.
73 Deutsch, *Judaism in Christian Eyes*, 251, 252.

Jewish books of customs ["minhag literature"]),[74] other Christian works on Jews and Judaism, first-hand observation, and personal knowledge.[75] It is, of course, in these two latter categories of sources that ex-Jews had an advantage. Able to rely on personal knowledge, they could provide great details about rituals, and they tended to focus on what they considered to be superstitious and present it as worthy of mockery. For example, in *Speculum Religionis Judaicœ*, Löwe writes about *tashlich* and says:

> Hwad är icke detta för en grufwelig synd och widskepelse; ty det är ogiörligit sina synder at bortskaka/ vtan ett slikt syndsens afläggiande/ måste ske genom en sann bättring och omwändelse.[76]
>
> [What sort of horrible sin and superstition is this because it is impossible to shake off one's sins? Rather such an absolution of sins has to take place by means of true repentance and conversion.]

On the ritual of makkot, Johannes Pfefferkorn in Poul Ræff's Danish translation in *Nouiter in lucem data* [Recently Drawn into the Light] writes that Jews believe they can expell their sins through their backsides:

> Han slar ha*n*nu*m* i hanss bagstak met eth belthæ oc wendher ringhen til/ eller met e*n* andhen swøbæ wel xxxix serdelwghe slag i then myening/ at er ther noge*n* synd igen vti thet me*n*nisckæ/ tha scal hwn swo vd driffues aff hanss gomp/ oc sidhen regner han sig at waræ alsamen reen/ pwr oc skær aff alle syndher.[77]
>
> [He beats him on the behind with a belt using the end with the buckle or with some other scourge, lashing him a good thirty-nine individual times in the belief that if there is any sin left in the man, then it can be driven out of his rump. And then he considers himself to be completely clean, pure and cleansed of any sins.]

And in his *Jüdischer Ceremonien* [About Jewish Ceremones], Christian Gottlieb Seeligmann writes about a superstition during Hoshana Rabba:

---

74 For example, in *Speculum Religionis Judaicœ*, Löwe mentions among others the Yiddish אײן שױן מעשה־בוך, *ayn shoyn mayse-bukh* [A Beautiful Book of Fairy-Tales]; and medieval Hebrew and Aramaic works such as אקדמות, *aḳdamut* [the Akdamut]; ילקוט ראובני, *yalḳuṭ Re'uveni* [Collection of Reuben]; ילקוט שמעוני, *yalḳuṭ Šim'oni* [Collection of Simon]; ספר לב טוב, *sefer lev ṭov* [The Book of the Good Heart]; קיצור שני לוחות הברית, *ḳiẓur šnei luḥot ha-brit* [Abbreviation of the Two Tablets of the Covenant]; and Jewish scholars such as David Kimhi and Rashi.

75 Deutsch, *Judaism in Christian Eyes*, 240.

76 *Spec.* (Sthlm, 1732), 50–51.

77 Adams, *Lessons in Contempt*, 226–27, 283–84.

> Am aller *curieuse*sten ist/ daß sie an diesem Tage frühe bey hellem Mondschein aufstehen/ und zwar gantz nackend/ nehmen ein Bett-Laken um ihrem Leib/ und stellen sich damit in Mondschein/ werffen das Bett-Laken von sich/ und breiten sich aus. Wann nun einer seinen Kopff in den Schatten des Monds nicht siehet/ so dencket er/ er sterbe dasselbige Jahr; siehet er aber ein Arm oder ein Bein nicht von seinem Leibe/ so bedeutet es einem von seinen nähesten Befreunden. Da siehest du/ lieber Christ/ was vor ein schrecklicher Aberglauben unter den Jüden vorgehe/ wi sie GOtt versuchen/ und seine Geheimniß wissen wollen: Dafür GOtt dich und mich in Gnaden bewahre.[78]

> [The most curious thing is that they get up early that day in the bright moonlight and, completely naked, take a bed sheet around their body and stand with it in the moonlight; they throw off the bed sheet and spread it out. If someone does not see his head in the shadow of the moon, he thinks that he will die during that year; but if he does not see an arm or a leg from his body, it means that for one of his closest friends. There you see, dear Christian, what terrible superstitions have currency among the Jews, how they tempt God and want to know his secret. May God keep you and me in his mercy.]

Sometimes, they included a description of ceremonies that they had taken part in themselves. For example, in Löwe's *Speculum Religionis Judaicæ* (p. 50), he writes about the Priestly Blessing:

> Sedan lyfta de vp händerna/ och *Cantorn* siunger för dem HERrans wälsignelse. Der wid hafwa de och en *Fabel*, det jag sielf försökt och *proberat* hafwer/ och sedt at det vti ingen sanning är. De betäckia sina hufwuden med en yllen-duk när Arons slächt siunger wälsignelsen/ och föregifwa; at den som då ser på dem/ han skal blifwa blind/ derföre hålla både små och stora för ögonen. Och har jag äfwen den tid jag en Jude war/ tagit mig den dristigheten på/ och under wälsignelsens förrättande sedt på dem/ och är doch Gudi lof! icke blind worden.

> [Then they raise their hands, and the cantor sings the Lord's blessing to them. They also have a fairy-tale about this, which I myself have tried and experienced, and seen that there is no truth in. They cover their heads with a woollen cloth when the family of Aaron sing the blessing, and they allege that whoever looks at them during this moment will go blind. For this reason, both young and old cover their eyes. And when I was also a Jew, I had the audacity to look at them while the blessing was being performed, and – praise be to God! – I did not turn blind.]

There are several reasons why this genre appeared at the end of the fifteenth century and why it continued to be popular until the turn of the nineteenth century.

---

78 Christian Gottlieb Seeligmann, ספר מנהגים של יום טוב וחתנות *Jüdischer Ceremonien Von der Jüden Hochzeiten/ Fest- und Feyer-Tagen Durchs gantze Jahr. Nebst ihrem dabey habenden Aberglauben/ Zum Dienst der Warheit vorgestellt* (Stockholm: Johan Laurentius Horrn, 1725), 18. Löwe includes a Swedish translation of this passage in his *Speculum Religionis Judaicæ*, pp. 58–59.

Ronnie Po-Chia Hsia places the turning point as the blood libel of Trent (now Trento in northern Italy) in 1475 because for the first time the investigation of an alleged murder took particular interest in Jewish customs and rituals.[79] However, as both Elisheva Carlebach and Yaacov Deutsch have argued, Christian writers already showed an interest in Jewish worship before Trent (e.g., the Dominican inquisitor Bernard Gui, 1261/62–1331), and furthermore the blood-libel investigation in Trent does not explain why ethnography about Jews became so popular in Germany and the north.[80]

Among the reasons for the genre's appearance at the turn of the sixteenth century, it is important to note that the beginning of the modern age also marked a subtle, gradual change in how Jews were being perceived.[81] They were viewed as human beings (albeit failed ones) and their state of Jewishness was seen not as an innate condition, but instead as a learnt set of behaviours and attitudes.[82] It was these behaviours and attitudes that had to be uncovered and understood. Christian ethnographical works helped with this shift in focus away from writing about and theologically countering Judaism to writing about Jews. Furthermore, there was both a growing interest in Christian Hebraism and studying Hebrew for biblical scholarship and an increasing number of conversions from Judaism to Christianity who could act as sources and even writers.

There was already a long tradition of literature that described the unknown or the less-well-known. Indeed, one of the most popular works of the Middle Ages was *The Travels of Sir John Mandeville*, a fantastical travel memoire that appeared in the second half the fourteenth century and was translated into at least ten languages. However, whereas such travel literature often highlighted the unusual and the extraordinary, ethnographical works tended to focus on the quotidian, usual, ordinary, and customary; Löwe uses the word "brukelig" [customary, common, accepted, practised] to describe such phenomena.[83] This interest in customs is

79 Hsia, "Christian Ethnographies of Jews in Early Modern Europe," 224.

80 Carlebach, *Divided Souls*, 173; Deutsch, *Judaism in Christian Eyes*, 230–31.

81 Shmuel Ettinger, "The Beginnings of the Change in Attitude of European Society towards the Jews," *Scripta Hierosolymitana* 7 (1961): 193–217.

82 Carlebach, *Divided Souls*, 172.

83 Within earlier travel literature, there are, of course, exceptions. For example, in his *Itinerarium fratris Willielmi de Rubruquis de ordine fratrum Minorum, Galli, Anno gratiae 1253 ad partes Orientales* [The Itinerary of Brother William of Rubruquis of the order of the Friars Minor, France, in the Year of Grace 1253 to the Eastern Parts], the Flemish Franciscan missionary Willem van Rubroeck (fl. 1248–55) describes many details of everyday life among the Mongols. Similarly, the earlier account by Giovanni da Pian del Carpine (*c.* 1185–1252), *Ystoria Mongalorum quos nos Tartaros appellamus* [The History of the Mongols Whom We Call Tartars], although displaying more

also evident in contemporaneous Jewish scholarship: from the fifteenth century on there was a blossoming of the minhag literature in Ashkenaz.[84] Such literature described local traditions and folkways rather than an ideal vision of Jewish praxis and, in addition to having its intended audience of Jewish readers, acted as a source for writers of Christian ethnographic works about Jews. Finally, during the early modern period, there was a growing interest in ethnographic accounts of other peoples and religions with books appearing about other ethnic groups and cultures in the Old and New Worlds.[85] Interest in works about Jewish praxis only began to subside in the late eighteenth century with the emergence of the Enlightenment, when theological and biblical topics came to be replaced by philosophical concerns.

Writing ethnographical works about Jews and Judaism was largely a German phenomenon and there are several reasons why the genre arose, grew, and was particularly popular in the German lands. First, Jews had a long presence in some of these areas, and consequently there was also a large number of converts who could act both as informants and writers. Second, unlike countries such as Spain, Portugal, or France, the German lands did not have any overseas colonies, and so whereas inhabitants of the former countries looked to Central and South America, Africa, and Asia for subaltern natives, Germans had to look closer to home and Jews came to be their "other." Finally, Protestantism had strong roots in the German lands and was widespread, and with Protestant intellectuals' interest in Hebrew, the ground was fertile for literature about Jews. Moreover, ethnographic accounts of Jewish praxis were sometimes veiled criticisms of Catholicism with Jewish and Catholic rituals being paralleled. Rather than seeking salvation through faith alone, the Catholics, like the Jews, so it was claimed, had abandoned the Bible and followed invented rituals and various superstitions, and so absurd customs and traditions could be contrasted with Protestantism. This, too, was a reason why the genre was popular in Protestant circles and consequently in some German areas.[86]

Although the composition of these ethnographic works about Jews was largely driven by critical motives, even contempt, they do contain useful information for historians today about Jewish practices and history, the image of the Jews within a majority Christian culture, and Jewish–Christian relations at the time of writing. Occasionally, these works throw up surprising episodes from Jewish history. For

gullibility than in Willem's work, describes the everyday life, customs, food, clothing, and marriage of the Tartars.

84 Carlebach, *Divided Souls*, 175–77; Deutsch, *Judaism in Christian Eyes*, 236.

85 On ethnographical works in the early modern period, see Margaret T. Hodgen, *Early Anthropology in the Sixteenth and Seventeenth Centuries* (Philadelphia: University of Pennsylvania Press, 1964).

86 Carlebach, *Divided Souls*, 174.

example, in his *Speculum Religionis Judaicæ*, Löwe includes an account of the fraudulent summoning of the Shechinah by the false prophet Judah Leib Prossnitz (*c.* 1670–*c.* 1730/50), "which I myself remember and upon my conscience know to have truly happened."[87] Thus, Löwe's book provides us with a valuable insight into not only what Swedes at the beginning of the eighteenth century were being told about Jews, but also into Jewish ceremonies and folkways as practised at the time – albeit not in Sweden.

Speculum Religionis Judaicæ

Christian Petter Löwe

At the beginning of 1724, the converted Jew Christian Petter Löwe (his family name had probably been Lev/Lew or Levi/Lewi), originally from Poland, arrived in Sweden from Russia where he had spent a long time in prison.[88] In Turku (Åbo), he delivered a request to the Academy to teach Rabbinics, Hebrew, Chaldaic (Aramaic), and Syriac. However, as there was no evidence that he had any in-depth knowledge of these three languages nor was there evidence of him having taught before, his application was turned down. After travelling further west, his luck changed, and on 5 May 1724 the state commission decided to award him an annual income of 200 daler to teach Oriental languages. Just a few years later, in 1727, he took up the position of "master of Oriental languages" at the Royal Academy in Uppsala (Uppsala University) and began teaching Hebrew, Rabbinics, Polish, and Russian for an annual income of 300 daler. However, Löwe soon became notorious for his poor behaviour. In a letter about Jews in Stockholm from 1736, it is said of Löwe that although he was supposed to be a master in Oriental languages in Uppsala, he was often in Stockholm making all kinds of trouble. In the foreword to his *Speculum Religionis Judaicæ*, Löwe states that he has written this book on the Jews and their customs because such a work was not available in Swedish and he most certainly hoped it would sell well. To increase sales of the book he travelled the country and sold it himself, to the detriment of his work at the university. Because of "his bois-

87 *Spec.* (Sthlm, 1732), 80: "hwilket jag sielf mins och på mitt egit samwete/ wet at det vti sanning skedt är."
88 On Christian Petter Löwe, see Valentin, *Judarnas historia i Sverige*, 86–91.

terous and lecherous living and shaky finances [Löwe] had made himself totally impossible and was finally removed from office in 1739."[89]

Speculum Religionis Judaicæ

Löwe advertised his plan to write a description of Jewish customs and rituals in Swedish in a prospectus printed 30 August 1731 in which he asks those interested in such a work for subscriptions of three copper daler.[90] As soon as the book was published, subscribers would receive a copy. The chapters of the planned book are listed in the prospectus, and they are identical to the first edition in 1732.

This first edition of *Speculum Religionis Judaicæ* from 1732 was printed by Johan Laurentius Horrn (active in Stockholm 1717–41) and is an octavo comprising 154 pages (10 quires: a–b^{8}, c^{5}, A–G^{8} + one glued-in sheet and a flysheet at rear). Löwe's reason for publishing it is given in the preface to the work,[91] where he points out that there are a number of works describing Jewish customs and ceremonies in Latin and German, but none is available in Swedish.[92] As these foreign-language books are both expensive and written for a scholarly audience, he aims to publish a cheap work that will reveal the Jewish religion and customs that are currently being practised.[93] In his short preface, Löwe does make use of the phrase "draw into the light," commonly employed elsewhere by Christian writers to refer to their intentions of describing Jewish ceremonies and religion, but he is otherwise rather reticent in his preface about his condemnation of such rituals as superstition or false. Indeed, his principal focus here appears to be the book's affordability.[94]

---

89 Valentin, *Judarnas historia i Sverige*, 87: "till slut genom sitt bullersamma och liderliga liv och sina tilltrasslade affärer gjorde sig alldeles omöjlig och 1739 avsattes."
90 See Appendix 3.
91 *Spec.* (Sthlm, 1732), xxxiii–xxxviii.
92 *Spec.* (Sthlm, 1732), xxxiii: "[…] warandes de en del på *Latin* och en del på det Tyska Språket sammanskrefne, men ingen *Tractat* der om på Swenska, sedt vtkommen wara" [(…) some are compiled in Latin and some in German, but no treatise on the subject has been published in Swedish].
93 *Spec.* (Sthlm, 1732), xxxiv–xxxv: "ty hafwer jag det samma på Swenska korteligen vti Liuset welat frambringa, at der af ses och inhämtas kan hwad *Religion* och *Ceremonier* hos dem wid hwarje handa tilfällen brukade warda" [I have wanted to draw into the light the same (information) summarized in Swedish, from which can be seen and gathered what religion and ceremonies they perform in each case].
94 For example, this stands in stark contrast to the preface that Poul Ræff added to his *Nouiter in lucem data: iudeorum secreta* in 1516 – his Danish translation of Johannes Pfefferkorn's *Libellus de Judaica Confessione*. Here he writes: "Thenne bog er vtdraghen aff latinen oc vtsæth paa dansckæ/ til theris behoff som icke kwnne forstaa latinæ. Hwn tracterer oc indhæ holdher/ alle

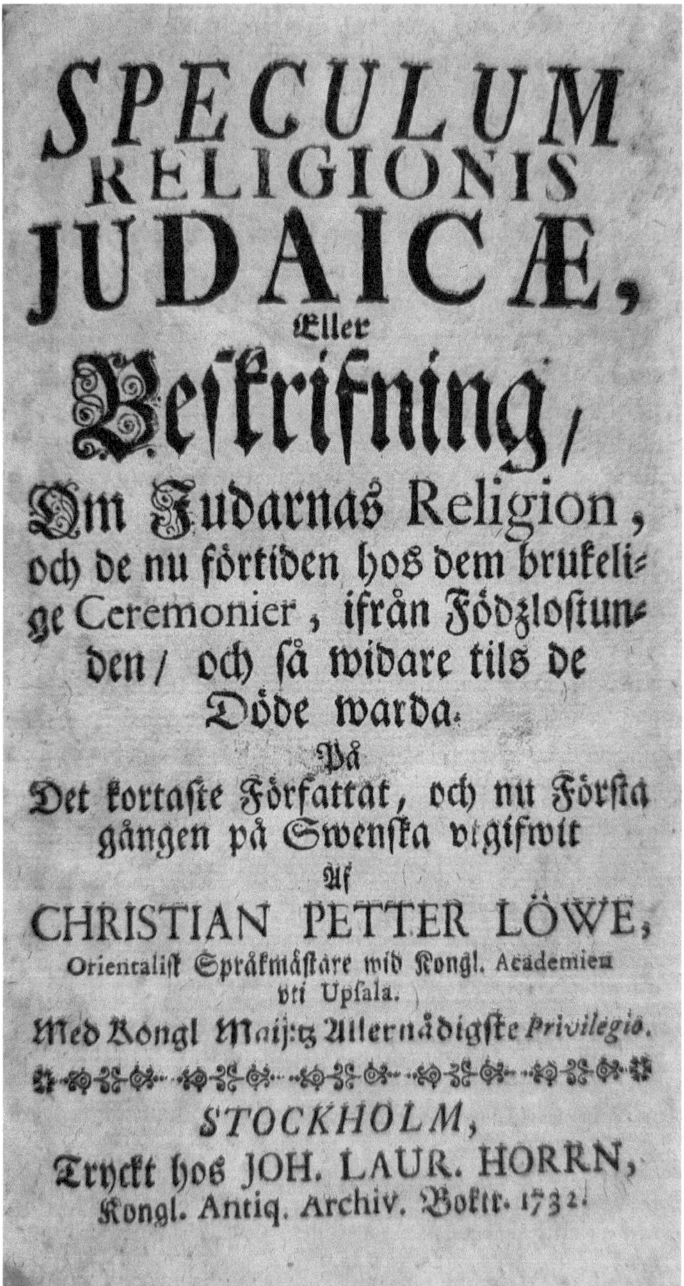
SPECULUM
RELIGIONIS
JUDAICÆ,
Eller
Beskrifning,
Om Judarnas Religion,
och de nu förtiden hos dem brukeli-
ge Ceremonier, ifrån Födzlostun-
den/ och så widare tils de
Döde warda.
På
Det kortaste Författat, och nu Första
gången på Swenska utgifwit
Af
CHRISTIAN PETTER LÖWE,
Orientalist Språkmästare wid Kongl. Academien
uti Upsala.
Med Kongl Maij:ts Allernådigste *Privilegio.*
STOCKHOLM,
Tryckt hos JOH. LAUR. HORRN,
Kongl. Antiq. Archiv. Boktr. 1732.

Fig. 2: Frontispiece of Christian Petter Löwe, *Speculum Religionis Judaicæ* (1732). Source: Author's own photograph.

Although Löwe certainly intended to make money from his book, it also functions as a personal testimony to the integrity of his own conversion. Throughout *Speculum Religionis Judaicœ*, Löwe is keen to present himself as a good Christian (and Swede), and he even devotes an entire chapter (ch. 12) to proving that Jesus is the true Messiah and son of God – arguments that would have been superfluous to his Christian readership but that underscore his sincerity and his own knowledge about Christianity. It is possible that in writing his book, Löwe is responding to suspicion directed against Jewish converts generally or against himself in particular. He clearly uses the language, images, and symbols of his new religion, and by doing so he rejects his former faith. In part at least, *Speculum* is meant to act as an affirmation of and passport to his new life as a Christian in Sweden. As we saw earlier, there was much resistance to Jews living in Sweden, and Löwe was doubtlessly eager to distance himself from his former coreligionists.[95] Löwe would have been keen to demonstrate that he had severed ties with the Jewish faith and people and was entirely sincere in his Lutheranism.

Contents

Speculum Religionis Judaicœ describes customs, rituals, and folklore connected with all life events beginning with birth and ending with death, the afterlife, and resurrection:

1. Birth
2. Day seven
3. Circumcision
4. Birth of a girl
5. Beginning school
6. Bar mitzvah
7. Tefillin
8. Praying
9. The Jews' religion
10. Dealings with Christians
11. Disbelief in Christ
12. Christ is the true Messiah
13. Anger at Christ
14. Kashrut
15. Teḳufot
16. Sabbath
17. Pesach
18. Shavuot

the hemelighæ stycker som the fwlæ iøder haffue mellom sig sielff/ baadhe i theris iødhætempel/ och i theris egnæ hws. Paa thet at cristnæ mennisckæ scullæ widhæ ath straffæ them" [This book is taken from Latin and translated into Danish to meet the needs of those who cannot understand Latin. It deals with and contains all the secret affairs that the bad Jews keep between themselves both in their Jewish temple and in their own houses. Thus shall Christian people know to reproach them]." Pfefferkorn, *Nouiter in lucem data*, p. 1; Adams, *Lessons in Contempt*, 202, 203. Ræff's and Löwe's prefaces reflect the changing polemical uses of Christian ethnographical texts about Jews and Judaism described above.

95 For example, between 1772 and 1786, around the time of Aron Isak's arrival in Sweden, there were no fewer than 273 articles and notices about Jews published in five large newspapers that on the whole presented them negatively. Carlsson, *Judarnas historia i Sverige*, 34–35.

19. Tisha beAv
20. Rosh Hashanah
21. Yom Kippur
22. Sukkot
23. Simchat Torah
24. Hanukkah
25. Purim
26. Engagements
27. Marriages and weddings
28. Divorce
29. Childless death
30. Meals
31. Food
32. Anger at Christians
33. Order and justice
34. Oath-taking
35. Maintenance of the poor
36. Shaving beards
37. Cutting nails
38. Mezuzot
39. Hatred of apostates
40. Confession by the sick
41. Last hour of death
42. Death
43. Torments of the dead
44. Mourners' arrival home
45. Paradise
46. Hell
47. Description of hell
48. Resurrection of the dead

In his *Judaism in Christian Eyes*, Yaacov Deutsch compares the topics covered in some forty-six ethnographical works about Judaism dating from 1508 to 1781.[96] Here, we can see that Löwe's topics are on the whole unexceptional; for example, along with thirty-five other works, he mentions customs of the Sabbath and along with twenty-seven other works the customs of the New Moon. Nonetheless, he also mentions some topics that are more unusual in Christian descriptions of Jews and Judaism; for example, he includes Grace after Meals (mentioned in five other works),[97] the Four Teḳufot (four others),[98] Ten Days of Repentance (four others),[99]

96 Deutsch, *Judaism in Christian Eyes*, 51–63.

97 *Spec.* (Sthlm, 1732), 43; Moses Marcus, *The Ceremonies of the Present Jews* (London: J. Roberts, 1728); Abraham Mears [Gamliel ben Pedahzur], *The Book of Religion, Ceremonies and Prayers of the Jews: In their Synagogues and Families on All Occasions* (London: J. Wilcox, 1738); Johann Christoph Georg Bodenschatz, *Kirchliche Verfassung der heutigen Juden sonderlich derer in Deutschland in IV. Haupt-Theile abgefasset aus ihren eigenen und anderen Schriften umständlich dargethan und mit 30 sauberen Kupfern erläutert*, 4 vols (Frankfurt [am Main]/Leipzig: Johann Friedrich Becker, 1748–49); Gottfried Selig, *Der Jude, eine Wochenschrift*, 9 vols (Leipzig, 1768–72); Gottfried Selig, *Der Jude, oder Altes und Neues Judenthum*, 3 vols (Leipzig: Rumpf, 1781–87).

98 *Spec.* (Sthlm, 1732), 30–31; Christoph Paul Majern, מינהגים. *Das ist derer heutigen Jüden Ceremonien, und Gebräuche* (Wittenberg: Johann Wilken, 1678); Giulio Morosini, דרך אמונה. *Via della fede mostrata a'gli ebrei* (Rome: Sacra Cong. de Prop. Fide, 1683); Johann Friedrich Guthertz, *Beschreibung der Jüdischen Ceremonien und Gebräuche der heutigen Juden, daß sie dabey Gottes Gebot hindansetzen, und die Aufsätze ihrer Väter weit höher achten* (Brieg: Tramp, 1747); Johann Friedrich Guthertz and Christian Gottlieb Hamburger, *Beschreibung derer Ceremonien und Gebräuche der heutigen Juden: daß sie dabey Gottes Gebot hindansetzen, und die Aufsätze ihrer Väter weit höher achten in einem kurzen Auszuge nach der Wahrheit vorgestellet* (Frankfurt [am Main]/Leipzig: s.n., 1755).

99 *Spec.* (Sthlm, 1732), 50–53; Majern, מינהגים. *Das ist derer heutigen Jüden Ceremonien, und Gebräuche*; Bernard Picart, *Cérémonies et coutumes religieuses de tous les peuples du monde*, 7 vols (Amsterdam: Bernard, 1723–37); Selig, *Der Jude, eine Wochenschrift*; Selig, Der *Jude, oder Altes und Neues Judenthum*.

and Bar Mitzvah (just two others).[100] However, his accounts of some these customs are not entirely trustworthy. For example, when writing about Grace (*birkat ha-mazon*) after the Passover seder, he uses the text from the song "Ḥad Gadya" as the blessing:

> siunga sedan en wisa/ som de kalla *Berkat Hamason*: om en Ichelein eller en killing och en katt/ som åt vp samma killing: hunden bet katten/ kiäppen slog hunden/ elden brände vp kiäppen/ watnet slächte elden/ oxen drack vt watnet/ Slachtaren slachta oxen/ döden slachta Slachtaren/ och Gud afskaffade döden.[101]
>
> [Then they all sing a song that is called *Berkat Hamason* about a *(z)ichelein* or a kid and a cat that ate this kid, the dog bit the cat, the stick beat the dog, the fire burned the stick, the water put out the fire, the ox drank the water, the slaughterer killed the ox, the Angel of Death slew the slaughterer, and God abolished death.]

Löwe's descriptions are based on Polish-Ashkenazi traditions and practices, and he includes some practices that are not mentioned elsewhere, e.g., children wear a certain number of garlic bulbs around their necks on Tisha beAv.[102]

Löwe provides two reasons for publishing his affordable work: (1) a source of pleasure and entertainment for his readers, and (2) a warning to avoid Jewish practices.[103] Although he does not aim to show that Jews are evil or demonic, there can be no doubt that *Speculum* aims to paint Jewish customs and practices in a negative light. Some traditions are depicted as merely foolish superstitions. So, for example, when writing about the description in Yeshayahu Halevi's *Ḳiẓur šnei luḥot ha-brit* of how a sinner after death is forced to eat poisonous herbs, Löwe adds the

100 *Spec.* (Sthlm, 1732), 8; Morosini, דרך אמונה. *Via della fede*; Carl Anton, *Kurzer Entwurf der Erklärung Jüdischer Gebräuche sowol geistlicher als weltlicher zum Gebrauch akademischer Vorlesungen entworfen* (Helmstadt: s.n., 1751).

101 *Spec.* (Sthlm, 1732), 43.

102 See pp. 135, 137*n*190 in this edition.

103 *Spec.* (Sthlm, 1732), xxxviii: "Jag har fördenskull det förnämsta vti största hastighet och korthet sammanskrifwit, så mycket jag i sanning wara wet och mig bekant är; warandes der om försäkrad, det den Gunstige Läsaren sin förnöijelse här vtinnan hafwa och finna skal" [Therefore, in the greatest haste and brevity, I have compiled what is most important, as much as I know to be true and am familiar with. The gracious reader can be reassured that he will enjoy and find pleasure within]; *Spec.* (Sthlm, 1732), 112: "Jag hafwer fördenskul allenast det förnämligaste af deras *Traditioner* och Fabler welat anföra/ tackandes GUD! som oß sitt ords klara lius gifwit hafwer/ så at wi icke byggia på en sådan lös sand eller grund/ vtan på alla werldenes Frälsare hwilken är den rätta grunden och wägledaren til Himmelen och saligheten" [Therefore, I have chosen to quote only the noblest of their traditions – thanks be to God! who has given us the clear light of his word, so that we might not build upon such unstable sand or foundation but rather upon the Saviour of the entire world who is the right foundation and guide to heaven and blessedness.]

following criticism: "Now, my gracious reader, we can also see their superstition here, because every single person who is of sound mind can understand and comprehend that it is impossible for whoever is dead to be able to chew and eat."[104] Similarly, the custom of tashlich is described as a "horrible sin and superstition."[105] Other practices are, however, described in more menacing terms. Chapter 10 is full of anti-Christian curses and swearwords ("*Erel*," "*Skäratz*," "*Capora*," "*Skedd*," "*Taf Orel Gemach Schemo*," and "*Taud Goi Mutter*"), while the prayer *Aleinu Leshabeach* is described in chapter 8 as being anti-Christian.[106] In chapter 9, we read that "They speak so contemptibly against the Christian religion and say that when their Messiah comes, they will become great and considerable lords, and the noble Christians will be like farmhands and maids for the Jews."[107] However, this is presented as a ridiculous belief rather than as a real threat to Christians.[108] What is noteworthy, is that Löwe restricts his criticisms of Jews to their "superstitious" religious practices. There is no mention of antisemitic canards such as ritual murder, host desecration, exploitative usury, the wandering Jew Ahasuerus, well poisoning, and even deicide, typically found in medieval and some early modern works. Furthermore, Löwe glorifies Christianity throughout and uses Christian doctrine to disprove Jewish beliefs.

The historiography on Löwe and *Speculum Religionis Judaicæ* is rather modest, and there are diverging views about the tone and intent of Löwe's work. Most recently, Carl Henrik Carlsson has claimed that Löwe describes Jews and their religion "in an extremely negative way" and that "Löwe was one of several authors spreading anti-Jewish ideas in Sweden long before Jews were allowed to settle in the country."[109] By contrast, Magnus Nyman wrote in his doctoral thesis (1988), that *Speculum* is written in a "popularized form" and "in long sections the book is an honest account of Jewish customs and traditions" but that it emphasized Jewish

---

104 *Spec.* (Sthlm, 1732), 110: "Nu min Gunstige Läsare/ kan man och här se deras wahntro/ ty hwar och en/ som af ett sundt förstånd är/ kan fatta och förstå/ at den som döder är kan ogiörligen tugga och äta."

105 *Spec.* (Sthlm, 1732), 50–51: "en grufwelig synd och widskepelse."

106 *Spec.* (Sthlm, 1732), 14–15 and 12 respectively. There is a long tradition in Christian polemical literature of describing the *Aleinu Leshabeach* as a particularly anti-Chistian prayer. See p. 85*n*60 in this edition for *Spec.* (Sthlm, 1732), 12.

107 *Spec.* (Sthlm, 1732), 12: " Emot den Christeliga *Religionen* hafwa de ett sådant försmädeligt tal och säija/ at när deras *Messias* kommandes warder/ skola de stora och ansenliga Herrar warda och de förnämlige af Christenheten för Judarna blifwa såsom drängar och Pigor."

108 Cf. the medieval belief that the Red Jews would accompany Antichrist at the End of Days and enslave the Christians of Europe. See Adams, *Jews in East Norse Literature*, vol. 1, 540–44.

109 Carlsson, *Judarnas historia i Sverige*, 28: "[…] ytterst negativt. Löwe var en av flera författare som spred antijudiska föreställningar i Sverige långt innan judar tilläts bosätta sig i landet."

hatred of Christians.[110] Finally, Hugo Valentin argued that Löwe writes at length about Jewish superstition and presents Judaism as "a religion of foolishness and as gruesome fairy-tales," and contrasts it with "an impartial and objective work" published in 1801 by another convert, Nathanaël Joëlsson, who criticized Löwe.[111]

It seems to me, that even though the account of Jewish customs and traditions in *Speculum* is anything but impartial and objective (in this I agree with all three of the historians mentioned above), it does not engage in an extremely negative vilification of Jews per se, but is rather an attempt to show that some religious practices are (allegedly) based on folk beliefs rather than the Bible. I would agree with Nyman that it includes much accurate (or as Nyman calls it, honest) information about the customs of Jews, which, although often dressed in critical language (as we would expect in Christian ethnographical writing about Jews), can provide us, as indeed the original readers, with a valuable insight into Judaism as practised in the early eighteenth century.

Popularity

Even before publication, the plan for *Speculum Religionis Judaicæ* as outlined in the 1731 prospectus was included in several German scholarly journals that summarized the year's work in Hebraism and Jewish studies. For example, it appears in both the *Neue Leipziger Gelehrte Zeitung* and *Niedersächsische Nachrichten*:

> Upsal. Hier lebt ein bekehrter Jude, Christian Peter Löwe genan*n*t, welcher in der Rabbinischen und andern Morgenländischen Sprachen wohl erfahren ist und nechstens ein Werck von 16 Bogen in 4 unter folgendem Titel herausgeben word: Speculum Religionis Judaicæ, Beskrifning an [*sic*] Judarnas Religion och nu brukelige Ceremonier, oder Beschreibund der Jüdischen Religion und ihrer heut zu Tage bräuchlichen Gewohnheiten. Es bestehet solches aus 48 kurtzen Capiteln [...][112]

> [Uppsala. Here lives a converted Jew, called Christian Peter Löwe, who is well versed in the rabbinical and other Oriental languages and will next publish a work of 16 quires in quarto under the following title: *Speculum Religionis Judaicæ*, Beskrifning om Judarnas Religion och

110 Magnus Nyman, *Press mot friheten: opinionsbildning i de svenska tidningarna och åsiktsbrytningar om minoriteter 1772–1786* (Uppsala University, PhD thesis, 1988), 110: "populariserad form [...] I långa stycken är boken en ärlig redogörelse för judiska seder och bruk."

111 Valentin, *Judarnas historia i Sverige*, 89, 91: "en dårskapens religion och som hiskliga fabler" and "ett sakligt och objektivt arbete."

112 *Neue Leipziger Gelehrte Zeitung* (1731): 884–85.

nu Brukelige Ceremonier, or "Description of the Jewish Religion and its Customs Currently in Use." It consists of 48 short chapters (...)]

Upsal. Der sich hieselbst schon viele Jahre aufhaltende Orientalische Sprach-Meister Hr. Christian Peter Löwe,* wird sich ehestens durch ein nützliches und bisher in Schwedischer Sprache noch nicht heraus gewesenes Buch, von etwa 16 Bogen in 4. bekannt machen, dem er den Titel geben wird: Beskrifning om Judarnas Religion och nu brukelige Ceremonier, d.i. Beschreibung von der Jüdischen Religion und ihren heut zu Tage gebräuchlichen Gewohnheiten. Auf lateinisch *Speculum Religionis Judaicæ*. Die gantze Erzehlung wird sich in 48 kurzen Capiteln darstellen: [...]

* Es könte sich jemand wundern, wie man in Schweden von den heutigen Gebräuchen der Juden etwas beglaubtes in Papier bringen könne, da man im gantzen Reiche so wenig Juden als Jesuiten dulde. Man muß also wissen, daß der Verfasser ein gebohrner Jude, der nachdem er lange Zeit unter den Juden als Mitgenoß gelebet, sich zum Christenthum bekehret. Dergleichen sich in unsern Gegenden in allem ohngefehr 5 bis 6 aufhalten. Er verstehet die Rabbinische und andere Morgenländische Sprachen ziemlich wol, und hat die Hrn. *Studiosos* bisher darin unterrichtet. Daher man diesen seinen Nachrichten desto mehr trauen kan.[113]

[Uppsala. The Oriental language master, who has been living there for many years, Mr Christian Peter Löwe,* will soon make himself known through a useful book, which has not yet been published in Swedish, of about 16 quires in quarto, to which he has given the title *Beskrifning om Judarnas Religion och nu brukelige Ceremonier*, that is "Description of the Jewish Religion and its Current Customs," in Latin *Speculum Religionis Judaicæ*. The whole story will be presented in 48 short chapters: (...)

* Someone might wonder how something certifiably true about the Jews' present-day customs can be put on paper in Sweden, because as few Jews as Jesuits are tolerated in the entire kingdom. It must be known that the author, a Jew by birth, who, after living among the Jews for a long time as a fellow citizen, converted to Christianity. There are about five to six people like that in our lands. He understands the Rabbinic and other Oriental languages fairly well and until now has taught them to students. Therefore, one can trust his news all the more.]

After its publication, the book is also recorded in Johann Christoph Wolf's extensive *Bibliotheca Hebræa*, although here too it seems only to be a planned publication:

קריסטיאן פיטר ליב CHRISTIANVS PETRVS LEBH, Ex-Judæus, qvi per plures annos Vpsaliæ literas Orientis docuit. Parat is librum Svecicum sub titulo: *Speculum religionis Judaicæ*, capitibus LVIII. [*sic*] comprehensum, qvo ritus Judæorum hodie receptos exponet. Eorum I. aget de festis Judæorum natalitiis. II. de ritibus ad puerum, septem dies natum pertinentibus. III. de

113 *Niedersächsische Nachrichten* (1731): 666–68.

circumcisione &c. & ultimum de resurrectione. Indicem omnium capitum leges, si placet, in Niedersächsischen Nachrichten [...] & Leipziger Gelehreten Zeitungen [...][114]

[קריסטיאן פיטר ליב Christianus Petrus Lebh, a former Jew, who for many years taught the writings of the East in Uppsala. He is preparing a Swedish book under the title *Speculum Religionis Judaicæ* (Mirror of the Jewish Religion), 58 (*sic*) comprehensive chapters, that should explain the rites of the Jews as practised today. The first of them will deal with the feasts of the Jews' days of birth; 2) on the rites pertaining to the seven-day-old child; 3) about circumcision and so on, and the last on the resurrection. Read the list of all chapters, if you like, in *Niedersächsischen Nachrichten* (...) & *Leipziger Gelehreten Zeitungen* (...)]

One of the reasons that Löwe was dismissed from his post in Uppsala was that he was spending far too much time travelling through the country peddling his book rather than teaching students. So, how successful an author was Löwe? How popular was his *Speculum*? It is difficult to say with any certainty. On the one hand, it is rarely referred to in other works as an authority and as the entry in Johann F. A. de le Roi's *Die evangelische Christenheit und die Juden* from 1884 shows its very existence was in doubt:[115]

Eine längere Reihe von Jahren hindurch war auch Christian Peter Löwe oder Lebh Docent der orientalischen Sprachen an der Universität Upsala. Er unterrichtete viele Studenten in diesem Fach. Später wollte er in schwedischer Sprache einen "Spiegel der jüdischen Religion" herausgeben, der, nach dem vorliegenden Plane, in 58 [*sic*] Kapiteln die Gebräuche der Juden jener Zeit schildern sollte. Ob das Buch, dessen Erscheinen damals die gelehreten Zeitungen vorbereiteten, wirklich herausgekommen ist, war nicht zu ermitteln.[116]

[Christian Peter Löwe or Lebh was also a lecturer in Oriental languages at the University of Uppsala for a number of years. He taught many students in this subject. Later he wanted to publish a *Mirror of the Jewish Religion* in Swedish, which, according to the plan he presented, should describe the customs of the Jews of that time in 58 (*sic*) chapters. It was not possible to determine whether the book, whose publication the scholarly newspapers were preparing for at the time, actually was published.]

---

114 Johann Christoph Wolf, *Bibliotheca Hebræa*, vol. 4 (Hamburg: Widow of Theodor Christoph Felginer, 1733), 966. Cf. Julius Fürst, *Bibliotheca Judaica*, vol. 3 (Leipzig: Wilhelm Engelmann, 1863), 80.
115 I have been able to find one reference, viz. *Heßisches Heb-Opfer Theologischer und Philologischer Anmerckungen* 21 (1739): 808*n*–09*n*. Löwe is referred to here as a source for information about fasting before a wedding: "So schreibet ferner der bekehrte Christian Peter Löwe in seinem *Speculo relig. Iud.* eller/ Beskrifning am [*sic*] Judarnas religion/ pag. 140 s." [Thus writes the convert Christian Petter Löwe in his *Speculum Religionis Judaicæ*, p. 140 seq.]. The page reference shows that the edition referred to must be Gothenburg 1732. More recently, *Speculum Religionis Judaicæ* is referenced in Miroslav Dyrčík, "Was Leibele Prossnitz a Charlatan?" *Judaica Olomucensia* 1 (2013): 23–35 (28*n*28).
116 Le Roi, *Die evangelische Christenheit und die Juden*, vol. 1, 432.

On the other hand, *Speculum Religionis Judaicæ* was expanded and reprinted twice: later in 1732 in Gothenburg and then again in 1735 in Stockholm (see below). This would suggest that the book did have readers: demand was high enough to warrant expanding and reprinting the work and sales were buoyant enough to pay for it.[117]

By the beginning of the nineteenth century, Löwe's *Speculum* was already being seen in a poor light by some scholars. In the introduction to his first volume of *Judiska lagstiftningen, eller Gamla testamentets stadgar* (1801), the Jewish convert to Christianity, Nathanaël Joëlsson (1775–?) appears to criticize Löwe and his book, although he does not mention the author specifically by name:

> Således wänte man icke här några upgifter, at bereda åtlöje öfwer den Judiska Nationen. Jag will icke härma några nychristna af mina Landsmän, hwilke snarere likna Muhammedanska Renegater, än döpta Christendomsbröder. Det är snarare til en wederläggning af deras tilmålen öfwer den Judiska Nationen, och de ännu wördnadswärda upppenbarelser [*sic*] de följa i sin Lära, som jag fattat til pennan; ty det är ömande at se, med hwad orättwisa denna alltid så beklaganswärda, och ofta så obilligt förtryckta, Nationen blifwit bemött af sina egna fordna Medbröder. Sådant har deremot wäckt min afsky. Mit hjerta är ännu brinnande för mina Landsmän; jag önskar dem alla godt; jag älskar många af dem, ty jag älskar dygden och redligheten hwar den finnes, utan at smäda Tros-bekännelsen; och hoppas samma rättwisa af dem tilbaka. De skola derföre här snarare finna en förswarsskrift, och kanske flera uplysningar just i de mål, som dem egentligen angå.[118]

> [Thus, you will not expect any information here that makes a mockery of the Jewish nation. I will not mimic some of the new Christians from among my countrymen, who are more like Mohammedan renegades than baptized Christian brothers. It is rather a refutation of their aims regarding the Jewish nation and the still venerable revelations that they follow in their teachings that I have committed to ink; for it is painful to see the injustice this wretched and often so unfairly oppressed nation has been met with by its former brethren. I wish them all well. I love many of them, as I love honesty and virtue wherever it exists without insulting the Creed. And I hope that (I will receive) back the same fair treatment from them. Therefore, they will rather find a letter of defence and perhaps more information about the affairs that actually concern them.]

117 The theologian, philosopher, and mystic Emanuel Swedenborg (1688–1772) was also interested in Judaism and alongside works, such as Buxtorf's *Lexicon Chaldaicum, Talmudicum et Rabbinicum* (1639) and Monsieur de la Créquinière's *Conformité des coutumes des Indiens orientaux avec celles des Juifs & des autres Peuples de l'Antiquité* (1704), we find Löwe's *Speculum* in his library. See Thomas Noack, "Die Bibelübersetzungen von Swedenborg und Tafel," *Offene Tore Jahrbuch* (2014): 131–87 (179*n*77).

118 Nathanaël Joëlsson, *Judiska lagstiftningen, eller Gamla testamentets stadgar, jämte de talmudiska tilläggningar och ceremonier, hwilka af hwarje jude iakttagas*, vol. 1 (Stockholm: Kumblinska, 1801), fol. a3r–v.

In a note a little later in his book, Joëlsson does name Löwe and writes:

> De många widskepliga bruk, hwilka Löwe i sin bok *Speculum Religionis Judaicæ*, tryckt i Stockholm 1735, tillägger Judarne i allmänhet, äro långt ifrån sanningen och rätta förhållandet, åtminstone til största delen. Det är rysligt at se, med hwad blindt nit och öfwerdrifwenhet han just röjer sin föresats at förklena sina fordna Bröder. Hans upgifter kunna wisst icke räknas bland *pias fraudes*. Hwad han anförer om Liloth, den han kallar Lillith, samt mycket annat, betygar jag inför Gud, at jag aldrig hört talas om. Men man syndar så ofta mot det ottonde budet och uttyder alt til det wärsta. Hwad skulle man wäl säga, om man anförde historien om Jerusalems Skomakare, Marcolphus, Ho[l]bergs Gubben, m. fl. som allmänt köpas och säljas, och upgaf dem såsom anledningar at döma om Lutheranismen?[119]
>
> [The many superstitious practices, which Löwe in his book *Speculum Religionis Judaicæ*, printed in Stockholm in 1735, apportions to the Jews in general, are far from the truth and correct state of affairs, at least for the most part. It is appalling to see with what blind zeal and arrogance he simply reveals his intention to belittle his former brethren. His information certainly cannot be counted among *pias fraudes*. What he states about Liloth, whom he calls Lilith, and much else, I testify before God that I have never heard of. But people so often sin against the eighth commandment and interpret everything as the worst. What would we say if the story of Jerusalem's cobbler, Marcolphus, Holberg's old man, and others, which are generally bought and sold, were cited and given as reasons to judge Lutheranism?]

It is thus possible that by the beginning of 1800s, less than three quarters of a century after it was published, Löwe's work was already being seen as untrustworthy, unjust, and unfair.

Later editions

The Gothenburg 1732 edition, printed by Lars Unge (active as *Gymnasii* printer in Gothenburg 1730–32), is an octavo comprising 272 pages (17 quires: A–R^8).[120] The Stockholm 1735 edition, printed by Frantz Philip Paulssen (active in Stockholm 1734–37), is an octavo comprising 242 pages (15 quires: A–P^8 + one flysheet at rear).[121] Both of the two later editions share many characteristics: most importantly, their

119 Joëlsson, *Judiska lagstiftningen*, vol. 1, 18.

120 "Och med *Autorns* bewilning andra gången vplagd, i Götheborg/ hos Kongl. *Gymnas*. Boktryckaren/ *Lars Unge*, 1732" [And with the author's permission published for a second time, in Gothenburg, at the Royal *Gymnasium* Book Printer, Lars Unge, 1732].

121 "Men nu Tredie Gången förökt Med en Tilökning om särskilte Judarnas *Antiquiteter* och Historier/ Tillika med ett behörigt Register öfwer hela Bokens innehållande *Materier*. Och efter mångens åstundan i Stockholm Uplagd och Tryckt hos Frantz Phil. Paulssen. Åhr 1735." [But now expanded for a third time with an addition about special Jewish antiquities and stories along with an appro-

expansions are in the form of appendices and neither of them therefore adds anything to the descriptions of the ceremonies found in the first edition. The Gothenburg 1732 edition contains the appendix "Kort vtdrag af *Michlall Jophis* och *Rabbi Salomo Jarchis* anmärkningar öfwer Propheten Jonas [A short excerpt from comments about the Prophet Jonah by Miklal Yofi (=Solomon ben Melech in מכלל יופי) and Rabbi Solomon Jarchi (=Rashi)], pp. 219–30. The Stockholm 1735 edition contains the same addition as Gothenburg 1732 (pp. 132–37) followed by a further 27 "Tilökningar utur Talmud och andre Rabbiniske *Antiquiteter* och Historie-Böcker utdragne" [Expansions Excerpted from the Talmud and Other Rabbinical Antiquities and History Books], pp. 137–200.[122] A noteworthy number of these additional readings in Stockholm 1735 concern Jews' opinions about demons ("dieflarna").

As far as the description of Jewish ceremonies is concerned both later editions reduplicate several printing mistakes from the first edition. For example, all three have "*Rosch Haschara*" instead of "*Rosch Haschana*" [Rosh Hashanah],[123] "*Hoschiana Raba*" instead of "*Hoschana Raba*" [Hoshana Rabba],[124] "Wattu-Källan" instead of "Wattn-Källan" [water spring],[125] and "orsaker skull" instead of "orsakers skull" [the sake of reasons].[126] When a correction has been made in Gothenburg 1732, it also appears in Stockholm 1735 which strongly suggests that Paulssen used Unge's edition as the basis for his own. For example, in both later editions, Stockholm 1732 "Fädrr" has been corrected to "Fäder" [fathers],[127] "Bäcker" to "Böcker" [books],[128] "siefwa" to "sielfwa" [self],[129] "wija" to "wilja" [want],[130] while Stockholm 1732 "förnöijese" has been corrected to "förnöijelse" [pleasure] in Gothenburg 1732 and "förnöjelse" [pleasure] in Stockholm 1732,[131] and "*scheuä*" has been corrected to "*schenä*" [two] in Gothenburg 1732 and "*schenâ*" [two] in Stockholm 1732.[132]

A further shared feature between the two later editions is that neither printer, Unge or Paulssen, appears to have had access to Hebrew type: no Hebrew letters

priate index of the subjects contained in the entire book, and, in accordance with the desire of many people, published and printed in Stockholm by Frantz Philip Paulssen].

122 See Appendix 4.

123 *Spec.* (Sthlm, 1732), 48; *Spec.* (Gbg, 1732), 93–94; *Spec.* (Sthlm, 1735), 62.

124 *Spec.* (Sthlm, 1732), 48; *Spec.* (Gbg, 1732), 94; *Spec.* (Sthlm, 1735), 62.

125 *Spec.* (Sthlm, 1732), 59; *Spec.* (Gbg, 1732), 117; *Spec.* (Sthlm, 1735), 75.

126 *Spec.* (Sthlm, 1732), 73; *Spec.* (Gbg, 1732), 145; *Spec.* (Sthlm, 1735), 92.

127 *Spec.* (Sthlm, 1732), 19; *Spec.* (Gbg, 1732), 36; *Spec.* (Sthlm, 1735), 25.

128 *Spec.* (Sthlm, 1732), 48; *Spec.* (Gbg, 1732), 94; *Spec.* (Sthlm, 1735), 62.

129 *Spec.* (Sthlm, 1732), 82; *Spec.* (Gbg, 1732), 163; *Spec.* (Sthlm, 1735), 101.

130 *Spec.* (Sthlm, 1732), 85; *Spec.* (Gbg, 1732), 168; *Spec.* (Sthlm, 1735), 104.

131 *Spec.* (Sthlm, 1732), xxxviii; *Spec.* (Gbg, 1732), C3v; *Spec.* (Sthlm, 1735), B7v.

132 *Spec.* (Sthlm, 1732), 104; *Spec.* (Gbg, 1732), 202; *Spec.* (Sthlm, 1735), 123.

appear in either book.[133] Instead of printing words in Hebrew type, the two printers either delete the Hebrew altogether or print a transliteration with Latin type. For example, deletion:

Stockholm 1732, 1:	och kallas på *Hebræiske Masseltof* מזל טוב
Gothenburg 1732, 1:	och kallas på *Hebræiske Masseltof*
Stockholm 1735, 1:	och kallas på Hebräiske *Masseltof*

Stockholm 1732, 1–2:	och kallas samma bön på *Hebræiska*: *Cadisch vegahm amen gehö* | *schemä raba* קדיש וגם אמן יהא שמי רבה
Gothenburg 1732, 2:	och kallas sam*m*a bön på *Hebræiska*: *Cadisch vegahm amen gehöschema raba*
Stockholm 1735, 2:	och kallas samma bön på Hebräiska: *Cadisch vegahm amen gehöschema raba*

Stockholm 1732, 15–16:	*Jmanuel*, det är/ Gud med oß הנה העלמה הרה וילדת בן Judarne wilja doch inwända at det or|det *Alma* עלמה intet skal betyda någon Jungfru
Gothenburg 1732, 29:	Jm*m*anuel/ det är/ Gud med oß. Judarne wilja doch inwända at det ordet *Alma* intet skal betyda någon Jungfru
Stockholm 1735, 20–21:	Jmmanuel/ det är/ Gud med oß. Judarne wilja doch inwän|da at det ordet *Alma* intet skal betyda någon Jungfru

For example, transliteration:

Stockholm 1732, 7:	at lära *a. b. c.* hwilket de kalla א ב ג ד.
Gothenburg 1732, 13–14:	at lära *a. b. c.* | hwilket de kalla *Aleph, Beth, Gimel.*
Stockholm 1735, 10:	at lära A B C, hwilket de kalla *Aleph*, *Beth*, *Gimel*.

Stockholm 1732, 22:	Och tu *Bethlehem Ephrata*, som liten äst ibland Juda städer/ vtaf tig skal den komma/ som i *Jsraël* en HErre wara skal hwilkens vtgång warit af begynnelsen och af ewighet. *Hebr*. ואתה בית לחם אפרתה צעיר אתה להיות באלפי יהודא ממך לי יצא מלכי בישראל ומוצאיו מקדם ימי עולם Deße alla *Prophetierna* af det gamla *Testamentet*, de wisa/ och lika såsom peka på Christum.

133 Indeed, Johan Laurentius Horrn was probably one of the few publishers in Sweden who had access to Hebrew letters for his printing press. As early as 1725, he made use of Hebrew type when he printed Christian Gottlieb Seeligmann's *Jüdischer Ceremonien*.

Gothenburg 1732, 42:	Och tu *Bethlehem, Ephrata*, som liten äst ibland Juda städer/ vtaf tig skal den komma/ som i Israel en HErre wara skal/ hwilkens vtgång warit af begynnelsen och af ewighet. *Hebr. Veat bait lechem Ephrata zair ata lehejot bealphe jehuda mimach jeze malche be Israel umo zaaph michedem jeme olam*. Deße alla *Prophetie*rna af gamla Testamentet/ de wisa/ och like såsom peka på Christum.
Stockholm 1735, 29:	Och tu Bethlehem/ *Ephrata*, som liten äst ibland Juda städer/ utaf tig skal den komma/ som i Israel en HErre wara skal/ hwilkens utgång warit af begynnelsen och af ewighet. *Hebr. Veat bait lechem Ephrata zair ata lehejot bealphe jehuda mimach jeze malche be Israel umo zaaph michedem jeme olam*. Desse alla *Prophetierna* af gamla Testamentet/ de wisa/ och like såsom peka på Christum.

Stockholm 1732, 23:	Ty Gud wil icke den ogudachtigas död/ vtan at han omwänder sig ock lefwer. *Hebr*. כי לא אחפוץ במת הרשע כי אם שובו וחי לעולם.
Gothenburg 1732, 43–44:	Ty Gud wil icke den ogudachti | gas död/ vtan at han omwänder sig ock lefwer. *Hebr. Chi lo ach puz bemet haracha chi im schu vu cachai le olam*.
Stockholm 1735, 30:	Ty Gud wil icke den ogudachtigas död/ utan at han omwänder sig och lefwer. *Hebr. Chi lo ach pur bemet haracha chi im schu vu cachai le olam*.

The transliterations in Stockholm 1735 are identical to those in Gothenburg 1732, although occasionally Paulssen has misread a letter.[134] The transliteration of the Hebrew may well have been made by Löwe himself in collaboration with Lars Unge. The mistakes it contains may be due to the lack of tradition for transliterating Hebrew,[135] to Löwe's inability to read Hebrew properly, or Unge's own mistakes at the press. In addition to those mistakes in the Hebrew that already appear in the Stockholm 1732 edition (e.g., all editions have "*Hrjom* [...] חיום" for "*Hajom* [...] היום"),[136] further errors are introduced in Gothenburg 1732 which are subsequently reproduced in Stockholm

134 For example, *Spec.* (Sthlm, 1732)'s "אחפוץ" (*aḥpuẓ*) is transliterated as "*ach puz*" in *Spec.* (Gbg, 1732), but the *z* has not been set properly and consequently not transferred the ink clearly resulting in an ambiguous letter form. In his 1735 edition, Paulssen has had to guess what this imperfect *z* could be and transliterates the word as "*ach pur*."

135 For instance, in the last two example above (*Spec.* [Gbg, 1732], 42, 43–44), we find "ch" used to transcribe four different Hebrew letters [ח *ḥet*, כ *kaf*, ק *ḳuf*, and ש *šin*]: ח (וחי "cachai" for *vaḥai*, אחפוץ "ach puz" for *aḥpuẓ*), כ (כי "chi" for *ki*), ק (מקדם "michedem" for *miḳedem*), and ש (הרשע "haracha" for *haraša*).

136 *Spec.* (Sthlm, 1732), 9; *Spec.* (Gbg, 1732), 17; *Spec.* (Sthlm, 1735), 12.

1735. For example, Stockholm 1732 has "*Rabbi David Kimki*" [Rabbi Daṿid Ḳimḥi], but the two later editions have "*Rabbi David Timki*,"[137] and Stockholm 1732 has "*Schadra* שעדרה" [spine], but the two later editions have "*Scadra*."[138]

The language of *Speculum Religionis Judaicæ*

Löwe's book is written in typical eighteenth-century Swedish: the sentences are rather wordy, with many participle phrases and numerous doublets.[139] The style is somewhat formal and the lexicon, perhaps reflecting the international nature of the book, contains many foreign words, which today all strikes the reader as unnecessarily pompous. For example, if we take Löwe's preface (pp. xxxiii–xxxviii), we can see that the average sentence length is just over sixty words per sentence; that is three to four times longer than in typical modern Swedish prose. Löwe uses foreign loanwords such as *ceremoni* [ceremony], *docent* [lecturer], *method* [method], *peregrination* [pilgrimage], *recommendera* [recommend],[140] *religion* [religion], and *tractat* [treatise]. The syntax of each sentence is relatively complex and also appears to be influenced by German with infinite verbs (e.g., past participles, infinitives) appearing towards or at the end of the clause.[141] Compare, for

137 *Spec.* (Sthlm, 1732), 8; *Spec.* (Gbg, 1732), 14; *Spec.* (Sthlm, 1735), 10.

138 *Spec.* (Sthlm, 1732), 12; *Spec.* (Gbg, 1732), 22; *Spec.* (Sthlm, 1735), 15.

139 On the typical traits of eighteenth-century Swedish, see the relevant sections in Gösta Holm, *Epoker och prosastilar: Några linjer och punkter i den svenska prosans stilhistoria*, Lundastudier i nordisk språkvetenskap, ser. A, vol. 17 (Lund: Studentlitteratur, 1970); Bengt Pamp, *Svensk språk- och stilhistoria* (Lund: Gleerup, 1971).

140 Generally, Löwe uses many *-era* verbs, that are often from Latin via German/French and tend to be found in more formal language, where it would have been possible to use a plainer Swedish word. For example, *continuera* (cf. Germ. *kontinuieren*/ Fr. *continuer* < Lat. *continuare* [continue], 67:21), *contribuera* (cf. Germ. *kontribuieren*/ Fr. *contribuer* < Lat. *contribuere* [contribute], 88:22, *copulera* (cf. Germ. *kopulieren* < Lat. *copulare* [unite, marry], 68:12), *destinera* (cf. Germ. *destinieren* < Fr. *destiner* < Lat. *destinare* [destine], 30:7), *musicera* (cf. Germ. *musizieren*/ Fr. *musiquer* < Lat. *musicare* [make music], 33:5), *ordinera* (< OSw. *ordinera* < Lat. *ordinare* [direct, arrange], 67:23), *prætendera* (cf. Germ. *prätendieren*/ Fr. *prétendre* < Lat. *prætendere* [pretend], 77:7), *recommendera* (cf. Germ. *rekommandieren*/ Fr. *recommander* < Lat. *recommendare* [recommend], xxxviii:78), *reformera* (cf. Germ. *reformieren*/ Fr. *réformer* < Lat. *reformare* [reform], 79:13–14), *studera* (< OSw. *studera* < Lat. *studere* [study], 71:23), and *tractera* (< OSw. *traktera* < Lat. *tractere* [treat, manage], 91:16;105:23). Of course, not all *-era* verbs used in *Speculum Religionis Judaicæ* are of Latin origin. For example, *broddera* (< Germ. *brodieren* [embroider], 10:2) and *ståffera* (< Germ. *stoffieren* < OFr. *estofer* [decorate], 33:29; also *vtståffera* 33:29).

141 Pamp, *Svensk språk- och stilhistoria*, 224. However, this syntactical convention was very common in early modern Swedish and likely not perceived as foreign influence by contemporaries, in

example, the position of the infinite verbs (here, *italicized*) in the three clauses in Löwe's first sentence – first in the original, and below that in modernized Swedish:

> Jag hafwer min Gunstige Läsare vti åtskillige Främmande Orter *sedt* mångahanda Beskrifningar om Judarnas Bruk och Ceremonier; warandes de en del på Latin och en del på det Tyska Språket *sammanskrefne*, men ingen Tractat der om på Swenska, *sedt vtkommen wara.*

> Jag har, min gunstige läsare, *sett* i åtskilliga främmande orter mångahanda beskrivningar om judarnas bruk och ceremonier, de är *sammanskrivna* en del på latin och en del på det tyska språket, men *sett* ingen traktat därom *vara utkommen* på svenska.

The learned style is enhanced by the smattering of Latin words that appear throughout the book, although they are generally restricted to the title of the work *Speculum Religionis Judaicæ* [Mirror of the Jewish Religion], to the short phrase *In summa* [in summary], and to the names of months of the year in giving dates (genitive forms: *Martii* [of March], 62:29), *Aprilis* [of April], 39:4, 40:13), *Maji* [of May], 45:14), *Junii* [of June], 45:20, 22), and *Septembris* [of September], 52:2).[142] The word *privilegio* (the ablative of *privilegium* [privilege], i:18) also appears once. There are a couple of German terms in Löwe's book: *in alles* [in total], 62:14) and *Widentag* (cf. *Weidentag* [Willow day], 58:2: a German term for Hoshana Rabba). These may be due to influence from his own language or from the written sources that he might have been using. For example, Christian Gottlieb Seeligmann uses the term "Groß-Weyden-Tag" [Great Willow day] to refer to Hoshana Rabba in *Jüdischer Ceremonien*, a book that Löwe clearly used as a source (see below). All of these features are typical of learned treatises written in an academic environment during the early part of the eighteenth century. It is remarkable that Löwe was able to master Swedish so well: indeed, we might wonder whether he received assistance from a native speaker.[143]

The Hebrew in *Speculum Religionis Judaicæ* is often transliterated which helps us to draw conclusions about Löwe's own pronunciation and knowledge of Hebrew.[144] However, caution needs to be taken as the transliteration is anything but systematic. The same word can be spelt in different ways ("*Kitzer*," "*Kitzor*," and "*Kitzur*" for קיצור, *ḳiẓur* [abbreviation])[145] and the same Latin letters are used to

contrast to the Latin and French words in the text which were printed in Roman type.

142 However, note "den 1. *September*" on p. 48:16.

143 Cf. p. xxxvii:5–9: "mig, det Swenska Språket at lära ombeflitat; på det at hwar och en som det samma förstå kan, må kunna denna *Tractat* läsa" [me, having worked hard to learn Swedish, so that each and every person who can understand Swedish will be able to read this treatise].

144 For an index of Hebrew, Aramaic, and Yiddish words used by Löwe, see Appendix 2.

145 *Spec.* (Sthlm, 1732): "*Kitzer*," 100; "*Kitzor*," 108, 109, and "*Kitzur*," 90.

transliterate different Hebrew letters with different sounds.[146] On the whole, Löwe transliterates the Hebrew text as a written language. Forms that might have had a different pronunciation when read aloud are transliterated as they are spelt in Hebrew rather than as they are pronounced in Ashkenazi Hebrew. For example, in *Spec.* (Sthlm, 1732) we find:

Spec. (Sthlm, 1732)	Transliteration as written[147]	pronounced[148]	Hebrew	Meaning
p. 65: *Catan*	*ḥatán*	*ḥósen*	חתן	groom
p. 4: *Mohel*	*mohél*	*móyəl*	מוהל	circumciser
p. 60: *Simkat Tora*	*simḥát toráh*	*símḥas tórah*	שמחת תורה	Simchat Torah
p. 49: *Thalit*	*ṭalít*	*táləs*	טלית	prayer shawl
p. 27: *Therepha*	*ṭerefáh*	*ṭréyfah*	טרפה	unkosher (f.)

A further example of the Hebrew being transliterated as a written language is Löwe's rendition of ביהוה (p. 9) as "*Bajehova.*" It is forbidden to use the name of God outside of the Temple (based on Exodus 20:7), so to avoid misusing God's name, the proper name is not usually pronounced or written. Instead, the tetragrammaton יהוה, YHVH is usually read as השם, *hašem* [the name] or אדוני, *adonai* [Lord]. Löwe's use of "*-jehova*" in his transliteration shows that he is not transcribing the prayer as it is spoken, but as he sees it written.

Nonetheless, a great many of Löwe's transliterated forms do reflect spoken forms with Ashkenazi or Yiddishified pronunciation. These forms can be grouped as follows:

1. Vowels

a) Weakening of unstressed vowels to [ə], usually written *e*:

Spec. (Sthlm, 1732)	Transliteration as written	pronounced	Hebrew	Meaning
p. 42: *Aref*	*'aróv*	*árəf*	ערוב	wild animals
p. 28: *Kalef*	*ḥaláf*	*ḥáləf*	חליף	knife
p. 42: *Kinem*	*kiním*	*kínəm*	כנים	lice
p. 100: *Kitzer*	*ḳiẓúr*	*ḳíẓər*	קיצור	abbreviation

146 See note 135 above.
147 An accent over a vowel marks the stress.
148 E.g., Ashkenazi pronunciation or Yiddish form.

p. 95: *Kopher*	*kufár*	*kúfər*	כופר	infidel
p. 42: *Macked Bekored*	*makát bechorót*	*mákəd‿bəchórət*	מכת בכורות	death of firstborn
p. 1: *Masseltof*	*mazál tov*	*mázəl tof*	מזל טוב	congratulations
p. 35: *Schakeret*	*šaḥarít*	*šaḥárəs*	שחרית	morning service
p. 49: *Schopher*	*šofár*	*šófər*	שופר	shofar, horn
p. 7: *Sider*	*sidúr*	*sídər*	סידור	siddur, prayer book

b) *Ḳameẓ gadol* (אָ) is pronounced [o], written *o*:

Spec.	Transliteration as		Hebrew	Meaning
(Sthlm, 1732)	written	pronounced		
p. 63: *Ador*	*adár*	*ádor*	אדר	Adar (month)
pp. 14, 52: *Capora*	*kaparáh*	*kapórə*	כפרה	expiation

2. Consonants

a) Devoicing of final obstruents:

Spec.	Transliteration as		Hebrew	Meaning
(Sthlm, 1732)	written	pronounced		
p. 42: *Aref*	*'aróv*	*árəf*	ערוב	wild animals
p. 42: *Barat*	*barád*	*bárat, bárət*	ברד	hail
p. 51: *Egos*	*egóz*	*égos*	אגוז	nut
p. 37: *Hafdala* (!)	*havdaláh*	*havdálah*	הבדלה	havdalah
p. 40: *Jom Tof*	*yóm ṭov*	*yóm tof*	יום טוב	festival, good day
p. 13: *Keset*	*ḥésed*	*ḥésət*	חסד	grace
p. 26: *Leftoff*	*lév ṭov*	*léf‿tof*	לב טוב	good heart
p. 1: *Masseltof*	*mazál tov*	*mázəl tof*	מזל טוב	congratulations
p. 95: *Meschomat*	*mešumád*	*mešúmət*	משומד	apostate

This final devoicing is particularly common in Western and Central Yiddish.[149]

b) The consonant ת (i.e., without dagesh) is pronounced as [s], written *s*:

Spec.	Transliteration as		Hebrew	Meaning
(Sthlm, 1732)	written	pronounced		
p. 39: *Pison*	*pitóm*	*píson*	פיתום	Pithom (town in Egypt; Exodus 1:11)

149 Neil G. Jacobs, *Yiddish: A Linguistic Introduction* (Cambridge: Cambridge University Press, 2005), 66, 132.

p. 85: *Zizzis*	*ẓiẓit*	*ẓiẓəs*	ציצית	knotted fringes on a tallit
p. 86: *Zeboos*	*ẓeva'ót*	*ẓevós*	צבאות	hosts

The spelling "*Ramset*" (p. 39) for Rameses (רעמסס, *ra'amses*, Exodus 1:11) may be a hypercorrection: Löwe has mistakenly "corrected" a final ס [s] to ת [s/t] believing that the final -s should be realized as -t. However, he writes "*Thalit*" (טלית, *ṭalit*, prayer shawl, p. 49), not "**Thalis*," "*Schevoot*" (שבועות, *šavu'ot*, Shavuot, p. 44), not "**Schevoos*," and "*et*" (את, *et*, direct object particle, p. 50), not "**es*."

c. The merger of *śin* (שׂ) and *šin* (שׁ) to give [s]:

Spec. (Sthlm, 1732)	Transliteration as written	pronounced	Hebrew	Meaning
p. 32: *Jaginkidos*[150]	*yáyin ḳidúš*	*yáyin ḳidus*	יין קידוש	kiddush wine
p. 30: [*Schamasch*] שמס	*šamáš*	*šáməs*	שמש	beadle

This merger is typically found in the area that today encompasses the Baltic States, Belarus, and parts of Russia and Ukraine. Regarding the word *Schamasch*, it is not so much Löwe's transliteration that is of interest, but rather his spelling of the Hebrew word שמש (*šamáš*) as שמס (*šáməs*) that reveals the merger between merger of *śin* (שׂ) and *šin* (שׁ) to give [s] (ס). In Yiddish, we would expect the spelling שמש (*šáməs*).

d. Glottal stop at the beginning of vowel-initial words:

Spec. (Sthlm, 1732)	Transliteration as written	pronounced	Hebrew	Meaning
p. 1: *gehö*	*yihe'*	*'ihe (?)*	יהא	shall be (Aramaic)
p. 15: *Gemach*	*yimḥaḳ*	*'imḥaḳ*	ימחק	shall obliterate
p. 64: *Gikack*	*yiḳaḥ*	*'iḳaḥ*	יקח	shall take

Although an initial glottal stop before a word beginning with a vowel is only found sporadically in Yiddish,[151] its appearance here in Löwe's transliterated Hebrew – where, of course, it does not mark an *'ayin* (ע) – must be a sign of spoken pronunciation. See also "Jaginkidos" above.

---

150 The *g* in the form "Jagin" (יין, *yáyin* [wine]) may be marking a glottal stop.

151 On the somewhat sporadic evidence for a weak glottal stop in vowel-initial words in Yiddish, see Jacobs, *Yiddish*, 122 (with references).

e. Consonant assimilation

Spec. (Sthlm, 1732)	Transliteration as written	pronounced	Hebrew	Meaning
p. 14: *Actamut*	*ʾaḳdamút*	*aḳtámut*	אקדמות	Akdamut (piyuṭ)

The assimilation [ḳd] > [ḳt] is not part of the written language but heard in spoken Hebrew. A transliteration of spoken pronunciation must also be behind the dissimilation [vd] > [fd] seen in "Hafdalah" (p. 37). Here, one can assume that the word was pronounced in such a way that the final [v] at the end of the first syllable was devoiced: [havdálah] > [haf-dálah].[152]

f. Reduction

Spec. (Sthlm, 1732)	Transliteration as written	pronounced	Hebrew	Meaning
p.: *Tarah*	*ṭaharáh*	*ṭára*	טהרה	ritual purity (in preparing a body for burial)

Löwe's spelling, if not merely a mistake, must reflect a reduction in the spoken language as it is not an accurate transliteration of the written Hebrew. Perhaps the reduction is due to the intervocalic [h] not being pronounced clearly. North-eastern and south-eastern Yiddish both lack the phoneme [h].[153]

Finally, it is worth noting that Löwe refers to the pulpit in a synagogue as "Halememer" (pp. 7, 8) and "Halmemer" (p. 58).[154] *Almemar* or *almemor* (from Arab. المنبر, *al-minbar*, "the platform," "the pulpit") is the term that was common throughout Ashkenaz to refer to the *bimah* (from Heb. בימה, *bimah*, "platform," "pulpit").

In referring to the false prophet Judah Leib Prossnitz, Löwe writes, "*Rabbi Löf Hanavi*, רבי לוי הנביא" (p. 80). Rather than writing "Levi" for לוי, he chooses the form "Löf" – much as he uses "Löwe" for his own surname. Notice also the devoicing of the final consonant in "Löf."

152 Usually, however, Yiddish demonstrates regressive (anticipatory) assimilation and we might expect pronunciations such as [agdamut] and [havdalə]. See Jacobs, *Yiddish*, 120–21. Regardless, Löwe's spellings here are not accurate transliterations of written Hebrew.

153 Jacobs, *Yiddish*, 114–15.

154 He also uses "*Cathedra*" and "*Catheder*" (< Lat. *cathedra*, Gk. *καθέδρα*, *kathédra* [chair]). See also p. 75*n*31 in this edition.

Christian Gottlieb Seeligmann and *Jüdischer Ceremonien*

Although Löwe's book is the first book written in Swedish that describes Jewish ceremonies, it is not the only publication on Jewish praxis to appear in Sweden in the first half of the eighteenth century. In 1722, Christian Gottlieb Seeligmann, a Jew who converted to Christianity in Lübeck in 1712 and who was a regular visitor to Sweden, published a short book called ספר מנהגים של יום טוב וחתנות *Jüdischer Ceremonien Von der Jüden Hochzeiten/ Fest- und Feyer-Tagen Durchs gantze Jahr* in Hamburg and Jena.[155] He then reprinted the book in both Stockholm (1725) and Lund (1737). The book concisely describes some of the most important ceremonies in Jewish tradition and makes for an interesting parallel to Löwe's *Speculum Religionis Judaicæ*, as are numerous instances where Löwe has copied information, for which reason the book has been edited in full in Appendix 6. For example, compare Löwe's *Speculum Religionis Judaicæ* with Seeligmann's *Jüdischer Ceremonien*:

Jüd. Ceremonier, 5:1–8

SIe glauben zwar, daß eine jede Ehe von GOTT gestifftet wird, weilen GOtt der HErr selbsten dem Adam im Paradies die Evam zur Ehe gegeben. Die Rabbinen aber setzen hinzu, daß so bald der Mensch gebohren werde, so werde im Himmel ausgeruffen: זה תלויי יקח ואח תלויי לכתו וגו das ist: dieser Mensch soll diese oder jene zur Ehe bekommen;

Indeed, they believe that every marriage is instituted by God, because the Lord God himself had given Eve to Adam in paradise. But the rabbis add that as soon as a person is born, there is a proclamation in heaven: זה פלוני יקח את פלונית לבתו וגו׳, that is "This person is going to be given this or that [person] in marriage."[156]

Spec. (Sthlm, 1732), 64:21–29

Judarna tro wäl/ at Äcktenskapet är af GUD insticktat och förordnadt/ hälst HERren GUD vti Paradis gifwit Evam Adam til Hustru och dem sammanwigt. Men *Rabbinerne* läggia det til/ at så snart en menniskia til werlden född warder/ skal vti Himmelen vtropat warda: *Se Pelona Gikack Et Bat Pelona*, det är: Hwem den eller den menniskian til Hustru eller Äckta få skal.

For sure, the Jews believe that marriage is instituted and ordained by God, not least because the Lord God had given Eve to Adam in paradise and married them. But the rabbis add that as soon as a person is born into the world, there is a proclamation in heaven: *Se Pelona Gikack Et Bat Pelona*, that is "This or that person who is going to be given [this person] as wife or husband."

155 Christian Gottlieb Seeligmann, ספר מנהגים של יום טוב וחתנות *Jüdischer Ceremonien Von der Jüden Hochzeiten/ Fest- und Feyer-Tagen Durchs gantze Jahr. Nebst ihrem dabey habenden Aberglauben/ Zum Dienst der Warheit vorgestellt* (Jena: Ritter, 1722; Hamburg: Rose, 1722; Stockholm: Johan Laurentius Horrn, 1725; Lund: Ludovig Decreaux, 1737).

156 Seeligmann adds "Da doch in der gantzen heiligen Schrifft nichts davon zu finden ist, noch weniger jemand im Himmel gewesen und es mit angehöret" [As none of this can be found in all of the Holy Scriptures, much less has anyone been in heaven and heard it] in order to support his case that Jewish ceremonies are essentially based on superstitution ("Aberglaube").

The passages in Seeligmann's *Jüdischer Ceremonien* that Löwe has translated into Swedish, usually word-for-word, in *Speculum Religionis Judaicæ* are the following:

Seeligmann, *Jüdischer Ceremonien*		Löwe, *Spec.* (Sthlm, 1732)	
5:1–8	Sie glauben zwar [...] zur Ehe bekommen	64:21–29	Judarna tro wäl [...] Äckta få skal.
5:11–22	2.) Wann Verlöbnis [...] vielfältig das Gegentheil	65:1–18	När Trolofningen skal [...] offta ske plägar.
5:23–31	3.) Von der zeit [...] nicht angefochten würden.	65:1–29	Ifrån samma Trolofning [...] intet kunna skada.
6:1–14	4.) Wann nun die [...] eine vergebliche Einbildung.	65:29–66:29	När nu tiden [...]en skiälig inbillning.
6:15–7:9	5.) Einen Tag vor der Hochzeit [...] Gesichte herunter hängt	66:29–67:25	Dagen för Brölloppet [...] betäcker hela ansichtet
7:27–8:31	7.) Die Trauung [...] im busen stecket.	68:10–70:11	När aftonen kommer [...] brefwet til henne
8:31–9:3	Nach diesem wird [...] welches er zertritt,	70:28–71:3	När nu Bruden [...] det han söndertrampar
9:11–16	So bald der Bräutigam [...] die Mahlzeit angehen soll	71:9–18	När de äro hemkomne [...] skal måltiden hållas.
9:16–17	Bey der Mahlzeit [...] schon studiret hat.	71:22–23	Vnder måltiden [...] en *Oration*
9:17–20	wann solche zu Ende [...] welcher es aufschreibet.	72:1–7	När måltiden ändad är [...] skrifwer dem alla vp
10:23–28	Den Abend vor Ostern [...] vor 10. (!) Uhr geschehen muß.	40:10–17	Aftonen för Påskadagen [...] klåckan är 9. [!] slagen
10:29–31	Am Oster-Fest [...] schicket sich zu Tisch.	40:23–25, 40:30–41:1	Om aftonen [...] läggiandes, wärden vti huset [...] sätter sig til bordz
11:5–12	1.) Stellen sie [...] wieder die Christen aus.	42:12–23	Der efter sättia de [...] emot de Christne.
11:13–17	2.) Haben sie [...] zu Bette legen.	43:17–23	De hafwa [...] vtan någon bön.
11:17–24	Ausser dem [...] des Creutzes geopffert.	44:14–21	Förutan detta [...] korßens trä vpoffrat hafwer.
11:27–12:1	und wird [...] mit Donner und Blitz durch Moses gegeben.	44:28–45:3	firandes [...] med stort dunder och blixt
12:6–13	Den 9ten *Abh* erinnern sich [...] die Zeit der Zerstörung vorbei ist.	45:20–46:14	den 9:de *Junii* [...] förn den tiden är framfaren [*Löwe's translation is expanded*]
12:13–16	Sonderlich haben sie [...] Israel *fatal*.	46:14–19	De hafwa [...] wara olyckelig.
12:16–21	Des Abends vorher [...] die Klag-Lieder der Jeremiä	46:21–30	Aftonen för [...] Jeremie klagowisor.
12:21–26	Den andern Morgen [...] und der Stadt Jerusalems.	46:30–47:4	Om morgonen [...] och Templets förstörande.

Seeligmann, *Jüdischer Ceremonien*		Löwe, *Spec.* (Sthlm, 1732)	
12:26–13:2	Bey Ausgang der *Synagoge* [...] Tag des Freudens haben würden.	47:8–10, 47:31–48:3	Sedan gå de [...] och fränder, at *Messias* snart komma [...] Fest och högtid.
13:5–22	An diesem Fest [...] ein Segen über das Horn	48:16–22, 49:2–22	Denna Fest [...] den inbillning, at om nyåhrsdagen [...] en wälsignelse der öfwer
13:27–14:16	Bey Ausgang [...] ein abscheulicher Aberglauben ist.	50:13–51:1	Wid deras vtgående [...] synd och widskepelse
14:21–24	Wir glauben vielmehr [...] erfordert	51:1–4	ty det är [...] omwändelse.
15:5–16	Den 9ten des Monats [...] um den Kopff herum.	52:3–13	Dagen för försonings dagen [...] kring om hufwudet.
15:20–23	Gleich darauf [...] bitten sollen	52:15–17	Sedan gå de [...] bedia skola
15:24–16:2	Nachmittag [...] gestraffet hat/ Schläge	53:8–19	Efter Middagen [...] slagit hafwer.
16:4–5	Hierauf gehen sie [...] das Mahl essen.	53:22–23	Der på gå de [...] Solen nedgår.
16:5–8	<N>ach dem Essen [...] mit ihren Nechsten	53:31–54:4	Efter måltiden [...] hwarandra försona.
16:9–11	Darauf gehen sie [...] 24. Stunden brennen müsten	54:6–8	Der på gå de [...] räckla vtl 24. timmar
16:19–21	Bey Ausgang [...] das Fest halten	55:4–8	Här på blåsa de [...] vti Jerusalem
16:22–28	und verrichten [...] anrühren können zum Bösen	55:11–19	När de komma [...] någon skada giöra.
17:16–23	Diese Fest [...] heraus zu gehen	56:20–57:2	hwilken högtid [...] äta vti sina hus
17:23–25	Ja etliche [...] Jung oder Alt	57:13–15	Ja somliga [...] gammal eller vng
17:28–30	Von selben glauben sie [...] gebähren wird.	57:26–29	De hafwa den inbillning [...] föda barn.
18:4–15	Dieser Groß-Weyden-Tag [...] austilgen könten.	57:31–58:21	Siette dagen [...] affallande warda.
18:15–23	Am aller *curieusesten* [...] wissen wollen.	58:25–59:12	Judarna hafwa [...] beslutit hafwer.
18:30–19:5	Dieses Fest [...] Obst-Werffen zu machen	59:29–60:18	den de på [...] kasta allahanda frukter på gatan.
19:8–10	welches 8. Tage [...] ein Zeichen oder *Miracul* wiederfahren	61:5–11	Denna Fest [...] händt ett Mirakel eller vnderwärck.
19:16–21	Dahero zünden die Jüden [...] so lang sie brennen.	61:26–30	Detta är orsaken hwarföre Judarna [...] intet arbete giöra
19:27–20:4	Dieses Fest [...] lesen hören.	63:11–19	Denna Fest [...] sig föreläsas.
20:4–6	In währenden lesen [...] das Haus einschlagen.	63:22–26	När *Cantorn* läser [...] Synagogan kullslå wille.
20:6–14	Und wann solches zu Ende ist [...] den Fluch Haman	63:28–64:11	När läsandet til ända är [...] Hamans förbannelse.

In total, translations of Seeligmann's book amount to about 16 % of Löwe's descriptions of all Jewish ceremonies, and about 55 % of Löwe's passages about the same ceremonies that are found in *Jüdischer Ceremonien*.[157]

Having printed his book to make money and pull himself out of poverty, Seeligmann travelled the country trying to sell it.[158] This too may have been an inspiration for Löwe who spent much of his time away from Uppsala travelling throughout Sweden trying to sell his book.

In 1740, Seeligmann had a second work printed in Lund: *Ein Tractätlein von denen jüdischen Fabeln, und Aberglauben*.[159] However, this *Tractätlein* was not written by him, even though he published it under his own name. It had already been published by Carl Gottlieb Willig, a Jew who converted in Greifswald in 1727, in Stockholm in 1736.[160] In turn, Willig had copied the work verbatim from Wilhelm Friedrich Reich who had composed and published the work in 1719![161]

This edition and translation

This edition presents the text of Christian Petter Löwe's *Speculum Religionis Judaicæ* from its first printing in Stockholm in 1732. The aim of the edition is to indicate to the reader precisely what appears in the original work. The punctuation, and cap-

157 Seeing as such large sections of Löwe's *Speculum* are identical to Seeligmann's *Jüdischer Ceremonien*, it is curious that Valentin calls Seeligmann's book "andefattig" [inane] and "torftig" [meagre] but Löwe's "populär" [popular] and "utförlig" [detailed], remarking that "även i denna antipatiska skildring från det judiska förfallets mörkaste tid kännetecknas det judiska livet glimtvis av en gripande än brusten skönhet" [even in this antipathetic depiction of the darkest period of Jewish decay, Jewish life is characterized by glimpses of a poignant albeit broken beauty]. Valentin, *Judarnas historia i Sverige*, 88–90.

158 Valentin, *Judarnas historia i Sverige*, 88–89.

159 Christian Gottlieb Seeligmann, *Ein Tractätlein von denen jüdischen Fabeln, und Aberglauben, so sie haben, von ihrer Geburth an, bis zur Beschneidung und Kirchen-Gang, was sie dabey vor Ceremonien gebrauchen, und wie diese Aberglauben widerleget werden; bestehend in: fünff Puncten Aberglauben, und eben so viel Wiederlegungen und Gegentheile, aufgesetzt* (Lund: Ludovig Decreaux, 1740).

160 Carl Gottlieb Willig, *Ein Tractätlein, von den jüdischen Fabeln und Aberglauben, so sie haben von ihrer Geburth an, biss zur Beschneidung und Kirchen-Gang, was sie dabey vor Ceremonien und Aberglauben, gebrauchen, und wie diese Aberglauben wiederlegt werden, bestehend: in fünff Puncten Aberglauben, und eben so viel Wiederlegungen und Gegentheile aufgesetzet* (Stockholm: s.n., 1736).

161 Wilhelm Friedrich Reich, *Das andere Tractätlein von denen Jüdischen Fabeln und Aberglauben, So sie haben von ihrer Geburt an, bis zur Beschneidung und Kirchgang, Was sie dabey vor Ceremonien und Aberglauben brauchen, Und Wie dieser Abergleuben widerlegt wird; Bestehend in fünff Puncten Aberglauben, Und eben so viel Widerlegungen oder Gegentheile* (Gotha: s.n., 1719).

italization have been retained in the transcription and page breaks are marked by a vertical bar. Allographs have not been differentiated, so, for example, long and short *s* have not been distinguished, nor have tall and round *r*. *Speculum* is printed using blackletter type, but foreign words are printed in Roman. In the transcription, *Speculum*'s blackletter appears as normal type, while Roman is rendered in italics. Expanded abbreviations – there are remarkably few – are also in italics. It can be difficult to distinguish being some of the Hebrew letters (particularly ב and כ, and ה, ח, and ת) in the original work, especially where the ink is smudged or has not taken properly. If in doubt, I have tended to use the letter that makes the most sense in the context.

The translation is intended to be as close to the Swedish as possible, following Löwe's wording and style, without sacrificing its meaning. Löwe's work is written in a rather typical, wordy style of formal Swedish used in the eighteenth century that includes many doublets and participles. In *Speculum*, doublets comprise two words (usually nouns or verbs) that have the same meaning and are connected by the conjunction "och" [and]. In the translation, I have tried to replicate this by using two synonyms:

wrår och wincklar	nooks and corners
lofwar och prisar	are praising and honouring
Tracterar och handterar	treats and deals with
stincker och lucktar	stinks and smells
belöner och bekröner	rewards and crowns

The participle constructions can sound rather unidiomatic if replicated in English. Although it is sometimes possible to translate the Swedish into English using a participle construction, I have tended to create a new clause beginning with "and" or "that" or to use an infinitive construction with "to":

Löwe:	[hon] spåttar honom 3. gånger vti ansichtet/ säijandes ...
Lit.:	[she] spits him three times in the face saying, ...
Transl.:	[she] spits in his face three times and says, ...

Löwe:	Ifrån denna Domstohl hördes en röst frågandes: ...
Lit.:	From this judgement seat was heard a voice asking, ...
Transl.:	From this judgement seat a voice was heard that asked ...

Löwe:	Det är hos dem äfwen brukeligit sig at förkläda/ hålla allahanda spel och *Comœdier*, giörandes hwar och en vti sina hus sig glade och lustige.
Lit.	It is for them also customary to dress up, perform all sorts of plays and comedies, making each and every person in their house themselves happy and joyful.
Transl.	It is also customary for them to dress up, to perform all sorts of plays and comedies, and for each and every person in their house to make themselves happy and joyful.

In order to avoid writing "one," which is becoming increasingly marked as affected formal in English, the Swedish indefinite pronoun "man" [one, a person] has been translated using constructions with "you," "we," or the passive voice:

Löwe: Ty man kan vti hela den Heliga Skrifft aldrig finna wid begynnelsen af twänne *versar*, at det ordet *Jehovah* altid står främst
Transl.: because in the entire Holy Scripture you never find at the beginning of two verses that the word *Jehovah* is always first

Löwe: *Taud Goi Mutter*, det är/ hwad orätt man giör en Christen/ det er tåfligit och Gudi behageligit.
Transl.: "*Taud Goi Mutter*," that is "Whatever wrong we do to a Christian, it is permitted and pleasing to God."

Löwe: och thetta skal wara hans namn/ thet man honom kalla skal
Transl: ... and this shall be his name whereby he shall be called,

However, for stylistic effect, the English pronoun "one" is used in translations of biblical quotations:

Löwe: när tig warder man sig glädiandes/ såsom man sig gläder i Skiördandene såsom man glad är när man skifftar byte.
Transl.: they rejoice near thee as one rejoices in harvest, and as one rejoices when one divides the spoil. (Isaiah 9:3)

Löwe's Bible translations are not always accurate. I have used the King James' Version (1611) as the starting point for my translations of Löwe's biblical quotations.

I have, of course, tried to avoid any inaccuracies, but at times I have had to render a word into English without the certainty that it fulfils Löwe's original intention. Some words are ambiguous, he occasionally uses German, Yiddish, and Hebrew terms as well as Latin, and there are misprints. In the translation, I have followed Löwe's spellings of Jewish ceremonies, concepts, and prayers, both in the Hebrew alphabet and in transliteration, but added a note with the correct spelling in order to help the reader avoid misunderstandings.

The apparatus contains corrections, explanations, and suggestions for further reading. Where relevant I have included readings from the Gothenburg 1732 and Stockholm 1735 editions.

Edition

https://doi.org/10.1515/9783110986938-002

p. i [a1r] *SPECULUM RELIGIONIS JUDAICÆ*, Eller Beskrifning/ Om Judarnas *Religion*, och de nu förtiden hos dem brukelige *Ceremonier*, ifrån Födzlostunden/ och så widare tils de Döde warda.

På Det kortaste Författat, och nu Första gången på Swenska vtgifwit Af *CHRISTIAN PETTER LÖWE*. Orientalisk Språkmästare wid Kongl. *Academien* vti *Upsala*. Med Kongl. Maij:tz Allernådigste *Privilegio*.

STOCKHOLM,

Tryckt hos *JOH. LAUR. HORRN*, Kongl. *Antiq. Archiv.* Boktr. 1732. |

Speculum religionis Judaicae or a description of the Jews' religion and the ceremonies practised by them nowadays from the moment of birth and so forth until they are dead.

Summarized briefly and now published in Swedish for the first time by Christian Petter Löwe, Master of Oriental Languages at the Royal Academy in Uppsala,[1] with his Royal Majesty's most merciful privilege.

Stockholm.

Printed by Johan Laurentius Horrn,[2] Royal Antiquarian Archival Book Printer, 1732.[3]

1 The Royal Academy in Uppsala refers to Uppsala University, founded 1477.
2 Originally from Nuremberg, Johan Laurentius Horrn (1683–1741) was active as a printer in Stockholm 1717–41. See Gustaf Edvard Klemming and Johan Gabriel Nordin, *Svensk boktryckerihistoria 1483–1883 med inledande allmän öfversigt* (Stockholm: P. A. Norstedt & söner, 1883–84), 227.
3 After the title page follow two pages (iii–iv) of copyright information. On behalf of King Fredrik I of Hessen, the *kanslikollegium* (specifically, Johan August Meijerfeldt the Elder, Claes Sparre af Söfdeborg, Gustaf Bonde, Johan Carl Strömfelt, Olof Törnflycht, Ture Gabriel Bielke, Ernst Johan Creutz the Younger, and Gustaf von Heland) endorse Christian Petter Löwe's treatise and in an open letter give him the copyright under the following terms: "for the next ten years, no one else may reprint the treatise in the Empire or import a reprint from abroad or they will incur a penalty of 500 silver daler." This copyright is followed by a series of dedications to Arvid Horn of Ekebyholm, Gustaf Cronhielm, Hans Henrik von Liewen, Casten Feif, Otto Reinhold Strömfelt, Johannes Steuchius, and Nicolaus Barchius on 27 pages (v–xxxii). See Appendix 1 for the text.

p. xxxiii [c1r] Förtal.

JAg hafwer min Gunstige Läsare vti åtskillige Främmande Orter sedt mångahanda Beskrifningar om Judarnas Bruk och *Ceremonier*; warandes de en del på *Latin* och en del på det Tyska Språket sammanskrefne, men ingen *Tractat* der om på Swens- p. xxxiv [c1v] ka, sedt vtkommen wara. För de Lärde | hafwer jag mig ei något företagit, at skrif- wa, hälst det dem, twifwels vtan bättre lärer bekant och kunnogt wara, så igenom Böckers läsande som *peregrinationer* och resor. Men aldenstund samma Böcker, något widlöftige och der jämte dyra och kostbara äro, så at hwar och en, som dem gierna åstundande, så många penningar ei påkosta och vtgifwa wil: ty hafwer jag det samma på Swenska korteligen vti Liuset welat frambringa, at der af ses och p. xxxv [c2r] inhämtas kan hwad *Religion* och *Ceremonier* hos dem wid hwarje | handa tilfällen brukade warda.

Det finnes wäl några små *Tractater* på Tyska vtgifne; men som man ingen wiß grund och vnderrättelse der om hafwa kan, huru det nu för tiden hos dem ifrån deras Födelse, til Dödsstunden tilgå månde; Ty har jag efter mångas inrådande en kort berättelse, angående de hos dem nu i bruk warande *Ceremonier*, på Trycket vtgå och framwisa welat; hade jag och det samma förr vtgå låtit, om jag warit af p. xxxvi [c2v] den förmögenhet, och det tilstånd, at jag mig på någon wiß ort kunnat | nedsättia och boende blifwa.

Men som GUD den Aldrahögsta genom sin Allwetande och Nådiga Försyn behagat, mig vti Swerge låta boende blifwa, rundeligen och dageligen den goda Gudens, och Wår Allernådigste Konungs Nåd och Hielp befunnit, och är här wid *Upsala Universitet*, såsom en *Docens* eller Språkmäster förordnadt, och mig derföre Lön och vnderhåld i Nåder gifwit blifwer; har jag fördenskull förmedelst och i krafft af den p. xxxvii [c3r] besynnerliga kiärlek, som jag til Swerges Crono hafwa mån | de, samt med största fog och billighet mitt Fädernes Land kalla kan; hälst här städes, mig mer än en Faderlig kiärlek dageligen bewist warder (mig, det Swenska Språket at lära ombeflitat; på det at hwar och en som det samma förstå kan, må kunna denna *Tractat* läsa, och billigt pris der på bekomma) samma *Tractat* på Swenska vtgå welat. Jag beder fördenskull den Gunstige Läsaren ei illa vptager om jag någon wiß *Method* och Ordning ei brukat hafwer. Jag har fördenskull det förnämsta vti största hastighet och p. xxxviii [c3v] kort | het sammanskrifwit, så mycket jag i sanning wara wet och mig bekant är; warandes der om försäkrad, det den Gunstige Läsaren sin förnöijelse här vtinnan hafwa och finna skal, och önskar at denna Lilla Bok, må af allom *Recommenderad* blifwa.

Stockholm den 25. Jan. Åhr 1732.

CHRISTIAN PETTER LÖWE. |

---

32 förnöijelse] förnöijese *Spec.* (Sthlm, 1732)*;* förnöijelse *Spec.* (Sthlm, 1735)*;* förnöjelse *Spec.* (Sthlm, 1735).

Preface

My gracious reader, in several foreign places I have seen many kinds of descriptions of the Jews' customs and ceremonies, some are compiled in Latin and some in German, but no treatise on the subject has been published in Swedish.[4] I have not undertaken to write anything for men of letters, but rather for those who without doubt learn familiarity and knowledge better from reading books than from pilgrimages and travels. But at the same time, these books are somewhat wordy and therefore expensive and costly, so that everyone, who sets their heart on them, does not want to lavish and spend so much money: so, I have wanted to draw into the light the same [information] summarized in Swedish, from which can be seen and gathered what religion and ceremonies are performed by them [i.e., Jews] in each case.

There are indeed some small treatises published in German, but as it is not possible to gain any certain reason or information about how they [i.e., Jews] act nowadays from birth until death, I have, after receiving encouragement from many people, wanted to publish and present in print a short account of the ceremonies that they perform nowadays. I would have had the same thing published earlier, had I been able and in a position where I could settle and remain in some certain place.

But as it has pleased God Most High through his omniscient and merciful providence to have me settle in Sweden, and I have unreservedly and daily found the mercy and assistance of good God and our most gracious king, and am appointed *docens* [lecturer] or language master at Uppsala University, and thus in grace am given a salary and maintenance, I have therefore, by the virtue and power of the particular love that I have for the Crown of Sweden and which I can with the greatest meekness and courtesy call my fatherland, as particularly here I am shown more than fatherly love every day (me, having worked hard to learn Swedish, so that each and every person who can understand Swedish will be able to read this treatise and acquire it at a cheap price), wanted to publish this treatise in Swedish. Therefore, in the greatest haste and brevity, I have compiled what is most important, as much as I know to be true and am familiar with. The gracious reader can be reassured that he will enjoy and find pleasure within. I wish that this little book may be recommended by everyone.

Stockholm, 25 January 1732.

Christian Petter Löwe.

4 Between 1500 and 1800, some eighty works were published in Europe on the customs and religious practices of Jews. The majority of these works were in Latin and German. See Chapter 1, pp. 22–30.

p. xxxix [c4r] *Capitlens* Innehåld På Denna Bok.

The contents of this book's chapters

p. 1 [A1r] CAP. I.

NÄr ett Barn hos *Judarna* födt warder/ om det är en Son/ önska de deß Fader och Moder mycken Lycka/ och kallas på *Hebræiske Masseltof* מזל טוב

Och när en Son född warder hafwa de twenne märckeliga och goda meningar der wid/ warandes ganska Lustige och glade. De säija at den Fadren/ som en Son född warder/ skal honom en gång vhr helfwetit frälsa kunna. Ty efter deras mening/ när en man dör och har vti denna werlden warit en ogudachtig och gudlös menniskia/ hwilken de på sitt språk kalla *Rascha* רשע och lemnar en Son efter sig/ och den samma Sonen/ så många gånger han går i *Synagogan* och beder til Gud för sin Fader/ så många trappor och steg skal han draga honom dermedelst vtur helfwetit/ och omsider frälsa honom der vtur in vti *Paradis*, och kallas samma bön p. 2 [A1v] på *Hebræiska*: *Cadisch vegahm amen gehö | schemä raba* קדיש וגם אמן יהא שמי רבה För det andra berätta de (hwilket jag och för en *Fabel* håller) och wilja bewisa det af en bok/ den de kalla *Masebok*, at det war en ogudachtig; och Gudlös man/ hwilken blifwit död vti sina synder vtan ringaste bot och bättring/ och ingen Son efterlemnat; har altså en man wid namn *Rabbi Eliesar*, mött honom vti des gestalt och skapnad רבי אליעזר och när han fick se honom/ huru han drog och släpade ett laß wed/ har han frågat honom huru det i den andra werlden tilstodo: derpå den andre swarat: Han måste alla dagar ett sådant laß släpa och draga/ och det samma sielf på elden läggia/ sig der på kasta och sedermera til aska förbränna. Mårgonen derefter får han åter sin förriga gestalt och skapnad igen och således måste han ewigt vti helfwetit pinad warda/ emedan han ingen Son efter sig qwarlemnadt. Fördenskul tilfrågade ofwannämde *Rabbi Eliesar* honom/ om han der ifrån ei

---

10 in] [i]n *Spec.* (Sthlm, 1732)*: the* i *is not visible on the printed surface;* in *Spec.* (Gbg, 1732; Sthlm, 1735). | **16** רבי אליעזר] רביאליעזר *Spec.* (Sthlm, 1732).

Chapter 1

When a child is born among the Jews, if it is a son, they wish the father and mother many congratulations and, as is said in Hebrew, *Masseltof* מזל טוב.[5]

And when a son is born, they have two particular and good opinions about it, and they are joyful and happy. They say that the father to whom a son is born will one day be able to be saved from hell, because they believe that when a man dies, and he has been an impious and godless person in this world, which in their language they call a *Rascha* רשע,[6] and leaves behind a son, then as many times as this son goes to the synagogue and prays to God for his father, so many stairs and steps will he thereby pull him out of hell, and finally save him from there and into paradise. And they call this prayer *Cadisch vegahm amen gehö schemä raba* קדיש וגם אמן יהא שמי רבה in Hebrew.[7] Second, they say (which I also maintain is a fairy-tale) and want to prove with a book that they call *Masebok*,[8] that there was an impious and godless man who died having sinned without the least penance and repentance, and he left no son behind. A man by the name of Rabbi Eliezer met him in this figure and shape רבי אליעזר,[9] and when he saw him and how he was pulling a load of firewood, he asked him how things were in the other world, upon which the other man answered that he had to drag and pull such a load and place it onto a fire all by himself, and throw himself onto it, and then be burnt to ash; the following morning, he takes his former figure and shape again, and thus he is to be punished for all eternity in hell as he did not leave a son behind. For this reason, the aforementioned Rabbi Eliezer asked him whether he could not be helped and

5 Heb.: מזל טוב, *mazal ṭov*, "congratulations." Löwe's transliteration can be explained by the Ashkenazi pronunciation of the phrase as *mazəl ṭov* or *mazəl ṭof* (with unvoiced final *v*).

6 Heb.: רשע, *raša'*, "someone who is evil, wicked."

7 Mistake for Heb.: קדיש וגם אמן יהא שמה רבא, *ḳadiš ve-gam amen yehei šmeh raba'*. "'Kaddish' and also 'Amen Yihei Shemi Raba' [May his name be blessed]" (Aram.). "The Mourner's Kaddish" (referred to here) is a prayer of praise to God that features in Jewish mourning rituals at all prayer services. "Amen Yihei Shemi Raba" is the beginning of the response said by the congregation after the *ḥazan* has completed the "Yitgadal" section of the prayer.

8 *Masebok*] This is possibly just a transliteration of the Yidd. מײַסע־בוך, *mayse-bukh*, "book of fairy tales," but it is more likely to be referring specifically to איין שוין מעשה־בוך, *ayn shoyn mayse-bukh*, a collection of 257 stories, mainly from the Midrash, the Talmud, and the oral tradition of the Ashkenazi Jews, that was first published in Basel in 1602. Tale no. 146, "The sinner who was released from hell through the kaddish prayer of his son," is very similar to the story told here.

9 Several different characters appear under the name *Rabi Eli'ezer*, Rabbi Eliezer, in the *Mayśe-bukh*: son of Azariah, of Zadok, and of Hyrcanus. The rabbi in tale no. 146, who meets a man carrying firewood upon which he will be burnt three times a day for dying without a son saying kaddish, is Akiva, not Eliezer. Löwe may be drawing upon a less well-known version of this tale or may have mixed up two or more stories to create his own tale.

kunde hulpen och befriad warda. Hwarpå han swarade/ Nei. Widare blef han tilfrågad/ om inga barn efter sig lemnadt hade; hwar til han swarade sig hafwa en dotter vti Staden *Cephat* och samma dotter en Son som wara 6. åhr gammal och när han förr omtalte bön skulle vti *Synagogan* läsa kunna hela åhret igenom/ så blefwo han från samma *marter* och qwal befriad. Bemälte *Eliesar* gick fördenskul p. 3 [A2r] til Staden *Cephat* lärandes samma dotterson bemälte bön i *Syna|gogan* at bedia. När ett åhr förbigångit war gick åter *Eliesar* vt på marken/ då samme man åter mötte honom klädd i hwita kläder lika såsom en Ängel til påseendes/ och sade til *Eliesar*: Tu hafwer en stol vti *Paradis*, emedan tu hulpit mig vhr *Gehenna* גיהנם eller helfwetit. Då tilfrågade *Eliesar* samma man huru det nu med honom tilstodo? Hwar på han swarade: Jag sitter ibland de vtwalda och rättferdiga vti *Paradis*.

Men min käre Christen/ nu kan man sij hwad ett *Fabel*-wärck det wara månde/ och huru förblindade och förståckade de arme och olycksalige *Judarne* äro der doch samme man en gång i helfwetit warit eller ännu wärkeligen är hwar ifrån ingen befrijelse och vprättelse wara månde. Ty ho wil tacka tig vti helfwetit? *Psal.* 16. *v.* 16. Och de fåkunnoge *Judarne* wilja doch lära/ inwända och säija at samma bön som kallas: *amen gehe schemä Raba,* skal hielpa och frälsa vhr det ewigtwarande helfwetit. Och detta är orsaken hwarföre *Judarne* sig så högeligen fägna när dem en Son hit til werlden född warder.

CAP. 2.

NÄr en Son är 7. dagar gammal waka de öfwer honom en hel natt och kalla den samma waknatt; ty de föregifwa den natten/ skola så för modren som Sonen wara den farligaste; kommer fördenskul hela granskapet tilsammans/ giörandes sig p. 4 [A2v] lustiga och | glade med dantzande siungande/ ätande och drickande.

freed from there, upon which he answered "no." He was asked further whether he had left no children behind, to which he answered that he had a daughter in the town of Safed[10] and this daughter had a son who was six years old, and when he [i.e., the man's grandson] is able to read the aforementioned prayer in synagogue throughout the year, then he will be freed from these ordeals and torments. The aforementioned Eliezer therefore went to the town of Safed and taught this grandson to pray the aforementioned prayer in the synagogue. When a year had passed, Eliezer went back out into the field where the same man, dressed in white clothes appearing like an angel, met him again and said to Eliezer, "You have a chair in paradise as you helped me out of *Gehenna* גיהנם (or hell)."[11] Then Eliezer asked this man what his situation was now, upon which he answered, "I am sitting among the chosen and righteous in paradise."

But, my dear Christian, now you can see what a fairy-tale this must be and how blind and stubborn the poor and unfortunate Jews are as this very man was once or even still is in hell from where no salvation or rehabilitation is possible. For who will thank you in hell? Psalm 16:[10].[12] And the ignorant Jews will however teach, object, and say that this very prayer that is called *amen gehe schemä Raba* will help and save them from eternal hell. And this is the reason why the Jews count themselves so very lucky when a son is born here into the world to them.

Chapter 2

When a son is seven days old, they watch over him for the entire night and call it "the night of watching,"[13] as they claim that this night is the most dangerous for both mother and son; for this reason, the whole community gathers and makes merry and is joyful, with dancing, singing, eating, and drinking.

---

10 The town of Safed ("*Cephat*"; Heb.: צפת, *Ẓefat*) is in the Galilee.

11 Heb. גיהנם, *gehinom*, "purgatory," "sense of intense shame," "place of purification for the Life to Come" ("*Gehenna*").

12 Löwe's "*Psal.* 16. *v.* 16" is presumably a mistake for Psalm 16:10: "For thou wilt not leave my soul in hell." Both later editions (Gbg, 1732; Sthlm, 1735) also refer to verse 16.

13 The night of watching (Heb. ליל שמרים, *leil šimurim*; Yidd. וואַך־נאַכט, *vakh-nakht*) probably developed from the habit of family and friends gathering to visit the new parents and the mohel checking the health of the infant the evening before circumcision. It evolved into a custom of eating a festive meal and then keeping watch over the infant through the night to protect him from evil spirits, especially from Lilith. See Elisheva Baumgarten, *Mothers and Children: Jewish Family Life in Medieval Europe*, Jews, Christians, and Muslims from the Ancient to the Modern World (Princeton and Oxford: Princeton University Press, 2007), 99–100.

CAP. 3.

DEn ottonde dagen kallas omskärelse dagen och då warder Barnet burit vti *Synagogan* af ett Qwinfolck/ hafwandes några med sig i föllje. När de komma til dören af *Synagogan*, komma en hop Mans-Personer tagandes emot barnet af dem (ty Qwinfolcken få ei gå vti samma *Synagoga* som Manfolcken vtan hafwa ett annat rum som dem tilslagit är) När mans Personerne barnet emottagit/ begynna samtelige *Scholæ*-Gåßarne ropa och skrija: *Baruch Haba* ברוּךְ הבא det är/ war wälkommen. Mitt vti *Synagogan* på högra handen står en stol med twänne rum/ vti hwilken twänne kunna sittia/ liggandes derpå kåsteliga och dyrbara hyender. Vti det högra rummet efterlåtes ingen at sittia/ ty de säija det samma skola wara *Prophetens Eliæ* rum/ föregifwandes honom/ när något barn skal omskiäras/ skola fast osynligen på samma rum altid sitta vti hela werlden derest ett Judiskt barn omskäres/ skönt 1000. barn på en tima och åtskillige orter omskurne blefwo. På wänstra sidan af Stolen sätter sig en/ hwilken Fader kallad warder/ tagandes barnet på sina knän/ då en annan den de kalla *Mohel* מוהל tilkommer/ hwilken wid

Chapter 3

The eighth day is called the day of circumcision and the infant is then carried to the synagogue by a woman accompanied by some others. When they arrive at the door of the synagogue a group of men take the infant from them (as women may not enter the synagogue like men, but have another room allotted to them).[14] When the men have taken the infant, all the schoolboys[15] start shouting and screaming, "*Baruch Haba* ברוך הבא,"[16] that is "welcome!" In the middle of the synagogue on the righthand side is a chair[17] with two compartments in which two people can sit, upon which there are precious and expensive cushions. No one is permitted to sit in the righthand compartment, as they say it is the Prophet Elijah's compartment,[18] claiming that whenever an infant is to be circumcised, he always sits quite invisible in this compartment, across the whole world wherever a Jewish infant is circumcised, even if a thousand children all at once and in different places were to be circumcised. On the lefthand side of the chair sits a man who is called the godfather,[19] and he takes the infant onto his knees. Then another man

14 The specially dedicated women's section of a synagogue known as *vaybershul* (ווײַבערשול, "women's synagogue") in Yidd. and *ʿəzrat našim* (עזרת נשים, "women's court") in Heb. The first mention of a division between men and women in Jewish houses of worship is found in the early medieval rabbinical text *Midraš Pirḳei Mašiaḥ* (מדרש פרקי משיח). See Adolph Jellinek, *Bet ha-Midrasch: Sammlung kleiner Midraschim und vermischter Abhandlungen aus der älteren jüdischen Literatur*, vol. 3 (Leipzig: F. Nies, 1853–77), 75; Yehuda Even-Shemuel, מדרשי גאולה. פרקי האפוקליפסה היהודית מחתימת התלמוד הבבלי ועד ראשית האלף השישי [*Midrashei Geula: Chapters of the Jewish Apocalypse Dating from the Completion of the Babylonian Talmud until the Sixth Millennium*] (Jerusalem: Mosad Bialiḳ, 1953/1954), 341; Lee I. Levine, *The Ancient Synagogue: The First Thousand Years* (New Haven: Yale University Press, 2000), 477*n*36.

15 Löwe's "*Scholæ*-Gåßarne" probably refers to "schoolboys" or "boys attending the *ḥeder*."

16 Heb.: *Baruch Haba*, ברוך הבא, *baruch haba'*, "Blessed is he."

17 On this chair, see Naomi Feuchtwanger-Sarig, "Synagoga Veritas? Johannes Pfefferkorn and his Synagogue Descriptions in the *buchlijn der iuden beicht*," in *Revealing the Secrets of the Jews: Johannes Pfefferkorn and Christian Writings about Jewish Life and Literature in Early Modern Europe*, ed. Jonathan Adams and Cordelia Heß (Berlin/Boston: De Gruyter, 2017), 109: "[W]hen a circumcision was performed in the synagogue, a bench, a special chair, two chairs, or a composite double-seat was brought into the hall for the ceremony, to accommodate the *sandaḳ* who held the infant on his lap during the surgical act. An additional seat was symbolically present for Elijah the Prophet."

18 A chair is designated for the Prophet Elijah, the "Angel of the Covenant" at every circumcision.

19 The godfather – the term used here is *fader* ("father") rather than *fadder* (godfather) – is usually referred to as סנדק, *sandaḳ* (Heb.) or *sandək* (Yidd.). The man who takes the infant from the mother and carries him into the room for the circumcision ceremony is the *kvatər* (Yidd. קוואַטער < Germ. *Gottvater* [godfather]).

omskärelsen skal noga tilse/ at han den samma lära skal/ och har en waß knif af p. 5 [A3r] stål/ | ett halft *Qvarter* lång/ warandes des skafft med en skön ädel sten infattat/ och omskär der med barnet Förhuden. Der efter kommer den tredie/ som de kalla *Baal Meziza* בעל מציצה, hwilken/ när barnet är omskurit/ utsuger bloden/ och har stora naglar giorde af silfwer/ hwilka sättias på tumman och äro mycket spitzige/ der med rifwer han det tunna skinnet utaf och warder kallat/ *Baal Peria,* בעל פריה den som blodet utsuger/ sprutar det uti en silfwerbägare med win och samma bägare warder på *Hebræi*ska kallad/ *Cosciel Bäraka* כוס של ברכה det är/ en wälsignad bägare. Denna förhud som afskuren är/ lägges uti ett litet silwerfat/ strax brede wid *Altaret,* som de kalla *Aron Hakodesch* ארון הקודש det är Förbundsens *Tabernakel.*

Samma dag om morgonen klockan 9/ hänga de en hwit förlåt för *Tabernaklet,* den de kalla *Paroket* פרוכת warandes der på med bokstäfwer påtryckt och med gullsnören ståfferat. Samma förbund som GUD med *Abraham* uprättat medelst omskärelsens insticktande. Den dagen som barnet omskäras skal/ ställer sig den som det förrätta skal för *Altaret,* beder och siunger/ bärandes barnet/ fram til *Altaret* och gifwer det namn/ samt tager 3 dråppar af det winet i hwilket bloden slagen war/ och släpper dem uti barnetz mun/ och wid det samma säger Fadren öfwer liudt: Wälsignad ware GUD! som låtit mitt barn blifwa uptagit uti *Abrahams* p. 6 [A3v] förbund/ sedan | warda wahlnötter öfwer hela *Synagogan* på gålfwet kastade/ at de närwarande barnen måge dem vpplåcka/ och så warder barnet til de wid dören stående Qwinfolcken lefwererat/ hwilka bära det til deß Moder.

Efter middagen ungefähr klåckan 2/ bereda de ett stort gästebud/ hwar til en ansenlig myckenhet af Judar budne warda/ så af Mans- som Qwins-Personer/

8 *Cosciel*] *Cos sciet Spec.* (Sthlm, 1732)*: in his list of errata (113:4; this edition 212:3), Löwe corrects "Cos sciet" to "Cosciel"; Cos sciel Spec.* (Gbg, 1732; Sthlm, 1735). | כוס של] כוסשל *Spec.* (Sthlm, 1732). *The same mistake is found in Seeligmann's* Jüdischer Ceremonien, *11:7.*

whom they call a *Mohel* מוהל[20] arrives, who is to make sure by circumcision that he [i.e., the infant] will have the same faith, and he has a sharp steel knife, half a quarter[21] of an ell [i.e., 7 cm or 3 in] long, with a beautiful precious stone mounted on its handle, with which he circumcises the infant's foreskin. Then a third man comes who they call *Baal Meziza* בעל מציצה,[22] who, when the infant has been circumcised, sucks out the blood and has long fingernails made of silver that are placed onto his thumbs and are very sharp with which he tears off the thin skin and is called *Baal Peria* בעל פריה[23] The man who sucks out the blood spits it into a silver cup containing wine, and in Hebrew this cup is called *Cosciel Bäraka* כוס של ברכה,[24] that is a "cup of blessing." This foreskin, which has been cut off, is placed onto a small silver tray, right next to the altar, which they call *Aron Hakodesch* ארון הקודש,[25] that is the tabernacle of the covenant.

That morning at nine o'clock they hang a white curtain in front of the tabernacle, which they call a *Paroket* פרוכת,[26] which has letters printed on it and is decorated with gold thread: the very covenant that God made with Abraham by which circumcision was established.[27] On the day the infant is circumcised, they stand the man who performs it before the altar, they pray and sing, carry the child to the altar and give it a name, and take three drops of the wine in which the blood was mixed, and let them fall into the infant's mouth, upon which the father says aloud, "Blessed art thou God, who let my child be brought into the covenant of Abraham!"[28] Then walnuts are thrown onto the floor around the whole synagogue so that those children who are present can pick them up, and then the infant is delivered to the women standing by the door who carry him to his mother.

20 Heb.: *Mohel*, מוהל, *mohel*, "circumciser".

21 Löwe's "*Qvarter*" is a quarter of a Swed. ell (Swed. *aln*), approx. 15 cm in total. A Swed. ell is equivalent to 59.38 cm (i.e., just under two feet in British imperial/US customary measure).

22 Heb.: *Baal Meziza*, בעל מציצה, *ba'al meẓiẓah*, "man responsible for carrying out *meẓiẓah be-peh*." The ritual of *meẓiẓah* (suction) is found in Shabbat 19:2 and requires the *mohel* or *ba'al meẓiẓah* to place his mouth directly onto the circumcision wound to suck blood away from the cut.

23 Heb.: *Baal Peria*, בעל פריה, *ba'al periah*, "man responsible for carrying out *periah*." The ritual of *periah* (uncovering) involves the removal of as much of the inner layer of the foreskin as possible.

24 Heb.: *Cosciel Bäraka*, כוס של ברכה, *kos šel barachah*, "cup of blessing."

25 Heb.: *Aron Hakodesch*, ארון הקודש, *aron ha-ḳodeš*, "the Holy Ark."

26 Heb.: *Paroket*, פרוכת, *paroket*, "curtain [of the Ark]."

27 Genesis 7:10–14.

28 Cf. the blessing that the father traditionally recites after the circumcision: ברוך אתה י-י אלהינו מלך העולם אשר קדשנו במצותיו וצונו להכניסו בבריתו של אברהם אבינו, "Blessed are You, O Lord, our God, King of the universe, who sanctified us by His commandments and commanded us to bring the child into the covenant of Abraham our forefather."

hwilka sittia wid hwar sina bord/ förnötandes tiden med lust och glädie. Öfwer måltiden warda åtskilliga *Orationer* af de unga *Studerande* Judar håldne/ warandes en lika *Pomp* och ståt så af de fattiga som rika hållen/ och måste de förmögne Judar der til *Contribuera.*

Barnen belangande/ så är den tredie för dem den swåraste och fahrligaste/ hälst månge då genom döden afgå. Om så hända skulle at barnet på ottonde dagen förmedelst siukdom och swaghet/ ei kan omskäras/ warder der med tiden utdragen til deß det kommer til sin hälsa igen. Men skulle hända at ett barn blifwer dödt före ottonde dagen/ så warder det af en Mans-Person med ett glas eller skarp sten wid grafwen omskurit.

Detta ware så korteligen talat om Piltebarn/ när det födt warder.

CAP. 4.

WIdare/ när ett Pigobarn födes/ äro de deremot ganska sörgse och bedröfwade/
p. 7 [A4r] hållandes före alla 4. wäggarna vti huset der|öfwer gråta/ och när det 4. weckor gammalt är gifwa de det namn. Fadren kommer vti *Synagogan*, stigandes på ett högt rum/ det de kalla *Halememer* הלממור och är med trappor giordt som en *Catheder*, och då ropar *Cantor* eller Siungaren Fadren wid namn och läser för honom ett *Capitel* vtur *Propheterna* och vnder det samma warder barnet kalladt wid namn.

Flere *Ceremonier* warda med Pigobarn ei öfwade.

In the afternoon, about two o'clock, they prepare a great feast to which a considerably large number of Jews are invited, both men and women, who sit at their separate tables, spending the time joyfully and happily. During the meal several speeches are delivered by the young Jewish students, and there is just as much pomp and pageantry among the poor as among the rich, and the wealthy Jews contribute to this.

As far as children are concerned, the third [day?] is the most difficult and dangerous for them as that is when very many of them pass away. If it so happens that the child cannot be circumcised on the eighth day due to illness and weakness, it will be postponed until he has returned to good health.[29] But should it so happen that an infant dies before the eighth day, then he is circumcised by a man using glass or a sharp stone.[30]

This was a brief account of infant boys when they are born.

Chapter 4

Furthermore, when an infant girl is born, they are on the contrary quite mournful and sad, and stay within the four walls of the house weeping. And when she is four weeks old, they give her a name. The father comes to the synagogue, stands on an elevated platform, which they call *Halememer* הלממור[31] and is equipped with stairs like a pulpit (*cathedra*), and then the cantor[32] or singer calls up the father by name and reads to him a chapter from the Prophets and during this the child is given her name.

No further ceremonies are practised concerning infant girls.

29 Yad, Milah 1:18; Arba'ah Ṭurim, Yoreh De'ah 262:2.

30 Genesis 34:14; Kol Bo 73; Hagohot Maimoni, Hilchot Milah 1:11; Talmud Sanhedrin 110b.

31 Heb.: *Halememer*, הלממור: *Almemar* or *almemor* (from Arab. المنبر, *al-minbar*, "the platform," "the pulpit") is a term used among some Ashkenazim for the *bimah* (from Heb. *bimah*, בימה, "platform," "pulpit"). The term *almemor* was common throughout Ashkenaz and is found, for example, two centuries earlier in Anthonius Margaritha, *Der gantz Jüdisch glaub*, 1530 (VD16 M 972), fol. T1r: "Nun merck was Almemor sey/ Almemor ist mitten in der kirchen ain viereckets gepew/ wie ein Altane sein möcht/ daran etlich stapflen gemacht/ auff wölchem man hinauff steiget" [Note what the *almemor* is. The *almemor* is a square structure in the middle of the church like a balcony up to which some steps have been built and on which one climbs.] On descriptions of the synagogue interiors in Christian ethnographical works about Jews, see Feuchtwanger-Sarig, "Synagoga Veritas?" 97–119.

32 The cantor (*ḥazan*) is a musically trained precentor who leads the congregation in prayer.

CAP. 5.

NÄr ett Piltebarn 4. eller 5. åhr gammalt är så at det kan tala/ lära de det en bön på *Hebræi*ska som så lyder: Mosis Lag är oß gifwen til arfs och *Jacobs* Församling: Hör min Son din Faders tucktan och öfwergif icke tin Moders Lag; Lagen skal tu hålla i sanning/ hos Gud Alsmächtig skal du sökia din hielp. När I hållen eder til Gud/ så lären I alla wißerligen lefwa *&c.*

När barnet är 6. åhr gammalt hafwes det först uti *Scholen* at lära *a. b. c.* hwilket de kalla א ב ג ד. När han detta wäl kan/ läres det stafwa uti en bönbok/ som kallas *Sider* eller *Thephila.* Sedan lära de dem 5. Mosis Böcker/ hwilka de kalla *Cumesch,* חומש, och när de dem wäl kunna förstå och uttyda/ begynna de at lära den så kallade *Mischna* som är något *facilere* och lättare än *Talmud.* Der efter läsa p. 8 [A4v] de *Talmud* som heter *Gemara, Continuerandes* seder|mera med andra *Rabbiners* läsande såsom: *Rabbi David Kimki, R. Salomon Jarcki, Tosephot,* och der jämte lära de det *Chaldai*ska språket med andra oräkneliga *Rabbiner.*

Chapter 5

When a boy is four or five years old, so that he can speak, they teach him a prayer in Hebrew that goes like this: “The Law of Moses has been given to us as an inheritance also of the congregation of Jacob.[33] Listen, my son, to your father’s chastisements and do not forsake your mother’s law.[34] You shall keep the law in truth. You shall seek your help from God Almighty. When you keep to God, you will indeed learn to live (and so on).”

Not until the child is six years old will he learn the *abc*, which they call the א ב ג ד,[35] at school. When he has learnt this well, he is taught to spell using a prayer-book that is called a *Sider*[36] or *Thephila*.[37] Then they learn the Pentateuch, which they call the *Cumesch* חומש,[38] and when they can understand and interpret it properly, they begin to learn the so-called *Mischna*,[39] which is somewhat simpler and easier than the *Talmud*.[40] Then they read the Talmud, which is called the *Gemara*,[41] then they continue with readings of other rabbis, such as Rabbi David Kimki,[42] Rabbi Salomon Jarcki,[43] the *Tosephot*,[44] and in addition the Chaldean language[45] with other innumerable rabbis.

---

33 Deuteronomy 33:4.

34 Proverbs 1:8.

35 Heb.: א ב ג ד, *alef bet gimel dalet*, (lit.) “a, b, g, d.”

36 Heb.: *Sider*, סדור, *sidur*, “prayerbook.”

37 Heb.: *Thephila*, תפילה, *tefilah*, “prayer.”

38 Heb.: *Cumesch*, חומש, *ḥumaš* (Heb.), “the Torah in printed book form.” Yidd. and Ashkenazi pronunciation: *khuməsh*.

39 Heb.: *Mischna*, משנה, *mišna*, “the Mishnah”: the first major written redaction of the Oral Torah.

40 Heb.: *Talmud*, תלמוד, *talmud*, “the Talmud”: a collection of writings (the Mishnah and the Gemara) that constitutes the central text of Rabbinical Judaism.

41 Heb.: *Gemara*, גמרא *gemara’*, “the Gemara”: the rabbinical analysis and commentary of the Mishnah.

42 “*David Kimki*” refers to Daṿid Ḳimḥi (1160–1235), rabbi, biblical commentator, philosopher, and Hebrew grammarian.

43 “*R. Salomon Jarcki*” refers to Shlomo Yitzchaki (*Šelomo Yiẓḥaḳi*, 1040–1105), known by the acronym Rashi, who wrote a comprehensive commentary on both the Talmud and the Tanach. The name Salomon Jarcki is a Christian name for Rashi. See Leopold Zunz, “Heißt Raschi Jarchi?” *Israelitische Annalen* (1839): 328, 335; reprinted in Leopold Zunz, *Gesammelte Schriften*, vol. 3 (Berlin: Louis Gerschel Verlag, 1875), 100–05.

44 Heb.: *Tosephot*, תוספות, *tosafot*, “the Tosafot”: the medieval commentaries on the Talmud.

45 Chaldean or Chaldaic was the language of the ancient Chaldeans. The term was first used by St Jerome to refer to the Aramaic found in the Hebrew Bible and this usage continued for centuries. However, Biblical Aramaic is not related to the ancient Chaldeans and their language, so the misnomer has been corrected by modern scholars, but Chaldean is found in nearly all older literature to refer to the Aramaic in the Hebrew Bible.

CAP. 6.

TIls en Son är ungefähr 13. åhr gammal warder han för ett barn ansedd/ och warda alla synder och fehlachtigheter efter deras mening/ som under samma tid ske/ Fadren tilräcknade; Men hwad han sedermera efter trettonde åhret syndande warder/ det blifwer barnet sielf tilräcknadt och måste derföre sielf lida och umgälla.

När nu Sonen til samma åhr kommen är/ går Fadren up uti den så kallade *Halememer* eller *Catheder*, då *Cantorn* honom åter wid namn ropar/ och läs för honom ett *Capitel* utur 5. Mosis Böcker eller ett stycke af *Propheterna*. Då säger Fadren med hög röst: Wälsignad ware HERren som förloßat mig ifrån ett slikt straff/ hwilket lyder på *Hebrœi*ska således/ ברוךְ שפטרנו מעונשו זו, der efter anrättes åter en måltid/ och om Sonen är af den *Capacite* och qwickhet/ håller han en *Oration*.

CAP. 7.

NÄr detta skedt är/ tager Sonen nogra remmar/ dem de kalla *Thephilim Scheliat*, *Thephilim Schelrosch*, det är; | Remmar som läggas öfwer handen/ och remmar som läggas öfwer hufwudet. På den ändan af remmen/ hwilken bindes på wänstra handen som är närmast hiertat/ är såsom ett litet *Muscat*; Samma rem lindar han 7. gånger omkring handen/ säijandes således: Wälsignad ware Gud! HERre Konung öfwer hela werlden/ som befalt oß binda *Thephilim* kring wåra händer. Och under det samma/ nämna de ett ord för hwart hwarf de den om handen wefwa/ hwilka ord tagas af en *vers* bestående af 7. ord/ så at hwart och ett hwarf swarar emot ett ord/ nämligen: I skolen hålla Eder til Gud i alla Edra lifzdagar och altid: *Hebrœi*ske:

p. 9 [A5r]

---

7 *Halememer*] *Hallemme Spec.* (Sthlm, 1732)*: in his list of errata (113:5; this edition 212:4), Löwe corrects "Halemme" to "Halememer"; Hallememer Spec.* (Gbg, 1732; Sthlm, 1735). | **10** ברוךְ שפטרנו] ברוךְשפטרנו *Spec.* (Sthlm, 1732).

Chapter 6

Until a son is about thirteen years old, he is considered a child, and they believe that all the sins and faults that happen during this time are counted as the father's; but whatever sins he then commits after his thirteenth year are counted as the child's own, and he must suffer and pay for them himself.

When the son reaches this year, the father goes onto the so-called *Halememer* or pulpit (*cathedra*), when the cantor calls him up by his name, and reads a chapter from the Pentateuch or a section from the Prophets. Then the father says in a loud voice, "Blessed be the Lord who exempted us from such a punishment," which in Hebrew goes ברוך שפטרנו מעונשו זו.[46] After this a meal is served again, and if the son is of such ability and intelligence, he gives a speech.

Chapter 7

When this has happened, the son takes some straps; they call them *Thephilim Scheliat*[47] and *Thephilim Schelrosch*,[48] that is "straps that are laid over the hand" and "straps that are laid over the head." On the end of the strap, which is tied around the left hand and is closest to the heart, is what resembles a small nutmeg seed. This strap is wound seven times around the hand while saying, "Blessed be God, Lord King of the whole world, who has commanded us to tie *Thephilim* around our hands";[49] and at the same time, they say a word for each wrap that they wind around the hand. These words are taken from a verse comprising seven words, so that each winding corresponds to one word, *viz.*. "You shall keep yourselves to God for all the days of your lives and always," In Hebrew: *Veattem*,

---

46 זו is possibly a mistake for של זה. This blessing is the abbreviated form, considered correct by most rabbis, of the full rabbinic blessing: ברוך אתה י-י אלהינו מלך העולם שפטרני מעונשו של זה "Blessed are You, O Lord, our God, King of the universe, who exempted me from this one's punishment." See Ivan G. Marcus, *The Jewish Life Cycle: Rites of Passage from Biblical to Modern Times* (Seattle: University of Washington Press, 2004), 90–92.

47 Heb.: *Thephilim Scheliat*, תפילין של יד, *tefilin šel yad*, "tefillin or phylacteries (for placing on the upper arm)."

48 Heb.: *Thephilim Schelrosch*, תפילין של ראש, *tefilin šel ro'š*, "tefillin or phylacteries (for placing above the forehead)."

49 The Hebrew blessing is: ברוך אתה י-י אלהינו מלך העולם, אשר קדשנו במצותיו וצונו להניח תפלין "Blessed are You, LORD, our God, King of the universe, Who has sanctified us with His commandments and has commanded us to put on tefillin."

Veattem, Hadvekim Bajehova Elohekim Kajm Kulekem Hajom ואתם הדבקים ביהוה אלהיכם חיים כולכם חיום. Der efter lägger han den andra remmen på hufwudet och binder den omkring/ hafwandes äfwen då ett *Muscat* fram uti pannan och en knut uti nacken/ och säger sålunda: Wälsignad ware GUD! Konung uti hela werlden som har helgat oß med tin bud/ och gifwit oß tin befallning om *Thephilim*.

När han om morgonen upstådt af sängen/ efterlåtes honom icke gå 4. alnar långt utan han icke twår sina händer/ och det måste ske innan klockan slagit 9/ hafwandes ei heller frihet hwarken äta eller dricka förr än samma remmar efter p. 10 [A5v] wahnligheten lagde äro/ och han giordt sin wederbörliga bön. När detta skedt | är/ tager han dem utaf sig/ läggiande dem til andra morgonen uti en *Brodderad* påßa/ och hänger den på wäggen/ och således måste han hela weckan *Continuera*, men om Sabbather och Festdagar är han derifrån befriad.

Om en/ som en rätt Jude är/ förlorar samma *Thephilim* och kan den ei innom några dagars förlopp igenskaffa/ så måste han få länge fasta; Men är det aldeles ogiörligit at han kan honom åter bekomma/ så är han efter deras Lag förbunden at giöra afbön til Gud när han äter. Ja om någon oförwarandes skulle dem släppa eller fälla/ så måste han med kyssande och annor wördnad dem uptaga/ och följande dagen fasta.

Denna *Thephilim* är hos Judarna den största heligdom. Remmarne belangande skola wara 3. alnar långa om händerna och 3. om hufwudet at de må räckia ned på sidorna/ samt en finger brede. Deßa remmar skola wara af rena *Creatur* och äro de utan til swarta men innan til bruna. Denna sin grund hafwa de tagit af *Exod. 13: 16.* derest står: Och det skal wara sig för ett teckn uti tine hand och en åminnelse för tin ögon/ at HERren hafwer fördt oß med mächtiga hand utur *Ægypten &c.* Warandes åfwannämde *vers* uti samma rem eller knut på *pargament* skrifwen och i den samma insydd och indbunden. Deß utan är och det der uti/ at alt förstfödt skulle höra HErranom til/ med mera. Ingen Mans-Person är efterlåtit at binda samp. 11 [A6r] ma | *Thephilim* för än han hint til 13. åhr; warandes Qwins-Personerne der ifrån befrijade/ emedan de med Hushåldz syßlor hafwa at giöra/ och kunna en sådan dyrbar skatt och heligdom ei wachta och i acht taga. Den warder och för en grof

1 *Hajom*] *Hrjom Spec.* (Sthlm, 1732; Gbg, 1732; Sthlm, 1735). | 3 knut] [k]nut *Spec.* (Sthlm, 1732): *the* k *is not visible on the printed surface;* knut *Spec.* (Gbg, 1732; Sthlm, 1735).

Hadvekim Bajehova[50] *Elohekim Kajm Kulekem Hajom* ואתם הדבקים ביהוה אלהיכם חיים כולכם חיום.[51] After this they lay the second strap on their head and tie it around, and they also have a nutmeg seed at the front on their forehead and a knot behind their neck, and they say thus: “Blessed be God! King of the whole world who has consecrated us with his commandment and given us the commandment of the *Thephilim*.”

When he gets out of bed in the morning, he may not go further than four ells [i.e., 2.4 m or 8 ft] unless he washes his hands, and this must happen before the clock strikes nine; he does not have the freedom either to eat nor drink until these straps have been laid out of habit and he has performed his necessary prayer. When this has taken place, he takes them off and places them in an embroidered bag and hangs it on the wall until the following morning. And so he must continue all week, but on the Sabbath and Holy Days he is relieved of doing this.

If someone who is a real Jew loses these *Thephilim* and is unable to recover them within a few days, then he must fast for a long time. But if it is entirely impossible for him ever to get them back, then he is obliged in accordance with their Law to apologize to God when he is eating. Indeed, if someone accidently lets go or drops them, then he must pick them up with kisses and other acts of reverence and fast the following day.

These *Thephilim* are the greatest sacred object for the Jews. As far as the straps are concerned, they should be three ells [i.e., 1.8 m or 6 ft] long on the hand and three [i.e., 1.8 m or 6 ft] on the head, so they may reach down his sides, and be one finger wide. These straps must be made from a clean animal, and they are black on the outside and brown on the inside. They have taken this from Exodus 13:16 where it says, “And it shall be for a token upon thine hand and a reminder for thine eyes, that the Lord has brought us with his mighty hand out of Egypt (and so on).” This aforementioned verse is written in the strap or knot on parchment and sewn into it and bound. Furthermore, it also says that every first born shall belong to the Lord and more. No male is allowed to bind these *Thephilim* before he is thirteen years old; women are spared this, as they have to do household chores and are unable to guard and keep an eye on such an expensive treasure and sacred object. The man who eats something before he has put them on is also

50 “*Bajehova*” is a Christianized transcription that does not reflect Jewish practice where God’s name – the Tetragrammaton יהוה – is usually replaced with another word, typically השם (*ha-šem*, “the name” or אדוני (*adonai*, “my Lord”). It is often printed as יי or י-י.

51 Deuteronomy 4:4: “But ye that did cleave unto the Lord your God are alive every one of you this day.” The typesetter has mistakenly used ח instead of ה in the final word.

mißgierningzman ansedd som något äter/ förr än han dem på sig tagit: hwilket heter på *Hebræ*iska *Posche Israel*, פושעי ישראל.

CAP. 8.

HWad Judarnas böner angår/ bedia de altid/ på *Hebræ*iska och ei på något annat tungomål. Gemene man förstå intet hwad de bedia; de tala/ men weta icke hwad de tala. *Cantorn* står wid *Altaret*, ropar och skrijar vtan någon *Concent* och *melodiè*. De öfrige siunga likaledes efter. Den första bönen de företaga/ inrätta de som den skal wara ett offer/ hwilket de hafwit ifrån den tiden deras *Tempel* war vti Jerusalem. Och när de skola bedia vti sin *Synagoga*, måste de wara 10. mans Personer och ingen vnder 13. åhr Gammal/ doch hindrar thet icke om de äro flere. Sina ansichten wända de til öster/ föregifwandes *Templet* hafwa stådt öster vt.

Deß vtan hafwa de ock en bön den de kalla *Schemonah Ehra* och innehåller 18. böner. Vnder det samma måste de buga sig 18. gånger. Derefter bruka de en bön p. 12 [A6v] som kallas *Modim* מודים då måste de buga sig neder til | jorden/ säijandes: Den menniskia som ei bugar sig neder til jorden vtaf hans ryggsena/ som på *Hebræ*iska kallas *Schadra* שעדרה, skal blifwa en orm/ och den samma skal Menniskian efter deß död qwälja och plåga. Widare brukas en bön den de kalla *Allenu le Schabeach* עלינו לשבח denna bönen bedia de twänne gånger om dagen/ morgon och afton/ lastandes och försmädandes dervtinnan de Christna och denna är deras *Ordinaire*

considered a coarse wrongdoer, which in Hebrew is called *Posche Israel*, פושעי ישראל.[52]

Chapter 8

As far as the Jews' prayers are concerned, they always pray in Hebrew and not in any other language.[53] Ordinary men understand nothing of what they are praying; they speak but do not know what they are saying. The cantor at the altar shouts and screams without any harmony and melody. The remainder sing along likewise. The first prayer they say, they set up as if it were a sacrifice which is a custom they have had from the time when their temple was in Jerusalem. And when they are to pray in their synagogue, there must be ten men and no one under the age of thirteen years old, but it does not stop them if there are more of them.[54] They turn their faces to the east, imagining that the Temple has stood in the east.

Moreover, they also have a prayer that the call *Schemonah Ehra*[55] and contains eighteen prayers. During this prayer, they have to bow down eighteen times. After this they say a prayer that is called *Modim* מודים,[56] when they have to bow down to the ground, saying, "The person who does not bow down to the ground, his spinal tendon," which in Hebrew is called *Schadra* שעדרה,[57] "shall become a snake, and it will choke and torment the person after his death."[58] Moreover, a prayer is said that they call *Allenu le Schabeach* עלינו לשבח.[59] They pray this prayer twice daily, morning and evening, in which they abuse and insult the Christians, and this is

52 Heb.: *Posche Israel*, פושעי ישראל, *pośe'i Yiśra'el*, "transgressors of Israel."

53 Actually this is not true. Some prayers, most notably Kaddish (already referred to on p. 2:1; this edition 66:11), are in Aramaic.

54 The requirement of a *minyan* or quorum of ten Jewish male adults is found in Talmud, Megilah 23b.

55 Heb.: *Schemonah Ehra*, שמנה עשרה, *šemoneh 'eśreh*, "the Eighteen," also known as the עמידה, *'Amidah* "Standing (Prayer)." The name of the prayer would have been familiar to Löwe, so the peculiar transcription "Ehra" is most probably due to a typesetting error. Both later editions (Gbg, 1732; Sthlm, 1735) also have *"Ehra."*

56 Heb.: *Modim*, מודים, *modim*, "[we] thank" is the name of a prayer of thanks.

57 A spelling mistake for שדרה (*šidrah*, "spine").

58 Cf. Talmud, Bava Ḳama 16a.

59 Heb.: *Allenu le Schabeach*, עלינו לשבח, *'aleinu lešabeaḥ*, "It is our duty to pray."

bön som de dageligen bedia. Om Festdagar bruka de andra böner/ om hwilka här efter berättas skal.

CAP. 9.

HWad deras tro och *Religion* anlangar/ tro de endast på Gud allena/ vteslutandes de andra twänne Personerna vti den guddomeliga warelsen. De wilja ei tro Christum wara den rätta och Sanna werldenes Frälsare och Saliggiörare; vtan förwänta en annan werldslig *Messiam,* at de må kunna hafwa glädie och andra jordiska förmåner. Emot den Christeliga *Religionen* hafwa de ett sådant försmädeligt tal och säija/ at när deras *Messias* kommandes warder/ skola de stora och ansenliga Herrar warda och de förnämlige af Christenheten för Judarna blifwa såsom drängar och Pigor.

Deß vtan tala de och mycken försmädelse emot Christum och den Christna läran/ hwilket är förskräckeligit at omtala. De wänta sin *Messiam* hwar dag och
p. 13 [A7r] tima/ *Hebr.* | *Messiah Ben Joseph*, *Messiah Ben David* משיח בן יוסף משיח בן דוד, och

13 משיח בן יוסף] משיחבן יוסף *Spec.* (Sthlm, 1732).

their ordinary prayer that they pray daily.[60] On holy days they use other prayers about which is told below.

Chapter 9

As far as their faith and religion are concerned, they believe only in God alone, excluding the other two persons in the divine being. They do not want to believe that Christ was the real and true saviour and beatifier of the world but anticipate another worldly Messiah so that they might receive joy and other earthly benefits. They speak so contemptibly against the Christian religion and say that when their Messiah comes, they will become great and considerable lords, and the noble Christians will be like farmhands and maids for the Jews.

Moreover, they also speak much that is contemptible against Christ and Christian teachings, which is terrible to describe. They anticipate their Messiah every day and hour – in Hebrew, *Messiah Ben Joseph*, *Messiah Ben David* משיח בן יוסף משיח בן דוד, and they say that the Messiah does not arrive in the world because of

---

60 The prayer *'Aleinu lešabeaḥ* is ascribed to Abba Arika (Rab) who lived in Babylon in the third century CE, but it is possibly older. The prayer praises God for having chosen the Jewish people to serve him, expresses the hope that non-Jews will recognize him and abandon their own idolatry (Isaiah 30:7 and 45:20). Originally the text included the lines: שהם משתחוים להבל וריק, ומתפללים אל אל לא יושיע "For they worship vanity and emptiness and pray to a god who cannot save." Even though the prayer was composed in a non-Christian land and most likely originates from the pre-Christian era, it was considered by Christians as being explicitly anti-Christian. Peter of Bohemia in the fourteenth century was the first to claim that the Jews thought of Christians as those worshipping vanity. See Joshua Trachtenberg, *The Devil and the Jews: The Medieval Conception of the Jew and its Relation to Modern Anti-Semitism*, rev. edn (Philadelphia: The Jewish Publication Society, 1993), 182–83. In the manual he prepared for the Inquisitors, the Dominican Bernhard Gui in Toulouse explained the lack of an explicit mention of Christians by making the distinction between the language of the prayer and its contextual intent. See Hans-Martin Kirn, *Das Bild vom Juden im Deutschland des frühen 16: Jahrhunderts. Dargestellt an den Schriften Johannes Pfefferkorns*, Texts and Studies in Medieval and Early Modern Judaism, vol. 3 (Tübingen: J. C. B. Mohr [Paul Siebeck], 1989), 46. Israel Yuval, however, has argued that at least as far as the twelfth century is concerned, the *'aleinu* prayer was in fact perceived by some Jews as an anti-Christian prayer of opposition, and particularly in the early Middle Ages, it often contained scathing additions directed at Christians. The passage was censored, but accusations of anti-Christianity continued. See Israel Jacob Yuval, *Two Nations in Your Womb: Perceptions of Jews and Christians in Late Antiquity and the Middle Ages*, trans. by Barbara Harshav and Jonathan Chipman [שני גויים בבטנך: יהודים ונוצרים - דימויים הדדיים] (Berkeley: University of California Press, 2006), 192–204.

säija at Messias intet kommer i werlden för de synder som de dageligen bedrifwa. En bok som de kalla *Medras Jalkut* מדרש ילקוט skrifwer jämte andra *Rabbiner*, at när de skola kunna rätt hålla och fira en *Sabbath* och icke bryta honom/ så skal deras *Messias* komma. De säija jämwäl at om söknedagarne är deras *Messias* bunden med en Jernkedia/ men om Sabbathen är han bunden med et hår/ och emedan han intet wil bryta Sabbathen och slita håret sönder/ kan han således intet komma. Men om Judarne rät skulle hålla Sabbathen/ så skulle deras *Messias* sielf håret sönderslita/ och dem vhr sitt fångenskap och Landsflychtighet förlåssa. De säija och at det goda som de Christne giöra Judarna förhindrar deras *Messiam* at han icke komma kan/ och heter på *Hebrœi*ska: *Keset Sekel umot katot Le Jsraël.* חסד של אומות עולם חטאות לישראל

De skrifwa och mycket annat om sin *Messia* hwilket är aldeles otroligit/ såsom: När deras *Messias* kommer/ skal den store Fisken *Leviathan* ליויתן slachtad warda och för de vtwalde och rättfärdige en måltid der af beredas/ och skola af des skin giöra sig tält och hyddor. De mindre fromme skola af samma skin giöra sig skor/ och de aldraminst fromme/ skoremmar. Men hwad *Leviathan* widkommer/ säija de honom wara slachtad från werldenes begynnelse och insaltad/ hwar af wid |
p. 14 [A7v] *Messiæ* ankomst en måltid anrättas skal. Theßlikes skola de och slachta den stora

9 de] d[e] *Spec.* (Sthlm, 1732)*: the* e *is not visible on the printed surface*; de *Spec.* (Gbg, 1732; Sthlm, 1735). | **12** De] de *Spec.* (Sthlm, 1732). | skrifwa] skri wa *Spec.* (Sthlm, 1732)*: in his list of errata (113:7; this edition 212:5), Löwe corrects* skriwa *to* skrifwa*;* skrifwa *Spec.* (Gbg, 1732; Sthlm, 1735).

the sins that they commit daily. A book called *Medras Jalkut* מדרש ילקוט,[61] along with other rabbis, says that when they are able to keep and celebrate a Sabbath correctly and not break it, then their Messiah will come.[62] Likewise, they say that on working days, their Messiah is bound with an iron chain,[63] but on the Sabbath, he is bound with a single hair, and as he does not want to break the Sabbath and snap the hair apart, he is thus unable to come. But were the Jews to keep the Sabbath correctly, then their Messiah would snap apart the hair by himself and release them from their imprisonment and exile. They also say that the good that the Christians do for the Jews hinders their Messiah, so that he cannot come, and in Hebrew is called *Keset Sekel umot katot Le Jsraël*[64] חסד של אומת עולם חטאות לישראל.[65]

They also write much else about their Messiah which is completely unbelievable, such as: When their Messiah comes, the great fish *Leviathan* ליויתן[66] will be slaughtered, and from it a meal will be prepared for the chosen and righteous, and from its skin they will make themselves tents and huts. The less pious will make shoes from this same skin, and the least pious shoelaces.[67] But as far as the leviathan is concerned, they say that it was slaughtered at the beginning of the world and preserved in salt, from which a meal will be prepared upon the arrival of the Messiah. Similarly, they will also slaughter the great ox that in Hebrew is called

61 Heb.: *Medras Jalkut*, מדרש ילקוט, *midraš yalkuṭ*, "Midrash collection." The Midrash is a collection of the rabbinical interpretations of and commentaries on the Talmud. Here, it is the *Yalkuṭ Šim'oni* (ילקוט שמעוני, "Collection of Simon") that is being referred to. This collection is an aggadic (non-legalistic exegetical) compilation on the books of the Bible (12–13 century CE?).

62 In the *Yalkuṭ Šim'oni* (תתנ"ב ה), it says: אמר רבי לוי אם משמרין ישראל אפילו שבת אחת כתקנה מיד בן דוד בא והן נגאלין "Rabbi Levy says, 'If Israel keeps even one Sabbath, as it was prescribed, the son of David will immediately come, and they will be redeemed.'" The same sentiment is found in the earlier Jerusalem Talmud, Ta'anit 3b.

63 The concept of the Messiah being delayed because a heavy iron chain has been placed upon his neck is found in several Jewish mystical works. See Morris M. Faierstain, ed., *Jewish Mystical Books: Book of Visions and Book of Secrets*, preface by Moshe Idel, The Classics of Western Spirituality (New York: Paulist Press, 1999), 62 and 257.

64 Löwe has missed the word עולם, *'olam* in his transliteration.

65 Heb.: "The grace of the nations of the world [are] sins to Israel."

66 Heb.: *Leviathan*, ליויתן, *leviatan* is a sea monster mentioned in Job 3:8, 40:15–41:26; Amos 9:3; Psalm 74:13–23, 104:26; Isaiah 27:1.

67 The leviathan plays a prominent role in haggadic literature in connection with the advent of the Messiah. Cf. Talmud, Bava Batra 75a where Rabbi Yoḥanan says that God will give a feast at the time of the resurrection to the righteous, at which the flesh of the leviathan will be served. Moreover, the skin of the leviathan will also be put to use: God will make tents (*sukot*) out of it for the righteous (*ẓedakim*) of the first rank, head coverings for those of the second, necklaces for those of the third, and amulets for those of the fourth. What skin is left over will be spread out on the walls of Jerusalem and illuminate the entire world.

oxan/ som på *Hebrœiska* kallas *Schor Habor* שור הבור samt föregifwa/ at de skola dricka win/ som hänger i samma drufwor som warit ifrån werldenes begynnelse; hwilket ses kan af en bok wid namn *Maxur* och *Actamut* מחזור אקדמות. Hwad mera *Fabler* de om sin Messia hafwa/ det är alt för widlyfftigt at omskrifwa/ men kan igenfinnas vti en bok som kallas *Madrasch Raba* och *Madrasch Jalkut.*

De tro och at the döde skola vpstå/ de tro den yttersta domen/ deras grundsatzar tagas vtur *Talmud* och ei uhr *Bibelen,* utan allenast 5. Mosis Böcker och några få af *Propheterna* bruka de at lära sina Barn.

CAP. 10.

HWad deras umgänge beträffar/ hafwa de af naturen en sky och leda til de Christna. De kalla dem på Hebræiska *Erel* ערל det är/ en förståckad/ och på det deras barn ei måge umgås med de Christna/ lära de dem hwarken *Latin* eller andra tungomåhl. Deras barn som Christne äro/ kalla de *Skäratz* שרץ, det är/ ett krypande diur/ och mena ei annat med en Christen än en falsk menniskia. Til den bästa Christen säija de *Capora*, det är/ han skal såsom ett slachtoffer omkomma. När de säija til en Christen wälkommen/ så säija de *Skedd*, det är/ war wälkommen
p. 15 [A7r] du | diefwul. När de wilja berömma en Christen och säija at det är en braf man/ så bruka de deße orden/ *Taf Orel Gemach Schemo*, det är/ en god förståckader/ hans namn skal blifwa utskrapat och utplånat. När en Christen går wäl/ säija de: Det går honom wäl Gudi klagat! för wåra synders skull. Men när de giöra en Christen

12 *Skäratz*] *Shärätz Spec.* (Gbg, 1732; Sthlm, 1735).

Schor Habor שור הבור[68] and claim that they will drink wine that hangs in the same grapes that have existed since the beginning of the world; which can all be seen in a book with the names *Maxur*[69] and *Actamut*.[70] What further fairy-tales do they have about their Messiah? It is far too extensive to write about but can be discovered in a book called *Madrasch Raba*[71] and *Madrasch Jalkut*.[72]

They also believe that the dead will rise on the Day of Judgement. Their tenets are taken from the Talmud and not from the Bible, except for the Pentateuch alone and some few of the Prophets that they teach their children.

Chapter 10

As far as social intercourse is concerned, they are by nature shy of and unpleasant towards Christians. In Hebrew they call them *Erel* ערל,[73] that is "an obdurate person." And as their children do not socialize with Christians, they do not teach them either Latin or other languages. The[74] children who are Christian they call *Skäratz* שרץ,[75] that is "a creeping animal," and they believe nothing else than that a Christian is a false person. About the best Christian they say "*Capora*,"[76] that is "he will die like a sacrificial offering." When they say "welcome" to a Christian, they say "*Skedd*,"[77] that is "welcome, you devil!" When they want to compliment a Christian man and say that he is a brave man, then they use these words "*Taf Orel Gemach Schemo*,"[78] that is "a good obdurate man, his name shall be erased and blotted out!" When a Christian fares well, they say: "He fares well, unfortunately,

68 Heb.: *Schor Habor*, שור הבר, *šor ha-bar*, "behemoth": a beast mentioned in Job 40:15–24.

69 Heb.: *Maxur*, מחזור, *maḥzor*, "machzor": a prayer book used during the High Holy Days (Rosh Hashanah and Yom Kippur). The usual prayer book, or siddur, is intended for weekday and Shabbat services, whereas the machzor is for festival prayer services. Machzorim are also sometimes used for the festivals of Passover, Shavuot, and Sukkot.

70 Aram.: *Actamut*, אקדמות, *aḳdamut*, "introduction": an Aramaic *piyuṭ* (liturgical poem) that includes a description (lines 75–84) of how the leviathan and the behemoth will be slaughtered and prepared by God as a banquet "for the righteous" (לצדיקי, Aram.).

71 Heb.: *Madrasch Raba*, מדרש רבה, *midraš rabah*, "Midrash Rabba": a collection of aggadic (non-legalistic, exegetical) works on the books of the Hebrew Bible.

72 On *Madrasch Jalkut*, see p. 87*n*61 in this edition for *Spec.* (Sthlm, 1732), 13.

73 Heb.: *Erel*, ערל, *'arel*, "uncircumcised."

74 In *Spec.* (Sthlm, 1732; Gbg, 1732; Sthlm, 1735), we find "deras," lit. "their."

75 Heb.: *Skäratz*, שרץ, *šereẓ*, "worm," "bug," "creepy-crawly."

76 Heb.: *Capora*, כפרה, *kaporah*, "atonement," "penance."

77 Heb.: *Skedd*, שד, *šed*, "demon," "devil," "fiend."

78 Heb.: טוב עורל ימחק שמו, *ṭov 'orel yimḥaḳ šemo*, "an uncircumcised good [man], may his name be obliterated."

orätt/ hålla de det för ingen synd/ utan säija: *Taud Goi Mutter*, det är/ hwad orätt man giör en Christen/ det er låfligit och Gudi behageligit. Icke heller wilja de bruka den knif/ hwar med en Christen ätit/ eller eljest brukat hafwer. Icke töras de dricka det win/ som är af en Christen präßat och handterat/ utan kalla det på *Hebræ*iska/ *Jain näsach* יין נסך eller et sådant som är afgudomen offrat och wigt. Och om en Jude hafwer ett glas win uti handen och en Christen rörer der wid törs han det sedermera intet dricka.

CAP. 11.

WIdare fara de vti sitt mörker och willfarelse fort föregifwandes Christum ei wara född af en ren och obefläckiad Jungfru/ der det doch vttryckeligen står vti *Esa.* 7. *v.* 14. Si en Jungfru skal warda hafwande och skal föda en Son och de skola kalla hans namn *Jmanuel*, det är/ Gud med oß הנה העלמה הרה וילדת בן Judarne wilja doch
p. 16 [A7v] inwända at det or|det *Alma* עלמה intet skal betyda någon Jungfru/ vtan en vnger Fru eller hustru/ der det doch klarligen står/ at *Rebecca* blef kallad *Alma*, då hon en Jungfru war. De wilja och *statuera*, at de hafwa ett rike och Regemente på andra sidan om röda hafwet/ derest alla 10. Juda slächter skola sin Konung hafwa/ hwilket doch är idel osanning/ hälst månge Siöfarande hafwa rest genom röda hafwet/ och aldrig ett sådant land warse blifwit/ hwarest något Judiskt Regemente och *Scepter* warit hafwer. De berätta fördenskul en grof osanning/ då de säija/ at ett haf skal finnas/ som warder kallat *Sambation Hanahar Hamit Gall Gall Koll Jom*

19 *Sambation*] *Sambacion Spec.* (Sthlm, 1735).

because of our sins!" But when they do wrong by a Christian, they do not consider it a sin, but say "*Taud Goi Mutter*,"[79] that is "Whatever wrong we do to a Christian, it is permitted and pleasing to God." Nor will they use the knife with which a Christian has eaten or has used in some other way. They do not dare to drink the wine that is pressed or handled by a Christian but call it in Hebrew *Jain näsach* יין נסך,[80] or "such a one that has been sacrificed for and consecrated to idolatry." And if a Jew has a glass of wine in his hand, and a Christian touches it, he does dare to drink any more of it.

Chapter 11

Furthermore, they descend quickly into darkness and delusion by asserting that Jesus was not born of a pure and immaculate virgin, as it states explicitly in Isaiah 7:14: "Behold, a virgin shall conceive and bear a son, and they shall call his name Immanuel, that is 'God [be] with us.'" הנה העלמה הרה וילדת בן[81] However, the Jews will object here that the word *Alma* עלמה does not mean a virgin, but a young woman or wife,[82] although it clearly says that Rebecca was called *Alma* when she was a virgin.

They will also assert that they have a kingdom and a government on the other side of the Red Sea, where all ten of the Jews' tribes are said to have a king,[83] which, however, is a sheer untruth. Very many sailors have travelled through the Red Sea and have never noticed any such a country where there has been Jewish governmental and royal power. Therefore, they tell a crude untruth when they say that there is a sea that is called *Sambation Hanahar Hamit Gall Gall Koll Jom*

79 Heb.: טעות גוי מותר, *ṭa'ut goy muter*, "wronging a gentile is permitted." The interpretation of Löwe's transliteration is uncertain.

80 Heb.: *Jain näsach*, יין נסך, *yayin nesech*, "wine libation."

81 Isaiah 7:14: "The virgin will conceive and give birth to a son" (Heb.).

82 On the dispute about the translation of עלמה in Isaiah 7:14 (*παρθένος*, *virgo*), see Naomi Seidman, *Faithful Renderings: Jewish-Christian Differences and the Politics of Translation* (Chicago: University of Chicago Press, 2006), 37–72; Jonathan Adams, *Jews in East Norse Literature: A Study in Othering in Medieval Denmark and Sweden*, vol. 1: *A Cultural Investigation*, Religious Minorities in the North: History, Politics, and Culture, vol. 4 (Berlin/Boston: De Gruyter, 2022), 349–52.

83 On the legend of these lost Jews, known as the Red Jews, see Andrew Colin Gow, *The Red Jews: Antisemitism in an Apocalyptic Age 1200–1600* (Leiden: Brill, 1995).

סאמבטיון הנהר המתגלגל כל יום det är/ en ström som vti hela 6. dagar sand och sten ifrån sig kastar/ och afskär öfwerfarten för de Resande/ så at ingen menniskia eller något annat Creatur dit komma kan/ men om Sabbatthen står den samme stilla/ och ingen sand eller sten ifrån sig kastar. Och de Judarna som äro på andra sidan om hafwet boende/ wilja icke bryta Sabbathen/ men eljest skulle de komma öfwer/ och dem vtur deras Landsflychtighet frälsa/ och vti sitt land å nyo insättia/ ändoch det klarligen står *Gen.* 49. *v.* 10. spiran skal icke tagen warda ifrån Juda ei heller en mästare från hans fötter til deß hielten kommer/ och honom skola folcken tilfalla. Och de hafwa doch hwarken *Scepter* spira eller Regemente/

p. 17 [B1r] Och äro doch icke desto mindre så | förblindade at de wänta en annan *Messiam* oachtadt *Prophetierna* vti gamla *Testamentet* ögonskenligen med det Nya öfwerensstämma at Christus är den rätta och sanna *Messias* och at flere än en Person vti Gudomen wara månde/ samt at alla 3. Personerne/ Gud Fader/ Son och then Helige Ande äro en warelse. Som ses af *Gen.* 1. *v.* 1. Derest står: I begynnelsen skapade Gud himmel *&c.* *Hebr:* *Berescit Bara Elohim*, hwarest det ordet *Elohim* talar om flere än en Person; ty eljest skulle det stå *El* och intet *Elohim*. Vti *Gen.* 1. *v.* 26. står: låter oß giöra menniskian til ett beläte som oß likt är; hwarest och tales mer än om en Person. I *Gen.* 2. *v.* 7. 8. 9. läser man: I 7. *versen* står: HErren Gud skapade menniskian/ I 8:de *versen* HErren planterade *etc.* Och i den 9:de *vers.*

---

1 סאמבטיון] סאמבטין *Spec.* (Sthlm, 1732). | המתגלגל] המגתלגל *Spec.* (Sthlm, 1732) | **2** menniskia] mennisk a *Spec.* (Sthlm, 1732); menniskia *Spec.* (Sthlm, 1735); Menniskia *Spec.* (Sthlm, 1735). **10** Och] och *Spec.* (Sthlm, 1732). | **19** *etc.*] ꝛc *Spec.* (Sthlm, 1732). *The* et *is abbreviated by an* r-*rotunda rather than the ampersand used in almost all other cases. Cf. 26:14 (this edition 104:15), 77:20 (174:5), and 94:2 (192:15).*

סאמבטיון הנהר המתגלגל כל יום,[84] that is a river that for six whole days throws up sand and stones and cuts off crossing for travellers, so that no person or any other creature can come there. But on the Sabbath, it stands still and does not throw up any sand or stones. And the Jews who live on the other side of the sea do not want to break the Sabbath, but otherwise they would cross and save themselves from their exile and settle again in their land, although it clearly says in Genesis 49:10: "The mace shall not be taken from Judah, nor a scholar from his feet, until his hero comes; and the people shall gather unto him." And yet they have neither sceptre, mace, nor government.

And nonetheless they are so blinded that they wait for another Messiah irrespective of the fact that the prophecies in the Old Testament obviously correspond with the New, that Christ is the correct and true Messiah and that there must be more than one person in the godhead, and that all three persons – God the Father, the Son, and the Holy Spirit – are one being. As is seen from Genesis 1:1, where it says, "In the beginning God created the heaven, etc." In Hebrew: *Berescit Bara Elohim*,[85] where the word *Elohim* speaks of more than one person, because otherwise it would say *El*, and not *Elohim*.[86] In Genesis 1:26 it says, "Let us make man in our image, after our likeness," where it also speaks of more than one person.[87] In Genesis 2:7–9 we read in verse 7: "The Lord God formed man,"[88] in verse 8: "The Lord God planted, etc.,"[89] and in verse 9: "The Lord God made to

84 Heb.: *Sambation Hanahar Hamit Gall Gall Koll Jom*, סאמבטיון הנהר המתגלגל כל יום, *sambaṭyon ha-nehar ha-mitgalgal kol yom*, "Sambation, the river that roars every day." According to rabbinical literature, the Sambation is a legendary river beyond which the Ten Lost Tribes were exiled by the Assyrian king Shalmaneser V. See Genesis Rabbah 73; Numbers Rabbah 16; Yalḳuṭ, Genesis 984; cf. Pliny, *Historia Naturalis*, 31.2. The river supposedly flowed strongly for six days per week, but on the seventh dried out. The tale of the river that ceased to flow on the Sabbath and the lost tribe of Israel imprisoned on the other side spread in both Jewish and gentile works. In medieval German (and subsequently, medieval Swedish) works, these isolated Jews were called the Red Jews. See Adams, *Jews in East Norse Literature*, vol. 1, 518–44.

85 Heb.: *Berescit Bara Elohim*, בראשית ברא אלהים, *bereišit bara' elohim*, "In the beginning God created…" (Genesis 1:1).

86 Heb.: *Elohim*, אלהים, *elohim*, "God" is a grammatical plural (of אל *el*, "God") but is understood as a singular and usually requires a verb in the (masculine) singular. This use of the plural may be to express greatness or excellence. Cf. also the Hebrew word בהמות *behemot* "a great beast," a plural form of the word בהמה *behemah* "beast" to express greatness that is also used with singular verb forms.

87 Genesis 1:26: נעשה אדם בצלמנו, "Let us make man in our image" (Heb.).

88 Genesis 2:7: וייצר יהוה אלהים את־האדם, "And the Lord God formed man" (Heb.).

89 Genesis 2:8: ויטע יהוה אלהים, "And the Lord God planted" (Heb.).

HErren/ Gud lät vpwäxa; hwarest står 3. gånger *Jehovah* HERre/ och hade kunnat warit nog/ om det stådt en gång. Fördenskull hwarest *Jehovah* står 3. gånger efter hwarannan så betyder det en Treenighet. Ty man kan vti hela den Heliga Skrifft aldrig finna wid begynnelsen af twänne *versar*, at det ordet *Jehovah* altid står främst/ vtan allenast då Adam Vti Paradiset syndade/ så står äfwen *Jehovah Elohim* 3. gånger efter hwarannan i begynnelsen på *verserne Gen.* 3. *v.* 21. 22. 23. Och HErren Gud giorde til Adam och hans hustru kiortlar. *Vers* 21. Och HErren Gud p. 18 [B1v] sade: si/ Adam | är worden såsom en af oß *v.* 22. Tå lät HErren Gud honom vtur Lustgården *Eden v.* 23. Här af är ofelbart at inhämta/ at 3. Personer äro oemotsäijeligen vti Gudomen. Då Gud säger: Menniskian är worden lika som en en af oß/ så synes det klart at det måste wara mera än en Person/ hälst han säger En af oß. Änskiönt *Judarna* efter sin medfödda arghet och förstockade wilja bewisa och påstå/ at Gud vnder det samma warit i samtal med Änglarna/ så är det aldeles orimeligit och vtan grund. Ty om jag en sak som ingen grund hafwer anföra wil/ så kan jag taga det första Ordet *Berescit*, hwilket hafwer 6. bokstäfwer/ nämligen ett *Bet, Resch, Alef, Schin, Jod, Tau.* Så kan jag säija: *Bet* heter *Ben*, det är/ Son. *Resch* heter *Ruach*, det är den Helige Anda/ *Alef* heter *Elohim*, eller *Av* det är Gud och Fader; *Schin* kan heta *Schemo*, det är namn; *Jod* kan säijas *Jeschua*, det är Frälsare; *Tau* kan kallas *Talu* eller korsfästa. Men ett slikt påfund och vpdichtande har ingen grund vti den Heliga Skrift/ vtan *auctorn* har allenast detta vti en god mening framfördt.

16 *Bet, Resch, Alef*] *Bet, Alef, Resch Spec.* (Sthlm, 1732)*: in his list of errata (113:8–9; this edition 212:6), Löwe corrects the order of the first three letters from* Bet, Alef, [Resch] *to* Bet, Resch, Alef*; Bet Resch Aleph Spec.* (Gbg, 1732; Sthlm, 1735). | **17** det är den Helige Anda] det är/ den Helige Anda *Spec.* (Sthlm, 1732)*: in his list of errata (113:10–12; this edition 212:7–8), Löwe corrects* det är *&c. to* det är Son. *Resch* heter *Ruach*, det är/ den Helige Anda *Spec.* (Sthlm, 1732)*;* det är Son/ *Resch* heter *RuacK*, det är den Helge Anda *Spec.* (Sthlm, 1735)*;* det är Son/ *Resch* heter *Ruack*, det är den Helge Anda *Spec.* (Sthlm, 1735).

grow,"[90] where it says *Jehovah*[91] three times, and it would have been enough if it just said once. Therefore, wherever it says *Jehovah* three times in a row then it means the Trinity, because in the entire Holy Scripture you never find at the beginning of two verses that the word *Jehovah* is always first except when Adam sinned in paradise, where it also says, *Jehovah Elohim*[92] three times in a row in the verses Genesis 3:21–23: "God made unto Adam and his wife coats," verse 21;[93] "And the Lord God said, 'Behold, Adam is become as one of us,'" verse 22;[94] "Therefore, the Lord God sent him forth from the garden of Eden," verse 23.[95] Hence, it is infallible to deduce that there are undeniably three persons in the godhead. When God says, "Man is become like one of us,"[96] it seems clear that there must be more than one person, not least as he says, "one of us." Even though the Jews from their innate fury and stubborn will justify and claim that God was conversing with the angels at the time, it is completely unreasonable and without cause. For if I want to allege something that is without reason, then I can take the first word *Berescit*,[97] which has six letters, viz. *Beth, Resch, Alef, Schin, Jod, Tau*.[98] So, I can say: *Bet* stands for *Ben*, that is "son";[99] *Resch* stands for *Ruach*, that is "the Holy Spirit";[100] *Alef* stands for *Elohim* or *Av*, that is "God" and "father";[101] *Schin* can mean *Schemo* that is "name";[102] *Jud* can be said *Jeschua*, that is "saviour";[103] *Tau* can be called "*Talu*" or "crucify."[104] But such an invention and concoction have no basis in the Holy Scripture, but the author alone has presented this in a good sense.

---

90 Genesis 2:9: ויצמח יהוה אלהים, "And [out of the ground] made the Lord God to grow" (Heb.).

91 *Jehovah* is a Latinization of the Hebrew יהוה, *YHṾH*, the Tetragrammaton, one of the seven names of God.

92 *Jehovah Elohim* is a Latinization of the Hebrew יהוה אלהים, *YHṾH elohim*, "the Lord God."

93 Genesis 3:21: ויעש יהוה אלהים לאדם ולאשתו כתנות, "Unto Adam also and to his wife did the Lord God make coats" (Heb.).

94 Genesis 3:22: ויאמר | יהוה אלהים הן האדם היה כאחד ממנו, "And the Lord God said, Behold, the man is become as one of us" (Heb.).

95 Genesis 3:23: וישלחהו יהוה אלהים מגן־עדן, "Therefore the Lord God sent him forth from the garden of Eden" (Heb.).

96 Genesis 3:22: הן האדם היה כאחד ממנו, "the man is become as one of us" (Heb.).

97 Heb.: *Berescit*, בראשית, *bereišit*, "In the beginning" (Genesis 1:1).

98 The letters of the Hebrew alphabet: *bet* (ב), *reš* (ר), *alef* (א), *šin* (ש), *yud* (י), *tav* (ת).

99 Heb.: *Ben*, בן, *ben*, "son."

100 Heb.: *Ruach*, רוח, *ruaḥ*, "spirit."

101 Heb.: *Elohim*, אלהים, *elohim*, "the Lord." Heb.: *Av*, אב, *av*, "father."

102 Heb.: *Schemo*, שמו, *šemo*, "his name."

103 Heb.: *Jeschua*, ישוע, *yešu'a*, "Jesus," derived from י־ש־ע, "save," "deliver," "help."

104 Heb: *Talu*, תליה, *teliyah*, "suspension, "hanging," and תלוי *talui*, "hanged," "suspended." התלוי *ha-talui*, "the hanged one" was used in some polemical Hebrew texts to refer to Jesus. See Jonathan Adams, "Hebraiske ord i *Jødernes hemmeligheder* (1516)," *Danske Studier*, 105 (2010): 31–50.

Finnas jämwäl andra ord der efter såsom *Bara* hwar af Treenigheten aftagas kan/ nemligen *Bet* heter *Ben* eller Son; *Resch* heter *Ruach* eller den Helige Anda *Alef*, heter *Av* eller Fader/ så at huru jag deße orden taga wil/ antingen fram eller tilbaka beteckna de doch Treenigheten.

p. 19 [B2r] Och til at bewisa at Christus är den/ som skal söndertrampa | ormsens hufwud/ är det vppenbart vti *Gen*. 3. *v*. 15. hwarest står: Jag skal sättia fiendskap emellan tig och qwinnona/ och emillan tina säd och hennes säd/ then samma skal söndertrampa titt hufwud och tu skalt stinga honom i hans häl. Och som Abraham vti trone hafwer wäntat uppå Christum/ ses vti *Gen*. 15. *v*. 6. Abraham trodde Gud/ och det wardt honom räknt til rättfärdighet. Warandes fördenskull och detta en förebild och afmålning til Christum/ då Gud sade til Abraham *Gen*. 22. *v*. 2. 3. 4. at han skulle vpoffra sin enda Son på *Moria* berg/ och är således Christus för wåra synder ett offer worden. Widare at *Messias* är Christus JEsus/ se wi äfwen vti *Num*. 24. 17. En stierna skal vpgå af *Jacob* och en spira skal vpkomma af *Jsraël*. Med hwilken stierna ingen annan förstås än Christus/ fast Judarna det ei wilja tilstå/ och det nogsamt kan af gamla Testamentet som 2. *Sam*. 7. *v*. 12. 13. 14. bewisas/ derest står: När nu tin tid förliden är/ at tu afsomnad är med tina Fäder/ skal jag vpwäckia tina säd efter tig/ som af titt lif komma skal/ honom skal jag stadfästa hans rike: Han skal byggia mino namne ett hus/ at jag skal stadfästa hans rikes stol til ewig tid/ jag skal wara hans Fader/ och han skal wara min Son. Ty här står ju klarligen/ at Gud wil af Dawidz stam och säd vpwäckia *Messiam*, och Gud wil wara
p. 20 [B2v] hans Fader och משיח Christus hans Son. Och vti *Es*. 9. Thet folck | som bo i mörkret skin thet klarligen. Tu giör folcket mycket ther med giör tu icke mycken glädie/ men när tig warder man sig glädiandes/ såsom man sig gläder i Skiördandene såsom man glad är när man skifftar byte. Ty tu hafwer sönderbrutit theras bördos ok och theras skuldrors ris och theras plågares staf/ lika som i *Midians* tid. Ty alt krig som sker med bång och blodig kläder skal vpbrännas och af eld förbrändt warda; Ty oß är födt ett barn/ en Son är oß gifwen/ hwilkens herredömme är vppå hans axlar/ och han heter Vnderlig/ Råd Gud/ Hielte/ Ewig Fader/ Fridfurste. På det hans Herradömme skal warda stort/ och på freden ingen ända/ på Dawidz säte och hans rike/ at han det bereda skal och stärckia med dom och rättfärdighet/ ifrån nu alt in til ewighet. Detta skal HErrans Zebaoths nitälskan giöra. Här är ock äfwen klart/ at ingen annan kan eller bör med detta barnet förstås/ än sielfwer wår

9 *Gen*. 15. *v*. 6] *Gen*. 15. *v*. 16 *Spec*. (Sthlm, 1732; Gbg, 1732; Sthlm, 1735). | **17** Fäder] Fädrr *Spec*. (Sthlm, 1732); Fäder *Spec*. (Gbg, 1732; Sthlm, 1735).

There are other words like this such as *Bara*,[105] from which the Holy Spirit can be deduced, viz. *Bet* stands for *Ben* or "son"; *Resch* stands for *Ruach* or "the Holy Spirit"; *Alef* stands for *Av* or "father," so no matter how I approach these words, either forwards or backwards, they nonetheless denote the Holy Trinity.

And to prove that Christ is the one who will trample upon the serpent's head, it is clear from Genesis 3:15 where it says: "I will put enmity between thee and the woman, and between thy seed and her seed; it shall trample upon thy head, and thou shalt sting his heel."[106] And that Abraham was faithfully waiting for Christ is seen in Genesis 15:6: "Abraham believed in God, and it was counted to him for righteousness." For this and the following reason he is also considered an archetype and prefiguration of Christ when God said to Abraham (Genesis 22:2–4) that he should sacrifice his only son on Mount Moriah, and Christ similarly became a sacrifice for our sins. Furthermore, we also see that the Messiah is Christus Jesus in Numbers 24:17: "there shall come a star out of Jacob, and a sceptre shall rise out of Israel." None other can be understood to be meant by this star than Christ, although the Jews will not admit it. And it can be clearly shown from the Old Testament as in 2 Samuel 7:12–14 where it says: "And when thy days be fulfilled, and thou shalt sleep with thy fathers, I will set up thy seed after thee, which shall proceed out of thy bowels, and I will establish his kingdom. He shall build a house for my name, and I will establish the throne of his kingdom for eternity. I will be his father, and he shall be my son." Indeed, for here it clearly says that God will set up the Messiah from David's house and seed, and God will be his father and משיח[107] Christ his son. And in Isaiah 9[:2–7]: "It shines clearly upon the people who dwell in the darkness. Thou hast multiplied the nation, and thereby not created much joy: they rejoice near thee as one rejoices in harvest, and as one rejoices when one divides the spoil. For thou hast broken the yoke of their burden and also the cane of their shoulders and the rod of their oppressor, as in the time of Midian.[108] For every war that takes place with noise and bloodied garments shall be burnt up and incinerated by fire. For unto us a child is born, unto us a son is given whose government shall be upon his shoulders: and his name shall be called Wonderful, Counsellor, God, Hero, Eternal Father, The Prince of Peace. Of the increase of his government and peace there shall be no end, upon the throne of David, and upon his kingdom, to prepare and strengthen it, and to establish it with judgement and justice from now until all eternity. The zeal of the Lord of Sabaoth [hosts] will perform this." Here it is also clear that none other than our Lord Jesus

105 Heb.: *Bara*, ברא, *bara'*, "created."

106 The "Protoevangelium" in Genesis 3:15; cf. Romans 16:20.

107 Heb.: משיח, *mašiaḥ*, "Messiah," "annointed one."

108 Midian was the fourth son of Abraham and Keturah (1 Chronicles 1:32).

HErre JEsus Christus: Hälst sådane ähre-titlar warda vti Ordspråks Bokenes 30. *v.* 4. Honom egenteligen tilägande. Wi finna äfwen ett klart skiäl derest står: Hwilken far vp til himmelen och neder? Ho fattar wädret i sina händer? Ho binder watnet vti ett kläde? Ho hafwer stadfäst alla werldenes ändar? Huru heter han? Och huru heter hans Son? Wetst tu thet? Och kan man äfwen se/ at det på ingen annan kan *appliceras*, än på Gudz Son. Vti *Es.* 40. *v.* 9. *Zion* tu predikar/ stig vp på ett högt p. 21 [B3r] berg/ *Je*|*rusalem*/ tu som predikar/ häf vp tin röst med macht/ häf vpp och fruchta tig intet/ Säg Juda städer: Si ther är eder Gud. Och *Esa.* 45. *v.* 8. Dryper i himlar åfwan efter och skyn rägne rättfärdighet jorden öpne sig och bäre salighet och rättferdighet wexa til med; Jag HErren Skapar honom. *Item Ezech.* 44. *v.* 2. HErren sade til mig/ thenna porten skal blifwa tillyckt och icke vplåten warda och ther skal ingen gå igenom/ vtan allena HErren *Jsraëls* Gud; och skal doch tillycht blifwa. *Item Esa.* 49. *v.* 6. Thet är en ringa ting at tu äst min tienare til at vprätta *Jacobs* slächter och igenföra det förskingrade vti *Jsraël* vtan jag hafwer ock giordt tig til hedningarnas Lius/ at du skal wara min salighet in til werldenes ända. *Jerem.* 23. *v.* 5. 6. Si then tiden kommer säger HErren/ at jag skal vpwäckia. Dawid rättfärdighetenes frucht/ och thet skal wara en Konung then wäl regera skal och skal vprätta rätt och rättfärdighet på jordene. På then tiden skal Juda hulpen warda och *Jsraël* säker bo/ och thetta skal wara hans namn/ thet man honom kalla skal HErren som oß rättfärdigar. *Jerem.* 30. *v.* 21. 22. Och hans wäldige skola af honom födde warda och hans herrar komma af honom sielfwom. Och jag skal låta honom för mig komma at han för mig offra skal: Ty hwilken är then eljest/ som mig så hiertans gierna offrar säger HErren/ och i skolen wara mitt folck och jag skal wara edar | p. 22 [B3v] Gud. *Dan.* 9. *v.* 24. Siuttijo weckor äro bestämda öfwer titt folck och öfwer tin helga stad/ så skal öfwerträdelsen blifwa förtagen och synden betäckt och mißgierningen försonad och then ewiga rättfärdigheten framhafd/ och synen och *Prophetian* besiglad/ och den aldrahelgaste smord warda. *Zach.* 9. *v.* 11. Tu vtsläpper och genom tins förbunds blod tina fångar vtur kulone ther intet watn vti är. *Mich.* 5. *v.* 2. Och tu *Bethlehem Ephrata*, som liten äst ibland Juda städer/ vtaf tig skal den komma/ som i *Jsraël* en HErre wara skal hwilkens vtgång warit af begynnelsen och af ewighet. *Hebr.* ואתה בית לחם אפרתה צעיר אתה להיות באלפי יהודא ממךְ יצא מלכי בישראל ומוצאיו מקדם ימי עולם

28 5. *v.* 2] 5. *v.* 1 *Spec.* (Sthlm, 1732; Gbg, 1732; Sthlm, 1735).

Christ can or ought to be meant by this child. Such honorary titles in Proverbs 30:4 are appropriate for him. We also find a clear reason where it says: “Who hath ascended up into heaven and descended? Who hath gathered the wind in his hands? Who hath bound the water in a garment? Who hath established all the ends of the earth? What is he called? And what is his son called? Dost thou know?” And we can even see that it cannot be applied to anyone other than the Son of God. In Isaiah 40:9: “O Zion, you preach, climb a high mountain; O Jerusalem, that preaches, lift up thy voice with strength; lift it up, be not afraid; say unto the cities of Judah, ‘Behold your God!’” And Isaiah 45:8: “Drop down, ye heavens, from above, and pour down righteousness: let the earth open, and let them bring forth salvation, and let righteousness spring up together; I the Lord have created it.” Similarly, Ezekiel 44:2: “‘The Lord said unto me, ‘This gate shall be shut and not be opened, and no one shall go through it except only the Lord, the God of Israel, therefore it shall be shut.’” Similarly, Isaiah 49:6: “It is a light thing that thou shouldest be my servant to raise up the tribes of Jacob and to restore the scattered people of Israel: but I have also given thee for a light to the Gentiles, that thou mayest be my salvation unto the end of the earth.” Jeremiah 23:5–6: “Behold, the day cometh, saith the Lord, that I will raise unto David a fruit of righteousness and it shall be a king that shall reign well and shall execute judgement and justice upon the earth. At this time, Judah shall be helped, and Israel shall dwell safely: and this shall be his name whereby he shall be called, The Lord Our Righteousness.” Jeremiah 30:21–22: “‘And his mighty shall be born of him, and his governors shall proceed from him himself; and I will allow him to draw near to me that he shall make an offering unto me: for who is this that engaged his heart to make an offering unto me?’ saith the Lord. ‘And ye shall be my people, and I will be your God.’” Daniel 9:24: “Seventy weeks are determined upon thy people and upon thy holy city, to finish the transgression, and to make an end of sins, and to make reconciliation for iniquity, and to bring in everlasting righteousness, and to seal up the vision and prophecy, and to anoint the most Holy.” Zechariah 9:11: “As for thee also, by the blood of thy covenant I have sent forth thy prisoners out of the pit wherein is no water.” Micah 5[:2]: “But thou, Bethlehem Ephratah, who is little among the cities of Judah, out of thee shall come forth he who is to be a lord in Israel; whose goings forth have been from the beginning and from eternity.” In Hebrew: ואתה בית לחם אפרתה צעיר אתה להיות באלפי יהודא ממךָ יצא מלכי בישראל ומוצאיו מקדם ימי עולם[109]

109 The correct Heb. biblical quotation is: ואתה בית לחם אפרתה צעיר להיות באלפי יהודה ממך לי יצא להיות מושל בישראל ומוצאתיו מקדם מימי עולם “But thou, Bethlehem Ephratah, though thou be little among the thousands of Judah, yet out of thee shall he come forth unto me that is to be ruler in Israel; whose goings forth have been from of old, from everlasting” (Micah 5:1).

Deße alla *Prophetierna* af det gamla *Testamentet*, de wisa/ och lika såsom peka på Christum. Ty han är födder vti Bethlehem. Han är af Dawidz slächt och stam. Han är född af en obesmittad Jungfru/ De 70. Daniels weckor äro ändade/ ehuru de derom *Calculera* och räkna. Alla *prophetierne* äro fullkomnade/ och doch äro Judarna så förblindade och förståckade icke annorledes än Pharao/ hwilken wiste at Gud honom med så många plågor straffade för *Jsraëls* barns skull. Så äro och de nu warande Judar/ som kring hela werlden vtspridde äro/ vti stort föracht och twång/ vtan något Rike och Regemente/ ingen Konung/ Präster eller Lewiter/ intet p. 23 [B4r] Tempel och Altare/ | ingen *Uhrim* och *Thumim*, ingen FörbundsArck/ inga offer och Propheter hafwandes. Och doch kunna de icke besinna och omwända sig/ falla JEsum til fot och sökia sin hälso och salighet vti deß sår: emedan nådenes dörr öpen står. Ty Gud wil icke den ogudachtigas död/ vtan at han omwänder sig ock lefwer. *Hebr.* כי לא אחפוץ במת הרשע כי אם שובו וחי לעולם derföre är det at önska; at Gud wille sig öfwer det arma folcket förbarma och til nåder taga/ och at de måtte låta sitt hierta beweka och sig omwända/ hälst de det nogsamt sig förskrifwit hafwa. Och wil jag ännu flera skiähl framföra.

CAP. 12.

AT Christus är Guds Son kan och bewisas af *Psal.* 2. *v.* 7. Tu äst min Son i dag hafwer jag födt tig. Eska af mig så wil jag gifwa tig Hedningarna til arfz och werldenes ändar til egendom. Tu skal sönderslå them med jernspiro/ såsom Lerpottor skal tu sönderkroßa them. Så låter nu vnderwisa eder I Konungar och låter tuchta eder i domare på jordene. Tiener HErranom med fruchtan och frögden eder med bäfwande. Hyller Sonen at han icke förtörnas och i förgås på wägenom. Ty hans wrede skal snart begynna at bränna; men salige äro alla the/ som trösta på honom. Änskiönt nu Judarna *interpretera* och vttyda detta språket om Salomon/ p. 24 [B4v] och at Dawid således sin Son Salomon vnder | det samma tiltalar/ så kan doch synas at ett slikt föregifwande är vtan någon grund; ty Salomons Rike och Rege-

All of these prophecies from the Old Testament show and equally point to Christ. For he was born in Bethlehem. He is of the house and tribe of David. He was born of an immaculate virgin. Daniel's seventy weeks[110] have ended no matter how they are calculated and determined. All the prophecies have been fulfilled and yet the Jews are blinded and stubborn, not unlike Pharaoh who knew that God was punishing him with so many plagues for the sake of the children of Israel. This is what present-day Jews are like who are scattered throughout the world, in great contempt and duress, without any kingdom or government, having no king, priests or Levites, no temple and altar, no *Urim* and *Thummim*,[111] no Ark of the Covenant, no sacrifices and prophets. And still, they cannot change their minds and convert, fall at the feet of Jesus and seek healing and blessing in his wounds while the door of mercy stands open. For God does not wish that the ungodly man dies but that he converts and lives. In Hebrew: כי לא אחפוץ במת הרשע כי אם שובו וחי לעולם.[112] Therefore it is to be wished for that God will take pity upon the poor people and show them mercy, and that they may allow their hearts to be awoken and convert, particularly those who have carefully requested this. And I will present even more reasons.

Chapter 12

That Christ is the Son of God can also be proved by Psalm 2:7–[12]: "Thou art my Son; this day have I begotten thee. Ask of me, then I shall give thee the heathens for thine inheritance, and the ends of the earth for thy possession. Thou shalt break them with a rod of iron; thou shalt dash them in pieces like clay pots. Learn now, ye kings; be instructed, ye judges of the earth. Serve the Lord with fear and rejoice with trembling. Praise the son, lest he be angry, and ye perish from the way, because his wrath shall soon begin to burn. But blessed are all they that put their trust in him." Although the Jews now interpret and decipher these words as being about Solomon, and that with them David is thus speaking to his son Solomon, it can nonetheless be shown that such a pretence is without any reason, as Solomon's empire and rule did not stretch any further than to the Land of

110 Daniel 9:24–27.

111 The Urim (אורים, *urim*) and Thummim (תומים, *tumim*) were elements of the breastplate (חושן, *ḥošen*) worn by the High Priest in the Temple and probably used in divination and cleromancy. See Exodus 28:30 and 1 Samuel *passim* (e.g., 14:41).

112 "As I do not wish the death of the evil one, unless he changes and lives forever" (Heb.). Cf. Shenei Luchot HaBerit, Aseret HaDibrot, Yoma, Ner Mitzva 4:36.

mente sträckte sig ei längre än vti Chanans Land. Skulle åter Judarna giöra det inkast: at Christenheten är ju den aldraminsta/ der doch en ganska stor myckenhet af Turkar och hedningar finnas/ och således/ at detta språk til de Christne ei *appliceras* kan; så måste de doch emot sin wilja tilstå; at det står hos Dawid: Förbannad ware den/ som sätter sin förtröstan på menniskior/ men wälsignad wara den/ som sätter sin förtröstan på HErranom. Nu står vti *Psalm.* 2. *versen* sidsta: Hyller Sonen at han icke förförtörnas. Wäl alla dem/ som sig på honom förlåta och hoppas. Ty om det skulle wara en menniskia/ så törs man ju intet på den samma förtrösta; följer fördenskul nödwändigt/ at Dawid vti samma *Psalm* talar ei om Salomon vtan om Christo. Vti *Malach.* 3. *v.* 1. står thet: Si jag wil vtsända min Ängel/ then ther wägen för mig bereda skal/ och med hast skal komma til sitt tempel HErren then I söken och förbundsens Ängel then i begären/ Si han kommer säger HErren Zebaoth. *Item. Zach.* 6. *v.* 12. Thetta säger HErren Zebaoth: Si thet är en man som heter *Zemah*, vnder honom skal det gro/ och han skal vpbyggia HErrans Tempel. |

p. 25 [B5r]

CAP. 13.

HÄr wid bör orsaken i acht tagas/ hwarföre *Judarna* så högeligen förarga sig öfwer *Messia.* Och är det til wetandes: at orsaken är denne/ emedan han ei fördt med sig ett jordiskt Rike/ vtan blifwit slagen/ hudflängd och korßfäst/ ja alla hans Apostlar och efterföljare hafwa ymkeligen omkommit. Men man måste weta at det war Guds Faders wilje/ at Christus skulle lida och dö/ ty eljest hade icke återlösnings wärcket warit gällande och fullkomligit/ hwilket jag med Dawids *Ps.* 49. 8. bewisa will/ derest det så lyder: Kan doch en broder ingen förlösa/ eller Gudi något försona? Ty thet kåstar förmycket at förlösa theras Siäl/ så at han måste låta det bestå ewinnerliga.

Canaan.[113] If the Jews object again that Christianity is the absolute smallest as there is a large number of Turks and pagans, and thus that these words cannot be applied to the Christians, then they must admit against their will that it says in connection with David: “Cursed be the man that trusteth in man, but blessed is the man that trusteth in the Lord.”[114] Now it says in the final verse of Psalm 2: “Praise the son, lest he be angry. Blessed are all they that ask his forgiveness and put their hope in him.”[115] Because if it were a person, then one does not dare to trust that person; it therefore necessarily follows that David in this Psalm was not talking about Solomon but about Christ. In Malachi 3:1 it says, “Behold, I will send my angel, who shall prepare the way before me: and the Lord, whom ye seek, and the angel of the covenant, whom ye delight in, shall suddenly come to his temple. Behold, he shall come, saith the Lord of hosts.” Likewise, Zechariah 6:12: “Thus speaketh the Lord of hosts: Behold there is a man called *Zemah*,[116] under him it shall grow up, and he shall build the Temple of the Lord.”

Chapter 13

Hereby we should observe the reason why the Jews become so tremendously annoyed about the Messiah, and it shall be known that the reason is this: because he did not bring an earthly realm with him, but was beaten, scourged, and crucified. Indeed, all his apostles and followers have died humbly. But we must know that it was the will of God the Father that Christ should suffer and die, as otherwise the work of redemption would not have been valid and complete, which I shall prove with David’s Psalm 49:[7–]8 which sounds like this: “But can no one redeem his brother nor give a ransom to God? For it costs much to redeem their soul, so that he must not let it cease forever.”

113 The Land of Canaan was the area of the Southern Levant comprising Phoenicia, Philistia, and Israel.

114 Jeremiah 17:5, 7.

115 Psalm 2:12.

116 Heb.: *Zemah*, צמח, *ẓemaḥ*, “branch.”

At Judarna föregifwa/ det twänne *Messier* komma skola/ den ena wid namn *Messias Ben Joseph* den andra *Messias Ben David*, deraf wilja de ei erkänna Christum fast det wärkeligen är den samma/ säijandes den ena skola omkomma lida och dö; men *Messias Ben Dawid* skal wara den sanna och rätta/ der utinnan de fara mycket wilse; Ty *Messias Ben Joseph* och *Messias Ben Dawid* är alt samma/ nämligen Christus JEsus. Detta kan klarligen inhämtas af den Hel. Skrifft; Ty *Messias Ben Joseph* warder han kallad i anseende til sin Fosterfader som het Joseph/ men *Messias Ben Dawid* warder han derföre kallad/ alldenstund | p. 26 [B5v] han war af Dawids *Familia* och slächt. Men at *Messias Ben Joseph*, skulle omkomma/ det är lida; bewises af *Dan.* 9. 26. derest står: Och efter de twå och sextio weckor skal Christus dödad warda och de skola icke wilja honom. *Item Zach.* 13. 7. Swärd vp öfwer min Herde och öfwer min Folcks Furste/ säger HERren Zebaoth: Slå Herdan så warda Fåhren förskingrad/ så will jag wända min hand til the små. At Christus är til Himla vpfaren och lefwer i ewighet/ som ei Judarna wilja tillstå/ ses af *Esa.* 53. Han är tagen vtur ångest och dom/ ho kan vttala hans lifslängd *etc.* ty han frälser them ifrån helfwete och den ewiga döden. *Hos.* 13. 14. Död jag skal wara tig ett förgifft helfwetit jag skal wara tig en plåga. Alt detta har Christus tilfyllest giordt och är för wåra synder död worden/ men Judarna wilja det ei tro/ vtan tala och vtsprida mer försmädelse mot Christum och deß helga lära. Jag will förden-skull önska/ at GUD sig öfwer detta arma Folcket wille förbarma/ dem vprätta och ögonen på dem öpna/ at de måge se hwem de hafwa Korßfästat och ehrkänna hans Heliga Ord och Lära/ och icke wänta på någon jordisk och wärdslig *Messia*, som stora rikedomar och härligheter med sig bringandes warder/ hälst det intet gagnar om man hade hela werlden/ när man lider skada til sin Siäl. Judarna hafwa och en *Tradition* vti en liten bok som kalles *Leftoff* der vil de säija/ at de | p. 27 [B6r] Christne

11 *Zach.* 13. 7] *Zach.* 13. 17 *Spec.* (Sthlm, 1732); *Zach.* 13. 7 *Spec.* (Gbg, 1732; Sthlm, 1735). | **15** *etc.*] ꝛc *Spec.* (Sthlm, 1732)*: the* et *is abbreviated by an* r-*rotunda rather than the ampersand used in almost all other cases. Cf. 17:18 (this edition 92:19), 77:20 (174:5), and 94:2 (192:15).*

The Jews pretend that two Messiahs will come, the one called Messiah Ben Joseph [son of Joseph][117] and the other Messiah Ben David [son of David],[118] which is why they will not recognize Christ even though he really was the very same; and they say the one will perish, suffer, and die, but Messiah Ben David will be the true and proper one. In this they are deluded as Messiah Ben Joseph and Messiah Ben David are one and the same, namely Christ Jesus. This can clearly be gathered from the Holy Scriptures, as Messiah Ben Joseph was named in honour of his foster father who was called Joseph, but he was named Messiah Ben David because he was of the family and line of David. But that Messiah Ben Joseph was to perish, that is suffer, is shown from Daniel 9:26 where it says: "And after two-and-sixty weeks Christ will be killed and they will not want him." Similarly, Zechariah 13:[7]: "'O sword, against my shepherd, and against the prince of my people,' saith the Lord of hosts: 'Smite the shepherd, and the sheep shall be scattered: and I will turn mine hand upon the little ones.'" That Christ has ascended to heaven and lives for eternity, which the Jews will not admit, is seen from Isaiah 53[:8]: "He was taken from anguish and from judgement: who shall declare his generation? etc."[119] for he saves them from hell and the eternal death. Hosea 13:14: "O death, I will be thy poisoned hell; I will be thy plague." Christ has done all these things to the full and has died for our sins, but the Jews will not believe it, but rather they speak and spread more contempt for Christ and his sacred teaching. For this reason, I wish that God would take pity upon this poor people, restore them and open their eyes that they might see whom they have crucified and recognize his holy words and teaching, and not wait for some earthly and worldly Messiah who will bring great riches and delights with him, especially as it is of no benefit to possess the whole world when your soul is suffering damage. The Jews also have a tradition in a little book called *Leftoff*,[120] where they say that the Christians who treat them well will

117 Messiah ben Joseph (משיח בן־יוסף, *Mašiaḥ ben-Yosef*) is a Jewish Messiah descended from Joseph through the tribe of Ephraim. In Jewish tradition, there are two, sometimes four, messianic figures: ben Joseph, ben David, and sometimes Elijah and the Righteous Priest. They will usher in the messianic age (Zechariah 1:21 [2:4]; Talmud Sukkah 52b). See also the following note. Traditionally, Christians have not argued that Jesus was Messiah ben Joseph, in spite of his father also being called Joseph, preferring instead to identify him solely with Messiah ben David.

118 Messiah ben David (משיח בן־דוד, *Mašiaḥ ben-Daṿid*) is a Jewish Messiah descended from the line of David through his father (Isaiah 1:1).

119 Isaiah 53:8.

120 *Leftoff* is a transliteration of לב טוב, *lev ṭov*, "good heart." *The Book of the Good Heart* (*Sefer Lev Ṭov*) is an ethical work by Yiẓḥaḳ ben Elyaḳum written in Yiddish and first printed in Prague in 1620. See Noga Rubin, "*Sefer Lev Tov*, Prague 1620: The First Edition of the Book?" *Zutot: Perspectives on Jewish Culture* 5, no. 1 (2008): 121–27.

som bewisa dem godt/ skola ei blifwa fördömde/ vtan för sin wälgerning bekomma det yttersta rummet vti Paradis.

CAP. 14.

FÖljer nu kårteligen at berätta om Judarnas mat. Hwad de Christnas mat angår/ efterlåtes icke Judarna den samma at äta/ vtan äro der wid strängeligen förbudne/ och warder af dem kallad *Therepha* טרפה, det betyder så mycket som en Warg skolat det samma sönderrifwit. De töra icke heller äta någon bakdel af något fyrfotat diur/ hwilket de tagit af *Gen.* 32. 32. derest står: Fördenskull äta *Jsraëls* barn än i dag ingen höffteseno/ efter Jacobs höfftes sena rörd war. De äro och vnderstundom så strängeligen förbudne/ at de ei vnderstå sig äta framdelarne/ vtan måste de dem bortkasta/ så framt ingen af de Christna dem kiöpa och behålla will/ och intet vtaf dem som äro twåklöfwade/ vtan och af andra som ei twåklöfwade äro. Men beträffande swinen som ock twåklöfwade äro/ töra de icke wid förlust af sitt lif äta eller widröra. De töra icke heller äta allahanda slags foglar/ och äro ibland dem följande låflige at äta: Sparfwar/ Rapphöns/ Anckor/ Giäß/ Dufwor och Höns. Deße foglar skola icke skiutas eller ihiälslås/ vtan skola lefwan-
p. 28 [B6v] de med nät och snaror fångade warda/ och efterlåtes icke hwad | Creatur det wara må at ihiälslå med yxa hammar/ sten eller staf/ och dem til någon spis bereda/ utan de måste hafwa en skarper knif ett qwarter lång/ så at icke den ringaste bräcka eller fel på honom wara skall/ vtan at han vnder strykandet fastnar wid nagelen. Denna knif warder kallad *Kalef* חליף och har hwar Bokstaf vti samma ord sin besynnerliga betydelse/ nemligen at samma knif skal wara vtan alla fel. Hafwandes der jemte det ordet *Kalef* den bemärkelse som en förwäxling och

7 *Gen.* 32. 32] *Gen.* 22. 32 *Spec.* (Sthlm, 1732; Gbg, 1732; Sthlm, 1735).

not be condemned, but rather receive the utmost place in paradise for the good deeds.[121]

Chapter 14

In the following I shall briefly talk about the Jews' food. As far as the Christians' food is concerned, the Jews are not permitted to eat of it; indeed, they are strictly forbidden to, and it is called by them *Therepha* טרפה,[122] that is the same as saying a wolf has ripped it apart. They do not dare to eat the hindquarters of any four-footed animal, which they take from Genesis 32:32 where it says: "Therefore, the children of Israel still today do not eat of the sinew of the thigh since the sinew of Jacob's thigh was touched." Sometimes they are so strictly forbidden that they do not even subject themselves to eating the forequarters but rather throw them away, unless some Christian wants to buy and have them, and not of those [animals] that have cloven hooves, but also of those that do not have cloven hooves. But with regard to pigs, that also have cloven hooves, they do not dare eat or touch it even if their lives depended on it. They also do not dare to eat all kinds of birds, and it is permitted to eat the following among them: sparrows, partridges, ducks, geese, pigeons, and chickens. These birds should not be shot or killed, but should be caught alive with nets and traps; and it is not allowed no matter what creature it is to kill it with an axe, a hammer, a stone, or a pole, and prepare it as food, but they must have a sharp knife, a quarter [of an ell; i.e., 15 cm or 6 in] long, so that not the smallest nick or blemish shall be upon it, so it does not stick to the nail when stroked. This knife is called a *Kalef* חליף,[123] and each letter of this very word has its own particular meaning, namely that this knife shall be completely without fault, as that word *Kalef* has the sense of a change or transformation from life to

121 Mishneh Torah, Sefer Shoftim, Melachim u-Milḥamot 8:11: כל המקבל שבע מצות ונזהר לעשותן הרי זה מחסידי אומות העולם ויש לו חלק לעולם הבא "Everyone who keeps these seven commandments [the Laws of Noah] and is careful in observing them is considered one of 'the pious among the gentiles' and will receive a share in the world to come."

122 Heb.: *Therepha*, טרפה, *ṭerefah*, "torn [by a beast of prey]." The term refers to meat from kosher animals that has been disqualified from being used as food because of defects such as disease or injury. In the following, Löwe confuses the Hebrew term with the Yiddish word טרייף (*ṭreyf*) that refers to all non-kosher animals and food.

123 The knife used for traditional slaughtering (שחיטה, *šeḥiṭah*) is usually just called a סכין *sakin* (the common word for any knife in Heb.) or שלאכטמעסער "slaughtering knife" in Yidd. However, here Löwe uses the Talmudic term חלף *ḥalaf* (or *ḥalif*) that is particularly common among Ashkenazi Jews.

ombytning från lifwet til döden. Med denna knif taga de lifwet af foglarna/ men til stora Creatur såsom oxar och kor/ warder en stor knif en aln lång och 3. finger bred af dem brukad/ och måste den wara så skarp äfwen som den förra och med den samma skola de allenast skära ett skärande. Icke få de aldeles afskära hals eller strupa/ utan allenast hälften både af foglar och andra Creatur. Detta slachtandet efterlåtes icke allom at förrätta/ ty Qwinfolcken är det aldeles förbudet; vtan är en wiß person som der på några åhr lära måste; och warder den samma kallad *Sioket*, det är/ Slachtare. De töras icke slackta om *Sabbather* och Festdagar/ vtan i nödfall eller då lifsfara är å färde. När han slacktat och hufwudet afskurit/ får man samma Creatur intet äta; och om någon vnder slacktandet drager knifwen fram och tilbaka/ eller vphörer och åter begynner/ så är det äfwen förbudit at äta. Ty | p. 29 [B7r] de föregifwa at dermedelst kommer bloden at stadna vti kroppen/ och kan hwarken med saltande eller wattnläggiande utdragas. Här med är ännu icke nog/ vtan när de slackta en oxe/ ko/ får eller lamb/ skal Slacktaren inwärtes känna dem wid refbenen/ lungor och lefwer/ om de äro wid refbenen anwuxne/ och om så befinnes, få de det ei äta/ vtan om ingen af de Christne det kiöper/ så måste det bortkastas. Finnas några swulnader och andra bräckligheter/ är det äfwen förbudit at äta; men när alt är befunnit wara sundt och vtan någon wanck/ efterlåtes dock ei äta mer än framdelen/ doch måste köttet först ligga en half tima vti watn/ och när det vhr watnet tagit är lägges det på en sned bänck at watnet må afrinna och sedan beströs det med salt/ så tiockt som en tunner sniö/ och så ligger det allenast en timma vti saltet/ at bloden dermedelst må vtdragas/ och widare warder det med rent watn afskiöldt. Hwad mera deras slacktande angår/ så är der om mycket til at skrifwa/ men man will låta der med bestå.

Eljest skola Judarna hafwa twänne knifwar/ twänne gafflar/ twänne grytor/ twänne skedar/ *in Summa*, vtaf alt det de bruka/ skola de hafwa twänne persedlar. Ty när de äta smör/ ost eller miölck/ töras de en tima der efter intet äta kött/ vtan måste wänta tils den är förbi. Och vti det kiärile som de haft miölck/ ost eller smör/ få de intet hafwa några köttwahror/ och med | p. 30 [B7v] samma knif som de skurit bakelse/ smör eller annat få de ei skära kött. Der så hända skulle at någon af förseende och hastighet/ skulle taga en sked eller knif som warit vti kött eller såppa/ och sätter den vti någon miölckmat/ så få de hwarken äta maten eller bruka kiärilet. Och de kiärile som äro *destinerande* til en wiß rätt/ äro med wißa streck vtmärckte. Detta hafwa de af gamla *Testamentet*, hwarest står/ at man intet lamb koka skal med deß Moders miölck.

death.[124] With this knife they take the life of birds, but for larger creatures like oxen and cows, a large knife, one ell [i.e., 60 cm or 2 ft] long and three fingers wide, is used by them, and it must be just as sharp as the aforementioned one and only with this is a cut to be made. They may not entirely cut the neck or throat, but only half of it, both for birds and other creatures. It is not permitted for all to perform this slaughter, as women are entirely forbidden; but it is a wise person who must study several years for this and he is called a *Sioket*,[125] that is a "slaughterer." They do not dare slaughter on the Sabbath and holidays unless there is an emergency or danger to life. When he has slaughtered and decapitated the creature, he may not eat it. And if during the slaughtering someone pulls the knife back and forth, or stops and begins again, then it is also forbidden to eat it, because they claim that this makes the blood clot within the body, and it cannot be drawn out either by salting or leaving it to soak in water. This is still not enough, but when they slaughter an ox, cow, sheep, or lamb, the slaughterer will feel inside along the ribs, lungs, and liver, and if there are any growths along the ribs, they may not eat it; if none of the Christians buys it, it must be thrown away. If there are any swellings and other ailments, it is also forbidden to eat it. But when everything is found to be healthy and without any defect, it is still not permitted to eat anything more than the forequarters; and the meat still has to soak in water for half an hour. And when it is taken out of the water, it is placed on a sloping board so that the water might run off and is then sprinkled with salt, as thick as a layer of snow. And it lies in this salt for at least an hour so that the blood will thereby be drawn out, and then it is further rinsed in clean water. As far as what else there is to say about their slaughtering, there is much that can be written, but I will leave it there.

Apart from that, the Jews have two knives, two forks, two pans, two spoons. In summary, with every object that they use they should have two of them. Because when they eat butter, cheese, or milk, they dare not eat meat for the next hour, but they must wait till it has passed. And in the vessel in which they have had milk, cheese, or butter, they may not have any meat products, and with the same knife that they have cut baked goods, butter or something else, they may not cut meat. Should it happen by mistake or through haste that someone takes a spoon or knife that was in meat or soup and puts it in dairy food, they may neither eat the food nor use the vessel. And the vessels that are intended for a certain dish are marked by certain stripes. They take this from the Old Testament where it says that a lamb should not be boiled in its mother's milk.[126]

---

124 In Heb., חלף means "pass through" and in Aram. "change, alter."

125 Heb.: *Sioket*, שוחט, *šoḥeṭ*, "ritual butcher": a butcher who is trained in religious law and the practice and regulations involved in traditional slaughtering.

126 Exodus 23:19; Exodus 34:26; Deuteronomy 14:21.

CAP. 15.

JUdarna hafwa wiſsa månader och synnerliga dagar om åhret i hwar månad/ på hwilka en Scholebetient den de kalla *Schamasch* שמש hwilken går hus från hus kring hela församlingen och ropar 8. dagar förut/ på denna *Dato*, timma och *minut* faller *Thekopha* תקופה det är efter Judarnas mening at en blodsdråppa skal vti hela werlden falla på ett wist ställe vti deras hus. Och när samma dråppa faller på några matwahror/ och en Jude äter af samma spis/ eller faller vti drickswahror/ så blifwer han der af från *Dato* til följande åhrs samma *Datum* vpswullen/ och när samma timma kommer måste han dö. Wed samma *Thekopha* är efter deras

Chapter 15

The Jews have certain months and particular days every month of the year on which a synagogue official,[127] whom they call *Schamasch* שמס,[128] who goes from house to house around the entire community and shouts eight days before "on this date, hour, and minute falls *Thekopha*";[129] in the Jews' opinion, that is when throughout the whole world a drop of blood shall fall upon a certain spot in their house. And when this drop falls upon food items, and a Jews eats of this same food, or it falls into beverages, then for one year from that date he will be swollen, and when the same hour comes, he must die. At this *Thekopha*, there is in their

---

127 Löwe calls the synagogue official a "Scholebetient," lit. "an official of the *schola*." The word *schola* should be understood as a Latinization of Yiddish *shul* (שול, "synagogue") and the phrase "en *Schole* Betient" means "a synagogue warden" or "*gabbai*." Cf. p. 118:1 for *Spec*. (Sthlm, 1732), 36:1–2 and p. 189*n*290 for *Spec*. (Sthlm, 1732), 89.

128 Heb./Yidd.: *Schamasch*, שמס, *šamaš*, "helper." The reading of the final Hebrew letter is uncertain here due to poor reproduction on the printed page. If it is indeed a *sameḥ* (ס), it may be an attempt to reproduce the Yiddish שאַמעס or שמש (*šaməs*), a "shamos" or "synagogue caretaker," "beadle," "sexton" rather than the standard Hebrew term שמש (*šamaš*).

129 Heb.: *Thekopha*, תקופה, *teḳufah*, "turning of the sun," i.e., an equinox. There was an unusual folk belief attached to the four equinoxes during which it was said a noxious precipitation or drops of blood fell from the sky and poisoned water and food. The superstition is first documented in *Maḥzor Viṭry* (twelfth century) where the original source of the blood is described thus:

Vernal equinox: God turned the waters of Egypt to blood (Exodus 7:14–25)

Summer equinox: Moses struck the rock and blood flowed (Targum Pseudo-Jonathan Numbers 20:11; Midrash Tehillim 105:12. There may be an echo of this tradition in the New Testament; cf. John 19:34)

Autumn equinox: Abraham prepared to sacrifice Isaac and blood appeared on his knife (cf. Edward Kessler, *Bound by the Bible: Jews, Christians and the Sacrifice of Isaac* [Cambridge: Cambridge University Press, 2004], 119–38)

Winter equinox: Jephtha sacrificed his daughter to fulfil his vow to God (Judges 11:29–40)

Other explanations of the source of the blood include Lilith's menses and bloody battles between constellations of stars. There were several possible measures to prevent water becoming contaminated during the *teḳufot*, such as suspending a piece of iron in the water (as described here by Löwe) – a practice that began in western Ashkenaz during the thirteenth century. On the superstitions associated with the *teḳufot*, see Joshua Trachtenberg, *Jewish Magic and Superstitions: A Study in Folk Religion*, foreword by Moshe Idel (Philadelphia: University of Pennsylvania Press, 2004 [first edn 1939]), 257–58. See also Elisheva Carlebach, *Palaces of Time: Jewish Calendar and Culture in Early Modern Europe* (Cambridge, MA: Harvard University Press, 2011), 169–88.

Descriptions of the four *teḳufot* are very unusual in Christian ethnographical works about Jews and Judaism. In extant Christian writings about Jewish beliefs dating from before Löwe's treatment, they are only mentioned twice: Christoph Paul Majern, *מנהגים: Das ist derer heutigen Jüden Cremonien und Gebräuche ins Gemein und insonderheit durch das gantze Jahr* (Wittemberg: Wilcken, 1687 [1st edn in 1678]), ff. E1r–E2r (ch. 9); Giulio Morosini, *דרך אמונה: Via della fede mostrata agli ebrei* (Rome: Propaganda Fide, 1683), 444–522 (ch. 24–26).

mening en sådan beskaffenhet: När de läggia en jernnagel eller något annat jern p. 31 [B8r] der vti så skadar det intet/ men sker det icke/ skadar det. Detta blodet | faller allenast öfwer Judarna och ei öfwer de Christne eller någon annan *Nation*. Hwad orsaken til samma blodsdråppa wara månde/ der om komma *Rabbinerna* intet öfwerens. En del säija det wara ett tekn från *Ægypten*, då HErren låtit genom mord-ängelen döda alt förstfödt/ eller då när watnet blifwit förwandlat vti blod. Andra mena det wara ett tekn at Gud wil straffa dem/ när de öfwerträda det förbund/ som Gud med Abraham ingådt medelst omskärelsen. Andra åter säija; det wara *Zachariæ Barachiæ* Sons blod/ som blef ihiälslagen emellan Templet och Altaret. Men ingen har här om någon wiß grund/ hwar wid han sig stödia kan. Men efter min mening är det troligast/ medan det blodet som Judarna kalla *Thekupha* warder öfwer dem fallandes och de deraf plågade och inga andra *Nationer*, så skal det wara det samma som Judarna wid Christi korßfästande ropade skulle komma öfwer dem och deras barn. *Matth*. 27. *v*. 25. Så mycket ware korteligen sagt om Judarnas *Thekupha*.

CAP. 16.

HWad Judarnas Festdagar angår/ så hafwa de alla weckor sin Sabbatsdag och warder af dem firad/ som är Lögerdagen/ men på Söndagen eller dagen der efter p. 32 [B8v] som hos de Christne firas/ giöra de allahanda arbete. | Sabbathen fira Judarna sålunda: Om wintren klåckan 4. efter middagen och klåckan 6. om Sommaren på Fredagen/ begynna de sina Sabbather. Men om Fredagen för middagen baka de twenne kakor af hwete-miölk/ och om han wore aldrig så fattig måste han det hafwa/ och samma kakor warda kallade *Kalla*, och til det aldraminsta måste han hafwa ett Qwarter Wijn som kallas *Jaginkidos* det är ett win/ som skal wälsignas at warda heligt. Qwinfolcken måste derwid hafwa twänne stora lius eller en lampa med twänne wekar vti. Orsaken til denna *Ceremonie* anföra *Rabbinerna* vti *Tal-*

25 *Ceremonie*] *Cermonie Spec.* (Sthlm, 1732); *Ceremonie Spec.* (Gbg, 1732; Sthlm, 1735).

opinion, such a condition: when they place an iron nail or some other iron item into it [i.e., whatever the blood has dripped into], then it will cause no harm; but if this does not happen, then it will cause harm. This blood only falls onto the Jews and not onto the Christians or any other nation. The rabbis cannot agree on what the cause of this drop of blood may be. Some say that it is a sign from Egypt, when the Lord had the first-born killed by the Angel of Death[130] or when the water was turned into blood.[131] Others think it is a sign that God will punish them when they violate the covenant that God entered into with Abraham about circumcision.[132] Yet others say that it is the blood of Zechariah son of Berekiah, who was killed between the Temple and the altar.[133] But no one has any firm reason with which to support himself. But in my opinion, it is most likely that as the blood that the Jews call *Thekupha* falls over them, and they and no other nation are tormented by this, then it must be the same [blood] as the Jews at Christ's crucifixion shouted should come over them and their children. Matthew 27:25. So much is to be said briefly about the Jews' *Thekupha.*

Chapter 16

As far as the Jews' holidays are concerned, every week they have their Sabbath day that is celebrated by them, which is on Saturday, but on Sunday (that is the following day that is celebrated by the Christians), they tend to all kinds of work. The Jews celebrate the Sabbath like this: on Fridays at 4 p.m. in the winter or 6 p.m. in the summer they begin their Sabbath. But on Friday before noon, they bake two loaves from wheat flour, and if he is not too poor, then he must have this; and these loaves are called *Kalla*,[134] and at the very least he must have a quart of wine, which is called *Jaginkidos*,[135] that is a wine that is blessed in order to become sacred. The women must have two large candles or a lamp with two wicks. The rabbis provide the reason for this in the Talmud, which is called *Scabath Perek*

130 Exodus 11:1–12:36.

131 Exodus 7:14–24.

132 Genesis 17:10–14.

133 Matthew 23:35; Luke 11:51.

134 Heb.: *Kalla*, חלה, *ḥalah*, "challah": the special bread (usually plaited) eaten on the Sabbath and other holidays.

135 Heb.: *Jaginkidos*, יין קידוש, *yayin ḳiduš*, "wine of sanctification." A blessing is recited over the wine to sanctify the Sabbath and other holidays.

mud, som kallas *Scabath Perek Bame Madliken*, hwar om jag wil på ett annat ställe widlöfftigare handla. När de nu hafwa winet/ kakorna och liusen tilreds/ warder bordet strax dukat/ och ligger duken der på tils Sabbathen framgången är/ prydandes och vtstofferandes sina rum/ hwar och en efter sin förmögenhet. Sedan gå alla de som giffta hustrur äro/ hafwandes twänne lius hwar för sig/ tända liusen vpp och dem strax på stunden vtsläckia. Der på tändes de åter strax igen och giöra de öfwer dem en wälsignelse. Orsaken hwarföre de liusen vtsläckia och åter antända/ är denna: Emedan Qwinnoslächtet/ hafwer genom syndafallet vtsläckt liuset ifrån denna werlden ock det förorsakat och åstad kommit; skola fördenskull p. 33 [C1r] det om Sabbatherna HErranom til ett | tackoffer åter vptända. När nu liusen äro vptände/ läggias twänne kakor på bordet/

Sedan gå de til *Synagogan*: berättandes sig skola Sabbathen icke annorledes än en drottning/ emottaga med Siungande och *Musicerande* från klockan 4. til klåckan 7. om afftonen. När Sabbathen emottagen är/ måste alla *Musicaliska Instrument* nedläggias och icke det ringaste widröras; hafwandes de doch frihet med kokande och stekande sig at bereda innan Sabbathen infaller/ eller de den emottaga. Men när de Sabbathen emottagit/ och hafwa afstådt med Spelande och siungande; töras de icke något lius eller eld i sina händer taga eller widröra/ vpgiöra/ koka och steka/ handel eller wandel drifwa. Icke dierfwas de taga penningar vti sin hand/ rida eller åka/ icke heller gå mer än 2000. alnar. Om det är en Stad/ som icke är med murar och wallar befäst/ få de icke bära det ringaste hos sig/ hwarken knif eller andra saker. Om Fredags afftonen då *Musiqven* är ändad/ ställer sig *Cantor* eller Siungaren för Altaret och beder. Gemene man bedia och läsa samma ord/ men förstå intet hwad de bedia. Vnder det samma taga de sina bästa kläder vppå/ och för Arken/ hwarvtinnan 10. Guds bud förwarade äro/ hänges en förlåt ganska kåstelig med Gull- och Silfwerbielror vtståfferad. De tända vp många lius vti sina p. 34 [C1v] hus och *Synagogor*. När nu bönen är ändad tager *Cantorn* en bägare | med win vti sin högra hand/ giörandes deröfwer wälsignelsen/ och helgar Sabbathen med deße orden/ som stå vti *Gen.* 2. *v.* 1. Himmel och jord wardt fullkomnad med all sin hähr; och Gud fullkomnade på Siunde dagen sin wärck som han giordt hade/ och hwilade på Siunde dagen. När detta skedt är/ siunga de/ och gifwa det winet som wälsignadt är/ åt Piltebarnen at vtdricka. Men Pigobarnen komma icke der in förn de äro giffta/ hafwandes då som förr sagt är/ ett särskildt rum för sig sielfwa. När

12 Sedan] sedan *Spec.* (Sthlm, 1732).

Bame Madliken,[136] which I shall deal with more extensively elsewhere. When they have the wine, loaves, and candles ready, the table is immediately set, and the tablecloth stays on [the table] until the Sabbath is over, [and they] decorate and adorn their rooms each in accordance with their means. Then all the married women, holding two candles in front of themselves, light the candles and extinguish them again immediately afterwards. Then they are lit again, and a blessing is made over them. The reason why they extinguish the candles and then light them again is this: just as womankind through the Fall has extinguished the light from this world by being the cause of it and bringing it about, so they should relight it on the Sabbath as an offering to the Lord. Now, when the candles have been lit, two loaves are placed on the table.

Then they go to the synagogue [and] say that they should receive the Sabbath no differently than [as if it were] a queen, with singing and playing music from 4 until seven o'clock in the evening. When the Sabbath has been received, all the musical instruments must be put down and not as much as touched. They have the freedom to boil and roast in order to prepare before the Sabbath begins or they receive it. But once they have received it and refrained from playing and singing, they do not dare to pick up or touch or light any candle or fire, boil or roast, do business or trade. They dare not take money in their hands, ride or travel, or walk more than 2000 ells [i.e., 1.2 km or three quarters of a mile]. If it is a town that is not fortified by walls or moats, they may not carry the smallest thing on their person, not a knife or other things. On Friday evening, when the music has ended, the cantor or singer stands before the altar and prays. Ordinary men pray and read the same words, but do not understand what they are praying.[137] During this they wear their best clothes. And in front of the ark, in which God's Ten Commandments are kept, there hangs a curtain, quite lavishly adorned with gold and silver bells. They light many candles in their houses and synagogues. When the prayer has ended, the cantor takes a cup of wine in his right hand, and, making the blessing over it, he consecrates the Sabbath with these words that are found in Genesis 2:1[–2]: "The heavens and the earth were finished, and all the host of them. And on the seventh day God finished his work which he had made and rested on the seventh day." When this has happened, they sing and give the wine that has been blessed to the young lads to drink up. But young women do not enter until they are married, [and] they have, as said previously, a special room to them-

136 Heb.: *Scabath Perek Bame Madliken*] שבת פרק במה מדליקין, *šabat pereḳ bameh madliḳin*, "[Talmud tractate] Shabbat, chapter 'With what may we light?'" The chapter deals with what is appropriate for lighting the Sabbath candles.
137 Cf. p. 82:3–5 for *Spec.* (Sthlm, 1732), 11:13–14.

Fredags afftonen framfaren är/ låta de *Cantorn* begynna en sång/ den de kalla *Adon Olam* אדון עולם, gångandes sedan vt/ önskandes hwar och en den andra en god Sabbath.

Wid Föräldrarnas hemkomst, stiga barnen emot Fadren/ då han således önskar öfwer dem: Gud wälsigne Eder såsom Ephraim och Manasse. Modren önskar sammaledes. Der på bäres watn fram (hälst ingen får äta med otwagna händer) och sedan sättia de sig til bords. Wärden/ eller Fadren sätter sig på en stol och de andra sättia sig der omkring/ wälsignandes han bägaren hwar vti winet är/ och gifwandes de andre med sig. Der efter wälsignar han en kaka/ och gifwer dem der af hwar och en ett litet stycke/ bäras sedan in de kräseligaste rätter/ med förtröstan/ at huru mycket de om Sabbathen förtähra/ skal GUD dem andra dagen p. 35 [C2r] igen gifwa; Ty giö | ra de sig ganska glade och lustige/ läggiandes bort all sorg och bekymmer; siungandes der wid andeliga wisor. Sedan gå de til sängs och låta liusen brinna hela natten: ty dem är förbudit något lius at widröra/ vtan om det ske skal; så bör det ske af en Christen eller någon af en annan *Nation*.

Om Fredagen giöres eld vp vti en vgn/ derest de insättia kött eller annor mat at beredas til Sabbathen; Warandes ingen efterlåtit at se på samma mat/ vtan när den insatt är/ warder han vti vgnen inklistrad/ och andra dagen eller Sabbathen får ingen/ hwarcken Man eller Qwinna vgnen vpbryta/ vtan måste der til betiena sig af en annan Person ware sig Christen eller af en annan *Nation*; men maten warder af Judarna sielfwa vtur kiärlet vttagen.

Om Lögerdagsmorgon sofwa de tils klockan 8/ då en *Schole* Betient kommer ropandes i alla gator: I *Schole*! När detta skedt är kläde de på sig/ gångandes vti *Synagogan*, och bedia twänne Böner. Den första kallas *Schakeret*, det är Morgon-Bön/ och när detta skiedt är/ läser *Cantorn* vtur 5. Mosis Böcker/ eller af Propheterna 7. *Capitel*, hwilket alt är på *Pergament* skrifwit och tilhopa rullat. Sedan ropar *Cantorn* med hög röst en Person för hwart *Cap*. han vtläsit. Den första heter *Cohen* eller af Arons slächt/ den andra *Leve* af Leviternas: Sedermehra vpropas p. 36 [C2v] alla slächterne vtan någon wiß ordning. Men förr än | de blifwa vpropade/ går en

selves.[138] When Friday evening has progressed, they have the cantor begin a song that they call *Adon Olam* אדון עולם,[139] and they leave wishing each other a good Sabbath.

Upon their parents' arrival, the children approach their father, [and he] makes this wish over them: "May God bless you like Ephraim and Manasseh." The mother makes the same wish. Then water is carried out – preferably no one should eat with unwashed hands – and then they go to the table. The host or the father sits on a chair and the others sit around him while he blesses the cup containing wine and gives it to the others. Then he blesses a loaf and gives each and every one of them a small piece of it. Then the most delicious dishes are carried in with the reassurance that no matter how much they devour on the Sabbath, God will also provide for them the following day. Therefore, they are quite joyful and make merry, and leave behind all their sorrow and worries, during which they sing spiritual songs. Then they go to bed and leave the candles burning the whole night, as they are forbidden to touch any candles unless it is absolutely necessary – then it should be done by a Christian or someone of another nation.

On Friday, a fire is lit in the oven where they put meat or some other food to be prepared for Shabbat. No one is left to watch this food, but when it has been put in, it is closed in the oven,[140] and on the following day (or the Sabbath), no one – neither man nor woman – may open the oven, but they must be served by another person, be it a Christian or of another nation, but the food is removed from the cooking pot by the Jews themselves.

On Saturday morning, they sleep until eight o'clock, when a synagogue warden comes shouting in all the streets: "To shul!" When this has happened, they get dressed, go to the synagogue, and pray two prayers. The first is called *Schakeret*,[141] that is the morning prayer. And when this has happened, the cantor reads seven chapters from the Pentateuch or the Prophets, which are all written on parchment and rolled up. Then, in a loud voice, the cantor calls up a person for each chapter that he has read aloud. The first is called Cohen (or of Aaron's lineage); the second, Levi (of the Levites); then all the families are called up without any particular order. But before they are called up, one of the synagogue wardens goes around

138 See p. 71*n*14 in this edition for *Spec.* (Sthlm, 1732), 4.

139 Heb.: *Adon Olam*, אדון עולם, *adon 'olam*, "Eternal Lord." This hymn is recited as part of the daily and Sabbath liturgy. It is sometimes attributed to the poet Solomon ibn Gabirol (1021–58) but is certainly much older.

140 Löwe uses the Swed. word "inklistrad" here, lit. "pasted in." This possibly means that the opening to the oven is closed over with clay that subsequently needs to be broken open by a non-Jew to remove the food from the oven.

141 Heb.: *Schakeret*, שחרית, *šaḥarit*, "morning [prayer]." Shacharit is the name of the morning prayer service.

af *Schole* Betienterne kring och frågar/ huru mycket de derföre wilja gifwa til Synagogan friwilleligen? Detta kan vnder tiden stiga til en ansenlig *Summa*. Judarna äro ock altid förbundne/ at 4. gånger om åhret låta sig vpropa/ och dagen der efter betala.

Vnder de gamla och ålderstegne Judarnas Gudztienst/ gå de vnga/ eller de som förlofwade äro til sina Fästemör/ *tracterandes* och förnöijandes sig med Pepparkakor och Brännewin. När nu 2. timmar förledne äro/ och med Bönen warit vphållit/ gå deße unga åter vti Synagogan/ då de alla tillika bedia den andra Bönen/ hwilket sker wid paß klåckan 12. Der på gå de hem/ äta/ dricka och giöra sig glade/ arbetandes icke det ringaste.

När nu middagen förbi är/ gå de klåckan 4. åter i Synagogan ock bedia en Bön/ den de kalla *Thephilat Mincka*. Om Sommaren slamra de åstad några Psalmer Assaph; men om wintern Läsa de en *Tractat*, wid namn *Pirki Avot*, det är: goda *Reglor* och Lärdomar/ som deras förfader gifwit hafwa; giörandes de Lärde der öfwer en Förklaring. Der på gå de åter hem at få mat/ och giöra sig lustige.

En del af deras *Rabbiner* säija: at de nödwändigt äro förplicktade at äta 3. gånger/ andra äter 4/ om Sabbathen. Der om är skrifwen en *Tractat*, som kallas *Jalkut Reuveni*, sålunda: Den som äter 3. rätter om Sabbathen/ han blifwer frälst p. 37 [C3r] från 3. | plågor; ty de föregifwa at när deras *Messias* kommer/ skal öfwer dem komma 3. plågor. 1. At många skola siuke och krancke warda; 2. Skal en komma som skal heta Gog och Magog/ hwilken mycken strid och blodz vtgiutelse/ i werlden åstad komma skal. 3. Helfwetis eld. Fördenskull förmenes at den som Sabbathen til ähra äter 3. gånger/ han blifwer från deße plågor befriad.

and asks how much they will freely donate to the synagogue for this. Over time, this can amount to a considerable sum. Jews are also always obliged to have themselves called up four times a year and pay on the following day.

During the service for the elderly and mature Jews, the young ones or those who are engaged to their fiancées are served and enjoy gingerbread biscuits and brandy.[142] When two hours have passed and the praying has come to an end, these young people return to the synagogue where they all pray the second prayer[143] together, which happens at about twelve o'clock. Then they go home, eat, drink, and make merry, doing no work in the slightest.

When the dinner is finished, they return to the synagogue at four o'clock and pray a prayer that they call *Thephilat Mincka.*[144] In the summertime, they rattle through some Psalms of Asaph,[145] but in the wintertime, they read a treatise by the name of *Pirki Avot,*[146] that is good rules and teachings that their ancestors have given them, and the learned provide an explanation of it. Then they return home to have some food and make merry.

A number of their rabbis say that on the Sabbath they are necessarily obliged to eat three times, others [say] four times. About this it says in a treatise called *Jalkut Reuveni,*[147] that he who eats three meals on the Sabbath will be saved from three plagues, because they claim that when their Messiah comes three plagues will befall them: 1) many will become ill and unwell; 2) someone called Gog and Magog will come who will bring about much strife and bloodshed in the world; 3) the fire of hell. Therefore, it is believed that whoever eats three times to honour the Sabbath will be saved from these plagues.

---

142 These "Pepparkakor" [gingerbread biscuits] possibly refer to honey cake (לעקעך, *lekech*), traditionally eaten at Rosh Hashanah. In the equivalent passage in *Jüdischer Ceremonien* (7:1–2, this edition 294:11), Seeligmann calls them "Lab-Kuchen" [gingerbread biscuits]. The Swed. "Brännewin" has here (and at 60:25 [152:20], 67:12 [160:35] "bränwin") been translated with "brandy" in its broader sense of a drink made from distilled mash, such as *aqua vitæ, eau de vie, Schnapps, pálinka*, etc. In the equivalent passage in *Jüdischer Ceremonien* (7:1), Seeligmann calls it "Brandtwein" [eau de vie, brandy].

143 This refers to the additional service, Mussaf (מוסף), that is recited on the Sabbath and usually combined with the Shacharit prayer service.

144 Heb.: *Thephilat Mincka*, תפילת מנחה, *tefilat minḥah*, "prayer of offering": the name of the afternoon prayer service.

145 Psalms 50 and 73–83 (49 and 72–82 *LXX*) attributed to Asaph, although the precise meaning of this attribution is uncertain.

146 Heb.: *Pirki Avot*, פרקי אבות, *pirḳei avot*, "Chapters of the Fathers": a didactic compilation of ethical and moral sayings and teachings passed down by the rabbis from Moses onwards.

147 Heb.: *Jalkut Reuveni*, ילקוט ראובני, *Yalḳuṭ Re'uveni*, "Collection of Reuben": a seventeenth-century collection of *midrashim* (rabbinical interpretations) and legends composed by Reuben Ha-Kohen Hoschke (d. 1673) and first published in Prague in 1660.

Om aftonen när Stiernorna synas/ gå de åter vti Synagogan och siunga den 67. Psalmen/ farandes hel långsamt med siungandet. Deras *Rabbiner* föregifwa/ at de ogudachtige menniskior skola vti helfwetit brinna hela weckan/ men om Sabbathen skal elden släckt warda/ och de således ifrån helfwetis qwal och pina befrijade warda: Men när Sabbathen ändad är/ skal samma eld åter begynna brinna och de ogudachtige gå vti helfwetet. Detta är nu orsaken hwarföre de med sången/ så länge *Continuera* och fortfara/ på det de ei förbittida måge komma til sitt qwal och pino. Der på giöra de sin afton bön/ och wid slutet tager *Cantor* 5. *a* 6. Waxlius tilhopa/ jämte en Bägare med Win och förrättar en wälsignelse/ den de kalla *Hafdala*, הבדלה det är/ de giöra en åtskildnad/ emellan en Söchn- och en Sabbaths-Dag/ gångandes der med hem hwar til sitt: och som *Cantorn* giordt vti Synagogan/ så giör Husfadren hemma/ tager en Bägare Win/ wälsignar den samma/ och gifwer p. 38 [C3v] sina barn der af | at dricka/ och tager en Dosa med allahanda wälluchtande Kryddor/ och äfwen som vti Synagogan/ håller den för de närwarande/ at de der på luckta måge. Ty Judarna hafwa den mening/ at de hafwa twänne siäler/ en som de hafwa om Söchnedagarne/ den andra om Sabbathsdagarne/ och när Sabbathen framgången är/ går den Heliga siälen dem ifrå/ blifwandes de der af krafftlöse och wanmächtige. Fördenskul lufta de på samma Kryddor/ at de må sina kraffter åter bekomma. Sedan tages duken vtaf/ och då sticka alla de närwarande de twänne längsta fingren/ vti något litet win/ som de vtspilt/ hwilket wälsignat är/ säijande deße ord: HErrans Ord vplysa ögonen; Siunga och många andeliga Wisor/ hafwandes der wid mycken wahntro och widskepelse. De ropa äfwen Elias *Thisbe*! 110. gånger/ der med de mena/ at Elias komma skal och föra *Messiam* med sig. Säijandes och det; at när Elias kommandes warder/ skal han wara en förridare/ wägen för honom at bereda; läsandes det 32. och 33. *Capitlet* vti *Gen*. Åter warder den tredie kakan skurin/ och bordet dukat/ då ätes litet der af hwad de til Sabbathen bakat hafwa. Det warder hos dem kallat *Mellave Malcka*, מלווה מלכה eller fölg vt Drottningen/ menandes der med Sabbathen. Hwad de eljest hafwa för *Fabler* och *Traditioner*, woro alt för widlöftigt at berätta/ finnes och wara onödigt. |

---

18 samma] sam̄a *Spec.* (Sthlm, 1732)*: the only occurrence of a nasal stroke to mark an abbreviation in the book;* samma *Spec.* (Gbg, 1732; Sthlm, 1735).

In the evening, when the stars are visible, they return to the synagogue and sing Psalm 67, singing extremely slowly. Their rabbis claim that the impious people in hell burn for the whole week, but on the Sabbath the fire is extinguished, and they are thus free of the torments and torture of hell; but once the Sabbath has ended, this fire begins to burn again and the impious enter hell. This is the reason why they draw out and continue the song for so long, so that they [i.e., the impious] might not come too early to their torment and torture. They then say their evening prayer and at the end, the cantor picks up five to six candles together with a cup of wine and performs a blessing; they call it *Hafdala* הבדלה,[148] that is they make a separation between a weekday and a Sabbath day, each going home to their house. And, just like the cantor did in the synagogue, the father of the house does at home. He takes a cup of wine, blesses it, and gives it to his children to drink from, and they take a box containing all kinds of fragrant spices,[149] and also just like in the synagogue, they hold it for those present to be able to smell it. The Jews believe they have two souls – one that they have on weekdays, the other on Sabbath days – and when the Sabbath is over, the holy soul leaves them, making them powerless and impotent. So, they smell these spices that they might regain their power. Then the cloth is removed and all those present put their longest fingers into a bit of the wine that they have spilt and that is blessed, and they say these words: "May the words of the Lord illuminate your eyes!" They also sing many spiritual sings about which they have many unfounded beliefs and superstitions. They also shout "Elijah Thisbe!"[150] 110 times with which they believe that Elijah will come bringing the Messiah with him. They also say that when Elijah comes, he will be an outrider who will prepare the way for him [the Messiah]; and they read chapters 32 and 33 in Genesis. Then the third loaf is cut, and the table set, and then they eat a bit of what had been baked for the Sabbath. They call it *Mellave Malcka* מלוות מלכה,[151] or "escorting out the queen," by which they mean the Sabbath. It is far too extensive to describe what other fairy-tales and traditions they entertain, and it is also unnecessary.

---

148 Heb.: *Hafdala*, הבדלה, *havdalah*, "separation": a ritual that marks the end of the Sabbath and the beginning of a new week.

149 The decorative box that contains the fragrant spices, *besamim* (בשמים), and that is passed around during the havdalah ceremony.

150 The prophet Elijah is thought to have come from the town of Tishbe and is known, among other things, as Eliyahu ha-Tishbi (אליהו התישבי) in Hebrew. Löwe may be mocking the hymn *Eliyahu ha-navi* (אליהו הנביא, Elijah the Prophet) which includes the line "Eliyahu ha-Tishbi" and is repeated several times.

151 Heb.: *Mellave Malcka*, מלוה מלכו, *melyeh malkah*, "escorting the queen": the name of the meal taken after the end of the Sabbath.

p. 39 [C4r] CAP. 17.

JUdarnas stora Fester och högtider/ wil jag wid Påsketiden begynna/ aldenstund de räkna och börja sina åhrtal vti *Aprilis* Månad. Wid denna Högtiden hafwa de mycken wantro. Påsk-Festen kalla de *Pesack*, det är öfwerhoppa eller öfwersprin-ga/ emedan HErren Gud har vtsändt Mord-Ängelen vti Egypten til at döda alla förstfödde/ och han sprungit eller farit förbi Israels hus. Til Påsketiden baka de kakor/ dem de kalla *Matzoth* מצוה de äro sålunda handterade: Miölet måste wara af hwete och ingen råg ibland/ ei heller får hwetet twättas. Samma miöl knådas vti kalt watn/ vtan salt eller smör/ och samma watn måste dagen förvt/ innan Solen nedgår hemtagas/ och med rena kläden betäckias. De få icke låta samma bröd giäsa/ på det ei några hål må blifwa der vti när det bakat är. Skulle och hända at något hwetekorn vti degen finnes/ hålla de före den samma wara surnad/ kastandes den samma antingen vti eld eller watn. Detta giöra de til en åminnelse af det swåra arbetet/ som de haft wid de twänne städer; *Pison* och *Ramset*, hwilka de för Konung Pharao vpbygdt. Och emedan de intet haft tid at baka bröd til sin resa vtur Egypten/ vtan warit twungne at taga osurat bröd med sig/ derföre baka de sådant bröd til en åminnelse/ samt Gud til ähra/ at han dem vnder Mosen genom det | p. 40 [C4v] Röda hafwet/ in vti det förlofwade Landet fördt hafwer.

Denna Högtiden fira de den 13. *Aprilis*, hwilken Månad kallas Nisan/ och warder denna Fest/ vti stor högachtning och wördnad tagen: så at vti hela 8. dagar icke en smola surt bröd vti deras hus funnit warder/ vtan allenast de osyrade kakor/ de mala sielfwa miölet/ och warder det af Karlar bakat/ och ei af Qwinfolck; hwilket doch alt är en menniskio*Tradition* och stadga.

Aftonen för Påskadagen/ söker Wärden med Waxlius vti alla wincklar och wrår/ om han något surt bröd finna skal. Finner han något/ det ware mycket eller

---

0 CAP. 17] Andra Dehlen. Cap. 17 *Spec.* (Gbg, 1732; Sthlm, 1735).

Chapter 17

I will begin the Jews' great festivals and holidays with Eastertime, as they calculate and begin their year in the month of April. They have many unfounded beliefs during this holiday. They call the Easter festival *Pesack* (that is, "hop" or "jump over"):[152] when God sent the Angel of Death to Egypt to kill all the first born, he jumped or passed over the houses of Israel. For Easter they bake loaves that are called *Matzoth* מצוה.[153] They are prepared like this: The flour must be made from wheat with no rye mixed into it; nor may the wheat be washed. This flour is kneaded with cold water, without salt or butter, and this water must have been brought home the previous day before sunset and be covered with clean cloths. They may not let this bread leaven so that no holes appear in it when it is baked. If it happens that there is a wheat kernel in the dough, they consider it as having turned leavened, and throw it either into the fire or into water. They do this to remember the hard labour that they had in the two places, *Pison* and *Ramset*,[154] which they constructed for King Pharaoh. And because they did not have time to bake bread for their journey out of Egypt, but had to take unleavened bread with them, they bake such bread as a reminder as well as in praise of God that he led them under [the leadership of] Moses through the Red Sea and into the Promised Land.

They celebrate this holiday on 13 April (they call this month Nisan) and this festival is held in great respect and reverence, so that not a crumb of leavened bread can be found in their houses for eight whole days, only the unleavened crackers. They mill the flour themselves and it is baked by men, and not by women – which, however, is all a fabricated tradition and regulation.

The evening before Easter Day, the head of the household searches in all the nooks and corners by candlelight to see whether he can find any leavened bread.[155] If he finds some, be it a lot or a little, it is kept until the following morning when it

---

152 Pesaḥ or (the festival of) Passover. The name is derived from the verb פ־ס־ח, *p-s-ḥ*, "to pass over, skip."

153 Löwe's מצוה is a mistake for מצות, *mazot*, "wafers/crackers made of unleaven bread."

154 The river Pishon (פישון), the first river of Eden (Genesis 2:1), is identified by the biblical commentator Rashi as the Nile. Löwe seems to be confusing the name of the river Pishon with the city Pithom (פיתום), one of the cities that was built for the Pharaoh through the forced labour of the Israelite slaves (Exodus 1:11). On the other hand, Löwe may well have intended Pithom, and his spelling Pison may be due to the Ashkenazi pronunciation of ת as [s]. Rameses (רעמסס) was the other city built by the Israelite slaves (Exodus 1:11) and from where they departed on their Exodus (Exodus 12:37; Numbers 33:3). Again, the spelling suggests fluctuation in Löwe's pronunciation of ת as either [s] or [t]. For example, his "Ramset" may be a hypercorrect spelling where he mistakenly "corrected" a final ס [s] to ת [s/t].

155 The evening before Passover, it is customary to make a formal search throughout the home by candlelight for leavened food items (חמץ, *ḥameẓ*).

litet/ förwares det til morgonen bittida/ då det offenteligen på gatan af eld förbrändt warder/ hwilket måste ske för än klåckan är 9. slagen. Dagen för Påska måste alla förstfödde af Mans-Personer fasta och ei äta förr än Solen nedergår/ förnämligen och i synnerhet de/ som sedt sina 13. åhr; emedan Gud har förskont alla förstfödningar vti Egypten för mord-ängelen.

Om aftonen då Påskadagen ingår/ warder hwar och en huswärd som gifter är/ en bädd wid bordet af det aldra kostbaraste läggiandes/ och så snart det warder litet mörckt/ kläda de sina bästa kläder på. Då säger den ene til den andra: *Jom Tof*, יום טוב det är en god och önskelig Högtid eller Festdag. Der på gå de hem/ oc wär- p. 41 [C5r] den vti huset tager sina dödekläder på sig/ och förr än han sätter sig til | bordz/ läggia de på ett stort tenfat 3. osyrade kakor vti en Sarwet/ hwilken kallas *Matzot*. Den första kakan kalla de *Cohen*, den andra *Leve*, och den tredie Israel. Vppå deße kakor lägges ett stekt ägg/ och ett ben hwar wid litet kött hänger/ som är hwarken hel eller half stekt; hwilket alt har sin bemärkelse. De säija; at som ägget är rundt/ så går och döden rundt om hela werlden. Den prächtiga sängen skal honom påminna; at han ei skal wara högfärdig. Det halfstekta benet/ skal påminna dem om Påskalambet.

När detta skedt är; tager hwar och en ett glas win i högra handen/ och alla tilsammans taga i fatet med den wänstra/ säijandes med hög röst: Detta är det Brödet/ som wåra Fäder hafwa ätit vti Egypten. Den som är hungrog han komme och äte. Detta åhret äro wi här/ ett annat äro wi vti Jerusalem: detta säijes på *Chaldai*ska. På fatet ligger och ett stycke Pepparrot/ der af de skära och äta hwar sitt stycke. Orsaken är denne: Emedan Pepparroten är amper och bitter/ påminna de sig der medelst sitt swåra arbete vti Egypten. På detta stora fatet står ett litet fat/ hwar på liggia sönderhackade Äpplen och Wahlnötter/ hwilka äro til vtseende som leer/ alt detta tienar til en åminnelse/ at de vti Egypten warit twungne at slå leer och tegel.

Der efter förtäljer den ena den andra/ Historien om deras vtgång vhr Egypten. p. 42 [C5v] Barnen fråga Föräldrarna om allahanda ting. Om det | än woro 30. *a* 40. Personer

---

3 Solen] Sol-n *Spec.* (Sthlm, 1732)*: in his list of errata (113:13; this edition 212:9), Löwe corrects* Sol-n *to* Solen; Solen *Spec.* (Gbg, 1732; Sthlm, 1735).

is publicly burnt in a fire in the street which has to take place before the clock strikes nine. The day before Easter, all first-born men must fast and not eat until the sun sets – mainly and in particular those who have had their thirteenth birthday – because God spared all the first-born in Egypt from the Angel of Death.

In the evening, when Easter Day begins, each and every married head of the household makes a very exquisite bed alongside the table, and as soon as it gets a little bit dark, they dress in their best clothes. Then they say to each other *Jom Tof* יום טוב,[156] that is "a good and desirable holiday or festival!" Then they go home and the head of the household dresses in his death robes,[157] and before he sits at the table, they put a large tin plate with three unleavened crackers, called *Matzot*, in a napkin.[158] They call the first cracker "Cohen,"[159] the second "Levi,"[160] and the third "Israel."[161] A roasted egg is placed on these crackers as well as a bone with a small amount of meat hanging off it that is neither completely nor half roasted;[162] each of them has its meaning. They say, that just like the egg is round, so death goes around the entire world. The luxurious bed shall remind him that he must not be haughty. The half-roasted bone shall remind them of the paschal lamb.

When this has happened, each and every one of them takes a glass of wine in his right hand and they all hold the plate with their left one and say in a loud voice: "This is the bread that our ancestors ate in Egypt. He who is hungry may come and eat. This year we are here, next [year] we shall be in Jerusalem!" This is said in Chaldean. On the plate there is also a piece of horseradish that each of them cuts pieces off and eats. The reason is this: as horseradish is sharp and bitter, it reminds them of their hard labour in Egypt. On this large plate there is a small dish in which are some chopped apples and walnuts, which has the appearance of clay; all this serves as a reminder that they were forced to shape clay into bricks in Egypt.

Afterwards, they all tell each other the story of their exodus from Egypt. The children ask the parents about all sorts of things. Even if there are thirty to forty

---

156 Heb.: *Jom Tof*, יום טוב, *yom ṭov*, "good day" and by extension a Jewish holiday or festival. The greeting Löwe is referring to is most probably גוט יום טוב, *gut yom tov*, "happy holiday!" (Yidd.).

157 Löwe uses the term "dödekläder" [death robes] – probably taken from Seeligmann's *Sterbekleider* in *Jüdischer Ceremonien* (6:5 [this edition 292:23], 8:2 [294:34], 10:31 [298:34], 16:6 [306:10]), – to refer to the kittel (קיטל, *kiṭəl*), a white linen robe worn by Ashkenazi men on holidays, when leading the Passover seder, and at their weddings. It is sometimes used as a shroud for the deceased – hence the name "death robes."

158 The three *maẓot* represent the three divisions of Jews.

159 The first *maẓah* is referred to as כהן, *kohen*, "Cohen: priest (descended from Aaron)."

160 The second *maẓah* is referred to as לוי, *levi*, "Levite: a Jewish male descended from Levi."

161 The third *maẓah* is referred to as ישראל, *yiśra'el*, "(the people of) Israel."

162 The roasted egg and shank bone are usually placed on the *seder* plate, not on the *maẓot*.

wid bordet/ taga de hwar för sig ett glas win/ som nödwändigt rödt wara måste/ det ware sig Man eller Qwinna/ liten eller stor; Dåppandes lilla fingret vti glaset/ och spilla 10. röda windråppar på bordet/ berättandes: de 10. Pharaos plågor med deße ord: *Dam*, Blod; *Cefardea*, Groder; *Kinem*, Löß; *Aref*, Ohyra; *Dever*, Päst; *Koschek*, Mörcker; *Skekin*, Skabb; *Barat*, Hagel; *Arbe*, Gräshoppor; *Macked Bekored*, Förstfödingars Dödande.

Der efter sättia de en *Apart* Bägare med win på bordet och säija: Detta är Elie Bäggare; hoppandes/ at Elias komma skal och hafwa *Messiam* med sig. Då låtes dörren op inbillandes sig/ at *Messias* komma skal/ på en åsna inridandes och ropandes med hög röst: Giut din wrede vt på Hedningarna/ som tig icke känna wilja/ eller ditt Namn anropa! Blifwer så dörren öppen ståendes; men när hon länge stådt öpen/ och *Messias* icke kommer/ slå de dörren igen och säija några försmädeliga ord emot de Christne.

Der på äta de åter/ och äro ganska lustige; och när de mätte äro; taga de af den tredie kakan/ hwilken kallas Jsrael. Bruta den sönder/ och gifwa hwar och en ett stycke/ hwilket de skola vpäta. Nu wil jag fråga: Hwad det betyda skal/ at när de

people at the table, they each – whether man or woman, young or old – have before them a glass of wine that must necessarily be red. They dip their little fingers into the wine and spill ten red drops of wine onto the table, recounting the ten plagues of Pharaoh, saying: "*Dam*, blood;[163] *Cefardea*, frogs;[164] *Kinem*, lice;[165] *Aref*, vermin;[166] *Dever*, pestilence;[167] *Koschek*, darkness;[168] *Skekin*, scabies;[169] *Barat*, hail;[170] *Arbe*, locusts;[171] *Maked Bekored*, death of firstborn."[172]

Then they set aside a cup of wine on the table and say, "This is Elijah's cup,"[173] in the hope that Elijah will come bringing the Messiah with him. Then the door is opened, imagining that the Messiah will come riding in on a donkey, and they shout in a loud voice: "Pour your fury onto the pagans who do not want to know you or call your name!" The door then remains open, but when it has stood ajar for a while and the Messiah has not come, they close the door again and say some scathing words aimed at the Christians.

Then they eat again and are quite merry. And when they have had their fill, they take the third cracker that is called Israel. They break it apart and give a piece to everyone, which they are to eat. Now I will ask: what does it mean that only

---

163 Heb.: *Dam*, דם, *dam*, "blood." Plague 1: God turned the waters of the Nile into blood (Exodus 7:14–24).

164 Heb.: *Cefardea*, צפרדע, *ẓefardea*, "frogs." Plague 2: God sent a plague of frogs throughout Egypt (Exodus 7:25–8:15).

165 Heb.: *Kinem*, כנים, *kinim*, "lice." Plague 3: God infested the people and animals of Egypt with lice (Exodus 8:16–19).

166 Heb.: *Aref*, ערוב, *'arov*, "mixture (of wild animals)." Plague 4: God sent a plague of creatures to hurt people and livestock (Exodus 8:20-32). The root (ע־ר־ב) implies a mixture, suggesting that there was a diversity of animals. Jewish scholars usually interpret it to mean wild animals; Christian scholars interpret it to mean flies. Löwe translates it as "Ohyra" [vormin].

167 Heb.: *Dever*, דבר, *dever*, "pestilence." Plague 5: God brought a terrible plague on livestock (Exodus 9:1–3).

168 Heb.: *Koschek*, חושך, *ḥošech*, "darkness." Plague 9: Moses spreads his arms and darkness descends over Egypt and lasts three days (Exodus 10:21–23). Note that Lowe's ordering of the plagues is not correct.

169 Heb.: *Skekin*, שחין, *šḥin*, "boils." Plague 6: Moses tosses soot in front of the Pharao and it becomes a dust that spreads throughout Egypt causing festering boils (Exodus 9:8–12).

170 Heb.: *Barat*, ברד, *barad*, "hail." Plague 7: God sent a terrible thunderstorm with hail and lightning over Egypt (Exodus 9:13–35).

171 Heb.: *Arbe*, ארבה, *arbeh*, "locusts." Plague 8: God sends a plague of locusts over Egypt that devour all the vegetation remaining after the hail (Exodus 10:3–6).

172 Heb.: *Macked Bekored*, מכת בכורות, *makat bechorot*, "death of firstborn." Plague 10: Every firstborn son in Egypt dies (Exodus 11:1 – 12:36).

173 "Elijah's cup" is the fifth cup of wine poured during the seder. It is set to one side and left untouched in honour of the prophet who will come one day in the future to herald the arrival of the Messiah.

äro hel mätte/ de då först skola wara skyldige at äta den kakan/ som osaltad är/ der p. 43 [C6r] de likwäl tilförene haft andra *Delicate* och kå | steliga rätter? Denna kaka kalla de *Efikomen*, det är en söt spis. Ock detta brödet som de äta wid slutet af sin måltid/ är så heligt: at de icke låta der af en bröd smola nedfalla. Här på kan jag mig icke förstå/ eller wet/ hwad det betyda och innebära skal.

Der efter börja de siunga om Templetz byggiande och ropa många hundrade gånger/ at *Messias* komma skal/ och siunga sedan en wisa/ som de kalla *Berkat Hamason*: om en Ichelein eller en killing och en katt/ som åt vp samma killing: hunden bet katten/ kiäppen slog hunden/ elden brände vp kiäppen/ watnet slächte elden/ oxen drack vt watnet/ Slachtaren slachta oxen/ döden slachta Slachtaren/ och Gud afskaffade döden. Detta skal wara såsom en liknelse/ huru det på yttersta dagen til gå skal. De hafwa der jämte den wahntron; at de/ om de twänne första Påske-nätterne/ skola befrijade wara ifrån de onda andar: och kalla de fördenskul samma nätter *Lel Schimurim*, det är/ bewarelses nätter; läggiandes sig deße twänne nätter vtan någon bön.

Deße förenämde *Ceremonier*, bruka de allenast de twänne första dagarna vti Påska/ de andra 6. dagarne warda såsom Festdagar brukade; men intet efterlåtes dem med handel och wandel sig något befatta. Påsketiden warder hos dem räck-

when they are completely full are they ready to eat the cracker, which is unsalted, having previously had other delicacies and exquisite courses? This cracker is called the *Efikomen*,[174] that is a "sweet food." And this bread, that they eat at the end of their meal, is so holy, that they do not let a single crumb fall onto the floor. I do not understand or know what is meant by this or what it signifies.

Then they begin singing about building the Temple and shout many hundreds of times that the Messiah will come. And then they all sing a song that is called *Berkat Hamason*[175] about an *Ichelein*[176] or a kid and a cat that ate this kid, the dog bit the cat, the stick beat the dog, the fire burned the stick, the water put out the fire, the ox drank the water, the slaughterer killed the ox, the Angel of Death slew the slaughterer, and God abolished death.[177] This is a metaphor of how things will happen on Doomsday.[178] They equally hold the superstition that for the first two Easter nights they are freed from evil spirits, and therefore they call these nights *Lel Schimurim*, that is "the nights of vigil." They go to bed these two nights without any prayers.[179]

They only perform these aforementioned ceremonies on the first two nights of Easter. The other six days are treated as holidays, but they are not allowed to

---

174 Heb.: *Efikomen*, אפיקומן, *afiḳoman* (from Gk. ἐπὶ κῶμον, *epíkṓmon*), "that which comes after." It originally referred to desserts after a meal but came to mean the piece of matzah that is broken in two during the seder and set aside to be eaten as dessert.

175 Heb.: *Berkat Hamason*, ברכת המזון, *birkat ha-mazon*: the set of blessings said as grace after meals.

176 Heb. The word "Ichelein" is either Löwe's or the printer's mistake for Yidd. ציקליין, *ẓikleyn* "little goat"; cf. Germ. *Zieglein*. The first appearance of the song "Ḥad Gadya" (see below) is found in the Prague Haggadah (1526). The text appears in both Aram. and Yidd., where the word used for "little goat" is ציקליין

177 This is a description of the cumulative song חד גדיא (*ḥad gadya*, "one little goat,") and not of the Birkat Hamazon. "Ḥad Gadya" is a popular song sung at the end of the Passover seder and describes over several verses how one little goat, "which my father bought for two zuzim," is eaten by a cat, that was bitten by a dog, that was beaten by a stick, that was burnt by fire, that was extinguished by water, that was drunk by an ox, that was slain by a slaughterer, who was smitten by the Angel of Death.

178 There are several interpretations of the song "Ḥad Gadya." For example, it is a symbolic of the history of Israel, the dangers one faces in life, the Passover rituals at the Temple, and, as here, the End of Days.

179 This is not correctly presented. The night of the first seder is known as ליל שמורים *leil šimurim*, a "night of vigil" or "a waking night" and marks the night that God brought the children of Israel out of Egypt (Exodus 12:42). Rabbi Avraham ibn Ezra (*c.* 1089–1164) wrote that one should be wakeful this night and refrain from sleeping to praise God. The Haggadah tells of the Sages of Bnei Barak who remained awake until it was time for the morning Shema prayer. Thus, Löwe might be referring to Jews who do not go to sleep and therefore do not say prayers before retiring to rest for the night.

nad 8. dagar/ och af alla de kiäril/ som de sig förra åhret betient hafwa/ så de sig ei p. 44 [C6v] betiena under Påsketiden/ så framt de icke wißa kiä | rile/ ifrån den ena Påskan til den andra/ der til endast hafwa *reserverat* och bewarat; Men hwad jernredskaper widkommer/ warda de allenast vti elden brände/ Teen och Sölfwer i watn kokadt/ skiöldt och skurat. Hwad de ofwannämde kakor widkommer; warda de med jernpinnar hackade/ at de ei skola vpswälla. Om en kaka vti vngnen faller vppå den andra och fastnar tilsammans/ få de den ei äta/ vtan måste bortkastas. Efterlåtes dem ei heller/ at dricka några andra drycker/ vtan win/ miöd och watn. De koka honungsträ vti watn/ som ei wilja dricka win; men af spanmål få de icke dricka. Förutan detta/ taga de sig mycket at giöra och syßla med *Rabbiniske* och *Talmudiske* Bud och stadgar/ och wänta ännu den tilkommande *Messiam*, skiönt han i sanning kommen är efter alla Propheternas enhålliga öfwerens stämmelse/ hwilka oß det rätta Påskalambet föreställa/ som sig för alla menniskior/ på korßens trä vpoffrat hafwer. Detta ware så nog om Judarnas Påska.

CAP. 18.

FÖljer nu i ordning at handla om Judarnas Pingesfest. Denna dagen warder hos dem kallad *Schevoot* שבועות, det är så mycket som 7. Ty de räkna ifrån Påsk til Pingest 7. weckor; firandes de vti samma Fest 2. dagar/ och kalla dem *Mattan Tora*, p. 45 [C7r] det är | then dagen; på hwilken lagen vtgifwen är af Gud på Sinai berg/ til Israels barn med stort dunder och blixt. Wid denna Fest är hos dem brukeligit at sättia biörk löf vti sina Synagogor och äfwen wid sina hus/ brukandes de merendels miölckmat eller annor söt spis; Hwilket är en bemärkelse at lagen för dem söt och

engage in trade and business. They count Easter as lasting eight days and of all the cooking vessels that they have used the previous year, they do not use any during Easter, so that certain vessels are reserved and kept from one Easter to another. But as far as iron utensils are concerned, they are only burnt in the fire, tin and silver boiled in water, rinsed, and scrubbed. As far as the aforementioned crackers are concerned, they are stabbed with iron needles so that they do not swell up. If a cracker in the oven falls onto another one and they stick together, they may not eat it, but it has to be thrown away. Nor are they allowed to drink any other drinks than wine, mead, and water. They boil honey tree in water for those who do not wish to drink wine, but they may not drink [drinks derived] from grain. Apart from this, they have much to do and busy themselves with rabbinic and Talmudic commandments and rules and still wait for the future Messiah, even though in truth he has come according to the unanimous agreement of all the prophets, who present us with the real paschal lamb who has sacrificed himself on the cross for all people. That is enough about the Jews' Easter.

Chapter 18

Following in order, we now deal with the Jews' festival of Pentecost.[180] They call this day *Schevoot*;[181] that means "seven," as they count seven weeks from Easter to Pentecost. They celebrate this festival for two days and call them *Mattan Tora*,[182] that is the day on which the Law was given by God on Mount Sinai to the children of Israel with much thunder and lightning. On this festival it is their custom to place birch leaves in their synagogues and also in their houses,[183] and to make mainly dairy foods or other such sweet food which symbolizes that for them the

180 By the "Jews' festival of Pentecost," Löwe means the festival of Shavuot. This occurs at the same time as the Christian holiday Pentecost (Whitsun), but they celebrate entirely different events.

181 Heb.: *Schevoot*, שבועות, *šavu'ot*, "weeks," from the Hebrew שבע "seven." This name of the festival comes from Exodus 34:22 and Deuteronomy 16:10.

182 Heb.: *Mattan Tora*, מתן תורה, *matan torah* "giving of [the] Torah."

183 Homes and synagogues are often decorated with flowers and greenery during Shavuot. There are two reasons for this. The Midrash says that Mount Sinai blossomed with flowers when the Torah was to be given to Moses on its summit. Also, Moses was surrounded by greenery (bulrushes) when he was placed in the River Nile at three months of age (Exodus 2:3), on the same day (6 Sivan) that he later took the children of Israel to Mount Sinai to receive the Torah.

liuflig är. Vnder samma tid gå de twänne gånger/ äfwen som andra Festdagar vti Synagogan; läsandes då Ruths Bok/ och Historien om Boas: siungandes der jämte åtskilliga wisor at betyga sin kärlek til lagen/ och hålla sig der wid lustige och glade. Denna dagen fira de gemenligen på den 7:de *Maji*, den de kalla *Sivon*. Men wi Christne fira denna Fest; aldenstund den Helige Anda på denna dagen är öfwer Apostlarna vtgutin.

CAP. 19.

NÄr Pingestiden förliden är/ infaller åter en Fest den 9:de *Junii*, på hwilken Jerusalems Tempel är wordet vpbrändt/ den de kalla *Tischebau*, det är 9:de dagen vti *Junii* Månad. Då påminna sig Judarna Jerusalems jämmerliga förstöring och Templets skiöflande/ hållandes den dagen åhrligen för en sörje-och klagodag. Nie dagar förr än denna dagen begynnes och samma månad ingår/ begynna de straxt at sörja/ underståendes sig icke vti deße 9. dagar at äta kött/ dricka win/ giöra | p. 46 [C7v] något Bröllup/ eller sig med någon trolåfwa; vtan hafwa de endast frihet at vti samma dagar bruka omskiärelsen/ doch med det förbehåld/ at inga flere än 10. Personer under samma måltid äro tilstädes/ och då warder dem efterlåtit at äta kött. De töras icke låta putsa skiägget/ klippa håret/ gå i Badstugo/ se sig vti någon

Law is sweet and delectable.[184] During this time, just like on other holidays, they go to the synagogue twice. They read the Book of Ruth and the story about Boaz[185] and furthermore sing numerous songs to express their love for the Law and keep themselves joyful and happy. They usually celebrate this day on 7 May, which they call *Sivon*.[186] However, we Christians celebrate this festival because on this day the Holy Spirit was poured out over the Apostles.

Chapter 19

When Pentecost has passed, there is yet another festival on 9 June, when the Temple in Jerusalem was burnt to the ground, which they call *Tischebau*,[187] that means "on the ninth day in the month of June." Then the Jews remember the lamentable destruction of Jerusalem and the devastation of the Temple, and they keep this day every year as a day of sorrow and lamentation. Nine days before this day[188] begins and this month commences, they immediately begin to mourn, and for these nine days they do not dare to eat meat, drink wine, hold weddings, or get engaged to anyone; rather they only have the freedom during these days to perform circumcisions, but only on the condition that no more than ten people are present at the meal, and then they are permitted to eat meat. They do not dare trim their beards, cut their hair, take a bath, look at themselves in a mirror, put on

184 Löwe's explanation of the tradition of consuming dairy foods at Shavuot derives from Solomon comparing the Torah to milk (Song of Songs 4:11). Other explanations are based on the dietary rules of kashrut, the numerical value of the word חלב, *ḥalav* "milk" in gematria as forty – corresponding to the forty days and nights Moses spent on Mount Sinai, and to the similarity between the word גבינה, *gvinah*, "cheese" and the word for Mount Sinai used in Psalms: הר גבנונים, *Har Gavnunim* "mountain of majestic peaks" (Psalm 68:16–17).

185 There are several explanations why the Book of Ruth is read at Shavuot. For example, the story, like the festival, takes place during the harvest (Exodus 23:16); Ruth's descendant David died on Shavuot (Yerushalmi Ḥagigah 2:3); Ruth's conversion to Judaism parallels the entrance of the Jewish people into the covenant of the Torah; in gematria, the numerical value of Ruth is 606 – add to this the number seven (the number of Noahide Laws) and the total is 613, the number of commandments in the Torah.

186 Heb.: *Sivon*, סיון, *siṿan*, "Sivan": the ninth month of the civil year and the third month of the religious year in the Hebrew calendar (around May–June in the Gregorian calendar). Shavuot falls on 6–7 Sivan.

187 Heb.: *Tischebau*, תשעה באב, *tiš'ah be'av*, "Tisha beAv": an annual day of fasting to mark the destruction of the First and Second Temple in Jerusalem.

188 The first nine days of the Hebrew month of Av (אב, *av*: around July–August in the Gregorian calendar) are an annual period of mourning in recognition of the many disasters that have befallen the Jewish people. Several activities are prohibited during this period that culminates in Tisha beAv (lit. the ninth [day] in Av).

spegel/ icke taga rena linkläder eller några *Musicali*ska *Instrument* höra låta. *In Summa*, alt hwad/ som wid sörjande brukeligit är/ måste de giöra/ och ei det ringaste som lustigt och frögdefult är höra låta/ så länge den tiden påstår/ på hwilken Jerusalems förstöring skied är/ förn den tiden är framfaren.

De hafwa och en sådan wantro/ at ingen af dem törs eller dristar sig någon för Rätta *Citera* eller föra någon *Process* med en Christen; vtan föregifwa at den samma månaden skal för dem wara olyckelig/ så at/ änskiönt de den rättmätigaste sak hade/ skola de doch den samma tappa och förlora.

Aftonen för den 9:de dagen draga de skona af sig (Ty det är hos dem brukeligit/ at när någon sörja skal/ måste han draga skona af sig) sättia sig på jorden/ strö aska på sitt bröd och äta det med sörjande och gråtande; endast af orsak för Jerusalems Förstöring. Sedan gå de vti Synagogan hafwandes på sina skor nedlagt bakstycken/ sättiandes sig ned och afdraga dem/ och siunges der wid Jeremie klagowisor.

Om morgonen gå de likaledes vti Synagogan/ siunga samma klagewisor och |
p. 47 [C8r] draga skona af sig/ fastandes vti 24. Timmar. Då läser *Cantorn* för dem Jeremie klagowisor/ och siunger en hop andra klagosånger/ angående Jerusalem och Templets förstörande. Under det samma hafwa de närwarande barnen små spiut och bågar vti sina händer/ och lära sig strida/ på det när *Messias* kommer skola de strida med *Gog* och *Magog*. Sedan gå de på de dödas grafwar/ i mening at hälsa på sina Föräldrar/ wänner och fränder/ hwilka för många åhr sedan döde äro/ och äro de der til efter deras stadga och lag förbundne och förplicktade. Men om Judarna ei äro på den ort stadde/ at de hafwa en sådan kyrckiogård/ derest deras förfäder begrafne äro/ måste de gå til den kyrckiogård/ som de närmast hafwa/ vti hwad landzort det wara må; skolandes sig der wid påminna huru många 1000. menniskior vti Jerusalem äro ihiälslagne. Der på gå barnen åstad/ bryta sina swärd sönder/ och skicka dem hwar och en vti sina anhörigas graf/ säijandes at de döda för dem strida och fächta skola. Barnen hafwa under det samma så många

clean linen clothes, or listen to any musical instruments. To summarize, everything that is usual during mourning they must do, and not listen to the slightest thing that is fun or joyous for as long as the period lasts when the destruction of Jerusalem took place, until that time has passed.

They also have a superstition that none of them dares or is bold enough to summon someone to attend court or bring a case against a Christian; but they allege that this month is unlucky for them, so that even if they had the most legitimate case, they would still be defeated and lose it.

On the evening of the ninth day, they remove their shoes (because it is their custom that when someone is to mourn, he must remove his shoes), they sit on the ground, scatter ashes on their bread, and eat it mourning and weeping, all because of the destruction of Jerusalem. Then they walk to the synagogue, having pushed flat the back part of their shoes, sit down, and remove them, and with that they sing Jeremiah's Lamentations.

In the morning they likewise walk to synagogue, sing the same lamentations and remove their shoes, and they fast for 24 hours. Then the cantor reads them Jeremiah's Lamentations and sings a load of other lamentations about Jerusalem and the destruction of the Temple. During this, the children who are present have small spears and bows in their hands and learn to fight,[189] so that when the Messiah comes, they will fight alongside Gog and Magog. Then they go to the graves of the deceased in order to greet their parents, friends, and relations, who died many years previously; and they are bound and obligated to do this by their regulations and law. But if the Jews find themselves not in a place where they have such a cemetery where their ancestors are buried, then they must go to the cemetery that is nearest to them in whatever town that might be, and by so doing remember how many thousands of people were killed in Jerusalem. With that the children go off, break their swords into pieces, and send each of them to their relatives' grave and they say that the dead will do battle and fight for them. During this, the children wear as many heads of garlic around their necks as the number of years

---

189 Bows and arrows are not associated with Tisha beAv but with the festival of Lag Ba'Omer, the 33rd day of the Omer Count. There is a connection between the *minhag* (custom) of playing with bows and arrows and the coming of the Messiah. According to the Zohar, the coming of the Messiah will be marked by a bright, radiant rainbow. As the Hebrew word for rainbow (קשת, *ḳešet*) is the same as the word for bow, bows and arrows are played with to mark the hope for the coming of the Messiah.

hwitlökar om halsen på sig/ som de til åhren komne äro; men hwad här med til förståendes är/ wet jag icke. De hänga en swart förlåt för sitt Altare/ och der brede wid ett swart lius som sättes på jorden. Sedan läggia de sig på de dödas grafwar/ gråta och sörja/ bönfallandes at de döda skola bedia för dem hos Gud/ at *Messias* p. 48 [C8v] snart komma och deras Tem|pel åter vpbyggia måtte/ samt vtfästandes och låfwandes/ sig af den dagen skola giöra den största Fest och högtid. Ty de föregifwa/ at när *Messias* kommandes warder/ skola alla deras Fest och högtidsdagar aldeles afskaffade warda; men allenast på den dagen en stor Fest och högtid hållas. Detta wara en stor Fabel/ lärer hwar och en kunna finna/ ty det är ju omöjeligit at de döda kunna någon hielpa och frälsa.

CAP. 20.

SEdan wi nu hafwa betrachtadt deße föregående Fester och högtider/ skridom wi til deras Nyåhr hwilket de kalla *Rosch Haschara,* ראש השנה Denna Fest fira de den 1. *September*, som kallas *Tischri*. Om den samma hafwa de mycken wahntro och

they have reached; but what is to be understood by this, I do not know.[190] They hang a black curtain in front of the altar and next to it a black candle is placed on the ground. Then they lie on top of the graves of the deceased, weep and mourn, beseeching the dead to pray for them before God, that the Messiah will soon come and their Temple might again be built, as well as committing themselves and promising to hold the greatest festival and holiday on that day. Because they allege that when the Messiah comes, all of their festivals will also be completely abolished, but only on that day will they have a great festival and holiday. This is a great fairy-tale, which everyone ought to be able to see, because it is impossible for the dead to be able to help and save anyone.

Chapter 20

As we have now observed these aforementioned festivals and holidays, let us advance to their New Year, which they call *Rosch Haschara* ראש השנה.[191] This festival is celebrated on 1 September, which they call *Tischri*.[192] They have many un-

---

190 The apotropaic use of garlic for the traditional visit to the cemetery is documented with people bringing garlic and salt with them to the graves, asking the deceased to intervene for them, and scattering garlic in the cemetery to keep evil spirits away; see Herman Pollack, *Jewish Folkways in Germanic Lands (1648–1806): Studies in Aspects of Jewish Life* (Cambridge, MA: The M.I.T. Press, 1971), 193–95. Paul Christian Kirchner, like Löwe a Jewish convert to Christianity, wrote in 1717 that Jews eat garlic on the fast day of Tisha beAv (even though it is a strict fast day):

> Why they keep the 9th of August [*sic*], [commemorating] the destruction of Jerusalem and eat garlic and carry garlic, salt and bread tied in a kerchief to their neck [...] They eat garlic because the smell of the garlic takes away the power of all those who don't eat any when it comes to them. So the smell is supposed to go from them to the Christians to weaken them and make the Jews powerful and strong.

Paul Christian Kirchner, *Jüdisches Ceremoniel, D. i. Allerhand Jüdische Gebräuche, Welche Die Juden in und ausser dem Tempel, bey allen und jeden Fest-Tagen, im Gebeth, in Opffern, in Bedeutungen, in Copulation, in Auslösung der Erstlinge, im Sterben und Begräbnissen, in Erbschafften, in Essen und Trincken und dergleichen mehr pflegen in acht zu nehmen* (Erfurt: Weinmann, 1717), 122–23; quoted from Maria Diemling, "'As the Jews Like to Eat Garlick': Garlic in Christian-Jewish Polemical Discourse in Early Modern Germany," in *Food and Judaism*, ed. Leonard J. Greenspoon, Ronald A. Simkins, and Gerald Shapiro, A Special Issue of Studies in Jewish Civilization, vol. 15 (Omaha, NE: Creighton University Press, 2005), 224. It has, nonetheless, not been possible to find a parallel to Löwe's claim that children wear as many heads of garlic around their necks as their years of age.

191 Heb.: *Rosch Haschara*, ראש השנה, "new year": The Jewish New Year – Rosh Hashanah (ראש השנה, *ro'š ha-šanah*) – begins on the first of Tishrei.

192 Heb.: *Tischri*, תשרי, *tišrei* or *tišri*, "Tishrei/Tishri": the first month of the civil year and the seventh month of the religious year in the Hebrew calendar (around September–October in the Gregorian calendar).

widskepelse; ty 14. dagar förvt bereda de sig med fastande och bediande/ stå om morgonen bittida vp för dagningen/ gå vti Synagogan och bedia Gud om syndernas förlåtelse. De hafwa och den inbillning/ at denna tiden skal i himmelen trenne Böcker öpnas/ då de ogudachtiga blifwa til en ewig fördömmelse inskrefne/ och de som mindre ogudachtige eller medelmåttige äro/ warda ei inskrefne/ vtan i hopp och wäntan af bättring/ warder med deras inskrifwande til en annan festdag opskutit/ som firas en månad der efter och kallas *Hoschiana Raba* הושענה רבא Men p. 49 [D1r] de Gudfruchtige skola | vpskrifne warda til ett ewinnerligit lif. Deras *Rabbiner* föregifwa och/ at om nyåhrsdagen skal i himmelen blifwa vpskrifwit/ hwad alla menniskior det åhret hända skal/ ja om man skal lefwa eller dö. De hafwa och ett horn det de kalla *Schopher*, שופר hwilket är af en wädur/ i den meningen och med en sådan vttydning; at Gud skal ihugkomma den wäduren/ som Abraham hafwer i sin Sons Isaks ställe vpoffrat/ och tänckia på det förbund/ som han med Abraham gjort hafwer/ och förlåta dem deras synder. De säjia: At när Satan hörer blåsas vti detta hornet/ måste han fly bort och wika vndan. Denna Fest warder hos dem äfwen som Pinges Festen 2. dagar firad/ tilbringandes den merendels med läsande och siungande. Icke heller törs någon äta/ han ware sig vng eller gammal/ innan de hördt vhr Synagogan blåsas i hornet/ hwilket sker på följande sätt. Först giör den mannen som i hornet blåsa skal/ en wälsignelse der öfwer/ och tager en duk af vll eller silke/ öfwer hufwudet; På samma duk hänga vllträdar vti alla 4. hörnen/ den de kalla *Zizit Schœl Thalit*, ציצית של טלית. Der efter gå alla de/ som äro af Arons slächte och stam/ på trappan wid Altaret/ och läsa HERrans wälsignelse öfwer folcket/ betäckiandes sina hufwuden med ett ylle-kläde hwilket kallas *Thalit* טלית p. 50 [D1v] hwar på vti alla 4. kantar och hörn hängia 3. ylle-trådar/ som tilförene om|talt är. Sedan lyfta de vp händerna/ och *Cantorn* siunger för dem HERrans wälsignelse. Der wid hafwa de och en *Fabel*, det jag sielf försökt och *proberat* hafwer/ och sedt at det vti ingen sanning är. De betäckia sina hufwuden med en yllen-duk när Arons slächt siunger wälsignelsen/ och föregifwa; at den som då ser på dem/ han skal blifwa blind/ derföre hålla både små och stora för ögonen. Och har jag äfwen den

4 Böcker] Bäcker *Spec.* (Sthlm, 1732); Böcker *Spec.* (Gbg, 1732; Sthlm, 1735).

founded beliefs and superstitions about this day; so, 14 days beforehand they prepare themselves with fasting and prayer, they get up early in the morning before sunrise, go to the synagogue, and pray to God to forgive their sins. They also have the delusion that three books are opened in heaven during this time, when the unfaithful will be inscribed for an eternal punishment, and those who are less unfaithful or mediocre will not be inscribed, but, in the hope and expectation of improvement, their inscription is put off until another holiday, which is celebrated a month later and is called *Hoschiana Raba* הושענה רבא.[193] However, the pious will be inscribed for an eternal life. Their rabbis also allege that on New Year's Day it is written in heaven what is going to happen to all people in that year, indeed, whether they will live or die. They also have a horn that they call a *Schopher* שופר,[194] which is made from a ram with the meaning and such interpretation that God will remember the ram that Abraham sacrificed in lieu of his son, Isaac, and forgive them their sins. They say that when Satan hears the horn being blown, he has to flee and avoid it. Like the holiday of Pentecost, this festival is also celebrated for two days, and they spend most of it reading and singing. No one, young or old, dares to eat until they have heard the horn being blown in the synagogue which happens in the following way. First, the man who is to blow in the horn performs a blessing over it and places a woollen or silk cloth over his head. On this cloth woollen threads hang in the four corners, they call them *Zizit Schœl Thalit* ציצית של טלית.[195] Afterwards, all those of the family and tribe of Aaron go to the steps by the altar and read the Lord's blessing[196] over the people, and they cover their heads with a woollen cloth called a *Thalit* טלית,[197] on which three woollen threads hang along the four edges and corners, as was mentioned previously. Then they raise their hands, and the cantor sings the Lord's blessing to them. They also have a fairy-tale about this, which I myself have tried and experienced, and seen that there is no truth in. They cover their heads with a woollen cloth when the family of Aaron sing the blessing, and they allege that whoever looks at them during this moment will go blind. For this reason, both young and old cover their eyes. And

---

193 Heb.: *Hoschiana Raba*, הושענא רבא, *hoša'na raba'*, "Hoshana Rabba": the festival falls on 21 Tishrei during the holiday of Sukkot. It is marked in the synagogue by reciting the Hoshanot while processing with the four species – citron (אתרוג, *etrog*), date palm (לולב, *lulav*), myrtle (הדס, *hadas*), and willow (ערבה, *'aravah*) – seven times around the bimah. The ceremony is an act of gratitude and rejoicing for a fruitful year.

194 Heb.: *Schopher*, שופר, *šofar*, "shofar": an instrument made from a ram's horn and used primarily during Rosh Hashanah and Yom Kippur.

195 Heb.: *Zizit Schœl Thalit*, ציצית של טלית, *ẓiẓit šel ṭalit*, "the tallit's tzitzit": the knotted fringes attached to the four corners of the tallit (note 4 below).

196 Numbers 6:23–27.

197 Heb.: *Thalit*, טלית, *ṭalit*, "tallit": a fringed garment worn as a prayer shawl.

tid jag en Jude war/ tagit mig den dristigheten på/ och under wälsignelsens förrättande sedt på dem/ och är doch Gudi lof! icke blind worden. Wid deras vtgående af Synagogan/ önska de hwar annan at de måge på detta nya åhret blifwa vti Himmelen vptecknade och vpskrefne. Sedan gå de hem/ äta och dricka; brukandes gemenligen under denna Fest hwita kläder; ty de säija/ at hwitt betyder syndernas förlåtelse. När middagen är ändad/ löpa både unga och gamla til rinnande watn/ skaka sina kläder/ lika som de något vti watnet kasta skulle; menandes der med sina synder i watnet at skaka/ och säija der wid deße ord: *Thaslech Et Koll Katotenu Bemsulot Hajam. &c.* תשליך את כל חטא במצלות הים. Det är/ wi kasta alla wåra synder i haffens diup och Israels folcks synder/ at de ewinnerligen ei skola påtänckte warda: de skaka åter en gång sina kläder/ på det deras synder aldeles i grund måga kastade blifwa. Hwad är icke detta för en grufwelig synd och |
p. 51 [D2r] widskepelse; ty det är ogiörligit sina synder at bortskaka/ vtan ett slikt syndsens afläggiande/ måste ske genom en sann bättring och omwändelse. Widare hafwa de en widskepelse/ at de vti denna Högtiden intet äta några nötter; ty en nött heter på Hebräiska *Egos* אגוז och när man räcknar det tilhopa/ hafwa samma bokstäfwer så mycket at betyda som synd. אגוז בגמ חטא. Och detta är orsaken hwarföre de ei töras äta nötter/ vtan se gierna/ at de kunna förskaffa sig andra friska fruckter/ öfwer hwilka de läsa en wälsignelse/ för än de dem äta. De gifwa och på denna Högtiden många allmosor til de fattige/ menandes sig der medelst det ewiga Lifwet kunna förwärfwa. Men förgäwes? ty det ewiga Lifwet bekommer man icke så lätt; vtan allenast genom en sann bot och lefwernes förbättring/ samt igenom en sann tro på JEsum Christum/ som för wåra synder lidit/ dödt/ ock från de döda åter vpstånden är: Hwilken nu sitter på Alsmächtig GUDz Faders högra hand/ der ifrån han på yttersta dagen åter kommandes warder/ til at dömma lefwande och döda. Således är på det kortaste om Judarnas Nyåhr handlat.

when I was also a Jew, I had the audacity to look at them while the blessing was being performed, and – praise be to God! – I did not turn blind. When they leave the synagogue, they wish each other that they might for the New Year be recorded and inscribed in heaven. Then they go home, eat, and drink. And during this holiday, they wear white clothes, because they say that white means the forgiveness of sins.[198] When the meal has concluded, both the young and old run to running water, shake their clothes as if they were throwing something into the water, by which they believe that they are shaking their sins into the water,[199] and they say these words during this *Thaslech Et Koll Katotenu*[200] *Bemsulot Hajam*, etc. תשליך את כל חטא במצלות הים,[201] that is "We throw all our sins and the sins of the people of Israel into the deep of the sea that they may never be thought of again." Then they shake their clothes once more so that their sins can be completely thrown into the depths. What sort of horrible sin and superstition is this because it is impossible to shake off one's sins? Rather such an absolution of sins has to take place by means of true repentance and conversion. Moreover, they have a superstition that they do not eat any nuts during this holiday, because in Hebrew a nut is called *Egos* אגוז,[202] and when you add it together, these letters mean the same as sin: אגוז בגמ חטא.[203] And this is the reason why they do not dare to eat nuts but prefer to procure other fresh fruits over which they read a blessing before they eat them. On this holiday they also give many alms to the poor believing that they can obtain eternal life by so doing. But in vain! Because you cannot receive eternal life so easily, but only through true penance and improving one's way of life and through a true belief in Jesus Christ, who suffered, died, and rose from the dead for our sins: who now sits on the right hand of Almighty God the Father, from where he will come on the Final Day to judge the living and dead. Thus has the Jews' New Year been dealt with in brief.

---

198 Cf. Isaiah 1:18.

199 The ritual of atonement called Tashlich (תשליך, *tašlich*,"casting off") is performed during the High Holy Days.

200 *Katotenu*] This is not an accurate transliteration of חטא, *ḥeṭ'* "sin." The intended word is probably חטאינו, *ḥeṭ'einu*, "our sins."

201 Cf. Micah 7:19: ותשליך במצלות ים, כל חטאותם ("and Thou wilt cast all their sins into the depths of the sea.")

202 Heb.: *Egos*, אגוז, *egoz*, "walnut," "nut."

203 Heb.: אגוז בגמ חטא, *egoz be-GM ḥeṭ'*, "a nut in G.M. is a sin." The word בגמ (*be-GM*) is probably an abbreviation for בגימטריה [in gematria]. In gematria, the numerical value of אגוז [nut] is 17 and חטא [sin] is 18. Another form of the word "sin" – חט – with a numerical value of 17, and thus reminiscent of the word "nut" in gematria, is used to explain why it is best to refrain from eating nuts.

CAP. 21.

TIjo dagar efter Judarnas Nyåhr/ följer deras Försonings Fest/ den de kalla p. 52 [D2v] Långdag/ eller på Hebreiska *Jom Kipor*. Den|na dagen hålla de ganska Helig: Han infaller på den 10. *Septembris*, hwilken Månad de kalla *Tisri*. Dagen för försonings dagen/ bereda de sig til Festen på följande sätt: 1. Hafwa de en sådan wahntro och sed; för en man taga de en tupp/ och för en qwinna en höna. Men är qwinnan hafwandes/ tages för henne allena både en tupp och höna. Der om säija de; at hanen skal för dem wara såsom ett offer. Denna hanen säger den ena til den andra/ skal gå til döden; men du skal gå til Lifwet och friden/ taga så hanen eller hönan och slänga den 3. gångor kring om hufwudet/ detta måste ske dagen förut klåckan 9. och kalla de det *Capora*. Sedan gå de på Kyrckiogården/ läggia sig på *Rabbinernas* griffter/ gråta och skrika/ bediandes at de för dem hos Gud bedia skola. De som hafwa *Disposition* om de fattigas medel/ sättia sig vti Porten och de fattige å både sidor/ innom på Kyrckiogården; hafwandes hwar och en ett litet fat för sig/ och alla de som på Kyrckiogården ingå/ måste på både sidor kasta penningar til de fattige/ och när detta skedt är/ gå alla samteliga fattige til den som med fattig penningarne hafwer at *Disponera* och handla; och då gifwer han dem/ hwad som hela åhret samlat är/ kallandes det *Pidron Näphäsch*, det är: kropparnas vtlösande ifrån döden. Lika som man kunde kiöpa det ewiga Lifwet för penningar. p. 53 [D3r] När detta är bestält/ gå de hela Kyrckiogården omkring. Der på gå de hem | med de slacktade hönßen/ som de kring om hufwudet weftat hafwa/ plåcka och koka dem; men inälfworna warda på taket kastade/ föregifwandes de/ at deras höns warit til äfwentyrs vti någon annan mans hus eller lada och ätit/ och detta är orsaken at de hwarken lefren eller magen äta wilja/ men köttet warder af dem ätit. Efter Middagen gå alla Mans Personer vti Synagogan/ hafwandes en giördel eller bälte giordt af Oxeläder/ då lägger sig den ena efter den andra til jorden på ansichtet/ slåendes då den ena den andra 39. slag på Ryggen med samma Rem eller

Chapter 21

Ten days after the Jews' New Year comes their festival of atonement, which they call Long Day or in Hebrew *Jom Kipor*.[204] They keep this day quite holy: it falls on 10 September, which month they call *Tisri*. The day before the Day of Atonement they prepare for the holiday thus: They have a superstition and custom like this: for a man they take a cockerel and for a woman they take a hen, but if the woman is pregnant, they take a cockerel and a hen just for her. About this they say that the cockerel will be like a sacrifice for them. "This cockerel," the one says to the other, "will go to death, but you will go to life and peace." They then take the cockerel or hen and swing it three times about their heads. This must happen before nine o'clock, and they call it *Capora*.[205] Then they go to the cemetery, lying on the tombs of the rabbis, weeping and screaming, and imploring them to pray for them before God. Those people who are in charge of funds for the poor sit by the gate with the poor on either side in the cemetery, and each of them has a small dish in front of them. And everyone who enters the cemetery has to throw money at the poor. And when this has happened, all of the poor people go to the one who is in charge of handing out and dealing with the poverty funds, and he gives them whatever has been collected throughout the year, and it is called *Pidron Näphäsch*,[206] that is "the bodies' redemption from death," as if you can buy eternal life with money. When this has been done, they walk around the entire cemetery. After this they go home with the slaughtered chickens that they have swung around their heads, pluck and boil them, but the giblets are thrown onto the roof, as they claim that their chickens might have been in another man's house or barn and eaten [something treyf]; and this is the reason that they will not eat either the liver or stomach, but the meat is eaten by them. After noon all the men go to the synagogue wearing a girdle or belt made of ox leather. Then each in turn lies face-down on the ground, beating one another 39 times on the back with this strap or girdle.[207] The one doing the

---

204 Heb.: *Jom Kipor*, יום כיפור, *yom kipur*, "Yom Kippur." Yom Kippur or the Day of Atonement falls on 10 Tishrei and concludes the High Holy Days.
205 Heb.: *Capora*, כפרות, *kaparot*, "Kapparot": a customary ritual of expiation in which a chicken is waved over someone's head before it is slaughtered.
206 Heb.: *Pidron Näphäsch*, פדיון נפש, *pidion nefeš*, "soul redemption." Pidyon Nefesh is a special prayer for which one "sacrifices" (i.e., pays) money.
207 The customary ritual of makkot (מכות, *makot*, "lashes") involves the beating of penitential community members by the "beadle" (שמש, *šamaš*), or some other pious man, as a symbolic punishment for their sins and a means to gain atonement (Temurah 3a–b). Each penitent is struck 39 times across the back to reflect the punishment by 39 lashes in the Torah for certain sins during the time of the Temple. During his beating, the penitent recites Psalm 78:38: והוא רחום׀ יכפר עון ולא־ישחית והרבה להשיב אפו ולא־יעיר כל־חמתו, "But He, being merciful, forgave iniquity and would

giördel/ den som slår räknar slagen/ men den som ligger på jorden/ slår sig för hwart slag för bröstet och bekänner sina synder. När nu den ena den andra slagit hafwer/ warder ett ombyte och omwäxling giordt/ och den som på jorden legat/ slår åter den som sig tilförene slagit hafwer. Orsaken är denna: Den som är skyldig til döden han får 40. slag/ och derföre gifwes de andra til en åtskilnad 39. Der på gå de hem/ på det de måge äta innan Solen nedgår. At jag ei må förgäta hwad deras försoning widkommer/ blifwer på denna dagen/ der stora Städer äro och många Judar/ några 1000:de höns slacktade: och efter swänskt mynt/ skal för hwar höna gifwas en styfwer åt den/ som dem slacktar; kastandes han penningarne vti en watnskåhl och aftwättar dem. Deße höns warda af dem samma qwäll ätne. Efter p. 54 [D3v] måltiden taga de | sina dödekläder på sig/ bediandes hwar och en den andra/ om han något honom emot brutit om förlåtelse/ och sig således med hwarandra försona. Ty de föregifwa sig ei skola bönhörde blifwa/ om de sig med hwarannan icke försona och förlika månde. Der på gå de åter vti Synagogan tända op stora waxlius/ skolandes det minsta räckia vti 24. timmar. Deße lius warda kallade Siälelius/ och de som giffte äro/ taga så många marcker wax i hwart lius/ som de åldrige eller gamle äro. Der wid hafwa de denna widskeppelse/ at när samma lius en gång vptändt är/ och det sedan warder vtsläckt/ afbrutit eller smältat/ så skal deras bön/ det åhret ei hörd warda/ vtan de skola på det samma åhret dö. Denna dagen warder hos dem så helgad och firad/ at han hålles för den största bot- och bättrings dag/ på hwilken de således fasta/ siunga och pina sina lemmar. Deße 24. timmar medan liusen brinna måste de stå/ så om natten/ som om dagen/ föregifwandes; at på samma dag warda vti himmelen deras synder försonade/ och beslutit hwad dem hela åhret hända skal. Hela åhret är hos dem förbudit at falla på sina knä/ doch giöra de det denna dagen twänne gånger. Men när *Cantorn* eller föresiungaren ropar/ *Mälek Malaka hoc est* alla Konungars Konung: då stiga de alla vpp. Wid slutet af deras bön/ när den förrättad är/ öpna och vplåta de

26 *hoc est*] *h. e. Spec.* (Sthlm, 1732; Gbg, 1732; Sthlm, 1735).

beating counts the lashes, but the one lying on the ground hits his chest with each lash and confesses his sins. When the one has beaten the other, they swap and switch places, and the one who had been lying on the ground, now beats the one who had previously beaten him. The reason is this: whoever is guilty of death is given 40 lashes, and this is why others are given 39 to make a difference. Then they go home so they can eat before sundown. That I may not forget what their atonement entails, on this day where there are large towns and many Jews, some thousands of chickens are slaughtered; and in Swedish currency, a styver must be paid to the slaughterer for each hen; he throws the money into a bowl of water to rinse it. These hens are eaten by them in the evening. After the meal, they put on their death robes,[208] each one asking the other for forgiveness if he has hurt him in some way, and thus they atone with each other. Because they allege that their prayers will not be heard if they have not atoned and reconciled with each other. Then they go back to the synagogue and light large candles that should last at least 24 hours. They call these candles "soul candles," and those who are married pay as many marks for the wax in each candle as they are aged or old. From this they have the superstition, that once the candle is lit and is subsequently extinguished, disrupted, or melted, then their prayers will not be heard for the year, but rather they will die during that year. This day is sanctified and celebrated by them so much, that it is considered the greatest day of penitence and penance on which they fast, sing, and torment their limbs. For these 24 hours while the candles are burning, they must stand, during the night as during the day, alleging that on this day their sins are being atoned in heaven and what will happen to them in the coming year is being decided. They are forbidden to fall to their knees throughout the whole year, but on this day they do so twice. But when the cantor or lead singer shouts *Mälek Malaka*, that is "King of Kings,"[209] then they all stand up. At the end of their prayers, when they have been performed, they open and unlock

---

not destroy; He restrained His wrath time and again and did not give vent to His fury." This verse has thirteen words in the Hebrew, so by repeating it three times, it was possible to keep count of the number of lashes. See Yaacov Deutsch, "Polemical Ethnographies: Descriptions of Yom Kippur in the Writings of Christian Hebraists and Jewish Converts to Christianity in Early Modern Europe," in *Hebraica Veritas? Christian Hebraists and the Study of Judaism in Early Modern Europe*, ed. Alison Coudert and Jeffrey S. Shoulson (Philadelphia: University of Pennsylvania, 2004), 215; Yaacov Deutsch, *Judaism in Christian Eyes: Ethnographic Descriptions of Jews and Judaism in Early Modern Europe*, trans. Avi Aronsky [יהדות בעיניים נוצריות] (New York: Oxford University Press, 2012), 90–92; Jonathan Adams, *Lessons in Contempt: Poul Ræff's Translation and Publication in 1516 of Johannes Pfefferkorn's* The Confession of the Jews, Universitets-Jubilæets danske Samfund, vol. 581 (Odense: Syddansk Universitetsforlag, 2013), 111, 190, 283–84.

208 See p. 125*n*157 in this edition for *Spec.* (Sthlm, 1732), 40.

209 The formulation "*Mälek Malaka*" is strange. One would expect מלך המלכים, *melech ha-melachim*, "king of kings." Both later editions (Gbg, 1732; Sthlm, 1735) have "Malek Malaka."

p. 55 [D4r] FörbundzArcken/ hwar vtinnan 10. Guds bud förwara | de äro/ och ropa alla med hög röst 4. gånger: Hör Israels Gud/ wår Gud är en ewig Gud. Åter ropa de deße orden 3. gånger: Han är wår Gud och ingen annan. Här på blåsa de ett starkt liudande vti samma horn som tilförene omtalt är/ säijandes der wid: Vti tilkommande åhr skola wi hålla wår Fest och högtid vti Jerusalem/ släckiandes så vt sina lius som öfwerblefne äro. Somlige taga de med sig hem/ några låta de blifwa qware/ til Synagogans widare tienst. När de komma vt om dörren/ at de få si nymånaden/ då säija de sig åter wilja giöra en god gierning/ wälsigna och Helga den samma/ hoppandes och springandes lika såsom de månaden fasttaga wilje/ och säija deße orden: Såsom jag emot dig springer/ och dig doch ei widröra kan; så skola och mina fiender ei det ringaste kunna anröra mig til ondo/ eller mig någon skada giöra. Der på gå de hem hwar til sitt hus. De som bo på Landet/ skiönt de bodde 50. mihl vtom Judiska Församlingen/ måste de likwäl wid samma Högtid sig infinna. Skulle ock någon Jude hos de Christne fången wara/ gå de andra Judarna för honom vti *Caution*/ at han doch må fira samma Fest/ och wara hos dem vti Synagogan. När nu hwar och en vti sitt hus kommen är/ skola de åter giöra en begynnelse samma afton til goda gierningar. Wärden går vti huset och söker vp ett
p. 56 [D4v] wackert rum til Löf Hyddo-Högtiden och slår der samma | städes neder en påla/ på det han samma rum desto bättre igen finna kan; til ett bewis/ at han sig om den ena goda gierningen efter den andra beflitar. Deße Ceremonier bruka de wid försoningsdagen och pina sina kroppar/ föregifwandes/ sig genom sådana goda wärck och gierningar från de synderna/ qwitte och ledige blifwa/ hwilka de hela åhret bedrifwit hafwa. Nei mine gode Judar/ jag råder eder allesammans/ emedan I ären mina bröder efter kiöttet/ at I gån til det rätta Försoningsoffret/ som är JEsus Christus/ hwilken är den endaste Medlaren emellan GUD och menniskian! Amen.

the Ark of the Covenant in which God's Ten Commandments are kept, and they all shout four times with a loud voice "Hear O God of Israel! Our God is an eternal God!" They shout these words again three times: "He is our God and no other!"[210] With that they blow a loud sound in the horn that was mentioned earlier and say, "In the coming year we will hold our festival and holiday in Jerusalem!"[211] and they extinguish their remaining candles. Some take them home, and some leave them behind for further use by the synagogue. When they go outside so they can see the new moon, they say that they would like to do another good deed, they praise and sanctify it, jumping and leaping about like they want to grab hold of the moon, and they say these words: "Just as I jump towards you but cannot touch you, so shall my enemies also not be able to touch me with evil or do me any harm." Then each of them goes home to his house. Those who live in the countryside, even if they live 50 miles from the Jewish congregation, also have to make an appearance on this holiday. Also, if some Jew has been captured by a Christian, then the other Jews make bail for him so that he may celebrate this festival and be with them in the synagogue. Now when everyone has returned home, they are to begin doing good deeds again that very evening. The head of the household goes into the house and finds a beautiful room for the Feast of Booths,[212] and in that place, he strikes down a pole so that he will be able to find this room more easily again as evidence that he manages to do the one good deed after the other. They perform these ceremonies and torment their bodies on the Day of Atonement and claim that through good works and deeds they can be absolved of and freed from the sins that they have committed throughout the year. No, my dear Jews, as you are my brothers in the flesh, I advise you all to go to the true atonement sacrifice, that is Jesus Christ, who is the only mediator between God and man! Amen.

210 Here, as elsewhere, the translation of the prayers is rather jumbled. Presumably this is meant to be the Shema benediction: שמע ישראל יהוה אלהינו יהוה אחד, "Hear, O Israel: the Lord is our God, the Lord is one" (Deuteronomy 6:4).

211 The prayer *Le-šanah haba'ah bi-Yrušalayim* (לשנה הבאה בירושלים, "Next year in Jerusalem") is usually sung at the end of the Yom Kippur service to express the desire to return to a rebuilt Jerusalem.

212 "The Feast of Booths" is the seven-day (eight-day in the diaspora) festival of Sukkot (סוכות, *sukot*) that begins on 15 Tishrei. It marks the end of the harvest (Exodus 34:22) and commemorates the end of the Exodus (Leviticus 23:42–43). See chapter 22 in *Spec.* (Sthlm, 1732).

CAP. 22.

EFter denna Fest följer nu i ordning löfhyddohögtiden den de kalla *Suca*. Denna Fest begynnes 5. dagar der efter/ och kallas derföre *Suca*; emedan det betyder en hydda/ hwilken högtid warder hos dem hållen 8. dagar. Vtom den tiden wil wäl hwar och en af dem gierna förse sig med en warm stuga/ Men i denna högtiden wilja de Gudi til ähra sittia vti kiölden; och byggia sig fördenskul hyddor af bräder på gatan/ på hwilka intet tak är/ vtan de äro allenast med löf betäckte. Der vti äta och dricka de/ och hafwa derstädes sitt tilhåld vti hela 7. dagar./ och så ingen p. 57 [D5r] annorstädes spisa det ringaste/ vtan i samma hydda; så | framt det icke rägnar och maten blifwer fördärfwad/ då få de äta vti sina hus. De säija/ at när det rägnar vti deße 7. dagar/ skal Gud wara wred på dem/ och intet wilja hafwa at de honom til behag skola vti samma hyddor sittia. Deße Festdagar ingå den 15. *Septembr.* då hösten begynnes och gemenligen plägar rägna och wara kalt wäder. Vti samma hydda få de icke hafwa något kiärille eller gryta som wid elden warit/ och om någon Person skulle med sådant vti hyddan inkomma/ måste de strax byggia en annan på ett annat ställe; Men orsaken der til wet jag icke. Ja somliga bruka och såfwa vti samma hydda.

Icke understår sig någon/ ware sig gammal eller vng/ til at smaka någon mat på deße 7. dagar/ undantagandes ett äpple som är nästan likt en Citron/ hwilket kallas *Etrog* אתרוג giörandes med största *Devotion* och andacht en wälsignelse der öfwer. *Rabbinerna* föregifwa; at det skal wara af samma slags äplen/ som Ewa gifwit åt Adam; och at döden genom samma äplens ätande kommit vti werlden. Deße äplen luckta ganska liufligen/ och warder på dem alla ett teckn befunnit/ som en menniskia med 3. tänder der vti bitit hade. De hafwa den inbillning; at om någon hafwande Qwinna biter stielcken af samma äple/ skal hon vtan någon sweda kunna föda barn. Denna Fest warder förnämligast hållen til åminnelse af det/ at de vti öknen bodt vti hyddor.

Chapter 22

The next in order after this festival is the Feast of Booths, which they call *Suca*.[213] This festival starts five days later, and it is called *Suca* as this means “a booth.” This holiday is kept by them for eight days. At any other time, each and every one of them would like to provide for themselves a warm room. But during this holiday, to honour God, they want to sit in the cold, and for this reason they build booths in the street made of planks, on which there are no roofs, rather they are only covered by foliage. They eat and drink outside in them and for an entire seven days have their abode there and do not eat the slightest thing anywhere else but in that very booth – as long as it does not rain and the food is ruined, then they are allowed to eat in their houses. They say that when it rains during these seven days, God is angry with them and does not want them to please him by sitting in these booths. These holidays start on the 15 September when autumn begins, and it is usually raining and there is cold weather. In these huts they may not have any vessel or pot that has been by the fire, and if someone brings such a thing into the booth, then they must immediately build another one in another place; but I do not know the reason for this. Indeed, some are even in the habit of sleeping in their booth.

During these seven days, no one, be they old or young, dares to taste any food except for an apple that is almost like a lemon, which they call an *Etrog* אתרוג,[214] and with exceedingly great devotion and piety they make a blessing over it. The rabbis claim that it is of the same species of apple as Eve gave to Adam, and that death came to the world through eating this very apple. These apples smell quite exquisite, and a mark can be found on all of them as if a person with three teeth has bitten into them. They are under the delusion that if a pregnant woman bites the stalk of this apple, then she will be able to bear her child without any pain.[215] This festival is principally held to commemorate their having lived in booths in the desert.

---

213 Heb.: *Suca*, סכה, *sukah*, “booth.” The seven-day holiday beginning on 15 Tishrei that marks the harvest (Exodus 34:22) and commemorates the Exodus (Leviticus 23:42–43) is usually referred to as Sukkot, סכות, lit. “booths.”

214 *Etrog*, אתרוג, *etrog*, “citron.” The citron is called the פרי עץ הדר, “fruit of majestic trees” in Leviticus 23:40 and is one of the four species used during the celebration of Sukkot.

215 There are several superstitions and traditions concerning women biting off an etrog’s style/stigma (פיטום, *piṭom*) and childbirth: as a *segulah* (סגולה, “remedy”) to alleviate labour pains, to give birth to a boy, or to have beautiful and fragrant children. See Chana Weisberg, *Expecting Miracles: Finding Meaning and Spirituality in Pregnancy through Judaism* (Jerusalem: Urim Publications, 2004), 34*n*17, 135*n*76, and 175 (quoting Talmud Ketubot 60b–61a).

p. 58 [D5v] Siette dagen vti | denna Fest kallas den stora Pildagen och *Hebr. Håschana Raba*; På Tyska Widentag. De taga qwällen förvt af deße bladen och giöra der af en liten qwast af vdda blad vti samma hydda/ och sättia dem vti watn til morgonen der efter. Då stå de äfwen så bittida vp som på Försoningsdagen/ gå vti Synagogan och förrätta sin bön. När bönen är ändad taga de 5. Mosis Böcker vtur Förbundsens Arck/ hwarest alla 10. Guds bud stå på *Pergament*, hållandes dem med sina händer på Predikostolen/ den Judarna kalla *Halmemer* och gå 7. gånger med samma äple och qwist om deras *Catheder*. Vti Förbunds Arcken insättia de ett waxlius och när de 7. gånger omkring gådt hafwa/ taga de samma qwastar/ som de aftonen förvt giordt hafwa/ fatta til sina knifwar och slå löfwen vtaf qwastarna/ at icke ett blifwer derpå sittiandes. De mena/ at som bladen affalla och afslås/ skola och deras synder afslagne och affallande warda. Och at de 7. gånger gå omkring Predikostolen sker til en åminnelse at Josua 7. gånger gådt kring om staden Jericho/ då de 7. murarne nedföllo och staden intogs.

Judarna hafwa och en förskräckelig fabel och wahntro/ hwar med de giöra Gudi ett stort mißhag; Ty på denna qwäll/ på hwilken är fullmånad/ gå de vti måneskinet/ taga ett lakan om sin kropp/ gå på ett ställe afsides; kasta där lakanet
p. 59 [D6r] ifrån sig och stå hel nakote/ Samt ställa sig der som Månan skiner/ bredan | des vt sig och bese sin egen skugga. När en vti månskenet intet ser skuggen af sitt hufwud/ menar han/ at han samma åhr dö skal. Felas honom vti skuggan/ hand/ fot eller någon annan lem/ skal en af deß närmaste slächt/ samma åhr genom döden afgå. Nu kan den gunstiga Läsaren sielf tänckia/ hwad det för en synd wara månde (hälst som Gud all widskeppelse högeligen förbudit) emedan de bär med intet annat wilja/ än försökia Gud och se in vti hans Råd-Cammar/ hwad Gud öfwer menniskiorna af sin allwetenhet beslutit hafwer. Jag wil för min del tacka den gode Guden/ at han mig/ som ett willfarande får/ ifrån en slik willfarelse förlossat/ frälsat/ och på den rätta wägen fördt hafwer/ til den rätta ängen och betet/ der jag kan föda och beta min Siäl med Guds Ord och dricka af den lefwande Wattn-Källan.

---

29 Wattn-Källan] Wattu-Källan *Spec.* (Sthlm, 1732; Gbg, 1732; Sthlm, 1735).

The sixth day of this festival is called Willow Day and in Hebrew *Håschana Raba*, in German *Widentag*.[216] In their booths the evening before, they take these leaves and make a small bundle of branches from pointed leaves and put them in water until the following morning. Then they also get up as early as on the Day of Atonement, go to the synagogue, and say their prayer. When the prayer has ended, they take the Five Books of Moses out of the Ark where all of God's Ten Commandments are written on parchment, and hold them in their hands on the pulpit, which the Jews called *Halmemer*[217] and walk seven times around this pulpit (*cathedra*) with this apple and bundle of branches. They place a wax candle in the Ark of the Covenant and when they have walked seven circuits, they take the branches that they made the evening before, and they grab their stems and beat the leaves off the branches so that not a single one remains upon them. They believe that just as the leaves fall off and are beaten off, so will their sins be beaten off and fall off. And the reason that they walk seven times around the pulpit is in memory of Joshua who walked seven times around the city of Jericho, when the seven walls fell down and the city was taken.

The Jews also have a terrible fairy-tale and superstition with which they do God a great displeasure; because on this evening, on which there is a full moon, they walk in the moonlight, with a sheet wrapped around their bodies, walk to a secluded spot, throw off the sheet, and stand completely naked, and stand where the moon is shining and, spreading out, they look at their shadows. When one of them does not see the shadow of his head in the moonlight, he believes that he will die that same year. If his shadow is missing a hand, foot, or some other limb, then a close family member will die that same year. Now, the gracious reader can think for himself what sort of a sin this must be (not least as God has strictly forbidden all superstition), yet they have no other desire than to test God and look into his council chamber to see what God in his omniscience has decided with regard to humanity. For my part, I want to thank the good God that he has redeemed me – like a lost lamb – from such delusion, saved me and lead to me to the right path, to the right meadow and pasture where I can nourish and feed my soul with God's words and drink of the living water spring.

216 Weidentag (Germ.), "willow day."
217 See p. 75*n*31 in this edition for *Spec.* (Sthlm, 1732), 7.

CAP. 23.

DEn ottonde dagen vti samma löfhyddohögtid/ hålla de sig ganska lustige och glade/ och samma dag bedia de en särskilt bön för fruchten vti landet/ at Gud dem en wälsignad wäderlek gifwa wille; det samma giöra de sedan vti sina böner 2. gånger om dagen/ hela åhret igenom. Nionde dagen är löfhyddohögtiden vte/ men p. 60 [D6v] de låta doch sina hyddor stå tils nionde dagen framfaren är/ den de på *Hebræi*|ska kalla *Simkat Tora,* שמחת תורה det är; de glädia sig der öfwer/ at lagen dem gifwen är.

På denna dag hafwa de en besynnerlig frögd och glädie öfwer de 10. Gudz bud/ hwilka de på Pergament skrefne i Synagogan förwara/ och när de dem framtaga wilja/ brukas der wid följande *Ceremonier.* Först betäckia och bekläda de dem med de aldrakåstbaraste och präktigaste sidentyger/ sedan taga de dem vtur Förbundsens Arck och dansa der med hela Synagogan omkring/ giörandes sig äfwen vti sina hus med ätande och drickande/ mer än som andra dagar/ lustige och glade.

De samla då tilhopa alt löf/ som de på sina hyddor haft hafwa/ och giöra der af på bergen frögde-eldar. För sina barn beställa de ock en besynnerlig glädie/ de kasta allahanda fruckter på gatan/ samt sättia på stora stänger allahanda *Baner* och Fahnor af papper eller tyg/ målade: På hwilka med gyllende Bokstäfwer skrifwit står: Detta är *Baner* för Juda stam/ för Lewi/ för Benjamin/ med flere dylike.

Vti Synagogan äro de ganska lustige/ och dricka der inne allahanda starcka dricker/ såsom win och brännewin; så at de offta vti sielfwa Synagogan/ på denna frögde Fästen slås/ så at bloden af dem rinna månde. *Summa*: i hela månaden äro idel Festdagar. |

p. 61 [D7r] CAP. 24.

EEt fierdedels åhr der efter/ hafwa de och en Fäst/ den de kalla *Kenuka* חנוכה wid paß samma tid som Juletiden hos oß plägar firas; nemligen den 25. *Decembr.*

Chapter 23

They remain joyful and happy on the eighth day of this Festival of Booths,[218] and on this day, they pray a special prayer for the fruits of the land, that God will give them blessed weather:[219] they then do the same thing while praying twice a day throughout the entire year. On the ninth day, the Festival of Booths is over, but they let their booths stand until the ninth day is over, which in Hebrew they call *Simkat Tora* שמחת תורה,[220] that is they are joyful that the Law was given to them.

On this day, they are particularly delighted and happy about God's Ten Commandments which they keep written on parchment in the synagogue, and when they want to take them out, they perform the following ceremonies. First, they cover and dress them with the most precious and most splendid silk fabrics. Then, they remove them from the Ark of the Covenant and dance with them around the whole synagogue. They are also more joyous and merrier in their houses while eating and drinking than on other days.

They then gather up all the leaves that they have had on their booths and make bonfires of joy from them on the mountain tops. For their children they also create a particular kind of joy: they throw all kinds of fruit into the street and hang all kinds of painted banners and flags made from paper or fabric on long poles; on these, written in gold letters, it says: "This is the banner for the tribe of Judah," "for Levi," "for Benjamin," with other such names

In the synagogue, they are rather merry and drink all kinds of strong drinks such as wine and brandy; so that in the synagogue itself on this festival of joy they often fight so that their blood runs. In summary, throughout the whole month there are festivals.

Chapter 24

A quarter of a year later, around the same time as Christmas is normally celebrated by us, namely 25 December, they also have a festival which they call *Kenuka*

218 Coming directly after the seven-day festival of Sukkot, Shemini Atzeret (שמיני עצרת, *šemini 'aẓeret*) is a separate, yet connected, holiday.

219 A special prayer for the fruits of the land, i.e., for rain (גשם, *gešem*), is sung on Shemini Atzeret.

220 Heb.: *Simkat Tora*, שמחת תורה, *simḥat torah*, "rejoicing of the Torah": a celebration to mark the end of the annual cycle of Torah readings in the synagogue.

Denna Fest fira de vti 8. dagar/ doch allenast efter middagarne/ och bruka vti samma dagar både handel och wandel/ samt förlusta sig med allahanda spel och *Comoedier*. De säija; at wid den åhrs tiden har deras Förfäder händt ett *Mirakel* och vnderwärck. Ty när den öfwerste Prästen Judas Machabeus/ en gång har fäcktat och stridt för deras Lära och Tempel/ hafwer den Heliga oljan warit med den öfwersta Prästens ring och Pitschafft förseglad/ hwilken Gudi til ähra vti Lamporna brinna skulle och aldrig vtslåckna; men fienden har kommit och samma olja förstördt och ohelgat/ så at allenast en liten flaska blifwit förwarad/ den fienden ei påfunnit/ hwilken ei hade kunnat brinna mer än en dag; den samma war och af öfwerste Prästen förseglad. Och än skiönt oljan ei war mehra/ har doch det *Mirakel* skedt: at hon blifwit förökad och sedan brunnit vti 8. dagar/ tils öfwersta Prästen fick tid at inwiga annan olja. Detta är orsaken hwarföre Judarna alla deße dagar vptända särskilte lius när det blifwer mörckt/ antingen af wax eller några
p. 62 [D7v] Lampor. Så länge liusen brinna/ töras de intet arbete giöra/ eller wid | något tilfälle betiena sig af dem samma sig til nytta/ vtan måste ett annat lius der til *apart* wara för handen. Sådane lius måste hwar och en vti sitt hus brinna låta/ hwilket och sker likaledes hwar afton vti Synagogan/ så länge denna Högtid warar. De sättia stora waxlius vti en staka med åtskillige rör och pipor/ giord/ som GUD Mose vti befallning gifwit hafwer den samma at giöra. Deße lius brännas på detta sättet: Första dagen ett/ andra dagen twå/ och så widare/ tils alla 8. dagarne framlidne äro; men på ottonde dagen måste de 8. lius på en gång antända: *In Summa*, de måste *in alles* hafwa 36. lius/ för vtan det liuset/ hwar med de andre vptände blifwa. Den som liusen hos dem vptänder warder kallad *Schamas* שמש det är/ en som tienar eller vptänder för de andra liusen. De 36. liusen som brinna vnder samma 8. dagar kallas/ *När Skel Kanuka*, det är/ wigde och helgade lius. Då berätta de lärde *Rabbinerna* hwar annan åtskillige gißningar vtur *Talmud* til at vttyda/ angående denna Festen חנוכה om hwilken är med det kortaste talat.

חנוכה.[221] They celebrate this festival for eight days, but only in the afternoons, and on these days, they usually trade and do business as well as make merry with all sorts of games and comedies. They say that at this time of year, a miracle and wonder occurred for their ancestors, because, when the high priest Judah Maccabee was fighting and doing battle for their faith and Temple, the holy oil, which was to burn in the lamps in honour of God and never be extinguished, had been sealed with the high priest's ring and seal. But the enemy had come and destroyed and desecrated this oil so that only a small bottle that the enemy had not discovered was left intact; it would not burn for more than a day and it was also sealed by the high priest. And even though there was no more oil, the miracle nonetheless happened: that it was increased and then burnt for eight days until the high priest had time to consecrate other oil. This is the reason why the Jews on these days light special candles, either wax or some lamps, when it becomes dark. As long as the candles are burning, they do not dare do any work or make use of them in any way, but they must have another candle at hand for this. Everyone must have such candles burning in their houses, which also happens in the same way every evening in the synagogue for as long as the holiday lasts. They place large candles in a holder made of tubes and pipes, the same that God commanded Moses to make. These candles burn in this way: on the first day one, on the second day two, and so on until all eight days have passed; but on the eighth day they must light the eight candles. In summary, they must have 36 candles *in alles*[222] in addition to the candle with which the others are lit. The one they use to light the candles is called *Schamas* שמס,[223] that is "one who serves or lights the other candles." The 36 candles that burn for these eight days are called *När Skel Kanuka*,[224] that is the "consecrated" or "blessed candles." Then the learned rabbis tell each other and interpret various conjectures from the Talmud concerning this festival חנוכה[225] about which has been very briefly written here.

221 Heb.: *Kenuka*, חנוכה, *ḥanukah*, "Hanukkah": an eight-day holiday beginning on 25 Kislev to celebrate the rededication of the Second Temple in Jerusalem. The holiday is observed by lighting candles on a nine-branched menorah.
222 Germ.: *in alles*, "in total."
223 See p. 111*n*127 in this edition for *Spec.* (Sthlm, 1732), 30.
224 Heb.: *När Skel Kanuka*, נר של חנוכה, *ner šel ḥanukah*, "Hanukkah candle."
225 Hanukkah (Heb.).

CAP. 25.

EFter denna Fest följer i ordning en annan/ den de kalla *Purim* פורים det är på *Hebræi*ska låttkastande. Denna Fest firas merendels den 11. *Martii*, til en p. 63 [D8r] åminnelse af | Konung Ahaswero och Ester/ då Haman hela Judiska slächtet vtrota och förderfwa wille/ och lät låttkasta ifrån den ena dagen til den andra/ tils han kom til *Martii* Månad/ som Judarna kalla *Ador*. Som *Hist.* beskrifwes i Esters B. 36. til at försökia om han Judarna på fall bringa kunde. Efter *Rabbinernes* mening hålles före at Moses är vti *Martii* månad död blefwen/ och derföre skulle Haman förment sig kunna Judarna vti denna månad aldeles vtrota. Denna Fest fira de allenast en half dag/ och bruka på den samma följande *Ceremonier*. Dagen förvt fasta de tils Solen nedergår/ och om aftonen gå de vti Synagogan läsandes Esters Bok/ samt giörandes sig lustige och glade. Morgonen der efter/ gå de åter vti Synagogen och läsa Esters Bok/ och töras icke äta/ förr än de hördt samma Bok sig föreläsas. Och at de fasta sker efter deras föregifwande; endast Gud til ähra och Ester til åminnelse/ som på samma dag fastat och hela Judiska slächtet frälst hafwer. När *Cantorn* läser samma Bok/ och Hamans namn nämnes/ begynna barnen med de hos sig hafwande hamrar af trä til at slå och klappa/ som de Synagogan kullslå wille; så at man icke det ringaste höra kan/ vtan då måste *Cantorn* med läsande vphöra. När läsandet til ända är/ skickar den ena den andra gåfwor och skäncker/ besynnerligen blifwer dem fattigom rundeligen gifwit/ och säija de p. 64 [D8v] det hos: Jag vpfyller la|gen/ som Gud befalt: du skal gifwa de fattige allmosor. Det är hos dem äfwen brukeligit sig at förkläda/ hålla allahanda spel och *Comœdier*, giörandes hwar och en vti sina hus sig glade och lustige. De hålla då en fri och öppen Taffel för hwem som komma kan/ och säija *Rabbinerna*, at det är en skyldighet/ och der med giöres Gudi ett wälbehag/ drickandes de sig den dagen så

Chapter 25

After this festival the next one to follow in order is the one that they call *Purim* פורים,[226] which means "casting lots" in Hebrew. This holiday is mostly celebrated on 11 March in remembrance of King Ahasuerus and Esther, when Haman wanted to annihilate and destroy the entire Jewish people, and had lots cast from the one day to the next until he arrived at the month of March, which the Jews call *Ador*,[227] as the story is described in the Book of Esther 36 to see whether he could bring the Jewish people to their downfall. According to the opinion of the rabbis, it is believed that Moses died during the month of March, and that is the reason why Haman thought that he would be able to annihilate the Jews during this month. This festival is only celebrated for half a day and usually comprises the following ceremonies. On the day before they fast until sunset,[228] and in the evening, they go to the synagogue and read the Book of Esther, and they are joyous and happy. The following morning, they go back to the synagogue and read the Book of Esther, and they dare not eat until they have heard this book read aloud. And according to their claims, fasting occurs to honour God and remember Esther who fasted on this day and saved the entire Jewish people. When the cantor reads this book and when Haman's name is mentioned, the children start banging and clapping with the wooden hammers they have brought with them as if they wanted to knock the synagogue over, so that you cannot hear anything else, and the cantor has to stop reading. When the reading has finished, they send gifts and presents to one another,[229] the poor in particular are generously provided for, and they say about this: "I am fulfilling the law that God commanded: 'Thou shalt give alms to the poor.'"[230] It is also customary for them to dress up, to perform all sorts of plays and comedies, and for each and every person in their house to make themselves happy and joyful. They have a free and open table for whoever can come, and the rabbis say that it is an obligation and by so doing they make a delight for God; and they drink

226 Heb.: *Purim*, פורים, *purim*, "(the festival of) lots". A holiday on 14 Adar to commemorate the saving of the Jewish people from Haman as told in the Book of Esther (מגילת אסתר, *megillat Ester*). The entire megillah is read aloud in the synagogue and people exchange gifts. See p. 157*n*229 in this edition for *Spec.* (Sthlm, 1732), 63.

227 Heb.: *Ador*, אדר, *adar*, "Adar": the sixth month of the civil year and the twelfth month of the religious year in the Hebrew calendar (around March in the Gregorian calendar).

228 In remembrance of Esther's fast in Esther 4:16.

229 During Purim, gifts of food and drink, called משלוח מנות, *mišloaḥ manot* (Heb.) or שלח־מנות, *shaləkh-monəs* (Yidd.), "sending of portions," are sent between family members and friends.

230 Cf. Deuteronomy 15:11.

druckne/ at de intet en gång wetta giöra åtskilnad emellan *Mardochai* wälsignelse ock Hamans förbannelse.

Huru behagelig denna deras gudstienst månde wara/ som stridet twärt emot Gudz befallning som så lyder: Du skal icke öfwerhopa tig med swalg och dryckenskap/ kan hwar ock en Christen nogsamt märckia. Detta är nu på det kortaste berättat om Judarnas *Purim* eller fastlag.

CAP. 26.

MEdan wi nu således beskådat Judarnas Festdagar/ wil jag och korteligen berätta om deras Bröllop. Judarna tro wäl/ at Äcktenskapet är af GUD insticktat och förordnadt/ hälst HERren GUD vti Paradis gifwit Evam Adam til Hustru och dem sammanwigt. Men *Rabbinerne* läggia det til/ at så snart en menniskia til werlden född warder/ skal vti Himmelen vtropat warda: *Se Pelona Gikack Et Bat Pelona*, det
p. 65 [E1r] är: Hwem den eller den menniskian til Hustru eller Äckta få skal. | När Trolofningen skal hållas/ tagas der til *Næe Manim* נאמנים eller trowärdige och beskedelige män: Och när Trolofningen bewiljad är/ vprätta de ett skriffteligit *Contract*, hwilket af samma trowärdiga män underskrifs. En af samma Mans Personer/ tager ett stycke af sina kläder vti sina händer och går til de både Trolofwade/ at de vti samma stycke med händerna taga skola; brukandes der wid deße ord: *Mekabel Kinjan* מקבל קנין det är; kiöpet är slutit. Der efter taga de twänne nya krukor och slå dem i gålfwet/ vti den Sahlen deräst Trolofningen skedd är/ med den bemärkelse; at så ogiörligit det är/ at samma krukor kunna hela warda; så omöjeligit skal det och wara/ at deras Trolofning skal blifwa om intet och tilbakas gå: fast det hos dem ganska offta ske plägar.

themselves so drunk on this day that they cannot even discern the difference between blessing Mordechai and cursing Haman.[231]

However pleasant this religious service of theirs may be, it is in conflict with God's commandment that sounds like this: "You shall not overwhelm yourself when swallowing and drinking," as each and every Christian carefully takes note of. Now has been told briefly about the Jew's Purim or Shrovetide.

Chapter 26

As we have now been looking at the Jews' festivals, I also want to talk briefly about their weddings. For sure, the Jews believe that marriage is instituted and ordained by God, not least because the Lord God had given Eve to Adam in paradise and married them. But the rabbis add that as soon as a person is born into the world, there is a proclamation in heaven: *Se Pelona Gikack Et Bat Pelona*,[232] that is "This or that person who is going to be given [this person] as wife or husband." When the engagement is to be held, *Nœe Manim* נאמנים[233] or trustworthy and humble men are consulted. And when the engagement has been granted, they draw up a written contract[234] that is signed by these same trustworthy men. One of these men takes a piece of his clothing into his hands and goes to the engaged couple so that they should take this garment with their hands, and when doing so use these words: *Mekabel Kinjan* מקבל קנין,[235] that is, "the sale is concluded." Afterwards, they take two new pots and throw them to the floor and break them in the hall where the engagement has taken place with this significance: just as impossible as it is that these pots can again become whole, so impossible is it also that their engagement shall come to nothing and be reverted – even though this often usually does happen for them.

231 The custom of drinking on Purim stems from a quotation in the Talmud attributed to the Babylonian rabbi Abba ben Joseph bar Ḥama (*c.* 280 – 352 CE, referred to as Rava): "One must drink on Purim until that person cannot distinguish between cursing Haman and blessing Mordechai" (Megillah 7b).

232 Heb.: *Se Pelona Gikack Et Bat Pelona*, זה פלוני יקח את בת פלוני, *ze peloni yikaḥ et bat peloni*, "so-and-so will take so-and-so's daughter." Cf. Bereishit Rabba 68:4.

233 Heb.: *Nœe Manim*, נאמנים, *ne'emanim*, "trustworthy," "faithful."

234 The engagement agreement (תנאים, *tena'im*) concerning the dates and costs of the wedding. It is usually agreed between the bride's parents and the groom's.

235 Heb.: *Mekabel Kinjan*, מקבל קנין, *mekabel kinyan*, "ownership is received." In order for the contract to take effect legally a symbolic transaction needs to take place. As the garment is touched, the other party is granted the engagement contract. In this way, both parties obtain a commitment from one another.

Ifrån samma Trolofning/ til den tiden då Brölloppet hållas skal/ kallas Brudgummen *Catan* eller Måg/ och Bruden *Calata* eller Sonehustru. Vnder samma Trolofningstid/ warda de fram för andra Vngkarlar mycket mer ährade och i wördning håldne. De låta icke Bruden eller Brudgummen om nattetid allena gå öfwer gatan; ty efter deras mening/ säija de: at om de äro allena/ skola de blifwa af de onda andar frestade och anfäcktade/ men är någor med dem/ skal dem intet kunna skada.

När nu tiden är inne på hwilken de skola hålla sitt Bröllop/ anställa de 7. dagar
p. 66 [E1v] för vt en dantz för vnga Personer/ och | Brudgummen gifwer Bruden efter sin förmögenhet och wilkohr några skäncker/ nemligen: En giördel af silfwer/ strumpor/ skor och andra wackra kläder.

Der är och hos dem brukeligit/ at när någon wijes/ skal Mannen hafwa sina döde kläder vppå/ dem han äfwen när han död är skal på sig hafwa. Döde kläderna bestå af en skiorta af Hållands/ eller annat fint Lärft/ med breda spetzar wid armarne: warandes giord som de nu hos oß brukelige kappråckar/ vndantagande det at hals qwalen eller linningen är helt smal. En hwit duk antingen af vll eller silke/ wid hwilken hängia på hwart hörn 8. ylle trådar/ som förr omtalt är.

Detta alt sker dagen för Brölloppet; men när *Copulationen* eller sammanwigningen ske skal/ drager Brudgummen döde kläderna vtan på de andra/ ock låter sig vti de samma wija. Deße döde kläder måste han som tilförene sagt är/ hwart åhr vppå sig hafwa/ vti Synagogan/ när Försoningsdagen är: en myßa hafwer han och/ hwilken är med guld och silfwer *Broderad*. Orsaken at han döde kläderna på sig tager är denna: At han vnder sin största glädie och medgång skal betänckia och sin dödelighet noga betrachta. *Rabbinerna* säija/ at sedan Jerusalems tempel förstördt är/ skola de ei lefwa vti stadig warande frögd och glädie/ hwilket och är en skiälig inbillning.

Dagen för Brölloppet warder en härlig måltid anrättad för Vngkarlar och
p. 67 [E2r] Jungfruur/ hwar wid | Brud och Brudgumme giöra sig ganska glade/ med dantzande och spelade/ aldenstund de vti ett annat stånd träda skola. Då sättias Brud och Brudgumme vti främsta rummet/ drickandes den/ som näst Brudgummen sitter/ honom til. Brudgummen gifwer honom handen/ och när det skiedt är/ tager han Brudgummens hand och Brudgummen omfamnar Bruden med det samma vti allas närwahro.

Om Bröllopsdagen warder en stol för Bruden ställd/ med sammet öfwerklädd/ med ett örnegått; der vppå/ sätties på bordet bränwin och Pepperkakor. Då komma först de giffta Hustrur och sättia Bruden på stolen; Sedan komma Jungfrurna/ fläta

From this engagement until when the wedding is to be held, the bridegroom is called *Catan*[236] or son-in-law and the bride is called *Calata*[237] or daughter-in-law. During this period of engagement, they are praised much more than other youngsters and held in reverence. They do not allow the bride or bridegroom to cross the street alone at night-time, because in their opinion they say that if they are alone, they will be tempted and beset by evil spirits, but if somebody is with them, then nothing will be able to harm them.

When the time approaches when they are to hold the wedding, they put on a dance for young people seven days before, and the bridegroom gives the bride some presents as far as his wealth and circumstances permit, namely: a silver belt, stockings, shoes, and other beautiful garments.

It is also their custom that when someone is to be married, the man wears his death robes,[238] that he will also wear when he dies. Death robes comprise a shirt of Dutch or other fine linen with wide points at the sleeves, made like the long coats that are common among us, except that the collar or waist is very narrow, [and] a white cloth either of wool or silk upon each corner of which hang eight woollen threads, as discussed earlier.

All this happens the day before the wedding, but when the nuptial or marriage is to take place, the bridegroom puts on the death robes over his other [clothes] and has himself wed in them. As said previously, he must wear these death robes every year in synagogue when it is the Day of Atonement. He also wears a cap that is embroidered with gold and silver. The reason that he wears death robes is this: that during moments of his greatest happiness and success, he must also reflect on and carefully contemplate his mortality. The rabbis say that since the Temple in Jerusalem has been destroyed, they ought not to live in constant joy and happiness, which is also a reasonable delusion.

The day before the wedding, a wonderful meal is prepared for the young men and women, at which the bride and bridegroom make merry with dancing and music, because they are to enter into another [marital] status. Then the bride and bridegroom are seated at the front of the room and toasted by the man sitting next to the bridegroom. The bridegroom gives him his hand and when this has happened, he takes the bridegroom's hand, and the bridegroom immediately embraces the bride in everyone's presence.

On the day of the wedding, a chair is put out for the bride, covered in velvet with a cushion. At the same time, brandy and gingerbread are placed on the table. Then the married women come first and seat the bride on the chair. Then the

---

236 Heb.: *Catan*, חתן, *ḥatan*, "bridegroom."

237 Heb.: *Calata*, כלה, *kalah*, "bride."

238 See p. 125*n*157 in this edition for *Spec.* (Sthlm, 1732), 40.

hennes hår och det åter vptaga/ siungandes vnder det samma allahanda wisor/ huru hon sig vti Äcktenskapsståndet skicka och ställa skal/ samt hwad beswårligheter hon vnder det samma hafwer at förwänta/ och siunga så länge; tils Bruden der öfwer börjar at gråta/ och detta *Continuerar* tils des deras *Rabbin* kommer tillika med de andra/ som der til *ordinerade* äro. Hwilken wid sin ankomst kastar ett silkes kläde på Brudens hufwud så at det betäcker hela ansichtet; hwilket skal betekna theras kyskhet och blygsamhet.

Förr än sielfwa wigslen går för sig/ måste hon samma dag vti en källa sig rentwaga/ än skiönt det den skarpaste kiöld och winter wara månde/ och töras de icke bada sig vti warmt watn; ja många warda der af både siuke och döde; p. 68 [E2v] jämrandes | de sig högeligen/ när de skola stå Brud/ för samma bad skul. När Bruden til samma bad gå skal/ följa henne en stor hop gamla kiäringar och påikar/ hafwandes med sig stora Mäßings-Kiätzlar/ klingandes der på med Nycklar/ häftigt ropandes: Bruden skal gå i bad! Detta bad är kringmurat/ och måste wara en rinnande källa/ derästingen inslipper/ vtan den/ som skal stå Brud. Detta bad kallas på *Hebræiska Mikve* מקוה, eller källa. När aftonen kommer warda de offenteligen på gatan *Copulerade* och sammanwigde.

CAP. 27.

CEremonierne Beträffande wid deras sammanwigande äro deße: Först warder en himmel af silke hållen öfwer Brudefolcken med 4. stänger/ hwilket sker af några närwarande vnga gåßar/ blifwandes samma wigsel gemenligen förrättad om Fredags aftonen förn de gå vti Synagogan. *Rabbinen* går främst/ der efter kommer *Cantorn* med de andra af slächten/ förandes Brudgummen vti sina Brudgums kläder/ hwar på han jemwäl hafwer sina döde kläder/ vnder samma himmel/ och ställer honom på högra handen. Wid det samma ropa gåßarne med hög röst/ *Barok Haba* ברוך הבא det är: wälsignad ware den som kommer. Här på begynner p. 69 [E3r] *Cantorn* och *Continuerar* wälsignelsen med siungande/ hwilket | sker med följande ord: *Baruk Elohenu Simen Tau Oma Sall tau, Baruk Hakatan Im Hakala.* סימן טוב

25 הבא] הבע *Spec.* (Sthlm, 1732).

unmarried women come and plait her hair and put it up while singing all kinds of songs about how she is to behave and conduct herself in marriage and what difficulties she can expect there. And they sing for a long time until it makes the bride start to cry. And this continues until the rabbi arrives with others who have been directed to [accompany him]. Upon their arrival, a silk cloth is thrown over the bride's head so that it covers her entire face, which is to symbolize her[239] chastity and modesty.

On the same day, before the actual wedding ceremony begins, she has to bathe in a spring,[240] even if it is freezing cold and wintertime. And they dare not bathe in warm water; indeed, many become ill and die from this. When they are to be brides, they lament loudly on account of this bath. When the bride is to go to this bath, a large group of old women and boys accompany her and they carry brass kettles and use keys to make them ring, shouting loudly: "The bride's on her way to the bath!" This bath is encircled by a wall and must be a running spring where no one enters except the one who is to be the bride. In Hebrew, this bath is called *Mikve* מקוה,[241] or "spring." When evening comes, they are publicly wed and married in the street.

Chapter 27

These are the ceremonies in connection with the wedding: First, a canopy of silk is held with four poles above the couple. This is done by some of the young men present and this wedding ceremony is commonly performed on a Friday evening before they go to the synagogue. The rabbi walks at the front, then comes the cantor with the other members of the family and they lead the bridegroom in his bridegroom outfit (over which he is also wearing his death robes)[242] under this canopy, and they stand him on the right-hand side. With that, the young men shout in a loud voice: *Barok Haba* ברוך הבע,[243] that is "Blessed be he who comes!" With that the cantor begins and continues to sing the blessing, which happens with the following words: *Baruk Elohenu Simen Tau Oma Sall tau, Baruk Hakatan Im*

239 In *Spec.* (Sthlm, 1732; Gbg, 1732; Sthlm, 1735), we find "theras," lit. "their."
240 See the following note in this edition for *Spec.* (Sthlm, 1732), 68.
241 Heb.: *Mikve,* מקוה, *miḳvah* or *miḳveh,* "mikvah": a bath used for ritual immersion.
242 See p. 125*n*157 in this edition for *Spec.* (Sthlm, 1732), 40.
243 Heb.: *Barok Haba,* ברוך הבא, (!)ברוך הבע, *baruch haba',* "blessed is he who comes" (Heb.).

ומזל טוב ברוך החתן עם הכלה Det är: wälsignad ware Gud! ett godt tekn och en god lycka; wälsignad ware Brudgummen och Bruden.

Här på hafwa Qwinfolcken Bruden fram vti sina Brude-kläder/ warandes hennes ansichte betäckt med en Silkesduk och föra henne under himmelen til Brudgummen/ gångandes hon sedan 3. gånger kring om honom/ och sedan ställa de henne wid wänstra sidan.

Der på tager *Rabbinen* ett glas win och giör en wälsignelse der öfwer/ gifwandes Brudgummen och Bruden der af at dricka. Sedan tager *Rabbinen* en gullring/ doch vtan någon sten/ den de kalla *Tabaat Kiduschin* טבעת קידושין det är/ en tro-ring. Denna ring gifwer han Brudgummen vti handen/ och *Rabbinen* låter Brudgummen sättia den på Brudens hand eller finger näst den minsta. *Rabbinen* säger deße orden för Brudgummen och han säger dem efter: *Häre At Mäkudeschet Libetabaat Kiduscham Kedat Mosche Vä Jsraël* הרי את מקודשת לי בטבעת קידושין כדת מושה וישראל det är; du är mig til hustru gifwen efter Mosis och Israels lag medelst denna tro-ring. Der på warder dem af de närwarande lycka och wälsignelse tilönskad.

Rabbinen tager sedan ett bref/ det de kalla *Ketuba* כתובה: det samma är på Per-
p. 70 [E3v] gament skrifwit/ hwar vtinnan vpteknadt warder/ huru många | Penningar den ena den andra tilfördt hafwer; hälst ingen Jude tager någon hustru/ vtan icke han tilförene får en wiß *Summa* penningar med henne. Det står ock vti samma bref förmält/ huru mycket han bruden i morgongåfwa gifwit hafwer/ samt om mannen skulle dö för'n hon/ huru mycket hon då på sin andehl bekomma skal. När brefwet är vpläst/ tager *Rabbinen* det samma och gifwer det åt en hustru som ledsagar Bruden/ hwilken lefwererar brefwet til henne/ förwarandes hon samma bref til sin yttermera säkerhet; Ty de hafwa ingen kyrckiobok/ hwar vti de något inskrifwa. Om någon wil weta huru gammal han är/ och hans föräldrar äro döde/ och de vti sina böcker barnets ålder ei *annoterat*, är det/ om deras föräldrar warit fattige/ swårt at igenfinna och weta. Men hafwa de warit rika/ skäncka de ett band til Synagogan vtaf linne/ med silke/ guld eller silfwer påsydt/ warandes der på Föräldrarnas namn/ och barnets/ jämte åhrtalet sömat/ när det födt är. Bandet kallas

1 ברוך] ברוף *Spec.* (Sthlm, 1732).

Hakala. סימן טוב ומזל טוב ברוך החתן עם הכלה.[244] That is, "Blessed be God! A good sign and good luck! Blessed be the bride and groom!"

With that, the womenfolk lead out the bride in her bridal outfit and her face is covered by a silk cloth [and they] lead her in under the canopy to the groom and walk her around him three times. And they stand her on the left-hand side.

With that, the rabbi takes a glass of wine and makes a blessing over it and gives it to the groom and bride to drink from. Then the rabbi takes a gold ring, but without any precious stone, which they call *Tabaat Kiduschin* טבעת קידושין,[245] that is "betrothal ring." He places this ring in the bridegroom's hand and the rabbi has the groom put it on the bride's hand or the finger next to the little one. The rabbi says these words to the bridegroom, and he repeats them: *Häre At Mäkudeschet Libetabaat Kiduscham Kedat Mosche Vä Jsraël* הרי את מקודשת לי בטבעת קידושין כדת מושה וישראל,[246] that is "With this ring you are given to me as a wife in accordance with the Law of Moses and Israel." With this, they are congratulated and wished happiness by those present.

Then the rabbi takes a letter – they call it *Ketuba* כתובה[247] – which is written on parchment, and in which is laid out how much money the one has given the other, for no Jew takes a wife unless he receives along with her a certain sum of money in advance. It also says in this letter how much he has given the bride as a morning gift,[248] and, should the man die before her, how much she will receive as her share. When the letter is read aloud, the rabbi takes it and gives it to a married woman who is accompanying the bride, who delivers the letter to her, and she keeps this letter for her additional security, as they have no parish register in which they record anything. If someone wants to know how old he is and his parents are dead and they did not note the child's age in their books, then, if their parents were poor, it is difficult to find out and know. But if they were rich, they sent a ribbon to the synagogue made of linen with silk, gold, or silver sewn into it, upon which the parents' and child's names are embroidered as well as the year

---

244 Heb.: *Baruk Elohenu Simen Tau Oma Sall tau, Baruk Hakatan Im Hakala*, סימן טוב ומזל טוב ברוך החתן עם הכלה, *siman ṭov u-mazal ṭov baruch ha-ḥatan ʿim ha-kalah*, "a good sign and congratulations to the groom and bride." Note that the Hebrew text is missing the first part of Löwe's transliteration: "*Baruk Elohenu*": ברוך אלוהנו, *baruch eloheinu*, "blessed be our Lord."

245 Heb.: *Tabaat Kiduschin*, טבעת קידושין, *ṭabaʿat ḳidušin*, "wedding ring."

246 Heb.: *Häre At Mäkudeschet Libetabaat Kiduscham Kedat Mosche Vä Jsraël*, הרי את מקודשת לי בטבעת קידושין כדת משה וישראל, *here meḳudešet li be-ṭabaʿat ḳidušin ke-dat Mošeh ve-Iśrael*, "Behold, you are consecrated to me with a wedding ring according to the religion of Moses and Israel."

247 Heb.: *Ketuba*, כתובה, *ketubah*, "marriage agreement." The contract outlines the husband's responsibilities in relation to his wife.

248 Cf. Germ. *Morgengabe*, "morning gift," "gift given by the husband to his wife on the morning after the wedding night." Similar to "dower."

på *Hebræiska Mapa.* מפה Detta band binda de omkring 5. Mosis Böcker/ som äro skrefne på Pergament/ och kunna således se/ om det 200. åhr tilbakas woro/ huru gammal en är.

Man wil nu åter komma til wigsel *Ceremonien.* När nu Bruden fått samma troskrift på Pergament/ tager *Rabbinen* åter en bägare win i högra handen/ giör en p. 71 [E4r] wälsignelse som *Continuerar* en rund tima/ kunnandes | man alla orden vti korthet ei anföra. Sedan lägges vnder Brudgummens fot ett nytt glas/ det han söndertrampar/ och har detta samma bemärkelse som krukorne/ om hwilka tilförene talat är. Wid och vnder deras *Copulerande* och sammanwigande/ bruka de ganska många facklor och der jämte allahanda lustigheter/ förandes Brudgummen dit Bruden boende är. När de äro hemkomne warder för Brudgummen och Bruden en kokad höna med såppan föresatt/ den de allena förtära skola/ emedan de hela den dagen/ på hwilken de skola *Copuleras*, fastande wara månde. Orsaken hwarföre dem en höna at äta gifwen warder/ är denna: At de som en höna skola fruchtsamme wara. När detta skedt är/ gifwes de andra Bröllopsgästerne tilkänna/ at de sig strax infinna skola/ och då skal måltiden hållas. Man- och Qwinfolcken sättias hwar för sig wid särskilte bord/ sittiandes Brudgummen i främsta rummet hos Manfolcken och Bruden hos Qwinfolcken. Vnder måltiden håller Brudgummen/ om han *studerad* är/ en *Oration*; och om han det icke kan; måste han til de andra *studerade* Judar och vnga Personer böta några kannor win/ då sedan en af dem *Orationen* förrättar. Brudgummen skäncker då til vngkarlarne Silkes Näsdukar/ och til Jungfrurne gifwer han röda band; doch komma de ogifta icke at sittia wid samma bord som de giffte; vtan vngkarlar och Jungfrur hafwa ett bord för sig p. 72 [E4v] sielfwa. | När Måltiden ändad är/ kommer *Tracteuren*, har en spira i handen med röda band bebunden/ ställer sig på en stol och ropar öfwerliudt vt/ hwad Bröllopsgästerne til Brudefolcken gifwa och skänckia wilja. Då räcker hwar och en efter sin förmögenhet sin skänck fram til *Tracteuren*, som skrifwer dem alla vp och huru mycket de gifwa. Dagen der efter lefwererar han altsammans Brudgummen i händer.

När måltiden ändad är/ och de efter wahnligheten wilja der på giöra bön/ bäres en tallrick omkring för de fattige/ hwilket och sker vti alla *Collationer* och samqwäm. Der på föra de Bruden til sängs/ warandes de andre hela natten vppe/ förlustandes sig således vti 3. dagar och nätter med dantzande och spelande/ och föres Brudgummen hwar qwäll til Bruden; men får icke nalkas til henne för än tredie natten; anförandes de en orsak der til af Tobie *Historia.* Skulle så hända/ at Bruden hafwer den *Passion*, som andra qwinnor hafwa/ får han icke liggia/ sittia

when he was born. The ribbon is called in Hebrew *Mapa* מפה.[249] They tie this ribbon around the Pentateuch, which is written on parchment, and so it can be seen – even if it is two hundred years ago – how old one is.

We shall now return to the wedding ceremony. When the bride has received this marriage document on parchment, the rabbi takes another glass of wine in his right hand, makes a blessing that lasts a good hour, and one cannot quote all the words concisely. Then, a new glass is placed under the bridegroom's foot. He tramples it underfoot and this has the same meaning as the pots mentioned earlier.[250] At and during their nuptial or wedding they use a great many torches. And along with all sorts of jesting, they lead the groom and bride to where they are to live. When they have arrived home, boiled chicken soup is provided, which they alone are to consume, as they were to fast for the whole day of their wedding. The reason that they are given a chicken to eat is this: that they should be fertile like a chicken. When this has happened, the other wedding guests are told that they are to show up right away and then the dinner can be served. Men and women are seated separately at different tables, [with] the bridegroom sitting in front with the men and the bride with the women. During the dinner, the bridegroom, if he is learned, gives a speech; and if he is not able to do so, then he must pay a fee of some jugs of wine to the other learned Jews and young people so that one of them then holds the speech. The bridegroom then presents silk handkerchiefs to the unmarried men and gives red ribbons to the unmarried women. However, those who are unmarried do not sit at the same table as those who are married; rather, unmarried men and unmarried women have a table of their own. When the dinner has finished, the master of ceremonies (*traiteur*) comes, carries a mace with a red ribbon attached in his hand, stands on a chair, and very loudly shouts out what the wedding guests will give and present to the bridal couple. Then, in accordance with their means, every one of them hands their present over to the master of ceremonies who notes them all down and how much they are giving. The following day he hands it all over to the bridegroom.

When the dinner has finished, and, as is their custom, they want to say their prayers afterwards, a plate for the poor is passed around; this also happens at all gatherings and get-togethers. Then they lead the bride to bed, while the others are up all night, entertaining themselves with dancing and music for three days and nights, and each evening the groom is led to the bride, but he may not approach her until the third night; the reason for which they say is in the story of Tobit. Should it so happen that the bride has the "passion," that other women have [i.e.,

249 Heb.: *Mapa*, מפה, *mapah*, "(Torah) binder."
250 See *Spec.* (Sthlm, 1732), 65:11–17 (this edition 158:18–22).

eller röra wid henne. Besinnes hon ei warit en ren Jungfru/ får han strax sig wid henne skilja.

Tager någor en änckia/ är deras Bröllop ganska tyst/ och få icke hafwa något *Instrument* at spela med; men lika *Ceremonier* warda wid deras wigsel brukade/ vtan allenast det; at Brudgummen får första natten komma i säng med Bruden/ och sker sammaledes med fattige och rike. Fast det sker offta at Brudgummen p. 73 [E5r] nalkas Bruden första | natten. Om Brudgummen der med beträdes måste han några Riksdahler til Synagogan eller de fattige vtgifwa.

Om Sabbathen der efter blifwer Brudgummen vpkallad vti *Cathedren*, 5. Mosis Böcker tagas åt honom vhr Arcken/ skrifne på *Pergament*, och kringweklade med kåstbaraste tyg/ jämte en Silfwer-Crona med ädla stenar besatt/ hwar wid en griffel af silfwer med en silfwerplåt är på kiädiorna hängandes. Sedan läsa de ett *Capitel* vtaf 5. Mosis Böcker/ och måste han derföre gifwa några Riksdahler til Synagogan och 5. til *Rabbinen*. Är Brudgummen *studerad* gifwer *Rabbinen* honom en större *Character* och ähre-tittel; ty hos dem gifwa *Rabbinerna* vt *Characterer*, hafwandes han derföre 10. men *Cantorn* en Riksdahler. De hafwa wäl wid sina Bröllop många andra vptog och äfwentyr/ dem man/ at Läsaren ei förtörnas må/ och Vngdommen förargas/ vtesluta wil. Detta ware om Judarnas Bröllop och des beskaffenhet få kortteligen handlat och talat.

CAP. 28.

FRån Judarnas Bröllop och *Copulerande* wil man skrida til deras ächtenskaps skilnad. Hos dem är det brukeligit/ för ringa orsakers skull skilja sig från sina hustrur. Ty 1. om en Man finner en främmande karl ståendes eller sittiandes vti p. 74 [E5v] någon Cammare med deß | hustru allena/ och han den samma ei känner/ samt flere Personer ei tilstädes äro/ hafwer han frihet at skiljas ifrån henne. 2. Om någon hustru/ när hon/ som andra qwinnor hafwa månde/ lägger sig hos sin man/ omgås/ äter och dricker med honom/ eller sitter med honom på samma stol/ och säger ei sin man til/ få de äfwen skiljas/ och warda de barnen som wid samma tilfälle aflade blifwa/ kallade *Mamser Ben Hanida* ממזר בן הנידה; det är ett förachtadt barn/ som skal vtur Judiska församblingen vtrotas. 3. När en Man inga barn eller arfwingar med sin hustru hafwa kan/ står det honom fritt om han behagar/ henne at öfwergifwa. 4. Är det honom och efterlåtit/ om hon löper vt och

21 orsakers] orsaker *Spec.* (Sthlm, 1732; Gbg, 1732; Sthlm, 1735).

she is menstruating], then he may not lie with her, sit by her, or touch her. If it is seen that she is not a virgin, then he may divorce her straightaway.

If someone marries a widow, then their wedding is quite quiet and there may not be any instruments to play music on. But otherwise, similar ceremonies are usual at their wedding, apart from this: on the first night the groom may go to bed with his bride. And the same thing happens for poor and rich alike. Although it often happens that the groom approaches the bride on the first night. If the groom is caught doing so, then he must pay some riksdaler to the synagogue or to the poor.

On the following Sabbath, the bridegroom is called to the pulpit (*cathedra*), and he is given the Pentateuch from the ark, written on parchment, and wrapped in expensive cloth, and with a silver crown beset with precious stones, upon which hangs a silver stylus[251] with silverplate on chains. Then they read a chapter from the Pentateuch and for this he must give some riksdaler to the synagogue and five to the rabbi. If the bridegroom is learned, the rabbi gives him a higher rank and honorary title, because among them the rabbis give out ranks. For this, the rabbi takes ten riksdaler and the cantor one. They also have many other escapades and capers at their weddings, which in order not to enrage the reader and anger the young, I shall leave out. So was briefly treated and spoken about the Jews' weddings and their nature.

Chapter 28

And from the Jews' wedding and union we move on to their marital divorce. It is their habit to divorce their wives for bad reasons: (1) If a husband finds a strange man standing or sitting alone in a room with his wife, and he does not know him, and other people are not present, then he is free to divorce her. (2) If any wife, when she is in the same way as other women might be [i.e., she is menstruating], lies with her husband, socializes, eats, and drinks with him, or sits with him on the same chair, and does not tell her husband [that she is menstruating], they may also divorce, and the children who are conceived under such circumstances are called *Mamser Ben Hanida* ממזר בן הנידה;[252] that is "a despised child who shall be eradicated from the Jewish congregation." (3) When a man is unable to have any children or heirs with his wife, then he is free – should it be pleasing to him – to abandon her. (4) It is also permitted for him to do so if she runs away and does not remain

251 Löwe's "griffel" [stylus] must be here referring to the Torah pointer (יד, *yad*).

252 Heb.: *Mamser Ben Hanida*, ממזר בן הנידה, *mamzer ben ha-nidah*, "illegitimate son of an impure woman."

icke blifwer hemma i huset. 5. Om hustrun något mannen owetterligen borttager och förstörer. 6. När hon bedrifwer hor med någon annan/ hwilket hos dem ganska sällan ske plägar/ och hålles det för den aldrastörsta skam. 7. Om hon icke är någon god hushållerska/ vtan mansens goda förslöser och ei är renlig vti sina syßlor eller eljest ohyggelig: *In Summa*; för åtskillige andra ringa saker kan en man skilja sig ifrån en hustru och en hustru ifrån sin man.

Skilnaden dem emellan sker på följande sätt: 1. vti den staden de åtskiljas skola/ skal wara 3. strömmar af åtskillige namn/ skolandes de äfwen flyta tilsammans. *Rabbinen* skrifwer åt henne ett skiljo-bref på Pergament vti andra lärda Personers
p. 75 [E6r] närwah|ro; warandes der på 12. rader skrifne/ och skola alla rader och bokstäfwer wara lika; ty än skiönt han det samma 10. resor skrifwit/ och de ei äro lika/ så skal han det å nyo renskrifwa. Wid skilnaden skola de wara vti ett rum/ hwar på äro twänne dörar; mannen står wid den ena och hustrun wid den andra. Han tager skiljobrefwet/ och hon skal stå med vplyfta händer/ och när han det til henne kastar/ skal hon det emottaga. Skulle så hända at hon ei kan brefwet emottaga/ vtan det faller ned på gålfwet/ så skal det åter renskrifwas/ tils des hon en gång/ kan det med händerna omfatta. Vti detta skiljobref/ stå deße orden: Du är från mig bortdrifwen/ du är från mig bortskickad; Jag är intet din man/ du är icke min hustru/ du är lösgifwen at taga tig til man ehwem du wil/ med annat mera/ som der wid brukeligit är. Der på går han vt igenom den ena dörren/ och hon igenom den andra/ och så äro de ifrån hwar annan skilde. Det sker och offta at de hwar annan igen begiära/ men det är dem icke efter låtit. När nu skillnaden skedd är/ måste mannen henne så många penningar och annor egendom/ som hon med sig/ då hon med honom kom tilsamman/ haft hafwer/ strax återlefwerera. Men om hustrun wil skiljas ifrån mannen/ så gifwer han henne intet något tilbakas/ af det hon med sig til honom hafwer haft/ derföre han henne under deras sammanlefnad
p. 76 [E6v] födt och försörgt hafwer. Om det hända skulle | at de hafwa barn sins emellan/ tager han gåssarna och hon flickorne; men hafwa de vdda/ så tager han största delen. Detta ware nog om Judarnas skiljobref/ som de kalla *Get*.

at home in their house. (5) If the wife unbeknown to her husband takes something from him and destroys it. (6) When she commits adultery with another, which only very rarely occurs among them and is considered the greatest dishonour of all. (7) If she is not a good housekeeper but wastes her husband's assets and is not clean in performing her chores or is otherwise unpleasant. In summary, a husband may divorce his wife or a wife her husband for several other trifling reasons.

Their divorce happens in the following manner: (1) In the town where they are to be divorced, there must be three streams with different names that also flow into one another.[253] The rabbi writes a letter of divorce[254] on parchment to her in the presence of other learned people; twelve lines are written on this, and all the lines and letters must be alike, because even if he has written the same thing ten times, and they are not alike, then he must re-write it again from scratch. For the divorce, they must be present in one room in which there are two doors; the husband stands by the one and the wife by the other. He takes the letter of divorce, and she is to stand with her hands in the air, and when he throws it to her, she is to catch it. If it so happens that she does not catch the letter, but instead it falls to the floor, then it is to be re-written until she is able to catch it with her hands. These words are written in the letter of divorce: "You are driven away from me. You are sent away from me. I am not your husband. You are not my wife. You are set free to take whom you will as your husband," with other further things that are their custom. Upon this he walks out through the one door, and she through the other, and then they are divorced from each other. It also often happens that they desire each other again, but that is not permitted for them. When the divorce has taken place, the man must immediately hand over to her as much money and other property as she had when she married him. However, if the wife wishes to divorce her husband, then he does not return to her any of the things that she brought him, as he has fed and provided for her during their life together. If it should so happen that they have children together, he takes the boys and she the girls; but if they have an unequal number, then he takes most of them. This is enough on the subject of the Jews' letter of divorce which they call a *Get*.[255]

253 This is a very strange sentence and may be the result of Löwe having misunderstood his source. The three "streams" ("strömmar") might be referring to a court comprising three judges ("domare"). The three streams are also mentioned in the description of halitzah (chapter 29), a ritual that must also be performed before a court of three.

254 See the following note in this edition for *Spec.* (Sthlm, 1732), 76.

255 Aram.: *Get*, גט, *geṭ*. A get is the official document that effectuates a divorce and frees the woman to remarry.

CAP. 29.

NU wil man handla om dem/ som inga barn efter sig lemnat hafwa. Dermed är hos dem så beskaffat: Enckian får intet giffta sig/ vtan hon först skal taga *Kelitza* חליצה det är afdragning. Detta måste ske på samma sätt som förr sagt är; at 3. strömmar skola wara vti samma stad. Enckian går til *Rabbinen* tillika med deß swåger/ och är en ansenlig hop folck derstädes församlade/ säijandes: Min man är blefwen död och inga barn efter sig lemnat. Nu är min Swåger närwarande; ty beder jag/ at han må sinom Broder säd vpwäckia/ eljest wil jeg hafwa *Kelitza*. Swågern tager vppå sig en sko på wänstra foten. Skon är rund giord med en såla/ vtan någon klack. På samma sko sitter bak på en lång rem/ och der spännen sittia skola/ är en liten rem. Den långa remmen lindar han 5. *a* 6. gånger omkring benet. Fram til binder han igen med twenne knutar/ dem änckian med tänderna vplösa skal. Sedan drager hon skon af honom/ och när det skedt är/ kastar han skon öfwer hufwudet och hon p. 77 [E7r] gifwer honom den samma strax igen. Således sker det 3. gånger. Der | på begynna alla närwarande med hög röst at ropa: *Kalutz Nal*, חלוץ נעל 3. gånger/ det är: skon är afdragen. Sedan går hon vti allas närwahro til honom och spåttar honom 3. gånger vti ansichtet/ säijandes: En sådan som ei sinom Broder säd vpwäckia wil/ skal icke wara vti Israel. Om han af henne *Prætenderar* och påstår/ måste hon gifwa honom en wiß *Summa* penningar; Men wil han ei gifwa henne *Kelitza*, så får hon ei giffta sig. Nog om detta.

Chapter 29

Now, we will deal with those who have not left any children behind. This is how it is arranged for them: The widow may not marry unless she first performs *Kelitza* חליצה,[256] that is "removal." This must happen as has previously been described: that there must be three streams in the same place.[257] The widow goes to the rabbi together with her brother-in-law and a considerable crowd of people who are gathered there and says: "My husband has died and left no children. Now my brother-in-law is present, so I ask that he may awaken his seed unto my brother; otherwise, I wish to have *Kelitza.*" The brother-in-law puts on a shoe on his left foot.[258] The shoe is made round with a sole but no heel. On the back of this shoe is a long strap and where the buckle should be, there is a small strap. He winds the long strap five to six times around his leg. At the front [of the shoe] he ties it with two knots which the widow is to undo with her teeth.[259] Then she pulls the shoe off him and when this has happened, she throws it over her head and straightaway gives it back to him. This happens three times, upon which all those present begin to shout with a loud voice: "*Kalutz Nal*, חלוץ נעל"[260] three times; that is, "the shoe is pulled off." Then, in the presence of everyone, she walks up to him and spits in his face[261] three times and says, "Such a [man] who will not awaken his seed unto his brother is not part of Israel." If he makes a claim or demand of her, then she must give him a certain sum of money. But if he will not give her *Kelitza*, then she may not marry. Enough about this.

---

256 Heb.: *Kelitza*, חליצה, *ḥaliẓah*, "pulling off, removal, extraction": the ritualized process by which a widow and her brother-in-law can avoid the requirement to enter a levirate marriage (יבום, *yibum*). Ḥaliẓah frees the woman to marry whomever she wishes. The process is described in Deuteronomy 25:5–10 and expanded in the Talmud and commentaries (see, e.g., the Talmudic tractate Yevamot). It involves the widow having to remove a shoe from her brother-in-law's foot and spitting on the floor. Löwe's description of the ceremony contains several practices not prescribed by law.

257 See p. 171*n*253 in this edition for *Spec.* (Sthlm, 1732), 74.

258 In fact, the shoe is usually placed upon the right foot.

259 In reality, the widow undoes the strap with her right hand. The scene as described by Löwe is not in accordance with the precepts of law. It may be an attempt on his part to make the *ḥaliẓah* ceremony seem comical or ridiculous.

260 Heb.: *Kalutz Nal*, חלוץ נעל, *ḥaluẓ na'al*, "shoe [is] removed."

261 During the *ḥaliẓah* ceremony, the widow spits on the floor in front of her brother-in-law, not in his face.

CAP. 30.

HÄr wid bör man ei förbigå at något handla om Judarnas *Ceremonier*, när de skola gå til bordß/ eller äta. Ingen Jude får gå til bordz förr än han twättat sina händer/ och då läsa de denna wälsignelsen/ säijandes: Wälsignad ware GUD/ som befalt oß twätta wåra händer; samt läsa den 23. Psalmen HErren är min Herde/ mig skal intet fattas *etc.* Brödet tager han med alle 10. fingrarne/ och den wälsignelsen som giöres öfwer brödet/ består af 10. ord/ nämligen *Bark Ata, Jehovah Elohenu Mälek Haolam Hamotzi Läkem Min* Det är: wälsignad ware wår GUD som låter wäxa bröd på jorden; warandes de äfwen förbundne at gifwa de fattige med sig när de hålla sina måltider och när de ätit/ skola de äfwen giöra wälsignelse. Flere *Ceremonier* | p. 78 [E7v] äro hos dem vnder eller wid måltiden intet brukelige/ hwilka at anföra nödigt synes.

CAP. 31.

HÄr wid håller jag ei för onödigt at berätta om Judarnas nähringsmedel/ dem de nu för tiden bruka månde/ så mycket mig bekant och witterligit är. De Judar äro ganska få/ som hafwa något at så eller vpskära; vtan de föda sig merendels med handel och wandel: hållandes det för ingen synd/ hwad orätt de en Christen giöra kunna. Vti Pohlen *arrendera* de merendels krogar och wärdshus. Gifwas och der af Judar allehanda handtwärkare/ vndantagandes grofsmeder. Vti Tyskland försörja de sig med Boskaps handel och penningars vtlånande åt de Christne. De Christne warda af dem gräseligen bedragne/ och sker detta på sådant sätt: de låta af gemena man/ som ei skrifwa kunna/ gifwa sig *Obligationer*; warandes samma *Obligationer* med Siffror skrefne; hwar vnder gemene man måste sina Bomärcken sättia. Af samma Siffror giöra Judarna sedermera större tahl och *Summa*: gå sedan der med til öfwerheten och låta samma *Summa* vtfordra och vtpanta. I Böhmen/ Mährn/ Schlesien/ Österrike och Ungern/ handla de merendels med allahanda kramwahror/ med *Wexel Cours*, med gull och silfwer; *Summa*, alt hwad de skola lefwa | p. 79 [E8r] vtaf/ hafwa de af de Christne/ och doch warda de Christne af dem så högeligen hatade och bedragne.

---

5 *etc.*] ꝛc *Spec.* (Sthlm, 1732). *The* et *is abbreviated by an* r-rotunda *rather than the ampersand used in almost all other cases. Cf. 17:18 (this edition 92:19), 26:14 (104:15), and 94:2 (192:15).* | **19** gräseligen] gråseligen *Spec.* (Sthlm, 1732)*;* gräseligen *Spec.* (Gbg, 1732; Sthlm, 1735).

Chapter 30

We ought not here to pass by dealing with the Jews' ceremonies when they are to go to table or eat. No Jew may go to table before he has washed his hands and then they read this blessing and say, "Blessed are you, God, who has commanded us to wash our hands," and reads Psalm 23, "The Lord is my shepherd, I shall not want, etc." He takes the bread with all ten fingers and the blessing that is made over the bread comprises ten words, namely: "*Bark Ata, Jehovah Elohenu Mälek Haolam Hamotzi Läkem Min*," that is, "Blessed are you our God who lets the bread grow upon the earth."[262] They are also obliged to take the poor with them when they have their meals. And when they have eaten, they also perform a blessing. There are no more ceremonies during or at mealtimes that are customary among them and deemed necessary to describe.

Chapter 31

I do not consider it unnecessary here to talk about the Jews' foodstuffs, that they use nowadays, in as far as it is familiar and known to me. Those Jews are few in number who have something to sow and reap, but for the most part they feed themselves through trading and commerce; they do not consider it a sin to commit whatever injustice they can towards a Christian. In Poland, they lease out the majority of taverns and inns. Jews also become all kinds of craftsmen, except blacksmiths, there. In Germany they provide for themselves by means of trading livestock and lending money to Christians. The Christians are cheated terribly by them, and this happens like this: they have a simple fellow who is unable to write issue himself promissory notes, these same promissory notes are written with figures and under which the simple man is to place his insignia. The Jews subsequently make these same figures into bigger numbers and total; they then take it to the authorities and have this total demanded and collected. In Bohemia, Moravia, Silesia, Austria, and Hungary they mainly trade in all kinds of small wares, with exchanging currency, with gold and silver. In summary, everything that they make a living from, they have from the Christians, and yet the Christians are so greatly hated and deceived by them.

---

262 Löwe has transliterated and translated this blessing incorrectly. It should read: ברוך אתה י-י אלהינו מלך העולם המוציא לחם מן הארץ, *baruch ata adonai yehovah/eloheinu melech ha-'olam hamoẓi leḥem min ha-areẓ*, "Blessed are You, Lord our God, King of the Universe, who brings forth bread from the earth."

CAP. 32.

ORsaken hwarföre Judarne sig öfwer de Christne så högeligen förarga/ är förnämligast stridigheten vti läran. När I Christne/ säija the: hafwen den rätta och sanna *Religionen*, hwarföre äro så många twistigheter vti Eder *Religion*, och den ena Christna förachtar den andra/ kallandes hwar annan kättare/ med mera? De Catholiske säija sig hafwa den rätta *Religionen*, de Lutherske/ *Reformerade*, Qwäkerne/ eller de så kallade Wederdöpare och flera andra/ säija och påstå äfwen det samma/ och kalla sig alla Christne/ talandes doch den ena emot den andra. Men Judarna förgäta sig sielfwa; påminnandes sig icke/ at de vti sin *Religion*, större twist och oenighet hafwa månde. De Pålska Judarna komma icke öfwerens med de Tyska; ty de Pålska äta intet det smör eller bröd/ som en Christen handterat och bakat hafwer: the bära ei eller de kläder/ som en Christen Skräddare sydt eller förfärdigat hafwer. De hafwa och andra bud/ seder och böner vti sina Synagogor än de Tyska Judarne. Der emot är det de Tyska Judarne lofgifwit at deße saker p. 80 [E8v] bruka och äta/ som de Pålska förbudit är. De | Portugisiske Judar/ hafwa hwarcken gemenskap eller vmgänge med de Tyska eller Pålske/ och äta icke hwad de andra Judarna kokat eller tilredt hafwa/ och så *vice versa*. Icke heller ingå de äckenskap med hwar annan. Hafwandes de en *Sect* ibland sig/ den ingen ehrkänna wil/ nemligen de *Caraiti*ska Judarna/ dem de kalla *Caraim*, hwilka hafwa helt åtskilda *Ceremonier* ifrån de andra. Så är och tilgår det äfwen hos de Turkiske. Det är och än i dag en wiß *Sect* som kallas *Sadekim*, och en som kallas *Cassidim*, warandes hos dem flere *Secter*, än hos de Christne; wore fördenskul alt för widlyftigt at om dem alla skrifwa och handla.

Jag wil allenast anföra en sak som hos Judarna *passerat* och förelupit/ hwilket jag sielf mins och på mitt egit samwete/ wet at det vti sanning skedt är. I en stad hwilken är belagen vti landskapet Mährn/ som kallas *Prosnitz*, war en man ibland Judarne/ den de på *Hebræ*iska kallade *Rabbi Löf Hanavi* רבי לוי הנביא hwilket

16 äckenskap] Ecktenskap *Spec.* (Gbg, 1732; Sthlm, 1735).

Chapter 32

The reason why the Jews are so very angry with the Christians is mainly due to the conflict in teaching. "If you Christians," they say, "have the right and true religion, why are there so many disputes in your religion, and why does the one Christian despise the other, calling each other a heretic and so on? The Catholics say that they have the right religion, the Lutherans, Reformed, Quakers, or the so-called Anabaptists[263] and many more say and claim the same thing, too, and they all call themselves Christians, yet the one speaks against the other!" But the Jews forget about themselves, and do not recall that they have greater disputes and disagreements in their religion. The Polish Jews do not agree with the German ones, because the Polish ones do not eat the butter or bread that a Christian has handled and baked; nor do they wear the clothes that a Christian tailor has sewn or made. They also have other commandments, customs, and prayers in their synagogues than the German Jews. On the contrary, it is lawful for the German Jews to use and eat these things that are forbidden to the Polish ones. The Portuguese Jews have neither a connection to nor association with the German or Polish ones, and do not eat what these other Jews have cooked or prepared, and likewise vice versa. Nor do they enter into marriage with one another. They have a sect among themselves that no one wants to recognize, namely the Karaites, the Jews called them *Caraim*,[264] who have completely separate ceremonies from one another. This is also how it is and is done among the Turkish [Jews]. There is also today a certain sect that is called *Sadekim*,[265] and one that is called *Cassidim*,[266] and so there are more sects among them than among the Christians. For this reason, it would be far too much to write about and deal with them all.

I only want to talk about one issue that has happened and taken place among the Jews, which I myself remember and upon my conscience know to have truly happened. In a town that is called Proßnitz [Prostějov][267] and that is located in Moravia, there was among the Jews a man whom they in Hebrew called *Rabbi Löf*

263 Löwe's "Wederdöpare" is a now archaic term for Anabaptists (Germ. *Wiedertäufer*).
264 Heb.: *Caraim*, קראים, *ḳara'im*, "Karaites." For Karaite Jews all the commandments that God gave to Moses are recorded in the the written Torah. Unlike in Rabbinic Judaism, Karaite Jews do not follow the teachings of the Oral Law (Talmud and Midrash).
265 Heb.: *Sadekim*, צדיקים, *ẓadiḳim*, "Tzadikim." Tzadikim are men who are believed to have achieved particular holiness and piety.
266 Heb.: *Cassidim*, חסידים, *ḥasidim*, "Hassidim." Followers of Hasidic Judaism, a spiritual revival movement that draws heavily on Lurianic kabbalah and has roots in western Ukraine. It spread rapidly throughout Eastern Europe in the eighteenth century.
267 Prostějov, "Prosnitz" (Germ. Proßnitz), is a city in Moravia.

betyder en Prophet. Den samma inbillade Judarne/ at han skulle alla dagar tala med *Schäkina* שכינה eller Gudz Anda/ och weta alt hwad som i himmelen skedde. Han sade och til Judarne at de bot och bättring giöra skulle/ säijandes: den tid förhanden wara/ på hwilken *Messias* komma skulle. De kallade honom *Navi* נביא p. 81 [F1r] eller en Prophet. Alla Judarne sände sina barn | til honom och lät wälsigna dem. Han lade sina händer på deras hufwud lika såsom Jacob på sin dödssäng; warandes Judarne aldeles vti den inbilningen/ at GUD dem en Prophet vpwäckt hade vtaf deras bröder/ den de höra skulle/ som det står vti 5:te Mosis Boks 18. *v.* 15. Ja/ jag har ock sielf warit med och låtit lägga händerna på mitt hufwud/ efter min Faders befallning/ den jag här vtinnan åtlyda måste. En tid der efter/ märckte Judarna hans bedrageri/ begärade af honom/ at han skulle wisa dem ett tekn/ eller låta dem se något vnder/ om det i sanning wore/ at han med GUD dageligen talade; hwilket han ock lofwade. Han satte dem en wiß tid före/ när det ske skulle/ doch med det förbehåll; at ingen af gemene man skulle vti samma rum inkomma/ vtan vteståendes blifwa/ och endast *Rabbinerna* af Arons slächte skulle få ingå/ men de andra som ei rene woro/ skulle ei få på samma heliga rum träda. Han wille och der frammanföre en hwit förlåt hänga låta/ skulle de då och få höra/ hwad GUD med honom talandes wordo/ samt huru han sig wiste vti dunder och eld. Alt detta skulle ske vnder stillatigande och skulle det ringaste wid förlåten icke röras/ hälst om någon der wid röra skulle/ worde de lika som wid Sinai Berg dödade och p. 82 [F1v] ihälslagne. Efter samma *Rabbins* befallning tilreddes en stor sahl/ och | hängdes den hwita förlåten derföre; de andra *Rabbinerne* twättade och helgade sig. När nu denna bedragaren kom gångandes/ föllo de alla på sina ansichten. Då han en liten stund vti Sahlen warit/ hafwer han bak om samma förlåt hafft fnyske vti en dosa liggiandes/ hwilket hafwer luft hafft/ at elden ei skulle vtsläckas/ samt krut/ hwilket ingen smäll af sig gifwa månde/ vtan allenast en *Flam* och låga. Då mente denna bedragaren at de närwarande tänckia skulle/ det GUD sig för honom vti samma eld wisat hade/ förwände så sin röst/ gifwandes sielf både tal och swar/ så at de andre tänckia skulle det han med GUD talade. Sahlen blef der wid full med rök och stanck af krutet. Då kunde de förstå hans bedrägeri/ och kastade samma

Hanavi, רבי לוי הנביא,[268] which means "a prophet." This man made the Jews believe that every day he spoke to *Schäkina*, שכינה,[269] or "God's spirit," and knew everything about what was happening in heaven. He also said to the Jews that they should perform penance and repentance, and he said that the time was nigh when the Messiah was to come. They called him *Navi*, נביא,[270] or a "prophet." All the Jews sent their children to him and had them blessed. He placed his hands on their heads, like Jacob on his deathbed; the Jews were completely convinced that God had awoken a prophet from among their brothers, whom they should listen to, as it is written in Deuteronomy 18:15.[271] Yes, I myself have also been there and, upon my father's orders (which in this respect I had to obey), had his hands placed upon my head. Sometime later, the Jews noticed his deceit, demanded from him that he show them a sign or let them see a miracle whether it was true that he spoke to God daily, which he also promised to do. He told them a certain time when it would happen, but on the condition that no ordinary men were to enter the room but were to remain standing outside, and only the rabbis of the house of Aaron would be allowed to enter, but the others, who were not pure, should not step into this holy room. He would also have a white curtain hanging in front of himself, but they would also get to hear what God was talking to him about as well as how he showed himself in thunder and lightning. All this was to happen in silence and the curtain should not be touched in the slightest: were someone to touch it, they would be killed and struck down just like at Mount Sinai. In accordance with this rabbi's orders a great hall was prepared, and the white curtain was hung in front of it. The other rabbis washed and blessed themselves. When this trickster entered, they all fell upon their faces. When he had been in the hall a short while, behind this curtain he had tinder fungus [i.e., amadou] lying in a tin that had been exposed to the air, so the fire would not be extinguished, as well as gunpowder which did not give off any bang but just a flame and fire. So, this trickster, thinking that those present would believe that God had shown himself to him in this very fire, disguised his voice giving himself both the statements and replies, so that the others would think that he was talking to God. The hall was filled with smoke and

268 Heb.: *Rabbi Löf Hanavi*, רבי לוי הנביא, *rabi Levi ha-navi'*, "Rabbi Löb the Prophet." The Sabbatian prophet Judah Leib ben Jacob Holleschau (*c.* 1670–1730), who settled in Prostějov after his marriage. See Gotthard Deutsch and Henry Malter, "Prossnitz, Löbele (Prosṭiẓ)," *The Jewish Encyclopedia*, vol. 10, ed. Isidore Singer et al. (New York: Funk & Wagnalls, 1901–06), 225, col. b.

269 Heb.: *Schäkina*, שכינה, *šechinah*, "dwelling." The Shechinah is the dwelling of the presence of God and refers to places where one is nearer to God. Particularly in the Talmud, it can refer to the feminine attributes of the divine presence.

270 Heb.: *Navi*, נביא, *navi*, "prophet."

271 Deuteronomy 18:15: "The Lord thy God will raise up unto thee a Prophet from the midst of thee, of thy brethren, like unto me; unto him ye shall hearken."

man vti boijor och fängelse/ förbannandes och straffandes honom; måste han således sedan gå vti ett rum och giöra bot och bättring; hafwandes sedermera innom en månad der efter i fängelset blifwit död/ och icke på någon Kyrckioplatz begrafwen. Flere andra sådane bedragare kunde man wäl anföra; men låter med denna allenast bestå; kunnandes hwar och en Christen nogsamt skönja/ huru Judarne af sine egne bedragne warda/ och äro doch så hårdnackade/ at de sig öfwer de Christne förarga/ tagandes icke sielfwa bielckan vtur sitt egit öga. |

p. 83 [F2r] CAP. 33.

JUdarnas *Politie* eller *Justitie* följer nu i ordning at betracktas/ warandes den samma sålunda inrättad: När någon sig emot GUD swårligen försyndat/ samt brutit emot werldzlig lag/ stämpla de at han genom förgifft blifwer af daga tagen/ eller på ett annat sätt hemligen dödad/ kunnandes de det samma behändigt fördölja och intet angifwa hos den Christeliga Öfwerheten/ på hwad ort det ock wara må. Ty sedan Templet blef förstördt/ hafwa de sina *Privilegier* och friheter förlorat/ och hafwa ingen macht/ til döden någon at dömma/ gifwandes förden-skull de det ei an hos den Christeliga Öfwerheten. Om någon bedrifwer dubbelt hor/ hålles det för den aldrastörsta synd/ och warda de som det bedrifwa således straffade: Den som der til största orsaken wara månde han blifwer ifrån sin Hustru skild/ och när witnen/ (ty inga andra få witna hos dem/ så framt de icke äro från tiugonde led) honom öfwertygat; måste han sig på döde båren lefwandes läggia/ blifwandes han betäckt med en swart yllen duk/ och twänne swarta lius ställas wid hufwudet/ jämte twänne horn hwar vti de blåsa för honom. Detta alt-sammans sker vti Synagogan. Til den brotzlige säija de: Det och det har du syndat.
p. 84 [F2v] När detta skedt är/ står han åter vp af likbåren/ | och måste sedermera vnder alla bönstunder ett helt åhr igenom sittia på en bänck strax wid dörren den de kalla *Ævel*: det är en sörjebänck/ och hafwa en yllen duk öfwer hufwudet med en stor swart fläck/ och måste ett swart lius brinna hela åhret igenom/ warandes liuset vti muren inmurat med ett glas der vtan före. Han måste och vndergå andra straff/ som *Rabbinerna* honom pålägga. Han måste liggia wid dörren för Synagogan på trappan och säija: Jag hafwer syndat emot Gud; derföre beder jag eder at I skolen trampa på mig: men de giöra det intet/ hwilket skal wara honom til större straff. Til Synagogan och de fattige skal han och en ansenlig *Summa* penningar gifwa. På samma sätt warder och med den handlat/ som af wåda eller oförwarandes någon ihiälslår. När någon sig icke så swårligen förser och förbryter/ sättia de den samma

---

7 sielfwa] siefwa *Spec.* (Sthlm, 1732); sielfwa *Spec.* (Gbg, 1732; Sthlm, 1735).

the stench of gunpowder. Then they could understand his deceit and threw this man into chains and prison, cursing and punishing him; he then had to go to a room and perform penance and penitence. Within a month he had died in prison and was not buried in a cemetery. We could mention several other such deceivers but will leave it with this one. Each and every Christian will be able to discern clearly how the Jews are deceived by their very own and yet are so stiff-necked that they are angry at the Christians and do not take the log out of their own eyes.[272]

Chapter 33

Next in order to be looked at is the Jews' system of order or justice, and it is organized in this way. When someone gravely sins against God and breaks a secular law, they forge a scheme to do away with him by poisoning or to kill him in some other way, and they can conveniently conceal this and report nothing to the Christian authorities, in whatever place it may be. Seeing as they have lost their privileges and freedoms ever since the Temple was destroyed and have no power to condemn someone to death, they do not inform the Christian authorities about it [i.e., the crime]. If someone commits double adultery, it is considered the greatest of sins, and those who commit it are punished in this way: the one who is most to blame is divorced from his wife, and when the witnesses – as no other may testify among them unless they are from the twentieth generation – have persuaded him, he must lie down alive on the bier and is covered by a black woollen cloth and two black candles are placed by his head as well as two horns in which they blow for him. All of this happens in the synagogue. They say to the criminal, "You have sinned by doing this and that." When this has happened, he rises from the bier and then at all prayer services throughout the following year he has to sit on a bench right next to the door which they call *Ævel*[273] – that is "a mourning bench" – and wear a woollen cloth over his head on which there is a large black patch. And a black candle must burn throughout the entire year, and this candle is placed within the wall with glass in front of it. He must also undergo other punishments that the rabbis subject him to. He must lie by the door of the synagogue on the steps and say, "I have sinned against God, for which reason I beg you to tread on me." But they do not do so, which is meant as an even greater punishment for him. He is also to give a considerable sum of money to the synagogue and to the poor. Whoever kills someone through misadventure or unintentionally is dealt with in the same manner. When someone makes a mistake or commits a

272 Cf. Matthew 7:1–5.

273 Heb.: *Ævel*, עבל, *'evel*, "wrong-doing," "unrighteousness."

vti fängelse och måste han böta til Synagogan efter gottfinnande: andra straff hafwa de icke. Hänga/ bränna och halshugga töras de icke giöra/ vtan de förtiga merendels saken/ at den Christeliga Öfwerheten/ ei den ringaste kundskap få kan. Om någon af Judarne/ en sak för den Christeliga Öfwerheten til känna gifwa skulle/ kalla de den samma *Moser* מסיר det är en förrädare; och hafwer den samma p. 85 [F3r] ingen *Pardon* eller nåd at förwänta/ emedan han Judarnas penningar | vnder de Christne bringa månde. Om någon dem förrådt hafwer/ kommer en *Rabbin* om nattetid med twå eller tre starcka karlar af Judarna/ stoppa ett kläde vti munnen/ at han icke ropa och skria skal/ bindandes sedan en handduk om halsen och strypa honom. Om någon hos Judarna sig ei så grufweligen försyndat/ måste han gifwa en mark wax til Synagogan; och om någon skulle så halsstarrig wara och ei betala wilja/ ledes han vti Synagogan/ skolandes han då swärja/ at han der vtinnan oskyldig är. Hos Judarne hafwa de eljest ingen annan rätt och *Justitie.*

CAP. 34.

NÄr Judarna skola giöra eed sins emellan/ måste de vti Synagogan taga de wanliga 5. Mosis Böcker vtur Arcken/ på *Pergament* skrefna/ dem de kalla; *Kaschar Sepher Tora,* כשר ספר תורה men intet den Tryckta Bibelen/ den de kalla *Chumaseh*: Judarne måste sin *Coschere* eller rätta *Thephilim* och Bönerim på hufwudet och wänstra armen läggia tillika med sin *Tallis* och *Zizzis*; det är en wiß hufwudduk/

12 wilja] wija *Spec.* (Sthlm, 1732); wilja *Spec.* (Gbg, 1732; Sthlm, 1735).

crime that is not as serious, they put him in prison, and he must pay a fine at their discretion to the synagogue. They do not have any other punishment. They dare not hang, burn, or behead but rather keep quiet about most things so that the Christian authorities will not have the slightest knowledge of them. If one of the Jews does make the Christian authorities aware of something, they call him *Moser* מסיר,[274] that is "a traitor." And he can expect no pardon or mercy, because he brought the Jews' money to the Christians. If someone has betrayed them, a rabbi comes in the night with two or three strong Jewish fellows, they stuff a rag into his mouth so that he will not shout and scream, then tie a towel around his throat and strangle him. If one of the Jews has not sinned particularly badly, then he must give one mark of wax to the synagogue. And should someone be so stubborn and not pay, he is led to the synagogue and is to swear that he is innocent of any [crime]. Apart from this, there is no other system of law or justice among the Jews.

Chapter 34

Among themselves, when the Jews are to swear an oath,[275] they usually have to take the Pentateuch out of the ark in the synagogue. Written on parchment, they call them *Kaschar Sepher Tora*, כשר ספר תורה,[276] but not the printed Bible which they call *Chumaseh*.[277] The Jews must put on their *Coschere*[278] or correct *Thephi lim*[279] and prayer-straps upon their heads and left arms as well as their *Tallis*[280]

274 Heb.: *Moser* מסיר(!), מוסר, *moser*, "informer," "one who engages in *mesirah* (i.e., an action in which one Jew reports the conduct of another to a non-rabbinic authority in a manner and under circumstances forbidden by rabbinical law)."

275 What follows is a description of the Jewish oath that Jews were forced to take in Christian European courts. It follows the format outlined by the German imperial court in 1555 in which the oath-swearer calls various curses, diseases, and catastrophes upon himself while standing on a pigskin.

276 Heb.: *Kaschar Sepher Tora*, כשר ספר תורה, *kašer sefer torah*, "kosher Torah roll." The phrase is ungrammatical in Hebrew; it is probably meant as a rendering of Yidd.: *koshər sefər tora*, "kosher Torah roll".

277 Heb.: *Chumaseh*, חומש, *ḥumaš*, "the Five Books of Moses."

278 Heb.: *Coschere*, כשר, *kašer* (Heb.), *koshər* (Yidd.), "kosher, proper, lawful."

279 Heb.: *Thephilim*, תפלין, *tefilin*, "phylacteries": two small black leather boxes containing parchment scrolls inscribed with verses from Exodus 13:9, 16; Deuteronomy 6:8, 11:18. Phylacteries are worn by adult men during weekday morning prayers, one on the upper arm and the other just above the forehead.

280 Heb.: *Tallis*, טלית, *ṭalit* (Heb.), *talis* (Yidd.), "tallit, prayer shawl": a rectangular garment of wool, cotton, or silk, with knotted fringes (tzitzit) attached to each of each of its four corners. Its design and use are based on the biblical commandments in Numbers 15:38 and Deuteronomy 22:12.

hwar wid äro otta trådar/ och den samma öfwer hufwudet draga. Förr än en Jude begynner at swärja måste han twätta sina händer/ och sedan tager han *Sepher* p. 86 [F3v] *Thora* ספר תורה eller 10. Gudz Bud/ och när han dem kyst | hafwer lägger han dem på sin högra arm och den wänstra der vppå/ wändandes han sitt ansichte åt Öster och lika såsom emot Jerusalem. När han swärjer säger han: Jag swär wid GUD Alsmächtig/ Abrahams/ Isaks och Jacobs GUD/ hwilken warder kallad *Adonai Elohim Zeboos El Schadai Ehich Ascher Ehich* אדוני אלהים צבאות אל שדי אהיה אשר אהיה. Wid det stora Gudomeliga Namnet/ Gudz wäsenteliga Namn *Jehovah*, som Himmel och Jord och alt hwad ther vti är skapat/ och betygar hos alla Änglar: Genom den Domens Lof som i Himmelen är/ och genom den Domens Lof som på Jorden är. Jag tager och på mig en förbannelse/ jag wil warda den samma som Josua förbannat hafwer/ och den allestädes närwarande stora Gudens förbannelse. Jag tager GUD Alsmächtig til witne och wil deße tre förbannelser på mig/ taga/ at jag i sanning swär vtan falskhet och ringaste ond tancka/ som jag efter min lära tänckia kunde. Om jag falskt swär/ eller falska tanckar vti mitt hierta hafwer/ så wil jag ingen syndernas förlåtelse af GUD hafwa/ och ingen förlåtelse eller försoning/ på försoningens dag/ hwarken i denna/ eller den tilkommande werlden. Ingen omwändelse skal mig hielpa/ vtan GUD skal på mig skicka och sända alla p. 87 [F4r] förbannelser vtaf Bileam/ och önskar/ at GUD/ som lif och död/ Wälsig|nelse och Förbannelse ondt och godt vti sina händer hafwer/ bringar på mig de förbannelser som vti 3. Mosis Bok vpräknade warda/ samt alla Förbannelser som Moses vti sin 5. Bok omtalar. komme och öfwer mig alla tijo Egyptiska plågor/ och siunke jag för HErren ned på detta rum som Corah/ Datan och Abiram vti jorden nedsunckne äro. Komme Spitälskan på mig såsom Miriam och Naeman/ at hon/ om jag falskeligen swär vti alla mina lifsdagar icke helad warder. Komme alla onda andar och dieflar i mig om jag för HErranom ett falskt och osant ord talat eller talandes warder. Warde mitt hus och egendom/ hustru och barn med eld och swafwel straffade som Sodom och Gomorra straffade warit. Min *Portion* och del ware vti

and *Zizzis*[281] – that is a white headcloth upon which are eight threads – and pull this over their heads. Before a Jew begins to swear [an oath], he must wash his hands and then take the *Sepher Thora*, ספר תורה,[282] or the Ten Commandments of God, and, when he has kissed them, he places them on his right arm and his left arm upon it, and he turns his face to the east as if towards Jerusalem. When he swears, he says: "I swear by God Almighty, the God of Abraham, Isaac, and Jacob, who is called *Adonai Elohim Zeboos El Schadai Ehich Ascher Ehich* אדוני אלהים צבאות אל שדי אהיה אשר אהיה.[283] By the great divine name, God's great name, *Jehovah*, who created heaven and earth and everything that is in-between. I declare with all the angels, by the promise of judgement that is in heaven and the promise of judgement that is on earth. I also draw a curse upon myself. I will become the one whom Joshua cursed, and the omnipresent great God's curse. I take God Almighty as my witness and will take these three curses upon myself, that I truly swear without falseness and the slightest evil thought that I could think in accordance with my faith. If I swear falsely or have false thoughts in my heart, then I will receive no absolution of sins from God and no forgiveness or atonement on the Day of Atonement, neither in this world nor the one to come. No conversion will help me, but God will cast and send onto me all the curses of Balaam.[284] And [I] wish that God who has life and death, blessing and curse, bad and good in his hands will bring upon me those curses that are listed in Leviticus as well as all the curses that Moses speaks about in Deuteronomy. May the ten plagues of Egypt befall me and may I be swallowed up in this room like Korah, Dathan, and Abiram were drowned in the soil.[285] May leprosy come over me like Miriam and Naaman,[286] so that – if I swear falsely – I shall never be cured of it for as long as I live. May all evil spirits and demons descend on me, if I have spoken or speak a false and untrue word before the Lord. May my house and property, wife and children be punished by fire and brimstone like Sodom and Gomorrah were punished.[287]

281 Heb.: *Zizzis*, ציצית, *ẓiẓit* (Heb.), *ẓiẓis* (Yidd.), "tzitzit, fringes."

282 Heb.: *Sepher Thora*, ספר תורה, *sefer torah*, "the Torah, the (book of the) Pentateuch."

283 A list of different names for God in Judaism: אדוני, "My Lord" (in *pluralis majestatis*); אלוהים, "Deity, God" (the plural *-im* ending was originally probably to form an abstract term, but is often understood today as a respectful *pluralis majestatis*); צבאות, "Armies, Hosts"; אל "God"; שדי, "God Almighty" is the traditional translation, but the precise meaning of the name is uncertain; אהיה אשר אהיה, "I am that I am."

284 The diviner, Balaam ("Bileam"), who is offered money by Moab to curse Israel. Numbers 22–25.

285 Korah, Dathan and Abiram were swallowed up by the earth for rebelling against Moses: Numbers 16:31.

286 God strikes Miriam down with leprosy in Numbers 12:10 for opposing Moses. The story of Naaman, an army commander, and his leprosy and cure is recounted in 2 Kings 5.

287 God rains fire and brimstone upon Sodom and Gomorrah in Genesis 19.

den tilkommande werlden förlorad. Jag skal ewigt wara och blifwa vti helfwetit och wid de dödas vpståndelse intet vpstå. Jag skal wara vti alla werldenes förbannelser/ och om icke alt sammans hwad jag talat hafwer/ sant är/ skola alla werldenes förbannelser på mig komma. Detta bekräftar jag altsammans med GUDz Namn/ vtan något återkallande af min vtsago/ och andra vndflychter dem man vptänckia kan; så sant GUD Alsmächtig/ som Himmel och Jord skapat hafwer mig hielpe til lif och siäl: Hwar på de andre Judarne säija. Amen.

p. 88 [F4v] Men skulle så hända at Judarne någon ed | emot de Christne giöra/ och afläggia skola/ så pålägger den Christna Öfwerheten dem til spott och skam/ at de skola swärja på ett rätt swinskin/ så nämligen: at ett swinskin lägges på tröskelen af Synagogan/ hwar på Juden måste icke allenast stå på knän/ vtan ock ther på läggia händerna; hwilket de ei giärna vndergå/ vtan sökia hällre med de Christne at förlikte blifwa/ och än skiönt de sanningen swärja skulle/ hålla de det doch för en stor skam och wahnheder. Detta ware nu om Judarnas Edgång så korteligen talat.

CAP. 35.

HÄr wid wil man ei förbi gå/ at handla ock omröra/ på hwad sätt de sina fattige underhålla. När någon hos dem genom någon åkommen olycka blifwer aldeles vtfattig/ skiuta de andra Judarne 2. eller 3. gånger tilsammans/ at han åter må komma för sig igen. Om en Jude hafwer många döttrar/ at han dem med Brudeskatt ei förse kan/ så *Contribuerar* och skiuter hela landet tilsammans/ hållandes det för en stor skam och wahnheder at en Israels Dotter ei gifft och försedd blifwer/ hälst ingen hos dem får ogiffter wara/ eho hon wara må/ så framt hon icke är ofärdig och lam; Doch sker ganska sällan/ at de ofärdige/ ogiffte blifwa. När nu

p. 89 [F5r] någon så vtfattig är at ho|nom ingen hielpa kan/ eller någon hielp förslå månde/ tager han hustru och barn/ drager ifrån den ena staden til den andra/ deräst Judar boende äro/ hafwandes Judarne vti hwar stad/ den som allmosor vtdelar/ och

6 Himmel] Himmmel *Spec.* (Sthlm, 1732); Himmel *Spec.* (Gbg, 1732; Sthlm, 1735).

May my portion and share in the world to come be lost. I shall be and remain in hell for eternity and not rise at the resurrection of the dead. I shall be subject to the curses of the world. And if anything in everything that I have spoken is not true, all the curses of the world will be upon me. I confirm all of this in the name of God without any retractions of my statement and other evasions that can be thought up. So truly may God Almighty, who has created heaven and earth, help my life and soul."[288] Whereupon the other Jews say, "Amen."

But should it so happen that the Jews are to make and swear an oath against the Christians, then, in order to ridicule and mock them, the Christian authorities force them to swear on a real pigskin in this way:[289] a pigskin is laid on the threshold of the synagogue upon which the Jew must not only kneel but also lay his hands. This they do not do readily but would rather seek to be reconciled with the Christians, and even though they are to swear the truth, they consider it nonetheless a great shame and disgrace. This, then, was a brief description of the Jews' oath-swearing.

Chapter 35

We will not pass by here without dealing with and describing in what way they support their poor. When by some accident one of them becomes completely destitute the other Jews club together two or three times so that he may get back on his feet again. If a Jew has so many daughters that he is unable to provide them with a dowry, then the entire country contributes and clubs together as they consider it a great shame and disgrace if a daughter of Israel remains unmarried and not provided for. It is preferable that not one of them be unmarried whoever she may be, as long as she is not handicapped and lame; and nevertheless, it happens only rarely that the handicapped remain unmarried.

When someone is so destitute that no one is able to help him or proffer any help, then he takes his wife and children and wanders from one town to the next wherever there are Jewish inhabitants; and in every town, the Jews have a man

288 The long quotation that ends here – *Spec.* (Sthlm, 1732), 86:4–87:30 – is not how Jews swore an oath, but rather how Christian authorities forced Jews to swear oaths. It is very reminiscent of the text of the oath imposed on Jews in Frankfurt *c.* 1392 and quoted in English translation in Jacob Rader Marcus, *The Jew in the Medieval World. A Source Book: 315–1791*, rev. edn with intro. by Marc Saperstein (Cincinnati: Hebrew Union College Press, 1999), 56–58.

289 The *More Judaico*, "according to Jewish custom," was an invention of Christian authorities in order to denigrate Jews during court cases. The use of a pigskin during the oath-taking is intended as a humiliation.

warder den samma kallad *Gabba* גבא. Denne hafwer alla Judar/ som i staden boende äro/ vti en bok optecknade. Fattig-förståndaren gifwer den fattige en *Pollet*, och på sedelen står den och dens Judens namn/ huru många dagar han den fattige qwarter och vnderhåld skaffa skal. De mindre förmögne Judarne pålägges 2. eller 3. dagar dem at underhålla; men om det en rik Jude är/ har han offta wid sitt bord 30. *a* 40. Personer/ warandes honom icke efterlåtit at sättia dem wid ett annat bord/ vtan wid det han sielf äter/ han ware sig aldrig så rik/ eller de andra aldrig så fattige/ så framt icke den fattige är siuklig/ eller hafwer någon annan skadelig och smittosam siukdom. När de fattige skola resa ifrån samma stad/ gifwa de dem förtärningspenningar; men om de lamma och bräcklige äro/ låta de dem åka/ men äro de aldeles siuke/ föra de dem vti sitt Hospital/ deräst de hafwa sitt vnderhåld/ och af *Doctorer* och Fältskiärarne besökte warda.

De fattige gå ifrån det ena huset til det andra/ och hwar och en gifwer dem efter sin förmögenhet/ farandes de således kring så länge de lefwa. När de dö och p. 90 [F5v] begrafwas skola/ warda samma | *Ceremonier* med dem som de rike Judar brukade/ tagande de af samma penningar til begrafnings omkostnaden som til de fattige gifne äro.

Det gifwes ett slags folck ibland Judarne som de kalla *Gerim* גרים det är/ en främling/ som ifrån andras *Religion* affallit och den Judiska antagit/ åt hwilka de gifwa ett wist vnderhåld/ och giöra dem androm mycket godt/ icke allenast af den Judiska/ vtan och af andra *Nationer*.

CAP. 36.

NU wil jag ock något tala om Judarnas skäggputzande eller rakande. Hos dem är det strängeligen förbudit at raka sig/ besynnerligen håren wid tinningarne och skägget/ ty *Rabbinerna* föregifwa ett straff som der af förorsakas skal/ hwilket står vti en Bok benämd *Kitzur Schenä, Lucot Habrit Cap. 33.* קיצר שני לוחת הברית. De hafwa en Fabel: at vti en stad i Tyskland/ som heter Speir/ derest en Riker Jude bodt hafwer/ hwilken låtit raka sitt skägg/ och på den samma tid hafwer der warit en lärder man/ hwilken kallade sig *Rabbi* Juda/ han förmante samma rika man at

who distributes alms and who is called *Gabba*, גבא.[290] He has all the Jews, who are resident in the city, registered in a book. The welfare warden gives the poor man a token, and on the note is written the name of such-and-such a Jew and how many days he must provide accommodation and maintenance for the poor man. The less prosperous Jews are instructed to provide for him for two or three days; but if he is a rich Jew, he often has thirty to forty people at his table, and he is not allowed to seat them at another table but only at the one where he himself is eating – it makes no difference how rich he is or how poor the others are, as long as the poor man is not ill or has some harmful and contagious sickness. When the poor are to travel on from this city, they are given pocket money. If they are lame and infirm, they allow them to go, but if they are extremely ill, they take them to the hospital where they stay and are seen by doctors and barber-surgeons.

The poor go from one house to the next, and everyone gives them as much as they can, and so they travel about for as long as they live. When they die and are to be buried, the same ceremonies as for the rich Jews are used, and to cover the cost of the burial they use the same money as is given to the poor.

There is a kind of people among the Jews whom they call *Gerim*, גרים,[291] that is a stranger who has left one religion and adopted the Jewish one. They provide them with a certain maintenance, and they do much good for others, not just from among the Jews but also from other nations.

Chapter 36

Now I will say something about the Jews' trimming and shaving of their beards. It is strictly forbidden for them to shave, particularly their hair at the temples and their beards, because the rabbis claim there is a punishment caused by this which is written about in chapter 33 of a book called *Kitzur Schenä, Lucot Habrit*, קיצר שני לוחת הברית.[292] They have a fairy-tale: in a city in Germany that is called Speyer there lived a rich Jew who shaved his beard and at the same time there was a learned man whom they called Rabbi Juda. He cautioned this rich man not to

290 Heb.: *Gabba*, גבא(!), גבאי, *gabbai*, "gabbai, synagogue warden, sexton." The man who assists in the running of the synagogue and services.

291 Heb.: *Gerim*, גרים, *gerim*, "proselytes, converts to Judaism."

292 Heb.: *Kitzur Schenä, Lucot Habrit*, קיצור שני לוחות הברית, *ḳiẓur šnei luḥot ha-brit*, "Abbreviation of the Two Tablets of the Covenant." Written by one of the greatest rabbis of the seventeenth century, Yeshayahu Halevi (1558–1630) about two years after he immigrated to Israel, *The Two Tablets of the Covenant* was published in the decades after his death. It is an important book on morality and was very influential on Hasidism.

han sig ei raka skulle; ty vti den andra werlden worde han derföre ett stort straff lidandes och bekommandes. Men han achtade icke en slik förmaning/ vtan sade p. 91 [F6r] sig ei tåla kunna det håren honom i munnen | hänga skulle/ och wara så ohyggelig. Men hwad hände? Den rika mannen blef och omsider vti mångas närwaro död. Under det samma war och förenämde *Rabbi* Juda närwarande/ hwilken skref efter Cabbaliskt sätt en Sedel/ och kastade den samma på den döda. Strax stod den döda vp på sina fötter/ och alla de som der woro/ sprungo af förskräckelse och fruchtan bort/ men *Rabbi* Juda blef allena qwarsittiandes/ kallandes han åter de andra tilbakas. Då begynte den döda at rifwa håren af sig. *Rabbi* Juda frågade hwad det honom felade? Han swarade: We mig! at jag ditt råd ei efter kommit hafwer. *Rabbi* Juda frågade widare: Huru *Tractera* och handtera de din Siäl? Den rika mannen swarade: När min Siäl skildes ifrån min kropp/ som en ond anda/ hwilken war til anseende som en Koo med stora horn/ hafwandes samma anda haft med sig ett kiärile/ med swafwel/ beck och salt/ och vti det samma har han min Siäl emottagit/ och kan jag der vtur icke komma. Der efter är en Ängel kommen från högsta Domstol/ och tagit ifrån den onda andan samma kiärile/ hwar vti Siälen låg/ och sedan wist den fram för den högsta Domstolen och alla Siälars Skapare och Vhrsprung. Ifrån denna Domstohl hördes en röst frågandes: Har du läsit vti Bibelen? p. 92 [F6v] Der på jag swarade: Ja! Der på befal|tes/ at Bibelen fram hafwas skulle/ och blef til mig sagt: Läs der vti. När Bibelen af mig öpnad blef/ fant jag strax denna *versen* skrifwen: Du skal ditt skiägg/ och tina tinningar intet bortraka och vtskämma. Nu wiste jag intet hwad jag swara skulle/ och fick strax der på höra en röst som sade: Tag denna Siäl/ och för henne vti det diupaste rummet i helfwetit. När nu den rika mannen vttalat hade/ tog *Rabbi* Juda sitt Cabbaliska Papper igen/ som han på honom lagt hade; fallandes samma man åter neder och wardt död/ som tilförene.

Summa: Den som den Judiska *Religionen* rätt hålla wil/ han måste 613. bud *observera* och i acht taga/ och warda de hos dem kallade *Tarjag Mitzwig*, תר יג hwilka ganska swåra äro/ så at vtaf dem alla/ ogiörligit är at hålla hundrade/ mycket mindre hela lagen/ vpfylla kunna. Men GUD ware lof! Wi hafwa den korsfästa JEsum/ som Lagen för oß vpfylt hafwer/ och om wi hålla oß til honom; hafwa wi inga onda andar at befara och befruchta/ de må taga hwad gestalt och skapnad de wilja. Gifwe fördenskull Gud! at ingen större synd wore/ än sitt skiägg afskära. Ware detta nog om deras skiäggrakande. |

11 rika mannen] rikamannen *Spec.* (Sthlm, 1732); rika mannen *Spec.* (Gbg, 1732; Sthlm, 1735).

shave because he would suffer and receive a great punishment for this in the next world. But he did not pay any attention to this caution but said that he could not stand having hairs hanging into his mouth and that it was unpleasant. But what happened? In the end, the rich man died in the presence of many people. The aforementioned Rabbi Juda was also present there, and in accordance with kabbalistic custom he wrote a note and threw it onto the dead man. The dead man immediately rose to his feet and all those who were present ran away out of fright and fear, but Rabbi Juda remained alone sitting and calling the others back. Then the dead man began tearing out his hair. Rabbi Juda asked him what was wrong. He replied, "Woe is me that I did not follow your advice!" Rabbi Juda asked further, "How do they treat and handle your soul?" The rich man answered, "When my soul departed my body, [there was] an evil spirit that looked like a cow with large horns. This spirit had a vessel filled with brimstone, tar, and salt, into which he received my soul and from which I cannot get out. Then an angel arrived from the highest seat of judgement and took this vessel in which my soul lay from the evil spirit, and then displayed it to the highest seat of judgement and the creator and source of all souls. From this judgement seat a voice was heard that asked, 'Have you read the Bible?' To which I answered, 'Yes!' Upon which a Bible was ordered to be produced and I was told, 'Read from it!' When the Bible was opened by me, I immediately found this verse written: 'Ye shall not shave off and mar your beard and temples.'[293] Now I did not know what to answer and straightaway I heard a voice that said, 'Take this soul and lead it to the deepest chamber in hell!'" When the rich man had spoken, Rabbi Juda picked up his kabbalistic piece of paper that he had laid on top of him, and this man fell back down and was dead like before.

In summary, he who wishes to follow the Jewish religion correctly must pay attention to and observe 613 commandments, and they call them *Tarjag Mitzwig*, תר יג,[294] which are rather difficult, so that out of all of them, it is impracticable to keep a hundred let alone be able to fulfil the entire law. But God be praised! We have the crucified Jesus who fulfilled the law for us, and if we follow him, we have no evil spirits to fear or dread. They may take whatever shape and form they wish! May God grant for this reason that there be no greater sin than to shave off your beard! This is enough about their beard-shaving.

---

293 Leviticus 19:27.

294 Heb.: *Tarjag Mitzwig*, תר יג: The numerical value of תרי״ג (*t-r-y-g*, "*Tarjag*") is 613 – the number of commandments according to *The Guide for the Perplexed* by Rambam (Moses ben Maimonides, 1135–1204), one of the most influential and prolific scholars of the Torah during the Middle Ages. The word "mitzwig" appears to be a mistake for *miẓvot* (מצוות, commandments). It is highly unlikely that Löwe was not familiar with the word *miẓvot*, so this spelling mistake is probably due to a typesẹtting error.

p. 93 [F7r] CAP. 37.

JUdarna hafwa och en *Ceremonie* och antagit bruk angående deras naglars afskiärande. När de dem afskära/ måste de ei förfaras/ vtan läggias vti ett pạpper/ och sedan vpbrännas/ föregifwandes; at när de dem bortkasta/ måste de dem efter sin död åter tilsamman skaffa. Det är ock hos dem så strängeligen förbudit/ at när en qwinna skal gå i kalla badet/ och hafwer det som qwinnor hafwa pläga/ skal hon sina naglar afskära; men om hon badar sig/ och de ei äro afskurne/ måste hon å nyo bada; föregifwandes de/ den onda andan/ när de ei afskurne äro/ sig infinna skola och närwarande wara/ och sig der emellan hwila. Intet mer om naglarnas Afskärande.

CAP. 38.

NÄr en Jude går in eller vt genom en dörr/ så är på högra dörpåsten ett hol/ warandes ett finger långt och ett finger bredt vthuggit. Vti samma hol sitter ett Pergament tilhopa rullat; för det samma är ett glas/ och läggia de fingret der vppå/ kyssandes Mans-Personerne det samma när de vt- och ingå; men Qwinfolcken äro
p. 94 [F7v] der ifrån befriade. Innehållet på samma Pergament | är detta: Du skal älska din nästa af alt dit hierta/ och all din Siäl *etc.* föregifwandes Judarne at samma Pergament som der vti stuckit är/ dem bewara skal för alla onda andar/ så at de vti deras hus intet inkomma skola. De äro mycket rädde och fruchtande at wara om nattetiden vte/ menandes de/ at den onda andan vnder den tiden macht och wåld hafwa skal; derföre de ock bära/ ett Pergament skrifwit af de lärda *Rabbiner*, hwar på äro alla helige Änglars namn efter *Cabbalisti*skt sätt skrefne/ samt GUDz Namn på en penning präglat. Detta Pergament insys vti en liten silkespung den de bära på halsen; giörandes sig der medelst förwißade/ at de ifrån de samma skola befrijade och oskadde warda. Detta Pergament warder af dem kallat *Komea*, קמיע. Nog här om.

15 *etc.*] ꝛc *Spec.* (Sthlm, 1732). *The* et *is abbreviated by an* r-*rotunda rather than the ampersand used in almost all other cases. Cf. 17:18 (this edition 92:19), 26:14 (104:15), and 77:20 (174:5).*

Chapter 37

The Jews have a ceremony and accepted custom concerning the cutting of their nails. When they cut them, they must not throw them away, but place them in a piece of paper and then burn them, believing that when they throw them away, they will have to gather them up again after their death. It is also so strictly forbidden for them that when a woman has to go to the cold bath and has that which women usually have [i.e., she is menstruating], she must cut her nails; but if she bathes and they are not cut, then she has to bathe again and rest inbetween as they believe that when they are not cut, the evil spirit will appear and be present. Nothing more about cutting nails.

Chapter 38

When a Jew enters or exits through a door, then there is a hole that is a finger long and a finger wide cut out on the right-hand doorpost. In this hole, there is some rolled up parchment in front of which is some glass, and they place their finger upon it. Men do this when they exit and enter, but women are spared doing this. The content on the parchment is this: "Thou shalt love thy neighbour with all thy heart and all thy soul, etc."[295] The Jews claim this very parchment that is stuck in side this will protect them from all evil spirits, so that nothing will happen to them in their houses. They are very afraid and fear being outside during the night, as they believe that at this time the evil spirit has power and potency; therefore, they also wear a piece of parchment written by the learned rabbis on which are written the names of all the holy angels in the kabbalistic manner as well as the name of God pressed into a penny. This piece of parchment is sewn into a little silk purse that they wear around their neck, and they assure themselves that they will be spared and left unharmed by these same [spirits]. They call this piece of parchment *Komea* קמיע.[296] Enough about this.

295 The text used in a mezuza is Deuteronomy 6:4–9 (the *Shema* and *Ve-ahavta*) and Deuteronomy 11:13–21. Löwe's quotation here is misleading. Instead of the words from Deuteronomy 6:5, he is actually quoting Matthew 22:39 and Mark 12:31.

296 Heb.: *Komea*, קמיע, *ḳami'a*, "talisman," "amulet."

CAP. 39.

WIdare tilse wi/ huru den hatad och förachtad warder som den Judiska *Religionen* öfwergifwer och den Christeliga antager/ samt hwad straff en slik efter deras omdömmande få skal. De säija: den som antager den Christna läran och sig döpa låter/ at deß moder något vmgänge med en Christen haft hafwer/ och så snart de p. 95 [F8r] förmärckia/ at någon den Christeliga *Religionen* | antaga wil/ stämpla de så/ at han genom förgifft eller andra medel må af daga tagen blifwa. Och när des egna föräldrar/ af en medfödd kärlek det samma ei giöra wilja/ förskaffa de doch en annan arg bof/ som detta förrätta skal; föregifwandes: at de efter sin död skola vtur Paradis drefne blifwa/ slagne/ och sittia vnder en swart förlåt och blygas derföre at de en sådan Son hit til werlden födt och vpfostrat hafwa. Fördenskul räkna de det för den största wälgiärning/ och mena GUDi der med en tienst at giöra/ när en sådan Son eller dotter dödat blifwer/ warandes de der om aldeles försäkrade at de derföre hafwa en stol för sig vti Paradis beredd. Således hade och så med alla *Conversis Judæis* eller omwände Judar/ handlat warit/ der icke Gud af sin besynnerliga nåde dem bewarat/ på flyckten skaffat och dem från deras mordiska dödande frälsat. En sådan *Conversus* kallas af dem *Meschomat.* משומדים Det är; Han är aldeles wärd at vtrotas/ och kalla de en sådan äfwen *Kopher* כפר, det betyder en sådan/ som förnekar GUD. Den samma måste och wara Landsflycktig/ och får icke den ringaste af sina Föräldrar ärfwa; och wilja de icke känna/ eller weta vtaf dem/ mycket mindre dem se eller höra. De andra Judarna hafwa til samma Familia en sky och fasa in til tiugonde led/ och wilja intet ingå något p. 96 [F8v] Ecktenskap vti den samma; hål|landes icke det för så stor skam och blygd/ om någon af deras *Familie* kommo på stegel och hiul/ som om någon sin *Religion* öfwergifwa månde/ i synnerhet när någon den Christne antaga månde. De säija och/ at när en sådan *Conversus* dör/ blifwer af des siäl en ond anda/ hwilken Satan kastar ifrån den ena werldenes ända til den andra/ blifwandes des siäl sänd vti swin och hundar/ och på sidstone vti det diupaste helfwetit; at der sammastädes plågad warda. Men när en sådan/ wil åter sig til dem gifwa och bedia om förlåtelse/ med föregifwande/ at Satan honom förfördt och bedragit hafwer/ blifwer han nådigt vptagen/ men läggia honom samma straff vppå som ofwannämdt är/ och försäkra honom om det ewiga lifwet/ med den *Præcaution* och för behåld om han inga barn efter sig lemnat hafwer/ vnder den tid han i Christenheten lefwat. Men i annor händelse taga de icke emot honom/ så framt han icke tager sina barn med sig/ och låter dem vpfostras och läras vti samma *Religion*, och om han det giör/

16 משומדים] משוטדים *Spec.* (Sthlm, 1732).

Chapter 39

Furthermore, we notice how whoever renounces the Jewish religion and accepts the Christian one is hated and despised and what punishment such a person should be given according to their judgement. They say that whoever accepts Christian teaching and has himself baptized, that his mother has had intercourse with a Christian. And as soon as they notice that someone wants to accept the Christian religion, they denounce him in this way: he is dispatched by poison or some other means. And when, because of innate love, this person's own parents are unwilling to do this, they procure some other malicious scoundrel to carry this out. And they imagine that after their death they will be driven from paradise, beaten, and sit under a black cloth and be ashamed that they have born such a son into the world and raised him. For this reason, they consider it the greatest good deed and believe that they are doing God a service when such a son or daughter is killed, and they are completely sure that by so doing they have prepared a chair for themselves in paradise. And all *Conversis Judœis* or "converted Jews" would have been dealt with like this, had God through his mysterious grace not preserved them, secured their escape, and saved them from their murderous deaths. They call such a convert a *Meschomat*, משומדים,[297] that is, "he is completely worth being annihilated," and they also call such a person *Kopher*, כפר,[298] which means, "someone who denies God." Such a person must also be exiled and may not inherit a thing from his parents. And they do not wish to hear or know anything about them, even less see or hear them. The other Jews shun and feel horror towards this family until the twentieth generation and do not wish to enter into marriage with them; they do consider it less shameful and embarrassing if one of their family ends up on the execution wheel than one of them abandons his religion, particularly when one of them adopts Christianity. They also say that when such a convert dies, his soul becomes an evil spirit that Satan throws from one end of the world to the other, and his soul is consigned to pigs and dogs and finally to the deepest hell where it is tortured. But when such a man wishes to return to them and asks for forgiveness, pretending that Satan seduced and deceived him, he is mercifully admitted, but they place the same punishment upon him as is mentioned above and assure him of the eternal life with the precaution and condition that he has not left any children behind from when he lived in Christendom. Otherwise, they do not admit him unless he brings his children with him and has them raised and instructed in

297 Heb.: *Meschomat*, משומדים, *mešumadim*, "apostates." Note that the Heb. is in the plural, but Löwe's transliteration ("Meschomat") is in the singular.

298 Heb.: *Kopher*, כפר(!), כופר, *kufar* (Heb.), *kofər* (Yidd.), "infidel, heretic."

hafwer han en stor löhn i Himmelen efter deras försäkran och berättelse at förwänta. Nog om detta. |

p. 97 [G1r] CAP. 40.

HÄr wid wil man ei förbi gå/ huru hos Judarne brukeligit är/ när någon siuk liggia månde/ eller de skiönja at han dö skal. Detta sker på följande sätt: De sända til honom twänne lärda män/ om de för hand äro/ och de dem få kunna/ samt om den siuke något litet tala kan. Deße twänne skriffta honom/ och samma skrifftermåhl warder kalladt *Widdu*, med det samma *Continuera* de til hans dödzstund och lyder det sålunda: Jag tror på den sanna Guden/ som ingen kropp är/ som warit för all ting/ och honom allena och ingen annan bör man tiena. Jag tror och den sanfärdige Propheten Moses/ at han den förnämsta Prophet wara månde/ och at lagen genom hans händer/ oß ifrån Himmelen gifwen är/ och vti ingen måtto förandrat blifwen. Jag wet at GUD de rättferdige med mycket godt belöner och bekröner/ och de onda och ogudachtige med mycket ondt straffar/ samt at han oß/ den vtlofwade *Messiam* skickandes warder. Jag tror och de dödas vpståndelse och alt hwad wåra lärde sagt och skrifwit hafwa. Om någon tancka emot Gudz och des lärares Lag/ vpkommit vti mitt sinne/ ångrar jag det af hiertat/ och wil omwända/ bättra mig/ och begiära förlåtelse af GUD och hans Heliga Lag.

p. 98 [G1v] Der efter säger han således/ och följer | då den rätta synda bekännelsen: HERre öfwer hela werlden/ här ligger jag vti titt wåld/ mitt lif och död står i tine händer! Jag beder tig Alsmächtige GUD/ du heter ju en barmhertig GUD; Jag beder tig tu wille snart sända mig tin hielp vtaf Himmelen/ så wäl som andra krancka vti Israel. Ty jag ångrar af hiertans grund alla mina synder/ dem jag vti alla mina lifsdagar/ från det jag född war/ in til denna närwarande dag och stund/ ehwad synd det wara må/ wettandes eller owettandes/ med ord/ gierning och tanckar/ begådt och bedrifwit hafwer. Öfwer alt detta hafwer jag en hiertans ånger/ och om jag medelst din Gudomeliga hielp/ frisk och sund warder/ vtfäster jag mig högeligen/ hädan efter sådane synder aldrig mera begå skola. Men om så är/ at tu HERre täckes kalla mig hädan/ så låt mig gladeligen insomna/ och skicka emot min Siäl barmhertighetenes Änglar/ som den emottaga och til henne säilja: Frid ware din ankomst! Förandes henne sedan vti Paradis ibland andra rättferdige/ och låte på henne din Härlighets Glants Lysa och Skina. |

7 *Continuera*] *Cotinuera Spec.* (Sthlm, 1732); *Continuera Spec.* (Gbg, 1732; Sthlm, 1735).

this religion. And if he does so, he can, according to their assurances and stories, expect a great reward in heaven. Enough about this.

Chapter 40

Here we will not pass by what the Jews' practice is when someone is lying ill, or they determine that he will die. This happens in the following way. They send two learned men to him, if there are any such men available and they can get hold of them, and if the ill man can talk a little. These two hear his confession (this confession is called *Widdu*),[299] and they continue with this until his moment of death, and it sounds like this: "I believe in the true God who has no body who has existed before all things, and we should serve him alone and no other. I also believe in the truthful prophet Moses, that he is the foremost prophet and that through his hands the Law was given to us from heaven, and it may not be altered in any way. I know that God rewards and crowns the just with many good things and punishes the wicked and ungodly with many bad things, and that he will send the promised Messiah to us. I also believe in the resurrection of the dead and in everything that our scholars have said and written. If any thought against God and his teachers' Law has arisen in my mind, I repent from my heart, and will turn back, better myself, and ask for God and his holy law's forgiveness."

After this he says this, and then follows the real confession: "Lord of all the world, here I lie in your power, my life and death in your hands! I ask you, Almighty God – you are indeed called a merciful God – I ask that you soon will send your assistance from heaven to me as well as other ailing people in [the House of] Israel. As I repent from the bottom of my heart all my sins, those that I have committed and perpetrated during all my living days, from the moment I was born until this present day and moment, whatever sin it may be, [committed] wittingly or unwittingly with words, actions, or thoughts. For all of this I repent from the heart and if I through your divine assistance become well and healthy, I confirm absolutely that from now on I will never again commit such sins. But if it is the case that you, Lord, prefer to call me from this place, then let me die happily in my sleep and send my soul the angels of mercy, who will accept it and say to it, 'Peace be upon your arrival!' And then they lead it into paradise among the just and have the brilliance of your glory gleam and shine upon it."

---

299 Heb.: *Widdu*, וידוי, *vidui*, "confession," "shrift": the name of the prayer that is said when death is imminent.

p. 99 [G2r]

CAP. 41.

NÄr nu en Jude vti sidsta dödzstunden wara månde/ föregifwa och säija de/ at til honom 4. Änglar kommande warda. En helig/ en dödsens/ en som skrifwer/ och en som räcknar/ säijandes: Statt vp din dödzstund är nu förhanden. Då skal den siuke vti sitt sinne swara: Nei. Strax der på öpnar han ögonen/ och han ser en Ängel för sig stående/ räckiandes ifrån Jorden til Himmelen; warandes samme Ängel til anseende ifrån föttren alt til hufwudet/ som altsammans idel ögon woro/ samt hans kläder och mantel af eld. Denna Ängel har en knif vti sina händer/ och på knifsudden skal hänga en dråppa galla/ och af den samma blifwer han dödlik/ stincker och lucktar. De säija och/ at ingen dör förr än han sedt Gudz Ansichte. Är han en Gudfruchtig man/ lefwererar han sin Siäl til GUD; men om han ogudachtig är/ wil han icke gierna dö. *Rabbinerna* föregifwa at det intet är nog der med, vtan när den timma och stund kommer/ at menniskian skal skiljas ifrån werlden/ så skal den som dö måste/ blifwa förskräckt för dödsens ängel/ som öfwer alt med ögon full är/ ett dragit swärd vti sina händer hafwer/ och tilfrågar? Har du vpfylt Gudz Lag? Har du giordt goda wärck ock gierningar? Har du giordt din morgon- p. 100 [G2v] och | affton bön? Har du vti alla dina lifsdagar bemött din nästa med sachtmodighet och höflighet? Skulle då befinnas/ at han här vtinnan ei bråttzlig är/ kastar han den samma droppan/ som på swärdet eller knifsudden hängande är/ den siuka vti munnen/ och då går hans Siäl vtan någon wärck och pina vtur des kropp/ som man ett hår vtur miölken draga wille. Men befinnes den siuke wara bråttzlig; går des Siäl vt/ som man törne vtdraga wille/ och vll der med vtkommer. Detta kan ses vti en Bok/ som warder kallad/ *Kitzer Schenä Lucot, Habrit Capite* 21.

CAP. 42.

NÄr nu den siuke döder är/ taga de/ hwilka honom vhr sängen lyfta skola/ kroppen och läggia honom på ganska litet halm; ty de säija: Så många halmstrå som den döda ligger vppå/ så många styng skal han få af halmstrå'n/ och känna dem som han wore lefwandes. De säija der jämte/ at så länge den döda är hemma och är på halmen liggiande/ skal han höra alt hwad de närwarande säija och tala månde. De ställa ett lius wid hans hufwud och det brinner så länge han på jorden liggiandes är. Då komma hans wänner/ gråtandes/ skriandes samt läggiandes sig på den döde; p. 101 [G3r] | Bediandes om förlåtelse/ och at han vti den andra werlden för dem bedia skal. De läggia på honom ett swart täcke/ taga ett rått ägg och slå det wid deß hufwud

Chapter 41

When a Jew is in his last moment of dying, they claim and say that four angels come for him: a holy one, one of death, one that writes, and one that counts. And they say, "Stand up, your moment of death has come!" Then the sick man must answer in his mind, "No!" Upon this he immediately opens his eyes and see an angel standing in front of him, stretching from earth to heaven; this angel appears from his feet to head as if he were just eyes and his clothes and cape made of fire. This angel has a knife in his hands and on the edge of the knife hangs a drop of bile and from which he is made lethal, stinks, and smells. They also say that no one dies before they have seen God's face. If he is a God-fearing man, he delivers his soul to God, but if he is ungodly, he does not want to die. The rabbis claim that this is not enough in itself, but when the hour and moment arrive that the person is to depart this world, then the one who must die is to be terrified by the Angel of Death who is covered with eyes, has a drawn sword in his hand, and asks, "Have you fulfilled God's law? Have you done good works and deeds? Have you done your morning and evening prayers? Have you treated your neighbour with meekness and courtesy all the days of your life? Should it then be found that he is not culpable in these things, then he throws this drop [of bile] that is hanging on his sword or knife edge into the mouth of the sick person whose soul then leaves the body without any torment or pain, just like you would pull a hair out of milk. But if the sick person is found to be culpable, the soul departs like you would pull out a thorn and wool comes out with it. This can be seen in chapter 21 of a book that is called *Kitzer Schenä Lucot, Habrit.*[300]

Chapter 42

When the ill man has died, the ones who are to lift him out of bed, take his body and lay him on a small amount of straw, as they say, "The dead man will be pricked by the stalks of straw as many times as the number of stalks that he is lying on, and he will feel them as if he were alive." Likewise, they say that for as long as the dead man is at home and is lying on the straw, he hears everything that those present say and talk about. They place a candle by his head, and it burns as long as he is lying on the ground. Then his friends arrive, weeping and screaming, and lying on top of the dead man, praying for forgiveness and that he will pray for them in the other world. They lay a black cover over him, take a raw egg and crack it open by his head. This is meant as a reminder that just as the egg is round, so

300 See p. 189*n*292 in this edition for *Spec.* (Sthlm, 1732), 90.

sönder. Detta skal wara til en påminnelse/ at som ägget rundt är/ går ock döden kring om hela werlden och skonar ingen. Sedan läggia de honom på ett långt bord/ twätta och kamma/ men intet raka honom/ hwilket de efter sitt språk kalla *Tarah* טהרה det är en rening. Der efter kläda de på honom döde kläderne/ men läggia honom intet vti någon kista/ vtan som han klädder är/ lägges han på båren och bäres til grafwen hwilken såsom andra grafwar giord är. Der wid är ett slags folck tilstädes som de kalla *Cabranim* קברנים, det är så mycket som dödgräfware. En liten stund förr än de komma med den döda til grafwen/ giöra de en kista af Bräder/ vtan någon botn/ och måste den döda liggia der vti på bara jorden/ och för grafwen intet wara tom och ledig/ vtan måste der wid wara folck tilstädes som henne wachta skola. När den döda kommen är/ läggia de honom vti grafwen/ hafwandes samma sina döde kläder vppå sig som han brukat när han war Brudgumme/ och läggia de allenast en stor swepeduk der til. Den yllne duken som har på alle 4. hörn 8. vllträdar/ lägges kring om hans hufwud efter Mosis lag vti
p. 102 *Numer.* 15. *v.* 38. 39. | 40. derest står at alla Judar skulle hafwa wippor på sina
[G3v] kläder. Sedan den döda vti grafwen nedsatt är; rifwa de vt en tråd af hwart hörn/ och föregifwa at samma vllknutar eller wippor skola vti andra werlden gifwa dem witnesbörd/ om de vnder begrafningen efter GUDz befallning hafwa lefwat wäl eller illa; och detta är orsaken/ hwarföre de en tråd vtaf hwart hörn vtdraga/ på det samma duk ei fullkomlig och giltig wara skal/ och något witnesmåhl widare gifwa kunna.

Sedan giöra de twänne trästickor/ dem de sättia emellan den dödas tummar/ och om den som död är warit en rik och lärd man/ hålla de wid hans graf en Lik-*Sermon*; och kalla den samma kistan/ som är vtan botn *Aron.* ארון Sedan läggia de honom vti grafwen/ hafwandes en liten linne påße/ den de fylla med jord som vhr grafwen opkastad är/ hwilken lägges vnder den dödas hufwud och sedan lägges några bräder der vppå/ kastandes de vti största hastighet grafwen igen. Betydelsen til samma mullpåßa är denna: At hela hans winning/ som han här i werlden haft hafwer/ har han altsammans vnder hufwudet/ och tager intet mera med sig. De wachta sig och granneligen/ at ingen får det ringaste af jorden som wid grafwen är/ hwarken med hand eller sina skor bortföra och draga; ty de säija: at den döde
p. 103 skal sam|ma mull/ när grafwen tilsluten är/ åter igenskaffa och tilhopa samla. När
[G4r]

death walks around the whole world and spares no one. Then they lay him on a long table, wash him and comb [his hair], but they do not shave him, which in their language they call *Tarah* טהרה,[301] that is "purification." After this, they dress him in death robes, but do not place him in a coffin, but dressed like this he is laid on a bier and carried to the grave, which has been prepared like any other grave. There are a kind of people present here who are called *Cabranim* קברנים,[302] that means "gravediggers." Shortly before they arrive at the grave with the dead man, they make a coffin of planks, with no bottom, and the dead man must lie in this on the bare earth, and as the grave cannot be empty and free, people must always be present to keep vigil. When the dead man arrives, they lay him in the grave wearing the same death robes that he used when he was a bridegroom, and they lay just a large cloth over him. The woollen cloth that has eight woollen threads at each of its four corners is placed around his head in accordance with the Law of Moses in Numbers 15:38–39,[303] where it says that all Jews are to have fringes on their clothes. When the dead man has been lowered into the grave, they pull out a thread from each corner and claim that these woollen knots or fringes will bear witness for them in the world to come, whether during the burial they have lived well or badly according to God's commandments. And this is the reason why they pull a thread out of each corner of this cloth so that it will not be complete and [ritually] acceptable and able to bear witness.

Then they make two wooden sticks. They place them between the dead man's thumbs and, if the dead man was a rich and learned man, they hold a funeral sermon. And they call this coffin that does not have a bottom *Aron* ארון.[304] Then they place him in the grave and have a small linen bag that they fill with soil that has been dug out from the grave which they place under the dead man's head. Then they lay some planks on top of this and fill the grave as quickly as possible. The meaning of this bag of soil is this: that all of his wealth that he has made here on earth, he has under his head, and he takes nothing more with him. They also take great care to make sure that no one takes away or brings the slightest amount of soil from the grave with them, either on their hands or their shoes, as they say: when the grave is closed, the dead man will reacquire and gather up this soil again. When the dead man, as is described in the first chapter, has left a son, he

301 Heb.: *Tarah*, טהרה, *ṭaharah*, "ritual purity."
302 Heb.: *Cabranim*, קברנים, *ḳabranim*, "grave-diggers."
303 Numbers 15:38–39: "Speak unto the children of Israel, and bid them that they make them fringes in the borders of their garments throughout their generations, and that they put upon the fringe of the borders a ribband of blue: And it shall be unto you for a fringe, that ye may look upon it, and remember all the commandments of the Lord, and do them; and that ye seek not after your own heart and your own eyes, after which ye use to go a whoring."
304 Heb.: *Aron*, ארון, *aron*, "coffin, casket."

nu den döde/ som vti det första Capitlet omtalt är/ en Son efter sig lemnat hafwer/ giör han en bön wid grafwen den de kalla/ *Amen Jehe Scheme Raba*; men hafwer den afledne ingen Son/ så giör en annan samma bön. Der på gå de hem; twätta sine händer/ och förmena den döda wara oren; doch innan de gå från grafwen/ skära alla samtelige den dödas anhörige ett hol fram vti bröstet på sina kläder.

Men til at komma igen til det/ hwar om wi tilförna talat hafwa/ nämligen de dödas orenhet; så törs eller vnderstår sig ingen/ som af Arons stam och slächte är/ röra det minsta wid de döda och gå vti det huset/ som den döde ligger/ eller på det ställe de begrafne äro; ja om det wore deras egen fader eller moder/ är det dem icke efterlåtit at wara vti samma hus. Sammaledes måste alla de/ som vti granskapet boende äro/ slå alt sitt watn bort/ och sig rent åter igenskaffa och hämta. Nu min kära Christen/ de hålla de döda för orene/ och gå doch om sina Fest- och Försoningsdagar til deras grafwar med gråtande och bediande/ at de för dem bedia och godt hos GUD mana skola: Må icke deras dårskap äfwen der af skönjes. |

p. 104 [G4v] CAP. 43.

NÄr de nu hemkomne äro/ berätta *Rabbinerne*, hwad för en swår pina och ängslan den döde wid deras bortgående lida och vtstå måste/ hwilket ses kan vti en bok som kallas *Kitzer, Schenä Lucot Habrit* Cap. 21. de säija at när menniskian död är/ så kommer dödsens Ängel och sätter sig på grafwen/ slåendes der på med sin hand. Ängelen säger til den döda: Statt vp/ säg mig hwad är titt namn. Den döda swarar: det är vppenbart och kunnogt för GUD/ som Himmel och jord skapat hafwer/ men jag wet intet mitt namn. Strax bringar samma Ängel des siäl vti kroppen/ reser honom vp/ giörandes honom skyldig vnder domen. Wid och vnder det samma har han eldröda pilar och jernkiädior vti sin hand. Första gången slår han til den döda ett hårdt slag/ så at alla lemmar skiljas ifrån hwar annan. Andra slaget: warda des ben sönderkroßade/ och komma då strax andra Änglar/ som dem tilhopa plåcka/ giörandes honom åter lefwande. Sedan slår Ängelen honom åter det tredie slaget/ begärandes af honom räckenskap/ för hwar och en giärning han giordt och bedrifwit hafwer. Första dagen warda ögonen på honom vtslagne; emedan han här i tiden talat det han aldrig sedt hafwer; Sedan öronen; emedan
p. 105 han talat det han | aldrig hördt. Så läpparne eller munnen/ aldenstund han talat
[G5r] oanständiga och ohöfwiska ord. Der näst tungan/ emedan han burit falskt witnes-

---

17 *Kitzer*] *Kitzner Spec.* (Sthlm, 1732; Gbg, 1732; Sthlm, 1735). | *Schenä*] *Scheuä Spec.* (Sthlm, 1732); *Schenä Spec.* (Sthlm, 1735); *Schenâ Spec.* (Sthlm, 1735).

[i.e., the son] says a prayer by the graveside that they call *Amen Jehe Scheme Raba.*[305] But if the deceased does not have a son, then another person says the same prayer. Then they go home, wash their hands, and consider the dead man to be unclean. However, before they leave the grave, all of the dead man's relatives cut a hole in their clothes in front of their chests.

But to return to what we were talking about before, namely the impurity of the dead man: none of those of the tribe or family of Aaron dare or venture to touch the dead at all or enter the house in which the dead man is lying or the place where they are buried. Indeed, even if it were their own father or mother, they are not permitted to be in the same house. Likewise, all those who live in the neighbourhood must throw all their water out and retrieve and fetch some clean [i.e., fresh water] again. Now, my dear Christian, they consider the dead to be unclean, and yet on their festivals and Days of Atonement, they go to their graves, weeping and praying, that they will pray for them and exhort God on their behalf: from this we can also discern their foolishness.

Chapter 43

When they have returned home, the rabbis talk about what harsh torment and fear the dead must suffer and endure at their passing away, which can be seen in chapter 21 of a book that is called *Kitzer*, *Schenä Lucot Habrit.*[306] They say that when a person dies, the Angel of Death comes and sits by the grave, hitting it with his hand. The angel says to the dead man, "Rise and tell me your name!" The dead man replies, "It's evident and known to God who has created heaven and earth, but I do not know my name." Immediately, this angel takes his soul out of his body, lifts it up, and judges him guilty. During this he has flaming-red arrows and iron chains in his hand. The first time, he strikes the dead man a harsh blow so that all of his limbs are separated from one another. The second blow: his bones are crushed. And then the other angels arrive and gather them all up and bring him back to life again. Then the angel deals him the third blow and demands of him an account of every single deed he has done and undertaken. On the first day, his eyes are knocked out, because he has spoken about what he has not seen. Then his ears, because he has spoken about what he has never heard. Then his lips or mouth, because he has spoken indecent and discourteous words. After this, his tongue,

305 Heb. *Amen Jehe Scheme Raba*, אמן יהא שמה רבא, *amen yehei' šemeih raba'*, "Amen, may his great name." This is taken from one of the lines of the Mourner's Kaddish ("May his great name be blessed.")

306 See p. 189*n*292 in this edition for *Spec.* (Sthlm, 1732), 90.

börd/ lugit och baktalat. Fötterne; emedan han gådt många syndiga och orätta wägar. Sidst slå de honom öfwer magan/ så at inälfworne der vtur fara månde/ tager dem och slår honom der med vti ansichtet/ säijandes: Detta har du syndiga menniskia/ för det du ätit och druckit vti werlden och icke tient tin GUD. Ty *Rabbinerna* föregifwa/ at om han warit from och Gudfruchtig/ så wet han sitt namn på *Hebræi*ska; men om han warit ogudachtig/ hafwer han det samma förglömt/ blifwer fördenskul den/ som sitt namn ei weta kan/ så hårdeligen pint och plågad. Der på skal den onda ängelen honom vpsluka och kasta ifrån den ena werldenes ända til den andra/ och säija: at samma menniskios siäl skal sedermera fara vti något Creatur eller stenklippa. De säija och/ at den onda ängelen/ som så *Tracterar* och handterar de ogudachtige/ skal på deras språk kallas *Doma* דומה. Här af kan den Gunstige Läsaren aftaga/ hwad för widskeppelser *Rabbinerna* hafwa månde/ hälst de tro alt hwad Fabel-wärck för dem kan skrifwit wara.

Det är doch wist och otwifwelachtigt/ at när menniskian dör/ kommer siälen vti Himmelen eller helfwetit; hälst emedan/ der som trädet faller blifwer det
p. 106 lig|giandes/ och måste siälen först lida och intet kroppen/ och ei som de för-
[G5v] blindade Judar förmena; at kroppen säija skal huru han heta månde. Judarne hafwa och der jämte en wahntro/ at när någon är siuk eller eljest vti lifsfahra; löpa de strax på de dödas grafwar/ och läggia sig på dem som för många hundrade åhr tilbakas döde äro/ gråtandes och ropandes. Ja jag säger/ det wore bättre/ at de vti nödernes tid/ den allena rådande och lefwande Guden för Christi skul om hielp anropa wille/ ty han allena är den rätta hielparen och förloßaren.

CAP. 44.

NU kommer man åter til den förriga Materien angående de döda. När de sina döda begrafwa/ och hafwa kommit hem vti sina hus/ sättia sig alla den dödas slächt och wänner/ såsom Broder och Syster/ Son eller Dotter på Jorden/ til at sörja och begråta honom vti 7. dagar. De töras inga skor hafwa vppå sig/ och intet äta af den mat/ som de sielfwa vti huset hafwa/ vtan allenast det/ som deras grannar och annat folck dem tilsända. De vptända ett lius/ hwilket ei får slåckias innan 4.

because he has borne false witness, lied, and gossiped. His feet, because he has walked along many sinful and wrong roads. Finally, they strike him on the stomach, so that his intestines pour out. They pick them up and hit him in the face with them, saying, "This is what you're getting, sinful human, because you have eaten and drunk in the world and not served your God." As the rabbis believe that if he had been pious and God-fearing, he would know his name in Hebrew, but if he had been impious, he would have forgotten it; whoever does not know his name is harshly tortured and tormented. Then the Evil Angel will devour him and throw him from one end of the world to the other and say that this person's soul will enter some creature or rock. They also say that the Evil Angel who treats and deals with the impious is called in their language *Doma* דומה.[307] From this the gracious reader can deduce what sorts of superstitions the rabbis have as they believe whatever fairy-tales have been written for them.

It is, however, certain and without doubt that when a person dies, his soul goes to heaven or hell, because just as when a tree falls, it remains lying, so it is also the soul that suffers and not the body; and not as the blinded Jews believe, that the body is to say what he is called. Likewise, the Jews also have the superstition that when someone is ill or in some other way at risk of dying, they immediately run to the graves of the dead and lie on the ones belonging to those who died many hundreds of years ago, weeping and shouting. Indeed, I say that it would be better if in their hour of need they called for Christ's sake upon the one ruling and living God for assistance, as he alone is the true helper and saviour.

Chapter 44

Now we return to the previous subject about the dead. When they bury their dead and have returned home to their houses, all the family and friends of the deceased, such as brother and sister, son or daughter, sit upon the ground to grieve and mourn him for seven days.[308] They dare not wear shoes and eat nothing of the food that they themselves have in the house, only that what their neighbours and other people send to them. They light a candle that may not be extinguished until

307 Heb.: *Doma*, דומה, *dumah*, "Dumah": the name of the angel in charge of the spirits of the dead, is hinted at in Isaiah 21:11: "The burden of Dumah. He calleth to me out of Seir, Watchman, what of the night? Watchman, what of the night?" (משא דומה אלי קרא משעיר שמר מה מלילה שמר מה מליל). The name is also mentioned in Genesis 25:14 (a son of Ishmael) and as an angel in the Talmud (Sanhedrin 4:1, Berachot 18:2), the Zohar, and in midrashim. Dumah is a popular figure in Yidd. folklore.

308 The week-long period of mourning, known as *shiva*, for close relatives of the deceased during which the mourners – those sitting shiva – do not leave the house.

weckor förbi gångne äro/ och samma lius måste brinna och aldrig under samma p. 107 [G6r] tid vtsläckias. Är det rikt och förmögit folck/ låta de liuset brinna ett helt | åhr igenom/ och måste sörjefolcket blifwa inne vti huset i 7. dagar och vnderstå sig icke at gå vt. De kalla hwar morgon och afton 10. Personer af granskapet in til sig vti en hel månad/ och förrätta vnder samma tid sin bön hemma vti huset/ läsandes då samma bön som åfwan anförd är. Der komma och andra Judar til at trösta dem/ sättiandes hela månaden igenom hwar morgon/ en hand-duk och en skål med watn wid hufwud-giärden/ der den afledne död blifwit/ i den tancka och mening/ at han hwar afton hemkomma och sig twätta skal. Eljest säija de och; at den som den ogudachtigaste menniskia warit hafwer/ allenast han ei öfwergifwer sin Judiska lära/ vtan sig wid den samma fast och oryggelig håller/ så skal han i helfwetit intet plågad warda/ vtan allenast lida ett åhr. När åhret framfarit är/ skal han der ifrån befriad warda och komma vti Paradis. Men om han den Christeliga Tron wedertagit hafwer/ så är han ewinnerligen förlorad och förtappad. De skrifwa eljest mycket vti en Bok/ som kallas *Menorat Hamaor*, huru mycket de arma siälarna plågade warda/ hwilket är alt för widlöftigt at anföra. |

p. 108 [G6v] CAP. 45.

DEnna ofwannämde Bok skrifwer äfwen huru stor frögd och glädie de rättfärdige och vtwalde vti Paradis hafwa skola. De berätta at hwar och en stol är af Saphir/ och för hwar och en stol skola flyta 7. strömar/ och skola de samma hafwa en obeskriflig härlighet. De säija och/ at GUD den Aldrahögsta/ skal sielf med de fromme och salige siälarne roa och förlusta sig/ samt en timma om dagen med them tilbringa. Den andra timman skal GUD sittia på Domstolen. Den tredie skal han höra/ när Judarna giöra sin bön/ och då skal HErren GUD sitt hufwud rista och säija: Wäl den Konung som man så lofwar och prisar/ som mitt heliga folck Israel mig giör. Den stora Guden skal mycket sörja och jämra sig/ at han förstördt sitt Tempel och sin wåning sina offer och *Altore*. Men min Gunstige Läsare/ det är ju wisserligen en Fabel och menniskio-dicht/ at GUD den Alsmächtige/ som all ting af ewighet sedt hafwer/ skal eller kan jämra sig öfwer det han giordt hafwer; och at det omöjeligit wara månde/ kan hwar och en förnuftig förstå och sinna/ hälst det

four weeks have passed, and this candle must burn and never be put out during this time. It they are rich and wealthy people, they let the candle burn for a whole year. And the mourners must remain in the house for seven days and do not go outside. Every morning and evening for a month, they call ten people from among their neighbours into their home. And during this time, they perform their prayers at home, and read the same prayers that are quoted above. Other Jews also come to comfort them. And every morning for the whole month they place a towel and a basin with water by the headboard of the bed where the deceased died, with the idea and belief, that he will come home every evening and wash. Apart from this, they also say that the man who has been an exceedingly impious person will not be tortured in hell, but just suffer for one year, as long as he did not abandon his Jewish faith even if not following it strictly and irrevocably. When the year has passed, he will be set free and come to paradise. But if he has adopted the Christian faith, then he is missing and lost forever. Otherwise, they write a great deal in a book that is called *Menorat Hamaor*[309] about how much the poor souls will be tortured, which is far too extensive to describe.

Chapter 45

This aforementioned book[310] also writes about how great a joy and happiness the just and the chosen will have in paradise. They say that every single chair is made of sapphire and before each and every chair there flow seven streams, and they are said to have an indescribable splendour. They also say that God the Highest himself will amuse himself and have fun with the pious and blessed souls and spend an hour a day with them. For the second hour, God sits on his judgement seat. For the third, he is said to be listening when the Jews say their prayers; and then God is said to shake his head and say, "Good for the king whom they are praising and honouring like this just like my holy people Israel did. The great God has much to mourn and despair about, that he destroyed his Temple and house, his sacrifices and altar!" But, my gracious reader, it is certainly a fairy-tale and manmade story that God Almighty, who has seen everything through eternity, will or can despair about something that he has done. Anybody who is sensible can understand and comprehend that this is impossible because it completely contra-

309 Heb.: *Menorat Hamaor*, מנורת המאור, *menorat ha-ma'or*, "the lamp of illumination." A Talmudic work by Rabbi Isaac ben Abraham Aboab (fl. 1300).

310 *Menorat ha-ma'or*. See the preceding note in this edition for *Spec*. (Sthlm, 1732), 107.

emot den Heliga Skrifft aldeles stridande är. Om denna deras ogrundade sagen skrifwa; så wäl *Menorat Hamaor*, som ock *Kitzor Schenä Lukot Habrit.* |

p. 109 [G7r] CAP. 46.

MEdan jag nu efter Judarnas beskrifning något handlat om Paradis/ wil jag ock något röra om helfwetit/ hwilket ses kan vti *Kitzor Schenä Lukot Habrit. Rabbinerna* berätta: at när en menniskia kommer för GUDz domstol/ skal GUD til henne säija: hafwer jag icke haft stor möda der med/ at jag skapat tig vti tin moders lif? At du intet blifwit död vti wädret? Har jag icke skaffat tig alt hwad tig nödigt warit hafwer? har du hållit min lag? Skulle då få wara at menniskian det samma giordt hafwer; blifwer hon lösgifwen och föres vti Paradis; men i annor händelse/ blifwer hon til fem förderfsens änglar antwardat och lefwererat/ och således swarar en ängel emot hwar Mosis Bok, som han öfwerträdt hafwer. Den första Ängelen slår honom/ den andra räknar/ den tredie kastar eld ifrån sig såsom en vgn; den fierde skaffar onda och ilaka kryddor/ stoppar honom der med munnen full säijandes således: Aldenstund du röfwat och tagit din nästa brödet ifrå/ och ätit det med tine tänder/ skal du nu deße bittra och onda kryddor tugga och nedswälja. Den femte slår des Fader och moder/ säijandes: hwarföre hafwen I icke bättre vpfostrat edra barn och tilhållit dem at läsa GUDz Lag/ och beflita sig om goda/ och fly onda p. 110 [G7v] giernin|gar. Nu min Gunstige Läsare/ kan man och här se deras wahntro/ ty hwar och en/ som af ett sundt förstånd är/ kan fatta och förstå/ at den som döder är kan ogiörligen tugga och äta.

CAP. 47.

HElfwetit warder af Judarne äfwen så beskrifwit/ som af förenämde Bok äfwen ses kan. De säija at GUD hafwer 7. helfweten skapat/ hafwandes hwart helfwete 7. Camrar/ hwar Cammar 7. strömmar af eld/ och 7. strömmar af hagel: warandes hwar och en af dem 1000. alnar bred/ 1000. alnar diup och 300. alnar lång/ och flyta hwar och en efter den andra/ och der igenom skola de ogudachtige och för-

dicts the Holy Scriptures. Both *Menorat Hamaor*[311] and *Kitzor Schenä Lukot Habrit*[312] write about this, their ill-founded tale.

Chapter 46

As I have now dealt with something about paradise according to the Jews' description, I will also touch upon something about hell, which can be seen in *Kitzor Schenä Lukot Habrit.*[313] The rabbis say that when a person comes before God's seat of judgement, God will say to him: "Have I not had much trouble by creating you in your mother's womb? That you did not die in the winds? Have I not provided everything for you, whatever you needed? Have you kept my law?" If the person has done so, then he is set free and led to paradise; but in the other instance, he is given and handed over to the five angels of perdition, and each angel thus corresponds to each book of Moses that he has transgressed. The first angel beats him; the second counts; the third throws out fire like an oven; the fourth gathers noxious and nasty herbs and stuffs them into his mouth saying this: "As you stole and took the bread from your neighbour and ate it with your teeth, you will now chew and swallow these bitter and noxious herbs." The fifth beats his [i.e., the dead man's] father and mother saying, "Why didn't you bring up your children better and urge them to read God's law and busy themselves with good deeds and flee bad ones?" Now, my gracious reader, we can also see their superstition here, because every single person who is of sound mind can understand and comprehend that it is impossible for whoever is dead to be able to chew and eat.

Chapter 47

Hell is also described by the Jews as can also be seen in the aforementioned book.[314] They say that God has created seven hells, each hell has seven chambers, and each chamber has seven rivers of fire and seven rivers of hail, and each one of them is a thousand ells [i.e., 600 m or 2000 ft] wide, a thousand ells [i.e., 600 m or 2000 ft] deep, and three hundred [i.e., 180 m or 600 ft] ells long, and they each flow one after the other, and the ungodly and the damned will travel upon them and be

311 See p. 207*n*309 in this edition for *Spec.* (Sthlm, 1732), 107.
312 See p. 189*n*292 in this edition for *Spec.* (Sthlm, 1732), 90.
313 See p. 189*n*292 in this edition for *Spec.* (Sthlm, 1732), 90.
314 קיצור שני לוחות הברית, *ḳiẓur šnei luḥot ha-brit*. See p. 189*n*292 in this edition for *Spec.* (Sthlm, 1732), 90.

dömde fara och pinade blifwa. Fördärfzens änglar som öfwer dem satte äro/ toga de ogudachtige åter fram och giöra dem lefwande/ ställandes dem til swars/ och måste de då/ alla onda gierningar och tanckar/ som de här vti tiden bedrifwit hafwa bekänna och vppenbara. De onda änglarne säija til dem: här in tils hafwen I gådt genom eld hagel och sniö emedan I icke hållit GUDz Lag/ som eder på Sinai berg gifwen är och icke fruchtadt för helfwetis eld. Kommer fördenskul och liden för edra onda gierningar/ och då föras de vti ett rum/ och vti hwart och ett rum
p. 111 [G8r] skal wara | 7000. wrår och wincklar/ vti hwar winckel skal wara 7000. Crocqdiler/ och hwar och en Crocodil skal spruta 300. gånger/ skolandes hwart sprutande innehålla 7000 krukor med förgifft. Der vtaf flyta 7. strömmar med dödsens kryddor/ och när en menniskia dem widrörer/ spricker hon sönder til alla ben och lemmar/ och måste således hela åhret igenom pint och plågad warda. Detta ware så korteligen talat om helfwetit och deß pina

CAP. 48.

OM de dödas vpståndelse *Fabulera* ock Judarna mycket. De föregifwa: at när *Messias* kommer/ skola wäl menniskiorna vpstå/ men doch icke alla/ vtan allenast de frome och Gudfruchtige och ei de ogudachtige/ at giöra redo och räkenskap; Ty som före sagt är/ måste den ogudachtige så snart han död blefwen är/ giöra räkenskap både med kropp och siäl tillika. De säija och at Keisare och Konungar/ som af de frommas och saligen dödas hufwud-skålar/ giordt sig drickes kiäril eller af andra ben/ knif-skaft: at samma ben wid det samma skola springa ifrån knifbladen/ samt hufwud-skålarne tagas och förswinna af borden och åter komma til sin graf när vpståndelsen ske skal; Skolandes den samma ingen annorstäds ske/
p. 112 [G8v] än vti Canans land. Men de som vti andra främman|de land boende äro/ skola wälta sig under jorden/ och ei kunna vpstå för än de komma til Canans land. De hafwa och eljest mycken wahntro och widskeppelse för sig som aldeles otrolig är/ och wore för den Gunstiga Läsaren alt för widlyftigt at omskrifwa. Jag hafwer fördenskul allenast det förnämligaste af deras *Traditioner* och Fabler welat anföra/ tackandes GUD! som oß sitt ords klara lius gifwit hafwer/ så at wi icke byggia på en sådan lös sand eller grund/ vtan på alla werldenes Frälsare hwilken är den rätta grunden och wägledaren til Himmelen och saligheten: Honom ware pris/ lof/ ähra och macht vti alla oändeliga och ewiga ewighet. Amen! |

punished. Angels of perdition that are placed above them march out the ungodly, bring them back to life, and hold them to account, and then they must confess and reveal all the evil deeds and thoughts that they have committed or had throughout all time. The evil angels say to them, "Until now you have walked through fire, hail, and snow, because you did not keep God's law that was given to you at Mount Sinai and did not fear the fires of hell. For this reason, come and suffer for your evil deeds!" And then they are led into a chamber, and in each chamber, there are said to be seven thousand nooks and corners, and in each corner, there are said to be seven thousand crocodiles, and each and every crocodile spews three hundred times, and each act of spewing contains seven thousand jars of poison. From here seven streams flow with the herbs of death, and when a person touches them, all of his bones and limbs shatter and he must be tortured and tormented like this for a whole year. This was a brief account of hell and its torments.

Chapter 48

The Jews also invent many tales about the resurrection of the dead. They maintain that when the Messiah comes, the people will rise from the dead, but not all, only the pious and God-fearing to prepare and make a reckoning. For, as it is said earlier, as soon as the ungodly man dies, he must make a reckoning with both his body and soul at the same time. They also say that emperors and kings, who have made drinking vessels from the skulls of the pious and blessed dead or knife-handles from other bones, that these bones will at the same time jump from the knife-blades and the skulls will be removed and disappear from the tables and return to their graves when the resurrection is to happen. This is only going to happen in the Land of Canaan. But those who live in other foreign countries will roll over under the ground and not be able to rise until they come to the Land of Canaan. Besides this, they also have much disbelief and superstition that is completely unbelievable, and which would be far too extensive to write about for the gracious reader. Therefore, I have chosen to quote only the noblest of their traditions – thanks be to God! who has given us the clear light of his word, so that we might not build upon such unstable sand or foundation but rather upon the Saviour of the entire world who is the right foundation and guide to heaven and blessedness: may there be unto him praise, honour, glory and power for ever and ever and all eternity. Amen!

p. 113 [H1r] De fehl, som vti denna Boken oförmodeligen inkommit/ behagar den Gunstige Läsaren på följande sätt benäget ändra.

Pag. 5. lin. 12. står *cos sciet*, läs *cosciel.*
Pag. 8. lin. 15. står *Halemme*, läs *Halememer*.
Pag. 13. lin. 21. står skriwa/ läs skrifwa.
Pag. 18. lin. 15. står *Bet, Alef*, läs *Bet, Resch, Alef*,
Ibid. lin. 19. står *Ben*, det är *&c.* läs *Ben*, det är en Son. *Resch* heter *Ruach*, det är/ den Helige Anda.
Pag. 40, lin. 19. står Sol-n/ läs Solen.

It will please the gracious reader to change the errors that have inconceivably occurred in this book in the following way:[315]

P. 5. l. 12: *cos sciet*, read *cosciel.*
P. 8. l. 15: *Halemme*, read *Halememer*.
P. 13. l. 21: skriwa, read: skrifwa.
P. 18. l. 15: *Bet, Alef*, read: *Bet, Resch, Alef,*
Ibid. l. 19: *Ben*, det är *&c.*, read *Ben*, det är en Son. *Resch* heter *Ruach*, det är/ den Helige Anda.
P. 40, l. 19: Sol-n, read: Solen.

315 The errata have been corrected and incorporated into the text of this edition.

Appendices

Appendix 1: King Frederik I's privilege and other dedications

1. King Fredrik I's privilege

Source: *Spec.* (Sthlm, 1732), iii–iv (a2r–a2v).

Text

WI *FRIEDRICH* med Gudz Nåde/ Sweriges/ Giöthes och Wändes Konung. *&c. &c. &c.* Landt Grefwe til Heßen. *&c. &c. &c.* Giöre witterligit: at Oß hafwer Wårt *Cancellie Collegium* i vnderdånighet wid handen gifwit, huru som det samma vppå *Orientaliske* Språkmästarens wid *Academien* i *Upsala* Oß Älskelig *Christian Petter Löwes* giorde ansökning til Wårt nådigste wälbehag bordt hemställa, om icke Oß skulle täckas at meddela bemälte *Löwe* Wårt nådige *Priviligium* vppå en *Tractat* kallad: *Speculum Religionis Judaicæ.*

I anseende til det arbete, som han wid denne Boks vpläggande anwändt; Och som Wi i betracktande af den flit, som merbemälte Språkmästare här wid wisat, til ofwannämdo Wårt *Collegii* underdånige hemställande för godt funnit at samtycka; Så wele Wi här med och i krafft af detta Wårt öpne Bref, nådeligen hafwa förvndt honom *Christian Petter Löwe*, Wårt *Privilegium* | på berörde *Tractat*, så at ingen den samma på Tijo åhrs tid, hwarcken här i Riket må eftertrycka, eller vt ifrån eftertryckt införa låta; wid Femhundrade Dahler Silferm:tz wite tilgiörandes.

Det alle som wederbör hafwa sig hörsameligen at efterrätta.

TIl yttermera wißo; hafwe Wi detta med egen hand vnderskrifwit och med Wårt Kongl. *Sigill* bekräffta låtit.

Stockholm i Råd-Cammaren den *11. Januarii 1732.*

Vti Hans Kongl. Maij:tz Wår Allernådigste Konungs och Herres frånwaro.

J. A. Meyerfeldt. Claes Sparre. Gustaf Bonde. J. L. Strömfelt. O. Törnflycht. T. G. Bielke. Ernst Johan Creutz. (L. S.) Gust. v. Heland.

https://doi.org/10.1515/9783110986938-003

Translation

We, Fredrik,[1] by the grace of God, King of Sweden, the Goths and Wends, etc., Landgrave of Hessen, etc. make known that our Chancellery College[2] has humbly passed on how they, upon the application for our most gracious pleasure from the Oriental language master at Uppsala Academy, the beloved to us Christian Petter Löwe, are to ask whether we would deign to notify the aforementioned Löwe of our gracious privilege for a treatise called *Speculum Religionis Judaicæ*.

In recognition of the work that he undertook in preparing this book and which we, in consideration of the diligence that this aforementioned language master has shown with this, have consented to the aforementioned request of our College, we hereby and by virtue of our open letter have graciously bestowed upon him, Christian Petter Löwe, our privilege for the treatise in question, so that no one else for the next ten years either here in the kingdom or beyond may reprint it under penalty of 500 daler silver.[3]

All who are concerned should obey this dutifully.

As further assurance we have signed this with our own hand and had it confirmed with our royal seal.

Stockholm, Council of Chambers, 11 January 1732.

In the absence of his Royal Majesty, our most gracious king and lord,

J. A. Meyerfeldt, Claes Sparre, Gustaf Bonde, J. L. Strömfelt, O. Törnflycht. T. G. Bielke, Ernst Johan Creutz, Gust. v. Heland.[4]

---

1 King Fredrik I of Hessen (1676–1751, r. 1720–51).

2 The Chancellery College (*Cancellie Collegium, kanslikollegium*) was the name for the chancellery during the Age of Empire (seventeenth and early eighteenth centuries).

3 500 silver daler was worth 167 riksdaler when the book was printed in 1732.

4 *J. A. Meyerfeldt*: Johan August Meijerfeldt the Elder (1666–1749) was a Swedish-Livonian general, member of the *Riksdag*, and a *rikskansliråd*. *Claes Sparre*: Claes Sparre af Söfdeborg (1673–1733) was *överamiral*, member of the *riksråd*, and president of the *amiralitetskollegium*. *Gustaf Bonde*: Gustaf Bonde (1682–1764) was *landshövding* in Östergötland, member of the *riksråd*, royal chamberlain, chancellor of Uppsala University, and an alchemist. *J. L. Strömfelt*: This possibly refers to Johan Carl Strömfelt (1678–1736) who was a Swedish *friherre* and baron, general lieutentant, and member of the *riksråd*. *O. Törnflycht*: Olof Törnflycht (1680–1737) was a Swedish *friherre* and baron, *landshövding* in Kronoberg and Stockholm, member of the *riksråd*, and chancellor of Uppsala University. *T. G. Bielke*: Ture Gabriel Bielke (1684–1763) was a Swedish *friherre* and baron, army major, member of the *riksdag*, and member of the *Kungliga Vetenskapsakademien*. *Ernst Johan Creutz*: Ernst Johan Creutz the Younger (1675–1742) was a baron, *landshövding* in Östergötland, member of the *riksråd*, and chancellor of the Royal Academy in Turku/Åbo (*Kungliga Akademien i Åbo*) founded in 1640. *Gust. v. Heland*: Gustaf von Heland (1680–1731) was active in the royal chancery and the *riksdag*, and he was appointed *kansliråd*.

2. Arvid Horn

Source: *Spec.* (Sthlm, 1732), v–viii (a3r–a4v).

Text

Kongl. Maij:ts Samt Sweriges Rikes Högtbetrodde Man och Råd/ Den Högwälborne Herre/ Herr Grefwe *ARVID HORN*, *Præsident* vti Kongl. Maij:ts och Riksens *Cancellie*, Åbo *Academie Canceller*, Samt *Præses Jllustris Societatis Literariæ & Scientiarum*. Nådigste Herre. |

Högwälborne Herr Grefwe Nådigste Herre.

AT jag denna Lilla *Tractat* och Beskrifning/ kallad *Speculum Religionis Judaicæ*, vnderstår mig at *dedicera* och tilskrifwa Eders Hög-Grefl. *Excellence*, för anlåter mig den högbeprislige Nåd/ som Eders Hög-Grefl. *Excellence* til min wälfärdz befrämjande bidragit; hwarföre och jag/ en vnderdån-ödmiuk tacksäijelse aflägger.

För öfrigt lefwer jag i det vnderdån-ödmiuka hopp/ at ei allenast få blifwa wärdig af en så hög Nåd och åtancka; Vtan och/ når Eders | Hög-Grefl. *Excellence* detta ringa wärck med milda och Nådiga ögon anser/ det befinnas lärer/ at mitt enfaldiga vpsåt här wid/ warit godt och wälmenande; än skiönt vtförandet ei torde wara på aldeles fullkommeligit.

Ty sedan jag/ som vti samma mörcker första gången hit til werlden kommit/ men nu efter den allwisa Gudens försyn och skickelse/ der ifrån til den Christeliga Tron och Läran brackt och på nytt födt blifwit/ eftersinnat/ med hwad för ett faseligit moln de samma betäckte äro: så har jag/ såsom om alt detta bekant/ vppå goda wänners inrådande och begiäran/ åtagit mig detta Wärcket på det Swenska Tungomåhlet/ til hwars och ens godtfinnande at lemna och af Trycket vtgå låta.

Gud den alldra högsta! som ett bättre Lius oß | i trona meddelat/ gifwe! at hwar och en måtte spegla sig vti detta och der af märckia/ at oß större nåd och klarhet/ än de fattige Judar wederfaren är; och derföre den stora Gudens Heliga Namn beprisa.

Den samma nådiga Guden/ vppehålle til många tider Eders Hög Grefl. *Excellence* wid lif och hälsa/ samt bekröne med nåd och wälsignelse/ hela den Hög-Grefl. *Familien* til Fädernes Landets stöd och de beträngdas hugnad och glädie.

Jag innesluter mig här med vti Eders Hög-Grefl. *Excellences* mycket Höga Nåd och framhärdar til dödstunden/ Eders Hög-Grefl. *Excellences* Vnderdån-ödmiukaste tienare *Christian Petter Löwe*.

Translation

His Royal Majesty's and the Kingdom of Sweden's highly trusted man and council, the noble lord, Count Arvid Horn.[5] President of his Royal Majesty's and the Kingdom's Privy Council Chancellery, Chancellor of Åbo Academy as well as President of the Illustrious Society of Literature and Sciences.[6] Most gracious Lord.

Noble Count, most gracious Sir:

That I presume to dedicate and ascribe this little treatise and description called *Speculum Religionis Judaicæ* to Your Excellency is due to the highly commendable grace that Your noble Excellency contributed to the promotion of my wellbeing, for which I also offer my humble thanks.

Moreover, I live in the humble hope that I not only may remain worthy of such great mercy and consideration, but also that when Your noble Excellency regards this modest work with mild and merciful eyes, that it will be found that my simple intent with it has been good and well meaning, even though its execution has not been entirely perfect.

Because ever since I, who first came hither to the world in the same darkness but who now after the providence and guidance of the all-wise God was brought thence to the Christian Faith and Teaching and was born again, have reflected upon what a ghastly cloud these same [Jews] are covered with, I have, as all this is familiar, on the advice and request of good friends, undertaken to have this work in the Swedish language released and printed for everyone's approval.

God Most High, who has shown us a better light in faith, make it so that everyone may reflect on this and thereby notice that we have greater grace and clarity than the poor Jews have experienced, and therefore praise the Holy Name of the Great God.

May the same gracious God sustain Your noble Excellency many times in life and health and crown with grace and blessing the whole of Your noble family for the support of the fatherland and comfort and joy of the beleaguered.

I hereby place myself under Your noble Excellency's very great mercy and persevere until the hour of my death. Your noble Excellency's most humble servant, Christian Petter Löwe.

---

5 Arvid Horn of Ekebyholm (1664–1742) was a soldier, diplomat, and member of the *riksdag* and appointed *rikskansliråd*.

6 Horn was the *Præses Societatis Literariæ & Scientiarum*, i.e., the chairperson of the Royal Society of Sciences in Uppsala (Kungliga Vetenskaps-Societeten i Uppsala), founded 1710.

3. Gustaf Cronhielm

Source: *Spec.* (Sthlm, 1732), ix–xii (a5r–a6v).

Text

Kongl. Maij:ts Högtbetrodde Man, Sweriges Rikes Råd, och *Præsident* vti Kongl. *Cancelliet* Samt Lag *Commission*, så och *Upsala Academiæ Canceller*, Högtwälborne Grefwe Herr *GUSTAF CRONHIELM* Nådigste Herre. |

Högwälborne Herr Grefwe Nådigste Herre.

MEd lika vnderdånighet/ tilskrifwer jag Eders Hög-Grefl. *Excellence* detta af mig på Swenska Tungomåhlet vtarbetade Lilla Wärck och Beskrifning/ om Judarnas *Ceremonie* ifrån deras födzlostund/ til des de döde warda; giörandes jag mig så mycket mehr försäkrad; at min vnderdånige wördnad här vtinnan intet onådigt vptages; hälst som Eders Hög-Grefl. *Excellences* | mig bewiste stora Nåd giör/ at jag näst GUD/ bör tilskrifwa all min timmeliga wälfärd och vpkomst/ Eders Hög-Grefl. *Excellence*, såsom min högste Herre och Förman wid Kongl. *Academien* i *Upsala*

Alt sådant har satt mig vti de otwifwelachtige tanckar/ at och hädan efter af Eders Hög-Grefl. *Excellences* Höga Nåd ei mindre än här tils få dehlachtig blifwa. Hwar emot jag med innerlig och trogen önskan til GUD ingalunda skal vphöra/ det han wille förlänga Eders Hög-Grefl. *Excellences* Lifstid än i många åhr/ och at en hwar beträngd vndersåte måtte få fägna sig af den nåden; at Eders Hög-Grefl. *Excellence* med hela den Hög-Grefl. *Familien*, vti ett begiärligit wälstånd | alt framgent *Florerar*. Det och jag i all min tid skal bedia om;

Som för öfrigit har den Nåden til mitt sidsta förblifwa/ Eders Hög-Grefl. *Excellences* Vnderdån-ödmiukaste tienare *Christian Petter Löwe*.

Translation

His Royal Majesty's highly trusted man, of the Privy Council of Sweden, President of the Royal Chancellery as well as the Law Commission and chancellor of Uppsala Academy, the noble lord, Lord Gustaf Cronhielm.[7] Most gracious Lord.

Noble Count, most gracious Sir:

---

7 Gustaf Cronhielm (1664–1737) was a diplomat, *landshövding* in Västmanland, member of the *riksråd*, and president of the *kammarkollegium*.

With similar humility, I dedicate to Your noble Excellency this little work and description of the Jews' ceremonies from the moment of their birth until they are dead, composed by me in the Swedish language. And it makes me all the more assured that my humble reverence in this will not be taken up ungraciously, but rather the mercy shown to me by Your noble Excellency means that I, after God, ought to attribute all of my worldly welfare and origin to Your noble Excellency as my greatest lord and leader at the Royal Academy in Uppsala.

All of which has given me the incontrovertible thoughts that I henceforth may partake no less in Your noble Excellency's great mercy than here. For which I will never cease to have a devoted and faithful wish for God: that he may prolong Your noble Excellency's life for many years to come and that every beleaguered subject may rejoice in the grace that Your entire noble family will flourish into the future with desirable prosperity. That is what I will pray for in all my days.

I who incidentally have the grace to remain until my final day Your noble Excellency's most humble servant, Christian Petter Löwe.

4. Hans Henrik von Liewen

Source: *Spec.* (Sthlm, 1732), xiii–xvi (a7r–a8v).

Text

Kongl. Maij:ts Högtbetrodde Man och Sweriges Rikes Råd, Högwälborne Grefwe Herr *HANS HINRICH von LIVEN*, Nådigste Herre. |

Högwälborne Herr Grefwe Nådigste Herre.

IBland andra höga Nådeteckn som mig bewiste blifwit, sedan jag blifwit en lem, vti den Christelige Lutherska Församlingen, samt Inwånare vti Sweriges Rike, är det icke det minsta, at Eders Hög-Grefl. *Excellence*, mig som en Fremling så nådigt behagat hägna. | Hwarföre jag wid detta tilfället har den Nåden, at vnderdån-ödmiukeligen *dedicera* och tilskrifwa Eders Hög-Grefl. *Excellence* efterföljande Lilla *Tractat*, kallad *Speculum Religionis Judaicæ*.

Min vnderdån-ödmiukaste bön och begiäran är: Det Eders Hög-Grefl. *Excellence* täcktes än widare förvnna mig den Höga Nåden. Hwaremot jag hos GUD skal stundeligen bönfalla, om alt hwad Eders Hög-Grefl. *Excellence* vti timmelig och andelig måtto kan förnöija, och at Eders Hög-Grefl. *Excellence* i mån|ga åhr, med hela des Höga *Familie* måtte säll hos oß lefwa.

Jag lefver, emot en så hög Nåd, til mitt sidsta, Eders Hög-Grefl. *Excellences* Vnderdån-ödmiukaste tienare *Christian Petter Löwe.*

Translation

His Royal Majesty's highly trusted man and of the Privy Council of Sweden, the noble count, Lord Hans Henrik von Liewen.[8] Most gracious Lord.

Noble Count, most gracious Sir:

Among the other signs of great mercy that have been shown to me since I became a member of the Christian Lutheran Congregation as well as an inhabitant of the Kingdom of Sweden, it is not least that Your noble Excellency has seen fit to protect me as a stranger. For which reason I at this moment have the grace to dedicate and humbly ascribe to Your noble Excellency the following little treatise called *Speculum Religionis Judaicæ*.

My most humble prayer and wish is this: that Your noble Excellency sees fit to continue to bestow Your high grace on me. For which I continually beseech God that Your noble Excellency may enjoy everything both in a worldly and spiritual manner, and that Your noble Excellency along with all Your noble family will live blissfully among us for many years to come.

In return for such great mercy, I live until my final day as Your noble Excellency's most humble servant, Christian Petter Löwe.

5. Casten Feif

Source: *Spec.* (Sthlm, 1732), xvii–xx (b1r–b2v).

Text

Kongl. Maij:ts Högtbetrodde Man och *Præsident*, vti Riksens Högloflige *Statz Contoir*, Högwälborne *Baron* Herr *CASTEN FEIFF*, Nådige Herre. |

Högwälborne Herr *Baron* och *Præsident*, Nådige Herre.

DEnne *Tractat* och beskrifning *Speculum Religionis Judaicæ* frambär jag i största vnderdån-ödmiukhet för Eders *Excellence* Herr *Baron* och *Præsidenten*, | som ibland andra Nådiga Herrar, i anseende til de många Nåde prof, som mig owärdigan bewiste blifwit, jag den nåden och friheten har aldeles at vtnämna och förklara, och näst GUD hela min vpkomst och timmeliga wälfärd tilskrifwa;

Hwarföre jag nu så wäl vnderdån-ödmiukast tackar, som och önskar, at alt framgent en dylik Nåd och åtancka få åtniuta: Hwilken höga Nåd, jag med oaflåtelig

8 Hans Henrik von Liewen (1664–1733) was an army officer and member of the *riksråd*.

plicht och wördnad til min död skal ihog | komma, och den stund jag lefwer, förblifwer Eders *Excellences* Vnderdån-ödmiukaste tienare *Christian Petter Löwe.*

Translation

His Royal Majesty's highly trusted man and President of the Kingdom's praiseworthy State Office, noble baron, Lord Casten Feif.[9] Gracious Lord.

Noble Lord Baron and President, gracious Sir:

I proffer this treatise and description, *Speculum Religionis Judaicæ*, in the greatest humility to Your Excellency Lord Baron and President, whom I, among other gracious lords in respect to the many acts of mercy that were shown to my unworthy self, have the grace and freedom to name and make completely clear and in accordance with God ascribe my entire origin and worldly welfare.

For which I now most humbly give thanks and also wish to enjoy a similar grace and consideration in the future. What high mercy I will remember with unwavering duty and reverence until my death! And while I am alive, I remain Your Excellency's most humble servant, Christian Petter Löwe.

6. Otto Reinhold Strömfelt

Source: *Spec.* (Sthlm, 1732), xxi–xxiv (b3r–b4v).

Text

Kongl. Maij:ts Högtbetrodde Man och *Præsident*, vti Riksens Högloflige Cammar *Collegio*, Högwälborne *Baron* Herr Otto Reinholt Strömfeldt/ Nådige Herre. |

Högwälborne Herr *Baron* och *Præsident*, Nådige Herre.

HÄr är en liten *Tractat*, vnder *Titul*, af *Speculum Religionis Judaicæ*, som jag likaledes har den Nåden at *dedicera* Eders *Excellence*. Min vnderdån | ödmiuka tancka här wid är, ingalunda vtan ordsak; ty när jag påminner mig de många Nåde prof, som Eders *Excellence* mig såsom en främling i mångahanda måtto wisat, fägnar det mig hierteligen, at jag til en vnderdån-ödmiuk tacksäijelses afläggiande, här medelst får tilfälle mitt vnderdån-ödmiukaste sinnelag at yttra.

9 Casten Feif (1662–1739) was a Swedish *friherre* and worked as Karl XII of Sweden's secretary.

Hoppandes som och allerödmiukast beder, hädan efter at äfwen få af samma Nåd mig hugna, såsom och, at detta Lilla Wärcket hos Eders *Excellence* må Nådigt vpta | gas;

Jag blifwer näst trogen an-önskan til GUDz milderika Nåd och wälsignelse, aldeles förbunden at framhärda, Eders *Excellences* Vnderdån-ödmiukaste tienare *Christian Petter Löwe.*

Translation

His Royal Majesty's highly trusted man and President of the Kingdom's praiseworthy *kammarkollegium*,[10] noble baron, Lord Otto Reinhold Strömfelt.[11] Gracious Lord.

Noble Lord Baron and President, gracious Sir:

Here is a little treatise with the title *Speculum Religionis Judaicæ*, which I likewise have the grace to dedicate to Your Excellency. My humble thought with this is not without reason, because when I remember the many acts of mercy that Your Excellency showed me as a stranger in many ways, it delights my heart that I, by submitting a humble thanks, have the opportunity to express my most humble disposition.

Hoping and most humbly praying that I henceforth will also be comforted by the same mercy, and also that this little work will be graciously taken up by Your Excellency.

Faithfully wishing for God's gracious mercy and blessing, I remain bound to persevere. Your Excellency's most humble servant, Christian Petter Löwe.

---

10 The "Cammar *Collegio*," or *kammarkollegium*, is the Swedish Chamber of Taxation and Auditing.

11 Otto Reinhold Strömfelt (1679–1744) was president of the *kammarkollegium*.

7. Johannes Steuchius

Source: *Spec.* (Sthlm, 1732), xxv–xxviii (b5r–b6v).

Text

Kongl. Maij:ts Tro Man, Sweriges Rikes Archi-Biscop, och *Pro-Canceller* Wid Kongl. *Academien* i *Upsala*, Then Högwördigste Herren HERR *Doct. JOANNES STEUCHIUS*, |

Höggunstige Herre Och Mächtige Befordrare.

Hwad som mig drifwit at i Liuset lämna och på Trycket vtgå låta denna Lilla *Tractat, Speculum Religionis Judaicæ* kallad/ eller Beskrifning om Judarnas *Ceremonier*, så wäl wid Födzlostunden/ som deras lefwerne och äntelige död; är intet någon blott *curiosite* af mig sielf vpfunnen/ vtan i den afsichten giordt/ at der igenom ställa wår Christna werld för ögonen/ huru den Aldrahögste | Gudens Nåd/ lyser på oß och wåra med Bröder vti denna Christeliga Lutherska Församlingen/ som ett sådant mörcker endtledigade äro/ för min dehl har jag ordsak hans Heliga Namn derföre prisa/ som mig vtur ett sådant mörcker tagit/ och en lem och medarfwinge til Gudz Rike och den ewiga Saligheten giordt hafwer.

Och som jag förhoppas at detta mitt företagande/ intet af Högwördigste Fadren Herr *Doctorn* och Erchie-Biskopen lärer ogunstigt vptagas; Ty har jag den samma i största ödmiukhet Högwördigste Fadren Herr *Doctorn* och Erchie-Biskopen *dedicera* och tilskrifwa welat/ med ödmiuk förtröstan/ at det igenom Högwördigste Fadrens Herr *Doctorns* och Erckie-Biskopens wahnliga gunst och Fader | liga omwårdnad Nådgunstigt befrämjes.

Hwar emot jag intet skal aflåta GUD den Aldrahögste at anropa/ han wille vti långa tider/ låta oß med hugnad och tröst få se/ Högwördigste Fadrens och Erchie-Biskopens förnöijeliga Lefnad/ til hela des Förnäma *Families* wälstånd!

Jag innesluter mig aldeles vti Högwördigste Fadrens Herr *Doctorens* och Erchie-Biskopens gunst. Förblifwande til mitt sidsta/

Högwördigste Fadrens Herr *Doctorens* och Erchie-Biscoppens Allerödmiukaste tienare *Christian Petter Löwe.*

Translation

His Royal Majesty's faithful man, the Kingdom of Sweden's Archbishop, and Vice-chancellor of the Royal Academy in Uppsala, the most reverend lord, Lord Dr Johannes Steuchius.[12]

Highly favourable Lord and mighty Patron:

What has driven me to draw into the light and have published in print this little treatise called *Speculum Religionis Judaicæ*, or a description of the Jews' ceremonies both from the moment of birth and their lives and eventual deaths, is not just some curiosity devised by myself, but rather has been done with the intention of hereby placing before the eyes of the Christian world how the grace of God Most High shines upon us in the Christian Lutheran Congregation who are freed of such a darkness. For my part, I therefore have reason to praise his holy name, who took me out of such darkness and made me a member and co-heir to the Kingdom of God and eternal bliss.

And as I hope that this undertaking of mine will not be unfavourably taken up by the Most Reverend Father, Doctor, and Archbishop, because I have wanted to dedicate and ascribe to this very person, with the humble confidence that it will be graciously promoted through the usual favour and paternal care of the Most Reverend Father, Doctor, and Archbishop.

Whereas I shall not refrain from calling upon God Most High that he will let us receive comfort and consolation for a long time by seeing the pleasant life of the Most Reverend Father and the Archbishop and the prosperity of his entire distinguished family!

I place myself completely in the favour of the Most Reverend Father, Doctor, and Archbishop.

Remaining to my final day, the Most Reverend Father, Doctor, and Archbishop's most humble servant, Christian Petter Löwe.

---

12 Johannes Steuchius (Jöns Steuch, 1676–1742) was a theologian, professor at Uppsala University, archbishop of Uppsala, and member of the *riksdag*.

8. Nicolaus Barchius

Source: *Spec.* (Sthlm, 1732), xix–xxxii (b7r–b8v).

Text

Kongl. Maij:ts Tro Man och Biskop öfwer Wästeråhs Stifft, Den Högwördige Herren HERR *D. NICOLAUS BARCHIUS*, |

Högwördige Fader, Gunstige Befordrare.

AT jag denne Lilla *Tractat Speculum Religionis Judaicæ* kallad/ vnderstår mig Högwördige Fadren Herr *Doctorn* och Biskopen *dedicera* och tilskrifwa; För anlåter mig den särdeles gunst och stora bewågenhet/ som Högwördige Fadren Herr Biskopen för mig låtit påskina.

Ordsaken/ hwarföre jag detta Lilla Arbetet antagit/ är förnämligast den; at jag som i samma mörcker warit inwecklad/ | finner mig nu högst-befogad det samma at vptäckia och androm enfalldigom för ögonen ställa.

Derföre/ som Gudz råd böra vppenbarliga prisas: har jag/ efter mitt ringa pund/ på mitt samwete och efter yttersta Förfarenhet/ sammanskrifwit och til Trycket vtfärdat detta mitt ringa Arbete. GUD! som benådat oß Christnom med ett fullkomligare Lius/ gifwe/ at hwar och en af oß må kunna wackta oß för en slik wantro.

Detta mitt ringa Arbete begiärer nu i ödmiukhet/ at få låhna några strålar af Högwördige Fadrens Herr *Doctorns* och Biskopens giällande Sohl/ hwar wid jag i ödmiukhet än ytterligare åstundar mig få hyggia och wärma.

At och GUD den Aldrahögste wille vppehålla Högwördige Fadren Herr | *Doctorn* och Biskopen/ samt hela des Förnäma *Familie* med nåd och krafft af Högden/ til sitt Namns ähra och hans Församlings vpbyggelse; Skal wara och blifwa min bön och önskan den stund jag lefwer/ som och med ödmiuk wördnad städze förblifwer/ Högwördige Fadrens Herr *Doctorns* och Biskoppens Ödmiukaste tienare *Christian Petter Löwe.*

Translation

His Royal Majesty's faithful man and Bishop of the Diocese of Västerås, the Reverend Lord, Dr Nicolaus Barchius.[13]

Reverend Father, favourable Patron:

---

13 Nicolaus Barchius (Nils Barchius, 1676–1733) was a priest and later bishop of Västerås.

That I presume to dedicate this little treatise, called *Speculum Religionis Judaicæ*, to the Reverend Father, Doctor, and Bishop, is due to the special favour and great consideration that the Reverend Father Bishop has let shine on me.

The reason that I have taken on this small task is principally this: that I, having been engulfed in the same darkness, now find myself perfectly qualified to uncover and place it before other simpleminded people's eyes.

Therefore, as God's counsel should be openly praised, I have in accordance with my little wealth, my conscience and extreme experience composed my small work and disseminated it in print. May God, who has graced us Christians with a more complete light, make it so that every one of us is able to guard ourselves from such superstition.

This small work of mine now humbly requests to be allowed to borrow some of the beams from the Reverend Father, Doctor, and Bishop's dazzling sun, by which I, in humility rather than further desires, may take care of and warm myself.

It will be and remain being my prayer and wish for as long as I live that God Most High will support the Reverend Father, Doctor, and Bishop as well as his entire noble family with grace and power from on high to honour his name and edify his congregation. I who also with humble reverence will always remain the Reverend Father, Doctor, and Bishop's most humble servant, Christian Petter Löwe.

Appendix 2: Hebrew, Aramaic, and Yiddish words, terms, and phrases found in *Speculum Religionis Judaicæ*

Untransliterated Hebrew

Spec. (Sthlm, 1732)	Standard Hebrew	Meaning (*Spec.* [Sthlm, 1732], page:line [this edition page:line])
אגוז בגמ חטא	אגוז בג"מ חטא	A nut in gematria is a sin (51:8–9 [140:17])
ברוךשפטרנו מעונשו זו	ברוך אתה י-י אלהינו מלך העולם שפטרני מעונשו של זה	Blessed are You, O Lord, our God, King of the universe, who exempted me from this one's punishment (8:21–22 [78:10])
הנה העלמה הרה וילדת בן	הנה העלמה הרה וילדת בן	The virgin will conceive and give birth to a son [Isaiah 7:14] (15:28–29 [90:11])
ואתה בית לחם אפרתה צעיר אתה להיות באלפי יהודא ממך יצא מלכי בישראל ומוצאיו מקדם ימי עולם	ואתה בית לחם אפרתה צעיר להיות באלפי יהודה ממך לי יצא להיות מושל בישראל ומוצאתיו מקדם מימי עולם	But thou, Bethlehem Ephratah, though thou be little among the thousands of Judah, yet out of thee shall he come forth unto me that is to be ruler in Israel; whose goings forth have been from of old, from everlasting [Micah 5:1] (22:14–16 [98:31–32])
חנוכה	חנוכה	Hanukkah (62:23 [154:27])
כי לא אחפוץ במת הרשע כי אם שובו וחי לעולם	כי לא אחפוץ במת הרשע כי אם בשוב וחי לעולם	As I do not wish the death of the evil one, unless he returns and lives forever [Shenei Luchot HaBerit, Aseret HaDibrot, Yoma, Ner Mitzva 4:36] (23:7–8 [100:13])
משיח	משיח	Messiah (19:30 [96:22])
רביאליעזר	רבי אליעזר	Rabbi Eliezer (2: 9 [66:16])

https://doi.org/10.1515/9783110986938-004

Transliterated Hebrew, Aramaic, and Yiddish

Spec. (Sthlm, 1732)	Hebrew, Aramaic, or Yiddish	Meaning	Language (*Spec.* [Sthlm, 1732], page:line [this edition page:line]) Notes
Actamut אקדמות	*akdamut* אקדמות	Akdamut	Aram. (14:7 [88:3]) Lit. “an introduction”: a liturgical poem (*piyuṭ*) recited during Shavuot
Adon Olam אדון עולם	*adon 'olam* אדון עולם	Adon Olam	Heb. (34:14 [116:2]) Lit. “eternal Lord, Lord of the universe”: a liturgical hymn
Adonai אדוני	*adonai* אדוני	My Lord, “God”	Heb. (86:7 [184:6–7])
Ador ––	*adar* אדר	Adar	Heb. (63:5 [156:5])
Ævel ––	*'evel* עבל	wrong-doing, unrighteousness	Heb. (84:3 [180:25])
Alef ––	*alef* א	the Hebrew letter א	Heb. (18:15, 17, 27 [94:16, 17; 96:3])
Allenu le Schabeach עלינו לשבח	*'aleinu lešabeaḥ* עלינו לשבח	Aleinu Leshabeach	Heb. (12:6 [82:16–17]) Lit. “it is our duty to praise”: a Jewish prayer
Alma עלמה	*'almah* עלמה	young woman, maiden	Heb. (16:1 [90:12])
Amen Jehe Scheme Raba ––	*amen yehei' šemeih raba'* אמן יהא שמה רבא	Amen, may his great name	Aram. (103:5–6 [202:2])
Arbe ––	*arbeh* ארבה	locusts	Heb. (42:10 [126:5])
Aref ––	*'arov* ערוב	wild animals	Heb. (42:8 [126:4])

Aron ארון	*aron* ארון	coffin	Heb. (102:18 [200:24])
Aron Hakodesch ארון הקודש	*aron ha-ḳodeš* ארון הקודש	the Holy Ark	Heb. (5:16 [72:10])
Av —	*av* אב	father	Heb. (18:17 [94:17])
Baal Meziza בעל מציצה	*ba'al meẓiẓah* בעל מציצה	man responsible for carrying out *meẓiẓah be-peh*	Heb. (5:4 [72:4])
Baal Peria בעל פריה	*ba'al periah* בעל פריה	man responsible for carrying out *periah*	Heb. (5:9 [72:6])
Bara —	*bara'* ברא	created	Heb. (18:25 [96:1])
Barat —	*barad* ברד	hail	Heb. (42:10 [126:5])
Bark Ata, Jehovah Elohenu Mälek Haolam Hamotzi Läkem Min —	*baruch atah Adonai, Eloheinu Melech Ha'olam hamoẓi leḥem min ha'aretz* ברוך אתה י-י אלהינו מלך העולם המוציא לחם מן הארץ	Blessed are You, Lord our God, King of the Universe, who brings forth bread from the earth	Heb. (77:23–25 [174:6–7])
Barok Haba ברוך הבא	*baruch haba'* ברוך הבא	blessed is he who comes, welcome	Heb. (68:26–27 [162:25])
Baruch Haba ברוך הבא	*baruch haba'* ברוך הבא	blessed is he who comes, welcome	Heb. (4:14 [70:6])
Baruk Elohenu Simen Tau Oma Sall tau. Baruk Hakatan Im Hakala סימן טוב ומזל טוב ברוף החתן עם הכלה	*siman ṭov u-mazal ṭov baruch ha-ḥatan 'im ha-kalah* סימן טוב ומזל טוב ברוך החתן עם הכלה	a good sign and congratulations to the groom and bride	Heb. (69:1–4 [162:27–164:1])
Ben —	*ben* בן	son	Heb. (18:16 [94:16])
Berescit Bara Elohim —	*bereišit bara' elohim* בראשית ברא אלהים	In the beginning God created (Genesis 1:1)	Heb. (17:10 [92:15])

Berkat Hamason --	*birkat ha-mazon* ברכת המזון	blessing of the food	Heb. (43:10 [128:7–8])
Bet --	*bet* ב	the Hebrew letter ב	Heb. (18:15 [94:16])
Cabranim קברנים	*ḳabranim* קברנים	kabranim, morticians	Heb. (101:16–17 [200:7])
Cadisch vegahm amen gehö schemä raba קדיש וגם אמן יהא שמי רבה	*ḳadiš ve-gam amen yehei šmeh raba'* קדיש וגם אמן יהא שמה רבא	Kaddish and amen. May his great name be great	Heb./Aram. (1:23–2:1 [66:11])
Calata --	*kalah* כלה	bride	Heb. (65:21 [160:2])
Capora --	*kaparah* כפרה	kaparah, expiation; penance; penitence, atonement	Heb. (14:26; 52:14 [88:14; 142:10])
Caraim --	*ḳara'im* קראים	Karaites	Heb. (80:8 [176:18])
Cassidim	*ḥasidim* חסידים	Hasidim	Heb. (80:12 [176:20])
Catan --	*ḥatan* חתן	groom	Heb. (65:20 [160:2])
Cefardea --	*ẓefardea* צפרדע	frogs	Heb. (42:7–8 [126:4])
Chumaseh חומש	*ḥumaš* חומש	Chumash, the Five (Books of Moses)	Heb. (85:20–21 [182:16])
Coschere --	*kašer* כשר	kosher, proper, lawful	Heb. (85:21 [182:17]) Transliteration in *Spec.*, cf. Yidd. *košər*
Cosciel Bäraka כוסשל ברכה	*kos šel barachah* כוס של ברכה	cup of blessing	Heb. (5:12 [72:8])
Cumesch --	*ḥumaš* חומש	Chumash	Heb. (7:26 [76:9]) Transliteration in *Spec.*, cf. Yidd. *ḥuməš*
Dam --	*dam* דם	blood	Heb. (42:7 [126:4])

Dever ––	*dever* דבר	pestilence	Heb. (42:9 [126:4])
Doma דומה	*dumah* דומה	Dumah	Aram. (105:24 [204:11]) Lit. "silence"
Efikomen ––	*afiḳoman* אפיקומן	that which comes after	Heb.(43:1–2 [128:3]) Cf. Gk. ἐπὶ κῶμον, *epíkṓmon*
Egos אגוז	*egoz* אגוז	nut	Heb. (51:6 [140:16])
Ehich Ascher Ehich אהיה אשר אהיה	*ehyeh ašer ehyeh* אהיה אשר אהיה	I am that I am	Heb. (86:8, 9 [184:7–8])
El אל	*el* אל	God	Heb. (86:7, 9 [184:7])
Elias *Thisbe* ––	*Eliyahu ha-tišbi* אליהו התישבי	Elijah from Tishbe	Heb. (38:18 [120:22])
Elohim אלוהים	*elohim* אלוהים	God, deity	Heb. (86:7, 8 [184:7])
Erel ערל	*'arel* ערל	uncircumcised	Heb. (14:19–20 [88:10])
Etrog אתרוג	*etrog* אתרוג	etrog, citron, *Citrus medica*	Heb. (57:18 [148:18])
Gabba גבא	*gabbai* גבאי	gabbai, synagogue warden, sexton	Heb. (89:6 [188:1])
Gehenna גיהנם	*gehinom* גיהנם	Gehenna, the realm of the unrepented dead	Heb. (3:6 [68:9])
Gemara ––	*gemara'* גמרא	Gemara	Aram. (7:30 [76:11])
Get ––	*geṭ* גט	get, divorce document	Aram. (76:4 [170:29])
Hafdala הבדלה	*havdalah* הבדלה	Havdalah	Heb. (37:25–26 [120:10]) Lit. "separation"

Halememer האלממר	*ha'almemar* האלמימר	the bimah, pulpit	Heb. (7:4 [74:15]) Cf. Yidd. אַלמימר, *almimer* from Arab. المنبر, *al-minbar*, "the platform," "the pulpit"
Halmemer ––	*ha'almemar* האלמימר	the bimah, pulpit	Heb. (58:12 [150:7]) Cf. Yidd. אַלמימר, *almimer* from Arab. المنبر, *al-minbar*, "the platform," "the pulpit"
Hüre At Mäkudeschet Libetabaat Kiduscham Kedat Mosche Vä Jsraël הרי את מקודשת לי בט־בעת קידושין כדת מושה וישראל	*here meḳudešet li be-ṭabaʿat ḳidušin ke-dat Mošeh ve-Iśrael* הרי את מקודשת לי בטבעת קידושין כדת משה וישראל	Behold, you are consecrated to me with a wedding ring according to the religion of Moses and Israel	Heb. (69:22–25 [164:12–14])
Håschana Raba ––	*hošaʿnaʾ rabaʾ* הושענא רבא	Hoshana Rabba	Heb. (58:2 [150:2]) Lit. "great supplication"
Hoschiana Raba הושענה רבא	*hošaʿnaʾ rabaʾ* הושענא רבא	Hoshana Rabba	Heb. (48:29–30 [138:7]) Lit. "great supplication"
Ichelein ––	*ẓiḳleyn* ציקליין	little goat	Yidd. (43:10 [128:8])
Jaginkidos ––	*yayin ḳiduš* יין קידוש	wine of sanctification, kiddush wine	Heb. (32:9 [112:23])
Jain näsach יין נסך	*yayin nesech* יין נסך	wine libation	Heb. (15:16 [90:5])
Jalkut Reuveni ––	*Yalḳuṭ Re'uveni* ילקוט ראובני	Yalkut Reubeni	Heb. (36:29–30 [118:18]) Lit. "the collection of Reuben"
Jeschua ––	*Yešuʿa* ישוע	saviour	Heb. (18:19 [94:18])
Jod ––	*yud* י	the Hebrew letter י	Heb. (18:15, 19 [94:16, 18])

Jom Kipor ––	*yom kipur* יום כיפור	Yom Kippur, Day of Atonement	Heb. (51:29 [142:2])
Jom Tof יום טוב	*yom ṭov* יום טוב	a good day, holiday	Heb. (40:28 [124:8–9]) Yidd. *yomṭof, yonṭof, yonṭif*
Kalef חלף	*ḥalaf, ḥalif* חלף	slaughterer's knife	Heb. (28:7, 11 [106:20, 22])
Kalla ––	*ḥalah* חלה	challah	Heb. (32:8 [112:22])
Kalutz Nal חלוץ נעל	*ḥaluẓ na'al* חלוץ נעל	shoe is removed	Heb. (77:2 [172:14])
Kaschar Sepher Tora כשר ספר תורה	*kašer sefer torah* כשר ספר תורה	kosher Torah scroll	Heb. (85:18–19 [182:15–16]) The syntax of the phrase is incorrect and more akin to Yidd.
Kelitza חליצה	*ḥaliẓah* חליצה	halitzah	Heb. (76:9, 18; 77:10 [172:2, 7, 18]) Lit. "pulling off, removal, extraction"
Kenuka חנוכה	*ḥanukah* חנוכה	Hanukkah	Heb. (xl:26; 61:3 [62:25; 152:23])
Keset Sekel umot katot Le Jsraël חסד של אומת עולם חטאות לישראל	*ḥesed šel umot 'olam ḥaṭot le-Yiśra'el* חסד של אומת עולם חטאות לישראל	The grace of the nations of the world are sins to Israel	Heb. (13:19–21 [86:10–11])
Ketuba כתובה	*ketubah* כתובה	ketubah, marriage agreement	Heb. (69:29–30 [164:16])
Kinem ––	*kinim* כנים	lice	Heb. (42:8 [126:4])
Kitzur Schenä, Lucot Habrit קיצור שני לוחת הברית	*ḳiẓur šnei luḥot ha-brit* קיצור שני לוחות הברית	Abbreviation of the Two Tablets of the Covenant	Heb. (90:18–19 [188:25]) Title of a work by Rabbi Yeshayahu Halevi.
Komea קמיע	*ḳami'a* קמיע	talisman, amulet	Heb. (94:18 [192:23])

Kopher כפר	*kufar* כופר	infidel	Heb. (95:23 [194:17]) Cf. כופר, *kofer*, denies.
Koschek —	*ḥošech* חושך	darkness	Heb. (42:9 [126:5])
Leftoff —	*lev ṭov* לב טוב	Book of the Good Heart	Heb. (26:31 [104:25])
Lel Schimurim —	*leil šimurim* ליל שמורים	night of vigil	Heb. (43:21 [128:13])
Macked Bekored —	*makat bechorot* מכת בכורות	death of the firstborn	Heb. (42:11 [126:5])
Madrasch Jalkut —	*midraš yalḳuṭ (Šim'oni)* מדרש ילקוט (שמעוני)	Midrash Yalkut (Shimoni)	Heb. (14:10–11 [88:5]) A collection of aggadic works on the books of the Bible
Madrasch Raba —	*midraš rabah* מדרש רבה	Midrash Rabba	Heb. (14:10 [88:5]) A collection of aggadic works on the books of the Bible
Mälek Malaka —	*melech ha-melachim* מלך המלכים	king of kings	Heb. (54:27–28 [144:26])
Mamser Ben Hanida ממזר בן הנידה	*mamzer ben ha-nidah* ממזר בן הנידה	illegitimate child born to a ritually unclean woman	Heb. (74:9–10 [168:28])
Mapa מפה	*mapah* מפה	(Torah) binder	Heb. (70:23 [160:1])
Masebok —	*mayse-bukh* מײַסע־בוך	book of fairy tales	Yidd. (2:4 [66:13])
Masseltof מזל טוב	*mazal ṭov* מזל טוב	congratulations	Heb. (1:7 [66:2]) Yidd. *mazəl tov*, *mazəl tof*
Mattan Tora מתן תורה	*matan torah* מתן תורה	Matan Torah, giving of the Torah	Heb. (44:29 [130:17])
Matzot —	*maẓot* מצות	matzot	Heb. (41:2 [124:11]) Unleavened flatbreads

Matzoth מצוה	*maẓot* מצות	matzot	Heb. (39:11 [122:6]) Unleavened flatbreads
Maxur מחזור	*maḥzor* מחזור	Machzor	Heb. (14:7 [88:3]) Prayer book for the High Holy Days
Medras Jalkut מדרש ילקוט	*midraš yalḳuṭ (Šim'oni)* מדרש ילקוט (שמעוני)	Midrash Yalkut (Shimoni)	Heb. (13:4–5 [86:2]) A collection of aggadic works on the books of the Bible
Mekabel Kinjan מקבל קנין	*meḳabel ḳinyan* מקבל קנין	ownership is received	Heb. (65:10 [158:17–18])
Mellave Malcka מלווה מלכו	*melaṿeh malkah* מלווה מלכה	Melaveh Malkah	Heb. (38:27 [120:27]) Lit. "escorting the queen"
Menorat Hamaor —	*menorat ha-ma'or* מנורת המאור	Menorat Hamaor	Heb. (107:24; 108:28–29 [206:15; 208:2]) Lit. "the lamp of illumination"
Meschomat משוטדים	*mešumad* משומד	the annihilated, destroyed	Heb. (95:21 [194:16]) Germ./Pol. (possibly Yidd.) influence seen in devoicing of final consonant (*meschomaṭ*)
Messiah Ben David משיח בן דוד	*mašiaḥ ben Daṿid* דוד בן משיח	Ben David the Messiah	Heb. (13:1, 2 [84:13])
Messiah Ben Joseph משיחבן יוסף	*mašiaḥ ben Yosef* משיח בן יוסף	Ben Joseph the Messiah	Heb. (13:1, 2 [84:13])
Mezuza —	*mezuzah* מזוזה	doorpost	Heb. (lxii:3 [64:3])
Mikve מקוה	*miḳṿah or miḳṿeh* מקווה	mikvah, ritual bath	Heb. (68:10 [162:16])
Mischna —	*mišnah* משנה	Mishnah	Heb. (7:28 [76:10])
Modim מודים	*modim* מודים	Modim	Heb. (11:30 [82:13]) Lit. "thanksgiving"

Mohel מוהל	*mohel* מוהל	mohel, ritual circum-ciser	Heb. (4:28 [70:14])
Moser מסיר	*musar* מוסר	informer	Heb. (84:29 [182:5])
Nœe Manim נאמנים	*ne'emanim* נאמנים	trustworthy, faithful (*masculine plural*)	Heb. (65:2 [158:13])
När Skel Kanuka ––	*ner šel ḥanukah* נר של חנוכה	Hanukka lamp	Heb. (62:19–20 [154:25])
Navi נביא	*navi'* נביא	prophet	Heb. (80:30 [178:4])
Paroket פרוכת	*paroket* פרוכת	curtain (of the ark)	Heb. (5:19 [72:13])
Pidron Näphäsch ––	*pidyon nefeš* פדיון נפש	redemption of the soul	Heb. (52:27 [142:17])
Pirki Avot ––	*pirḳei avot* פרקי אבות	Pirkei Avot	Heb. (36:22 [118:13]) Lit. "chapters of the fathers"
Posche Israel פושעי ישראל	*poše'i Yiśra'el* פושעי ישראל	sinful wrongdoer of Israel	Heb. (11:8–9 [82:2])
Purim פורים	*purim* פורים	Purim	Heb. (xli:1–2; 62:27; 64:17 [62:26; 156:1; 158:6]) Lit. "lots"
Rabbi Löf Hanavi רבי לוי הנביא	*rabi Levi ha-navi'* רבי לוי הנביא	Rabbi Levi the Prophet	Heb. (80:22–23 [176:26]) Judah Leibele Pros-nitz, *c.* 1670–*c.* 1730/50
Rascha רשע	*raša'* רשע	wicked, evil person, criminal	Heb. (1:16 [66:7])
Resch ––	*reš* ר	the Hebrew letter ר	Heb. (18:15, 16, 26 [94:16; 96:2])
Rosch Haschara ראש השנה	*ro'š ha-šanah* ראש השנה	Rosh Hashanah, New Year	Heb. (48:14–15 [136:12])

Ruach --	*ruaḥ* רוח	spirit; wind	Heb. (18:16, 27 [94:17; 96:2])
Sadekim --	*ẓadiḳim* צדיקים	Tzadikim	Heb. (80:12 [176:20])
Sambation Hanahar Hamit Gall Gall Koll Jom סאמבטיון הנהר המתגלגל כל יום	*Sambaṭyon ha-nehar ha-mitgalgal kol yom* סאמבטיון הנהר המתגלגל כל יום	Sambation, the river that roars every day	Heb. (16:14–15 [90:19–92:1])
Scabath Perek Bame Madliken --	*šabat pereḳ bameh madliḳin* שבת פרק במה מדליקין	Shabbat, chapter "With what may we light?"	Heb. (32:15 [114:1]) Chapter from the Talmud tractate *Shabbat*
Schadai שדי	*šadai* שדי	God Almighty	Heb. (86:7 [184:7])
Schadra שעדרה	*šidrah* שדרה	spine	Heb. (12:3 [82:15]) The use of *'ayin* as a vowel may be Yidd. influence
Schakeret --	*šaḥarit* שחרית	Shacharit	Heb. (35:22 [116:24]) Morning prayer service
Schäkina שכינה	*šechinah* שכינה	Shechinah	Heb. (80:25 [178:2]) Lit. "dwelling, settling": the divine presence of God
Schamas שמס	*šamaš* שמש	shamash, helper, synagogue beadle	Heb. (62:17 [154:23]) Cf. Yidd. שאַמעס, *šaməs*
Schamasch שמס	*šamaš* שמש	shamash, helper, synagogue beadle	Heb. (30:15–16 [110:2])
Schemo --	*šemo* שמו	his name	Heb. (18:18–19 [94:18])
Schemonah Ehra --	*šemoneh 'eśreh* שמנה עשרה	Shemoneh Esreh	Heb. (11:27 [82:11]) Lit. "eighteen": a central prayer of Jewish liturgy, also called Amidah

Schevoot שבועות	*šavu'ot* שבועות	Shavuot	Heb. (44:26 [130:16]) Lit. "weeks": the Feast of Weeks
Schin —	*šin* ש	the Hebrew letter ש	Heb. (18:15, 18 [94:16, 18])
Schopher שופר	*šofar* שופר	shofar	Heb. (49:6 [138:11])
Schor Habor שור הבור	*šor ha-bar* שור הבר	wild ox	Heb. (14:3 [88:1])
Se Pelona Gikack Et Bat Pelona —	*ze peloni yiḳaḥ et bat peloni* זה פלוני יקח את בת פלוני	so-and-so will take so-and-so's daughter	Heb. (64:27–28 [158:11])
Sider —	*sidur* סדור	Siddur	Heb. (7:24 [76:8]) Prayerbook
Simkat Tora שמחת תורה	*simḥat torah* שמחת תורה	Simchat Torah	Heb. (60:1 [152:6]) Lit. "rejoicing with/of the Torah"
Sioket —	*šoḥeṭ* שוחט	shochet, ritual slaughterer	Heb. (28:24 [108:8])
Sivon —	*siṿan* סיוון	Sivan	Heb. (45:15 [132:4])
Skäratz שרץ	*šereẓ* שרץ	creepy-crawly, bug; small inedible non-kosher creature	Heb. (14:23–24 [88:12])
Skedd —	*šed* שד	demon, devil	Heb. (14:29 [88:15])
Skekin —	*šḥin* שחין	boils	Heb. (42:9 [126:5])
Suca —	*suka* סוכה	booth	Heb. (56:17, 19 [148:1, 2]) Used by Löwe to refer to Sukkot, the Festival of Booths
Tabaat Kiduschin טבעת קידושין	*ṭaba'at ḳidušin* טבעת קידושין	wedding ring	Heb.-Aram. (69:16–17 [164:9])

Taf Orel Gemach Schemo —	*tov 'orel yimaḥ šemo* טוב ערל ימח שמו	an uncircumcised good man, may his name be obliterated	Heb. (15:3 [88:17])
Tallis —	*ṭalit* טלית	tallit, prayer shawl	Heb. (85:23 [182:18])
Talmud —	*talmud* תלמוד	Talmud	Heb. (7:29; 14:13; 32:14; 44:15–16 [*Talmudiske*]; 62:22 [76:11; 88:7; 112:25–114:1; 130:10–11 (*Talmudiske*); 154:26])
Talu —	*talui* תלוי	crucified	Heb. (18:20 [94:19])
Tarah טהרה	*ṭaharah* טהרה	taharah	Heb. (101:10 [200:3–4]) Lit. "purification": specifically, purifying a corpse before burial.
Tarjag Mitzwig תר יג	*t-r-y-g miẓẓot* תרי"ג מצוות	Taryag	Heb. (92:16–17 [190:27]) The 613 commandments
Tau —	*taṿ* ת	the Hebrew letter ת	Heb. (18:15, 20 [94:16, 19])
Taud Goi Mutter —	*ṭa'ut goy muter* טעות גוי מותר	wronging a gentile is permitted	Heb. (15:9–10 [90:1])
Thalit טלית	*ṭalit* טלית	tallit	Heb. (49:30 [138:23]) Prayer shawl
Thekopha —	*teḳufah* תקופה	Tekufa	Heb. (30:27 [110:4]) Turn, cycle; equinox
Thekupha —	*teḳufah* תקופה	Tekufa	Heb. (xl:12; 31:17, 23 [62:16; 112:11–12, 15]) Turn, cycle; equinox
Thephila —	*tefilah* תפילה	prayer	Heb. (7:24 [76:8])
Thephilat Mincka —	*tefilat minḥah* תפילת מנחה	Minchah	Heb. (36:19 [118:12]) Afternoon prayer-service

Thephilim —	*tefilin* תפילין	tefillin	Heb. (xxxix:20; 9:24; 10:7; 11:1; 85:22 [62:8; 78:18; 80:5, 13, 19, 28; 182:17]) Phylacteries
Thephilim Scheliat —	*tefilin šel yad* תפילין של יד	tefillin shel yad	Heb. (8:27–28 [78:13]) Phylacteries for placing on the upper arm
Thephilim Schelrosch —	*tefilin šel ro'š* תפילין של ראש	tefillin shel rosh	Heb. (8:28 [78:14]) Phylacteries for placing above the forehead
Therepha טרפה	*ṭerefah* טרפה	treyf	Heb. (27:9 [106:5]) Not kosher
Thumim —	*tumim* תומים	perfections(?)	Heb. (23:1 [100:9]) The meaning of the word is not known with certainty.
Tischebau —	*tiš'ah be'av* תשעה באב	Tishah beAv	Heb. (45:22 [132:8]) Lit. "the ninth of Av": a day of fasting to mark int. al. the destruction of the Temple
Tischri —	*tišri* תשרי	Tishri	Heb. (48:16 [136:13]) A month of the Jewish calendar (September–October)
Tisri —	*tišri* תשרי	Tishri	Heb. (52:3 [142:3]) A month of the Jewish calendar (September–October)
Tosephot —	*tosafot* תוספות	Tosafot	Heb. (8:3 [76:12]) Medieval commentaries on the Talmud
Uhrim —	*urim* אורים	lights	Heb. (23:1 [100:9]) Lit. "lights": part of the High Priest's breastplate

Veattem, Hadvekim Bajehova Elohekim Kajm Kulekem Hajom ואתם הדבקים ביהוה אלהיכם חיים כולכם חיום	*ve-atem ha-dvekim ba-YHVH eloheichem ḥayim kulechem ha-yom* ואתם הדבקים ביהוה אלהיכם חיים כולכם היום	But ye that did cleave unto the LORD your God are alive every one of you this day	Heb. (9:15–17 [80:1–2])
Widdu —	*vidui* ודוי	viddui	Heb. (97:10 [196:7]) Lit. “confession, shrift”
Zeboos צבאות	*ẓeva'ot* צבאות	Armies, Hosts	Heb. (86:7, 8 [184:7])
Zemah —	*ẓemaḥ* צמח	branch	Heb. (24:27 [102:14])
Zizit Schœl Thalit ציצית של טלית	*ẓiẓit šel ṭalit* ציצית של טלית	tzitzit	Heb. (49:24–25 [138:21]) Prayer-shawl fringe
Zizzis —	*ẓiẓit* ציצית	tzitzit	Heb. (85:24 [182:18]) Fringes

Hebrew, Aramaic, and Yiddish cross-references in Löwe's transcription

א → *Alef*; אב → *Av*; אגוז → *Egos*; אדון עולם → *Adon Olam*; אדוני → *Adonai*; אדר → *Ador*; אהיה אשר אהיה → *Ehich Ascher Ehich*; אורים → *Uhrim*; אל → *El*; אלוהים → *Elohim*; אליהו התישבי → Elias *Thisbe*; אמן יהא שמה רבא → *Amen Jehe Scheme Raba*; אפיקומן → *Efikomen*; אקדמות → *Actamut*; ארבה → *Arbe*; ארון → *Aron*; ארון הקודש → *Aron Hakodesch*; אתרוג → *Etrog*; ב → *Bet*; בן → *Ben*; בעל מציצה → *Baal Meziza*; בעל פריה → *Baal Peria*; ברא → *Bara*; בראשית ברא אלהים → *Berescit Bara Elohim*; ברד → *Barat*; ברוך אתה י-י אלהינו מלך העולם המוציא לחם מן הארץ → *Bark Ata, Jehovah Elohenu Mälek Haolam Hamotzi Läkem Min*; ברוך הבא → *Barok Haba, Baruch Haba*; ברכת המזון → *Berkat Hamason*; גבאי → *Gabba*; גיהנם → *Gehenna*; גמרא → *Gemara*; גט → *Get*; דבר → *Dever*; דומה → *Doma*; דם → *Dam*; האלמימר → *Halememer, Halmemer*; הבדלה → *Hafdala*; הושענא רבא → *Håschana Raba, Hoschiana Raba*; הרי את מקודשת לי בטבעת קידושין כדת משה וישראל → *Häre At Mäkudeschet Libetabaat Kiduscham Kedat Mosche Vä Jsraël*; ואתם הדבקים בי-י אלהיכם חיים כולכם היום → *Veattem, Hadvekim Bajehova Elohekim Kajm Kulekem Hajom*; ודוי → *Widdu*; זה פלוני יקח את בת פלוני → *Se Pelona Gikack Et Bat Pelona*; חומש → *Chumaseh, Cumesch*; חושך → *Koschek*; חלה → *Kalla*; חלוץ נעל → *Kalutz Nal*; חליצה → *Kelitza*; חלף → *Kalef*; חנוכה

→ *Kenuka*; חסד של אומת עולם חטאות לישראל → *Keset Sekel umot katot Le Jsraël*; חסידים → *Cassidim*; חתן → *Catan*; טבעת קידושין → *Tabaat Kiduschin*; טהרה → *Tarah*; טוב ערל ימח שמו → *Taf Orel Gemach Schemo*; טלית → *Tallis, Thalit*; טעות גוי מותר → *Taud Goi Mutter*; טרפה → *Therepha*; י → *Jod*; יום טוב → *Jom Tof*; יום כיפור → *Jom Kipor*; יין נסך → *Jain näsach*; יין קידוש → *Jaginkidos*; ילקוט ראובני → *Jalkut Reuveni*; ישוע → *Jeschua*; כופר → *Kopher*; כוס של ברכה → *Cosciel Bäraka*; כלה → *Calata*; כנים → *Kinem*; כפרה → *Capora*; כשר → *Coschere*; כשר ספר תורה → *Kaschar Sepher Tora*; כתובה → *Ketuba*; לב טוב → *Leftoff*; ליל שמורים → *Lel Schimurim*; מדרש ילקוט → *Madrasch Jalkut, Medras Jalkut*; מודים → *Modim*; מוהל → *Mohel*; מוסר → *Moser*; מזוזה → *Mezuza*; מזל טוב → *Masseltof*; מחזור → *Maxur*; מײַסע־בוך → *Masebok*; מכת בכורות → *Macked Bekored*; מלווה מלכה → *Mellave Malcka*; מלך המלכים → *Mälek Maluku*; ממזר בן הנידה → *Mamser Ben Hanida*; מנורת המאור → *Menorat Hamaor*; מפה → *Mapa*; מצות → *Matzot, Matzoth*; מקבל קנין → *Mekabel Kinjan*; מקווה → *Mikve*; משומדים → *Meschomat*; משיח בן דוד → *Messiah Ben David*; משיח בן יוסף → *Messiah Ben Joseph*; משנה → *Mischna*; מתן תורה → *Mattan Tora*; נאמנים → *Næe Manim*; נביא → *Navi*; נר של חנוכה → *När Skel Kanuka*; סאמבטיון הנהר המתגלגל כל יום → *Sambation Hanahar Hamit Gall Gall Koll Jom*; סדור → *Sider*; סוכה → *Suca*; סיוון → *Sivon*; סימן טוב ומזל טוב ברוך החתן עם הכלה → *Buruk Elohenu Simen Tau Oma Sall tau. Baruk Hakatan Im Hakala*; עבל → *Ævel*; עלינו לשבח → *Allenu le Schabeach*; עלמה → *Alma*; ערוב → *Aref*; ערל → *Erel*; פדיון נפש → *Pidron Näphäsch*; פורים → *Purim*; פושעי ישראל → *Posche Israel*; פרוכת → *Paroket*; פרקי אבות → *Pirki Avot*; צבאות → *Zeboos*; צדיקים → *Sadekim*; ציצית → *Zizzis*; ציצית של טלית → *Zizit Schœl Thalit*; ציקליין → Ichelein; צמח → *Zemah*; צפרדע → *Cefardea*; קברנים → *Cabranim*; קדיש וגם אמן יהא שמה רבא → *Cadisch vegahm amen gehö schemä raba*; קיצור שני לוחות הברית → *Kitzur Schenä, Lucot Habrit*; קמיע → *Komea*; קראים → *Caraim*; ר → *Resch*; ראש השנה → *Rosch Haschara*; מדרש רבה → *Madrasch Raba*; רבי לוי הנביא → *Rabbi Löf Hanavi*; רוח → *Ruuch*; רשע → *Rascha*; ש → *Schin*; שבועות → *Schevoot*; שבת פרק במה מדליקין → *Scabath Perek Bame Madliken*; שד → *Skedd*; שדי → *Schadai*; שדרה → *Schadra*; שוחט → *Sioket*; שופר → *Schopher*; שור הבר → *Schor Habor*; שחין → *Skekin*; שחרית → *Schakeret*; שכינה → *Schäkina*; שמו → *Schemo*; שמחת תורה → *Simkat Tora*; שמנה עשרה → *Schemonah Ehra*; שמש → *Schamas, Schamasch*; שרץ → *Skäratz*; ת → *Tau*; תומים → *Thumim*; תוספות → *Tosephot*; תלוי → *Talu*; תלמוד → *Talmud*; תפילה → *Thephila* ; תפילין → *Thephilim*; תפילין של יד → *Thephilim Scheliat*; תפילין של ראש → *Thephilim Schelrosch*; תפילת מנחה → *Thephilat Mincka*; תקופה → *Thekopha, Thekupha*; תרי״ג מצוות → *Tarjag Mitzwig*; תשעה באב → *Tischebau*; תשרי → *Tischri, Tisri*.

Appendix 3: Prospectus (30 August 1731)

Source: Stockholm, Kungliga biblioteket: Löwe, Christian Petter. *Gifwes Här Med Tilkänna, at Orientaliske Språkmästaren Wid Upsala Academie Herr Christian Peter Löwe ärnar Genom Trycket Låta Utgå, En Tractat, Kallad Speculum Religionis Judaicœ, Eller Beskrifning Om Judarnas Religion Och Nu Brukelige: Ceremonier, Pa [!] Swänska, Som Kommer at Bestå Af 16 Arck in Quarto, Af Hwilken Hela Bokens Innehåld Nu Följer:* = (Rubr.) S. Impr., 1731.

Text	**Translation**
Gıfwes här med tilkänna, at *Orientali*ske Språk-Mästaren wid *Upsala Academie* Herr *Christian Peter Löwe* ärnar genom trycket låta utgå, en *Tractat*, kallad *Speculum Religionis Judaicœ*, eller Beskrifning om Judarnas *Religion* och nu brukelige *Ceremonier*, pa Swänska, som kommer at bestå af 16 arck *in Quarto*, af hwilken hela Bokens innehåld nu följer:	It is hereby announced that the master of Oriental languages at Uppsala Academy, Mr Christian Petter Löwe intends to publish in print a treatise called *Speculum Religionis Judaįcœ* or *A Description of the Jews' Religion and Ceremonies Practised Nowadays*, in Swedish, which will comprise 16 quires in quarto. The contents of this book will be as now follows:
1. Om Judarnas födelse.	On the birth of the Jews
2. Om *Ceremonierne* när ett Barn 7. Dagar gammalt är.	On ceremonies when a child is seven days old
3. Om omskärelsen.	On circumcision
4. Om *Ceremonierne* som brukelige äro när ett Pigo-Barn födt warder.	On the ceremonies that are performed when a girl is born
5. Om *Ceremonierne* wid Barnens insättiande uti Skolen.	On the ceremonies when a child begins school
6. Om *Ceremonierne*, när ett Barn 13 åhr gammalt är.	On the ceremonies when a child is thirteen years old
7. Om Judarnas *Thephilim*.	On the Jews' *Thephilim* [i.e., tefillin]
8. Om Judarnas bönesätt.	On the Jews' way of praying
9. Om Judarnas Religion.	On the Jews' religion
10. Om Judarnas umgänge med the Christne.	On the Jews' dealings with Christians
11. Om deras willfarelse och mening om Christo.	On their delusion and belief about Christ

https://doi.org/10.1515/9783110986938-005

12.	Bewises at Christus är den rätta *Messias*.	It is proven that Christ is the true Messiah
13.	Om Orsakerne hwarföre de sig öfwer *Messia* förarga.	On the reason why they become enraged about the Messiah
14.	Om Judarnas matredande och ko-kande.	On the Jews' preparation of food and cooking
15.	Om Judarnas *Thekupha*.	On the Jews' *Thekupha* [i.e., teḳufah]
16.	Om Judarnas *Sabbath*.	On the Jews' Sabbath
17.	Om Judarnas Påska.	On the Jews' Easter
18.	Om Judarnas Pingest-Fest.	On the Jews' Pentecost
19.	Om *Jerusalems* förstöring.	On the destruction of Jerusalem
20.	Om Judarnas Nyåhr.	On the Jews' New Year
21.	Om Judarnas Försoningz-Fest.	On the Jews' Festival of Atonement
22.	Om Löfhyddo-Festen.	On the Festival of Booths
23.	Om Judarnas Frögde-Fest och Frög-de-Eldar öfwer Lagen.	On the Jews' Festival of Joy and Fires of Joy about the Law
24.	Om Judarnas *Kenuka*.	On the Jews' *Kenuka* [i.e., Hanukkah]
25.	Om en Fest som kallas *Purim* an-gående *Haman*, *Mardochai* och *Ester*.	On a festival called *Purim* concerning Haman, Mordechai, and Esther
26.	Om Judarnas trolåfningar.	On the Jews' engagements
27.	Om Judarnas sammanwigningar och Bröllop.	On the Jews' marriages and weddings
28.	Om Judarnas Skiljobref.	On the Jews' letters of divorce
29.	Om de Judars död, som ei Barn efter sig lemnat, och hafwa någon Broder efter sig uti lifwet.	On the death of Jews who do not leave a child after them and have no living brother
30.	Om Judarnas *Ceremonier* wid och under Måltiden.	On the Jews' ceremonies at and during meals
31.	Om Judarnas Nähringz-Medel.	On the Jews' food
32.	Hwarföre Judarne sig öfwer de Christne så högeligen förarga.	Why the Jews are so very angry with Christians
33.	Hwad Judarnas *Politie* och *Justitie* angå månde.	Concerning the Jews' system of order and justice
34.	Om Judarnas edzgång.	On the Jews' oath-taking
35.	Om de fattiga Judars underhållande.	On the maintenance of the poor Jews
36.	Om Judarnas skäggrakande.	On the Jews' shaving their beards
37.	Om Judarnas Naglars afskärande.	On the Jews' cutting their nails
38.	Om Judarnas *Mezuza* eller ut- och ingång.	On the Jews' *Mezuza* or exiting and entering

39. Om Judarnas haat til dem som ifrån deras Religion affalla.	On the Jews' hatred of those who leave their religion
40. Om Judarnas Skrifftermåhl wid de siuke.	On the Jews' confession by the sick
41. *Ceremonier*, när någon är uti sidsta dödzstunden.	Ceremonies when someone is at their last hour of death
42. *Ceremonierne* när någon död är.	Ceremonies when someone has died
43. Om den dödas pina, när sorgfolcket hemkommit är.	On the torments of the dead when the mourners have come home
44. *Ceremonierne* sedan de hemkommen äro.	Ceremonies when they have come home
45. Om Paradis.	On paradise
46. Om Helfwetit.	On hell
47. Om Helfwetis beskrifning.	On the description of hell
48. Om de dödas upståndelse.	On the resurrection of the dead
THE Herrar som til ett sådant Wärck lust hafwa, behaga med 3. Daler Kopparmynt theruppå *prænumerera*, här i *Stockholm* uti *Factorens* Herr *Lochners* Boklåda, och i *Upsala* hos *Auctoren*, som försäkrar, at Boken skyndsamligen skal på godt Tryck-Papper och med ren *Styl*, warda aftryckt, ock at hwar och en, på then ort, ther han *prænumerat*, skal sit *Exemplar* richtigt utbekomma, så snart therom i *Avisorne* kundgiöres.	Those gentlemen who wish to have such a work may like to subscribe to it with three copper dalers here in Stockholm at the bookshop of the commissioner Mr Lochner and in Uppsala with the author, who affirms that the book will be printed speedily on good printing paper and with a clean style, and that each and every person who has subscribed will correctly receive his copy at that place when it is announced in the newspapers.

Appendix 4: Extra material in *Speculum Religionis Judaicæ* (Stockholm: Frantz Philip Paulssen, 1735)

Source: *Spec.* (Sthlm, 1735), 204–08.

	Text	**Translation**	
	28. Tilökningar utur Talmud och andre Rabbiniske *Antiquiteter* och Historie-Böcker utdragne.	28 Expansions Excerpted from the Talmud and Other Rabbinical Antiquities and History Books	
1.	Kort utdrag af *Michlall Jophis* och *Rabbi Salomo Jarchis* anmärckningar öfwer Propheten Jonas.	Short excerpt from Michlall Jophi's and Rabbi Salomon Jarchi's comments on the Prophet Jonah.	132
2.	Judarnas berättelse om Menniskiorna för Syndafloden, tagen uthur *Medrasch i Jalkut*.	The Jews' story about the people before the Flood, taken from *Midrash Yalkut*.	137
3.	Judarnas berättelse om Mose och des Staf	The Jews' story about Moses and his staff.	139
4.	Sedan Gud i *I. Reg. 6. v. 7.* hade förbudit at bruka järnredskap till Templetz upbyggande, frågas billigt, huru man har kunnat sedan klyfwa eller sönderdela stenarne, som dertil nödige woro, hwarom Judarne i deras *Talmud* hafwa följande *Tradition*.	As God in 1 Kings 6:7 had forbidden the use of iron tools in the construction of the Temple, it is reasonably asked how it was possible to split or break the stones that were necessary for it, about which the Jews have the following tradition in their Talmud.	142
5.	Om Folcketz Synder i Sodom finnes följande berättelse i den *Talmudiska Tractaten Sanhedrin*.	The following story about the sins of the people in Sodom is found in the Talmudic tractate *Sanhedrin*.	147
6.	Om Mosis död tagit uhr *Decarem Rabba fol.* 246.	About the death of Moses taken from *Decarem Rabba*, fol. 246.	150
7.	Judarnas mening, hwarifrån dieflarna hafwa sitt ursprung.	The Jews' opinion about where demons have their origin.	157

https://doi.org/10.1515/9783110986938-006

16.	Huru Judarna uttyda the orden, som läsas i *Gen.* 12. v. 14. Tå Abraham kom i Egypten *etc.* och theras *Tradition* derom	How the Jews interpret the words that are read in Genesis 12:14: "When Abraham came to Egypt, etc." and their tradition about this.	175
17.	Om Elia, som skal warit förwandlad i en Ängel och hetat Sandalson, hafwa the förblindade Judar följande lustiga Historier	The blinded Jews have the following funny stories about Elijah who is supposed to have been transformed into an angel and is called Sandalphon.	176
18.	Om dieflarna hafwa Judarna följande mening:	The Jews have the following opinion about demons.	179
19.	Om Abraham hafwa Judarna i sin bok *Schalscheleth Nakkabala fol.* 2. följande *Tradition*	The Jews have the following tradition about Abraham in their book *Shalshelet Ha-Kabalah*, fol. 2.	180
20.	Huru Judarna uttyda de orden som läses i *Ezech.* 26. *v.* 20. Jag wil sättis the lefwandes prål och pracht *etc.*	How the Jews interpret the words in Ezek. 26:20: "I shall set pomp and splendour in the land of the living, etc."	183
21.	Om the twå stutar, som omtalas i Konung. bok. 18. v. 26. hwilka Elias och Baals Propheter skulle offra, hafwa Judarna en sådan *Tradition*, som följer:	The Jews have a tradition about the two bullocks that are mentioned in 1 Kings 18:26 which Elijah and the prophets of Baal were going to sacrifice, that is as follows.	185
22.	At diuren tala med hwarannan är i den *Talmudiska Tractaten Eruvin fol.* 100. *Col.* 2. på följande sätt at läsa:	In the Talmudic Tractate *Eruvin*, fol. 100, col. 2, it is possible to read the following about animals talking to one another.	186
23.	Om Konung David hafwa Judarne i den *Talmudiska Tractaten Sanhedrin fol.* 95. en sådan lustig lögn.	In the Talmudic tractate *Sanhedrin*, fol. 95, the Jews have a funny lie about King David.	186

24.	Judarnes mening om Og Konungen i Basan.	The Jews' opinion about Og, the king of Bashan.	189
25.	Judarnas mening, huru Davids ord i Psal. 22. v. 22. böra förstås: Hielp mig utur Leijons munn och frija mig ifrån Enhörningarne	The Jews' opinion about how David's words in Psalm 22:21 ought to be understood: "Help me from the lion's mouth and save me from the unicorns."	191
26.	Ofwantil är förmält, at Konung Salomon lät genom Benaja Jehoda Son gripa *Aschmedai*, dieflarnas öfwerste, och hålla honom fången efter Templets upbyggande, nu följer på hwad sätt *Aschmedai* har hämnas på Salomon therföre.	It is stated above that King Solomon had Asmodeus, the prince of the demons, arrested by Benaiah, son of Jehoiada, and kept him prisoner after the construction of the Temple. Now follows how Asmodeus took revenge on Solomon for this.	193
27.	När Judarna wilja wisa, at med the orden som stå i Esai. 63. v. 16. Tu äst wår Fader, Isaac warder förstånden, så giöra the thet med följande *Tradition*	When the Jews want to show that Isaac is to be understood in the words found in Isaiah 63:16 "You are our father," they do so with the following tradition.	198
28.	At Laban welat med förgifft af daga taga Elieser, tå han blef skickat af Abraham till at frija efter Rebecca, derom står i *Jalkut chadasch fol.* 83. följande handling.	The following act is written in *Yalkut Hadash*, fol. 83: that Laban wanted to kill Eliezer with poison, when he was sent by Abraham to marry Rebecca.	200

Appendix 5: Excerpts from Christophorus Bezelius' *Die Herrlichkeit des Christenthums* (Stockholm: Heinrich Käyser, 1684)

Excerpt 1: Cursing Jesus Christ

Source: Bezelius, *Die Herrlichkeit des Christenthums*, under "Historische Zugabe," 198–201 (§ 20).

Text

Haben sie JEsum von Nazareth den gecreutzigten gelästert.

[*Buxtorf. Synag. Jud. cap. V. pag. 133.*] In etlichen Gebett-Büchern der Jüden ist ein *Spatium* oder Weite einer halben Linien groß gelassen/ damit die Kinder/ und andere unwissende angemahnet werden zu fragen/ was daselbst mangele? Da sprechen sie ihnen die Wörter vor/ welche allhie mangeln (die sie auß Verbott der Christlichen Obrigkeit nicht dürffen drucken lassen/ weil sie lästerlich wider CHristum sind) oder schreiben sie ihnen neben zu an dem Rand deß Buchs. Wie ein gelehrter Mann sie beydes gedruckt und geschrieben gesehen hat. Sie lauten aber also: Welche knien und sich neigen zu dem/ das וריק Eitelkeit und Thorheit ist/ und beten an einen GOtt/ der nicht helffen kan (diß gehet auff Christum/ speyen auch auff die Erde/ nachdem sie diese Worte geredet haben) wir aber knien/ und neigen uns zu dem König/ der da ist ein König über alle Könige/ zu dem heiligen und gebenedeyeten GOTT/ der die Himmel außgebreitet/ und die Erde befästiget hat/ u.s.w.

[*Anton. Margar. de fide Jud. p. m. 156.*] Wenn die Jüden JEsum am allerhöchsten nennen/ daß sie etwa wegen der Christen thun müssen/ so heissen sie Jhesu ישו *Jeschu*, und so sie unter- und miteinander reden/ hengen sie die Worte hinan: ימח שמו das ist/ sein Nahme werde vertilget/ und ist gemein/ daß sie Jhesu *Jeschu* nennen/ welches schier lautet/ als ob sie ihm den rechten Nahmen *Jeschua* geben/ welches heisset ein Heyland; aber sie nennen ihn nicht vollkommen/ lassen ihm zur Schmach den besten Buchstaben aussen/ und nennen Ihn wie gedacht/ *Jeschu*, [*Wülfer. in Schekalim p. 41*] welches in der Hebreischen Zahl ist dreyhundert und sechszehen/ und gegen dem haben sie ein Wort וריק heist Eitel/ das auch in sich hat dreyhundert und sechszehen/ damit sie denn zu verstehen geben wollen/ daß/ wo *Jeschu* genennet wird/ nichts dann Eitelkeit/ Nichtigkeit und Torheit verstanden werde/ diesen und dergleichen Nahmen geben sie Christo.

https://doi.org/10.1515/9783110986938-007

[Joh. Ludw. Gottfrid/ *Chron. fol. 506.*] *Anno 1017.* bekamen die Jüden auff dem Charfreytag zu Rom ein Crucifix/ nahmen das Bild Christi vom Creutz/ schlugen/ verspeyeten/ und geiselten es/ hefften selbiges wiederumb an das Creutz und spieleten die *Passion* mit ihm/ wie ihre Vor-Eltern auff diesen Tag mit Christo. Sie würden aber über diesem Buben-Stück ergriffen/ und musten ihrer viel die Hälse hergeben. Solche Feinde Christi und seines Creutzes sind die Jüden; Daß freylich recht eine sonderliche grosse Gnade GOttes ist/ wenn ein Jüde bekehret wird/ Christum ehret/ und durch ihn sein Heyl suchet/ den er vorhin so sehr gelästert hat. Aber was bey Menschen unmüglich ist/ das ist bey GOTT müglich. [*Luc. XVIII, 27.*]

Translation

Have they blasphemed the crucified Jesus of Nazareth?

[Johannes Buxtorf, *Synagoga Judaica*, ch. [7], p. 133] In several of the Jews' prayer books a space or width of half a line is left empty, so that the children and other ignorant people are encouraged to ask what is missing there. Then they tell them the words that are missing here (which they are not allowed to have printed due to the Christian authorities' prohibition, because they are blasphemous against Christ) or next to the space in the margin of the book they write them down with the same wording that a learned man saw them both printed and written. But they read like this: "Those who kneel and bow to that which is ורִיק, vanity and folly, and pray to a God who cannot help" – this refers to Christ, they also spit on the ground after they have spoken these words – "but we kneel and bow to the king who is king above all kings, to the holy and blessed God who spread out the heavens and established the earth, etc."

[Antonius Margaritha, *De Fide Judaica*, middle of p. 156] When the Jews name Jesus Most High, which they have to do because of the Christians, then they call Jesus ישו, "Yeshu," and when they talk among themselves and to each other, they append the words ימח שמו, that is "may his name be erased!" And it is common that they call Jesus "Yeshu," which sounds just like they are giving him the right name "Yeshua," which means "a saviour," but they are not mentioning him in full. They leave out the best letter to mock him and call him as intended "Yeshu," [Johann Wülfer, *Schekalim*, p. 41] which in Hebrew numerals is 316, and against him they have a word וריק (it means "vanity"), which also totals 316; with this, they want to make it understood that where "Yeshu" is mentioned, nothing other than vanity, nothingness, and folly are to be understood. They give this and similar names to Christ.

[Johann Ludwig Gottfried (Johann Philipp Abelin), *Historische Chronica*, fol. 506] In the year 1017 on Good Friday, the Jews of Rome got a crucifix, removed the

image of Christ from the cross, beat it, spat on it, and scourged it; they reattached it to the cross and acted out the Passion with it like their ancestors did on this day with Christ. However, they were apprehended because of this act of roguery and many of them had to surrender their necks. The Jews are such enemies of Christ and his cross that it is of course a particularly great grace of God when a Jew is converted, honours Christ, and seeks his salvation through the one whom he had previously blasphemed so much. But what is impossible with man is possible with God. [Luke 18:27]

Excerpt 2: Believing what Jews say

Source: Bezelius, *Die Herrlichkeit des Christenthums*, under "Historische Zugabe," 211–17 (§ 26).

Text

Man soll den Jüden nicht heucheln und nach dem Munde reden.

Wie *Paulus Felgenhaueris, Isaacus Peyrerius*; und der seinen Nahmen unter den verwechselten Buchstaben *Habitò en Sion* verstecket/ [*Carpzov. in Ius Reg. Hebr. Schickardi p. 340*] wie auch *C. Barlæus*, der dem *Manasse Ben Israel gratuli*ret/ und unter andern diese Verse schreibet:

Si sapimus diversa; Deo vivamus amici,
Doctaque mens pretio constet ubique suo.
Hæc fidei vox summa meæ est, hæc crede Manasse,
Sic ego Christiades, sic eris Abramides.

[*Rumetsch de conjecturis ultimi temporis p. 111. 112*] Ja er/ der *Manasse Ben Israel* nennet unterschiedliche/ die doch Christen sind/ und heissen wollen/ *Nathan. Homesium SS. Theol. Doctorem, Heinricum Jesse*, und andere/ welche zum Theil ihm dem Jüdischen Rabbi ihre Schrifften *dediciret*, in gemein aber noch von grossen künfftigen Glück und Herrschafften gesaget/ bey ihrem Jüdenthum alle Liebe und Freundschaft angeboten haben. Welches aber nicht sein ist noch zu loben. Sie solten nur sehen/ was sie für Freunde an den Jüden hätten/ so sie die Macht bekämen/ wie sie dann offt ihre Löwen-Klauen blicken und sehen lassen.

[*Zeiler. Cent. 3. ep. LXXIX. f.*] Sie haben wol ehe grosses Geld gegeben/ dem *Cosroes* Könige in Persien *90000*. Christen abgekaufft/ und jämmerlich hingerichtet/ und da sie sie jetzo müssen etwas einziehen/ unterlassen sie doch nicht/ auch

in ihren Gebeten ihren Grimm wider uns außzuschütten. Von dem *4.* Vers deß *20.* Psalms/ der HErr gebe dir/ was dein Hertz wünschet/ schreiben sie in ihrem *Talmud* also: [*Anton. Margar. p. m. 152.*] Wenn sie für GOTT kommen und sprechen: O HERR und König/ wir bedürffen Nahrung und Speise/ so antwortet ihnen GOTT und spricht: Gehet hin und nehret euch/ und speiset euch/ einer von dem andern. Sprechen sie wiederumb zu GOTT: Ein Bäer/ so er sauget die Klauen/ kan er sich nehren/ Ein Löw aber gehet auß und raubet/ zerreiset und frisst andere Thiere/ diesen Löwen sind wir gleich/ wir können mit unsern Händen einer von dem andern unsern Mund nicht speisen/ wir müssen uns an die Schaaren der Völcker legen. Und wie eine Grube nicht voller Wasser wird/ darumb daß sie hohl ist; sondern wenn man Wasser anderswo darein leitet; also seind wir auch/ können von uns selbst nicht voll werden/ sondern von andern. So soll ihnen GOTT antworten: Gehet hin/ und leget eure Hände an die Schaaren. Hiebey mag ein jeglicher verständiger wol mercken/ was diesem Volck zu trauen sey/ weil sie so unverschämt schreiben und glauben/ daß sie nicht arbeiten dürffen/ sondern sich vom Raube/ wie ein Löwe/ behelffen und sprechen/ GOTT erlaube es ihnen/ und heisse es.

Darüber urtheile ein jeder selbst/ so sie die Gewalt hätten/ was sie thäten? Ja was? Weiß man doch Exempel/ daß Jüdische Ärtzte/ die an Fürsten-Höfen für andern wol gelitten/ und mit reicher Besoldung/ und grossen Gnaden beschenkket worden/ sich doch nicht haben enthalten können/ sondern wie die jungen Tigerthier endlich ihren Wolthäter zerrissen/ durch Gifft und andere Mittel ihre Herrschafft umgebracht und getödtet. So erzehlet *Joh. Cernitius* vom Churfürsten *Joachimo II.* zu Brandenburg/ daß er nach dem Nacht-Essen auff die Betrachtung deß bittern Leidens und Sterbens Christi gerathen/ und dieweil er keinen Mahler bey der Hand haben konte/ das Bildniß/ so ihm entweder vorgezeiget worden/ oder er ihm in sein Gemüth gefasst/ mit einer Kreide auff die Tafel gemahlet/ und in solchen Gedancken sich zur Ruhe geleget habe/ und bald darauff gestorben sey/ im Jahr Christi *1571*, denn sein *Medicus Lippoldus*, ein Jüd/ ihm Gifft im Malvasier zum Schlaff-Trunck gegeben hatte.

Es ist sich zu verwundern/ daß ein Christ einem Jüdischen Artzt mehr als einem Christlichen *Medico* vertrauen soll. Aber was thut Neugierigkeit nicht? Doch darff ich fast mehr sagen/ was thut Kaltsinningkeit im Christenthum nicht? Denn wäre er darinne rechtschaffen und eifferig/ er thäte es nimmermehr/ daß er einem geschwornen Feind JEsu von Nazareth sich so geheimmachte/ und seine Gesundheit ihm vertrauete. Darumb es mancher auch so haben muß zur Straffe seines Vorwitzes: Denn entweder versehen sie es/ oder thuns mit Fleiß/ daß der Mensch umb sein Leben kömmt.

[*Leg. D. Mülleri Judaism. detect. pag. 1435*] An einem *Medico* wird erfordert ein verständiges Haupt/ ein treues Hertz/ eine gesegnete Hand. Was haben aber die Jüden für Verstand in der Artzney? Auß der Geschicklichkeit in Metzgen/ und

Durchsuchung deß Viehes/ ob es innerliche Kranckheiten habe/ und Entäderung deß Fleisches entstehen die Ärtzte unter den Jüden. [*Buxtorf. Synag. Jud. c. XXVII. p. m 593.*] Denn gleicher gestalt wollen sie von dem Menschen/ seines Leibes Eigenschafften und Kranckheiten auch urtheilen/ welches mancher mit seinen Leben bezahlen muß/ schreibet ein gelerhter Mann.

[*Anton. Margarita de fide Jud. p. m. 68. 69.*] Und ein anderer gibt den Christen die Schuld/ daß so viel Jüden-Ärtzte sind/ denn weil sie bey den Christen im Beruff sind/ daß sie gute Ärtzte (als wenn kein GOtt in Israel wäre) so thäten sie wol närrisch/ wenn sie sich nicht wolten dafür außgeben. Aber/ schreibt er/ merck eben/ daß kein Jüde in Deutscher *Nation*, noch Böhmen/ Ungern wo gewesen sey/ der sein Lebenlang *Avicennam, Galenum, Hippocratem* und dergleichen in Hebreischer Sprach gesehen/ geschweige denn gelesen habe/ noch viel weniger Latein: Denn ihrer keiner in diesen Landen ists berichtet/ haben auch kein Buch das Artzney beschreibe/ *studi*ren auch nicht/ haben wol etwan kleine Büchlein mit Hebreischen Buchstaben Deutsch geschrieben/ und einig Erkändtniß der Kräuter und Wurtzeln/ wie sie es etwan von ihren Vätern gehöret und gelernet haben/ daher es mich verwundert hat/ daß wir Christen so thörichte Leute sind/ und ihnen glauben.

Wenn ein Jüde nicht gut thut/ das Seine verspielet/ versoffen/ mit andern Jüden verhadert/ oder sonst schändlich durchgebracht hat/ so zeucht er unter die Christen/ gibt sich für einen Artzt auß/ und auch gewöhnlich für einen Rabbi/ so überkömmt er Geld/ und wird viel von ihm gehalten. Und da dann gleich etliche die *Medicinam* verstünden/ wie in Hispanien und Italien/ was kan für Glück und Segen bey ihrer Cur seyn? Denn wie wolte GOTT die Hände segnen/ die seinen Sohn gecreuzigt haben/ und noch creutzigen mit ihren täglichen Fluch-Gebeten und Lästerungen. Ja viele, da sies gleich verstehen und helffen könten/ wollen doch nicht/ sondern verderbens vielmehr/ und befordern zum Grabe.

Zwar eine zeitlang halten sie an sich/ aber das geschicht/ wie auß Furcht/ so auch Ruhms und Gewinsts halber/ und daß sie die Leute sicher machen/ und desto mehr hin opffern mögen. Denn sie haben kein treues Hertz gegen einigen Christen. Könten sie mit einem Streich alle Christen hinrichten/ sie thäten es/ und hoffeten dafür einen fürnehmen Platz in dem Garten Eden.

Das/ meine ich nun/ solte ja die Christen abhalten/ den beharrenden verhärteten Jüden nicht zu heucheln und zu liebkosen. Auffrichtigkeit ist dir/ GOTT/ angenehm/ sagt David in seinem Gebet/ so sage man auch mit ihm in der Warheit: [*Psalm. CXXXIX, 20. 21. 22.*] GOTT sie reden von dir lästerlich/ und deine Feinde erheben sich ohne Ursach/ ich hasse ja/ HERR/ die dich hassen/ und verdreust mich auff sie/ daß sie sich wider dich setzen. Ich hasse sie in rechten Ernst/ darumb sind sie mir feind/ *139*. Psalm.

Translation

One should not lie in their favour and say what the Jews want to hear.

As Paul Felgenhauer, Isaac La Peyrère, and the man who hides his name under the mixed up letters *Habitè en Sion* [Johann Benedikt Carpzov, *Ius Regium Hebraeorum*, ed. Wilhelm Schickhard, p. 340] as well as Caspar Barlæus, who congratulates Menasseh ben Israel and among others writes these verses:

Even if we think differently, let's live like friends for God!
And the learned mind has its own value everywhere.
This is the highest statement of my faith, believe this Menasseh!
Thus, as I am a son of Christ, so you will be a son of Abraham.

Johann Christoph Rumetsch, *De Conjecturis ultimi temporis*, pp. 111–12] Indeed, this Menasse ben Israel mentions some people who, although they are Christians and want to be called such, Nathaniel Homesius (SS. Theol. Doct.), Henricus Jesse, and others who partly dedicated their writings to the Jewish rabbi but in common spoke of a great future happiness and power, they offered all their love and friendship in the name of their Judaism – which is, however, not to be praised. They should only see what kind of friends they would have in the Jews if they were to come to power, how they would then often let their lion claws show and be seen.

[Martin Zeiller, *Centuria Variarum Quaestionum, Oder, Ein Hundert Fragen*, ch. 3, fol. 79] They have indeed previously paid a lot of money, bought 90,000 Christians from Chosroes, the king of Persia, and miserably executed them, and as they now have to be somewhat withdrawn, they do not refrain from pouring out their wrath against us even in their prayers. On Psalm 20:4: "May the Lord give you what your heart desires," they write this in their Talmud: [Antonius Margaritha, middle of p. 152] When they come before God and say, "O Lord and King! We need food and sustenance!" God answers them and says: "Go and feed yourselves and sustain yourselves, one from the other." When they speak to God again: "If a bear sucks its claws, it can feed itself, but a lion goes out and steals, tears other animals to pieces, and eats them. We are like these lions. We cannot use our hands to feed our mouths one from the other. We must join the crowds of peoples. And as a pit does not fill up with water because it is hollow unless one directs water into it from somewhere else, so, too, are we. We cannot become full by ourselves, but only by others." This is how God is said to have answered them: "Go and lay your hands on the crowds!" From this, any sensible person can see how little this people should be trusted because they write so outrageously and believe that they are not allowed to work but should get by with robbery, like a lion, and they say that God allows them and commands them to do so.

Everyone may judge for himself just what they [the Jews] would do if they had power. Indeed, what? One knows examples of Jewish doctors, held in high regard by others at princely courts and presented with a rich salary and great favours, who still could not contain themselves, but who like young tigers finally tore their patrons to pieces, killed and slayed their rulers with poison and other means. This is what Johannes Cernitius tells about Joachim II Hector, Prince-elector of Brandenburg, who after supper was advised to contemplate the bitter suffering and death of Christ, and because he did not have a painter at hand, drew the image – either of what was shown to him or what he had pictured in his mind – on a board with a piece of chalk. And with such thoughts he laid himself to rest and soon afterwards died in the year of Christ 1571, because his *medicus* Lippold ben Chluchim, a Jew, had put poison in his nightcap of Malvasia wine.

It is astonishing that a Christian should trust a Jewish doctor more than a Christian *medicus*. But what does curiosity not do? However, I may say even more: what does callousness not do in Christianity? For if he were righteous and zealous in it [Christianity], he [a Christian] would never again confide in a sworn enemy of Jesus of Nazareth and entrust his health to him. That is why a good many people must be punished for their inquisitiveness: because either by mistake or on purpose, they [Jewish doctors] ensure that the person loses his life.

[Johannes Müller, *Judaism oder Judenthumb*, p. 1435] A *medicus* requires an understanding head, a faithful heart, a blessed hand. But what understanding do the Jews have of medicine? From their skill in butchering and searching cattle to see whether they have internal diseases, and deveining the meat, doctors came into being among the Jews. [Buxtorf, *Synagoga Judaica*, ch. 27. middle of p. 593] Because they want to judge the human being, his bodily properties and illnesses in the same way, many a man has had to pay with his life, writes a learned man.

[Antonius Margaritha, *De fide Judaica*, middle of pp. 68–69] And another man gives Christians the blame for there being so many Jewish doctors, as among Christians they are reputed to be good doctors (as if there were no God in Israel), so they would be stupid if they did not pretend to be. But, he writes, notice that no Jew in the German nation, nor Bohemia, Hungary or wherever else, has ever seen Avicenna, Galen, Hippocrates, and the like in the Hebrew language, let alone read them, even less so in Latin: Because not one of them has been reported in these countries, nor do they have a book that describes medicine, nor do they study it. They probably have some small book in German written with Hebrew letters and some recognition of herbs and roots that they have heard and learnt from their fathers. Therefore, it has astonished me that we Christians are such foolish people and believe them.

If a Jew does not do well, gambles away his belongings, drinks them away, loses them in quarrels with other Jews, or loses them in some other disgraceful way,

then he moves to be among the Christians, pretends to be a doctor, and usually also a rabbi, then he gets money and is held in high esteem. And because there would already be so many who understood medicine, as in Spain and Italy, what luck and blessing can there be in their cure? For how would God bless the hands that crucified his Son and continue to crucify him with their daily cursing prayers and blasphemies? Indeed, many [Jewish doctors], even though they could understand and help straightaway, do not want to but would rather make things worse and send them to the grave.

Indeed, for a while they contain themselves, but this happens out of fear and for the sake of fame and profit, and in order to make people feel safe and make them sacrifice even more. For they have no loyal heart for any Christians. If they could execute all Christians with one stroke, they would do it and hope for a privileged place in the Garden of Eden in return.

I now think that that should prevent the Christians from telling lies on their behalf and caressing the persistent, hardened Jews. "Sincerity is pleasant to you, God," says David in his prayer [cf. 1 Chronicles 29:17]; so we say with him in truth: [Psalm 139: 20–22] "God, they speak blasphemously against you, and your enemies rise up without cause. Yes, Lord, I hate those who hate you and am grieved with those that set themselves against you. I hate them in all seriousness. That's why they are my enemies." Psalm 139.

Excerpt 3: Drinking blood and killing children

Source: Bezelius, *Die Herrlichkeit des Christenthums*, under "Historische Zugabe," 217–22 (§ 26 [*sic*]).

Text

Ob die Jüden Christen Blut trincken/ oder auch sonst bey sich tragen und mißbrauchen?

Wol ist gewiß/ daß die Jüden nach der Christen Blut begierig sind. [*Joh. Lud. Gottfrid. Chronic. f. 586, 688.*] Noch mehr findet man in den Geschicht-Büchern/ daß sie sollen Christen-Kinder geraubet/ sie gemartert/ und das Blut ihnen abgezapfet haben. Ich will ein und ander Exempel anführen.

Im Jahr *1250.* kauffeten die Jüden zu Saragosa in Hispanien einen Christen Knaben/ den ein anderer Jüde gestohlen hatte/ dieses arme Kind von *7.* Jahren nagelten die boßhaftigen Jüden an ein Creutz/ durchstachen es mit einem Spies/ also am Creutz hangende/ und spielten die Passion mit ihm/ Christo zu Hohn.

Im Jahr *1475.* marterten die verfluchten Jüden zu *Trient* am Grünendonnerstag den *23. Martij* ein armes Knäblein/ Simon genant/ dritthalb Jahr alt/ zu todt/ fast auff diese Weise/ wie der HErr Christus gemartert worden/ dergleichen haben sie auch zu *Mota* in Friaul an einem armen Kinde gethan (dabey ein Christlicher Scribent diese Worte setzet/ ob sie wol ihren Lohn darumb empfangen/ so haben sie doch damit zuerkennen gegeben/ wie sie gegen uns und unsere Kinder gesinnet seyn/ und daß sie wohl werth/ daß man sie in den fürnehmsten Städten zu der Christen verderben mit so grosen Sorgen handhaben auffziehe/ und als nutzbare Kostgänger ernehre)

[*Zeil. in Itin. Germ. fol. 467.*] In der Stadt Ober-Wesel an der Mauer gegen dem Rhein ist ein Spittal/ in dessen Capelle eine hültzerne Seule/ an welche die Jüden ein Knäblein/ Werner genandt/ angebunden und getödtet haben/ dabey stehet: *Anno CCLXXXVII.* hat Wernericke de Wammenreid den Todt gelitten *XIII. Kal. Maij. Henricus Ranzovius* meldet/ daß dieser Knabe im 7. Jahr seines Alters am Charfreytag getödtet worden sey.

[*Dilherr Zeit- und Welt-Lauff p. 547.*] Im Jahr *1529.* den *20. Maij.* sind zu Bosing in Ungern bey *30.* Jüdische Manns- und Weibs-Personer lebendig verbrennet worden/ dieweil sie ein Kind gestohlen/ in einem Keller gemartert/ ihm alle Äderlein auffgeschnitten/ und das Blut mit Federkielen außgesogen/ hernach für das Thor getragen/ und in eine Hecke geworffen. Es wurde aber das todte Kind allda von einer Christlichen *Matron* gefunden/ und die Sache für die Obrigkeit gebracht/ welche nach fleissiger Erkundigung die Thäter erfuhr/ und wegen schrecklicher Händel/ so die Jüden in der Marter aussagten/ die gantze Jüdenschafft allda zum Feuer verdammet/ ohne die Kinder/ so unter *10.* Jahren ware/ welche fromme Christen auffnahmen/ tauffen liessen/ und aufferzogen.

So hat der Jüde Johann Pfefferkorn/ welcher zu Halle vor der Moritzburg verbrandt worden/ bekandt/ daß er zwey Christen-Kinder gestohlen/ deren eins er und andere Jüden also hingerichtet/ daß sie es sich zu todte bluten lassen/ welches Blut sie auffgefangen.

Da sind nun die Jüden beschuldigt worden/ daß sie solch Christen-Kinder Blut nicht allein zu allerhand bösen Händeln brauchten/ sondern auch gar kosteten und trincken/ welches sie aber nicht allein beständigt läugnen/ sondern auch viele Gelahrte erfahrne Christen halten sie deßfalls für unschuldig.

[*Carpzov in Ius Reg. Schickhardi c. IV. th. XV. p. 280.*] U[n]d möge diese Rede sich etwa daher verursachet haben/ weil ein Jüde geschrieben/ man solle nach der Christen דמים oder דמי stehen und trachten/ da dann das Wort דם vom Blut verstanden/ welches doch auch bey den Rabinen Geld und Güter heisset.

Sonst hat ein Jüde/ welcher sich zu Regensburg tauffen lassen/ außgesagt/ daß sie der Christen Kinder tödten/ und ihr Blut auffangen/ darein sie hernach ein Tüchlein tuncken/ und über den sterbenden legen/ mit den Worten: Sintemahl JEsus

der wahre Messias ist/ so komme das Blut dieses unschuldigen/ der im Glauben an Christum gestorben/ dir zu gut/ und gedeye dir zum ewigen Leben. Welches denn ein Zeugnis wäre ihres überzeugten Gewissens/ wenn man nur dessen gewiß sein könte/ wie eine gelehrte Feder schreibet.

[*Anton. Margarita de fide Jud. p. m. 71.*] Ich will noch hinzuthun/ was ein bekehrter Jüde von dem Blut essen auffgezeichnet hat: Es ist zuwissen/ schreibt er/ daß die Jüden kein Hintertheil essen/ darumb/ daß der Engel dem Jacob seinen Schenckel verrücket/ es sey denn daß sie alle Adern zuvor ausziehen/ und wie und welche man nehmen soll/ davon haben sie ein groß Buch geschrieben. So essen sie auch kein Blut/ darumb wässern und saltzen sie ein jedes Fleisch eine Stunde/ auff daß das Saltz das Blut heraus ziehen soll/ waschen hernach dasselbe Salz wol ab/ denn ihnen im Gesetz an vielen Orten verboten/ daß sie kein Blut essen sollen. Daher kommts auch/ wenn die Jüden ein Ey essen/ daß sie es nicht an der Seiten aufthun/ auch nicht am Boden/ sondern auff der Spitzen/ Ursach/ man findet etliche Eyer/ die haben einen Bluts-Tropfen in ihnen/ und derselbe liegt allewege an der Spitzen/ wenn er den solchen Bluts-Tropffen findet/ würfft er das Ey hinweg/ isset es nicht/ es ist unrein.

Wie denn auch ihre Väter vor dem Blut essen sich allezeit gräßlich gestellt/ daß auch die Apostel eine Zeitlang nachlassen müssen/ wie das Buch von ihren Geschichten zeuget.

Seind demnach die Jüden von solcher Beschuldigung/ als ob sie der Christen Kinder Blut trincken/ wol frey zuschelten. Nicht die Begierde das Blut zu trincken/ sondern die Bitterkeit/ der Christen-Blut zu vergiessen/ und zwar zur Schmach Christi am selbigen Tage/ hat sie zu solchen Mordthaten angetrieben.

Translation

Whether the Jews drink Christian blood or otherwise carry it around with them and abuse it.

It is certain that the Jews are greedy for the blood of the Christians. [Johann Ludwig Gottfried, *Chronica*, ff. 586, 688] One finds even more in the history books: they are said to have kidnapped Christian children, martyred them, and drained their blood. I want to cite one or two examples.

In the year 1250, the Jews in Saragossa in Spain bought a Christian boy whom another Jew had stolen. This poor seven-year-old child was nailed to a cross by the malicious Jews. While hanging from the cross, they pierced him with a spear and acted out the Passion with him to mock Christ.

On Maundy Thursday, 23 March, in the year 1475, the cursed Jews in Trent martyred a poor little boy called Simon, two and a half years old, to death, in the same

way as the Lord Christ was martyred. They also did the same thing to a poor child in Mota in Friuli. (A Christian writer writes these words about this: “Regardless of whether they received their reward for it, they have nevertheless acknowledged how they feel about us and our children, and that they are so valued that they are raised in the noblest cities – to the ruin of Christians – with such great care and they are honoured as if they were useful boarders.”)

[Martin Zeiller, *Itinerarium Germaniae Nov-Antiquae: Teutsches Reyßbuch durch Hoch und NiderTeutschland*, fol. 467] In the town of Ober-Wesel alongside the town wall facing the Rhine, there is a hospital. In its chapel there is a wooden pillar to which the Jews tied and killed a little boy called Werner. Next to it is says: “In the year [1]287, Wernericke de Wammenreid suffered death on 19 April.” Henricus Ranzovius reports that this boy was killed when he was seven years old on Good Friday.

[Johann Michael Dilherr, *Zeit- und Welt-Lauff*, p. 547] On 20 May in the year 1529, thirty Jewish men and women were burned alive in Bösing in Hungary [Pezinok, Slovakia] because they stole a child, martyred him in a cellar, cut open all of his veins, and sucked out the blood with quills. Afterwards they dragged him out the town gate and threw him in a hedge. But the dead child was found there by a Christian matron, and the matter was brought to the authorities, who, after diligent inquiries, found out who the perpetrators were. And because of terrible actions to which the Jews testified under torture, the entire Jewish community there was condemned to the fire with the exception of children under the age of ten whom pious Christians took in, had baptized, and raised.

Likewise, the Jew Johann Pfefferkorn, who was burned in front of Moritzburg Castle in Halle, confessed that he had stolen two Christian children, one of which he and other Jews executed by letting him bleed to death, which blood they collected.

The Jews have now been accused of not only needing such Christian children’s blood for all kinds of evil dealings, but also of savouring and drinking it, which they not only deny all the time, but also many learned Christians consider them to be innocent of this.

[Johann Benedikt Carpzov, *Ius Regium Hebraeorum*, ed. Wilhelm Schickhard, ch. 4, pt. 15, p. 280] And this talk may have been caused by this: a Jew wrote that one should demand and seek out the Christians’ דמים or דמי; as the word דם was understood to mean “blood,” but for the rabbis also means “money and goods.”

Alternatively, a Jew who was baptized in Regensburg testified that they killed the children of Christians and collected their blood, into which they then dunked a cloth and lay it over the dying with the words: “Since Jesus is the true Messiah, then the blood of this innocent one who died in faith in Christ will be for your good and will bring you eternal life.” As a learned pen writes: “What a testimony of their convinced conscience this would be, if only one could be sure of it!”

[Antonius Margaritha, *De Fide Judaica*, middle of p. 71] I also want to add what a converted Jew wrote about eating blood: "It is to be known," he writes, "that the Jews eat no hindquarters (because the angel dislocated Jacob's thigh) unless they extract all the veins beforehand. They wrote a big book about how and which ones to take. In order that they eat no blood, they soak and salt every piece of meat for an hour, so that the salt is supposed to draw out the blood. Afterwards, they wash off the same salt well, for it is forbidden many places in the Law for them to eat blood. That is why it is also so, that whenever the Jews eat an egg, they do not open it along the sides, not at the bottom, but at the top. The reason: several eggs can be found that have a drop of blood in them and everywhere this drop is found at the tip. When he finds such a drop of blood, he throws the egg away, does not eat it: it is unclean.

Just as their fathers imagined eating blood as always being abominable, the apostles also did not deviate from it for some time as the book of their stories testifies.

Accordingly, the Jews were exonerated from such things as drinking the blood of Christians' children. It was not the desire to drink the blood, but the bitterness to shed Christian blood and indeed to shame Christ on the same day that drove them to such murderous deeds.

Excerpt 4: Insincere conversion by Jews

Source: Bezelius, *Die Herrlichkeit des Christenthums*, under "Historische Zugabe," 226–30 (§ 27).

Text

Auß Furcht und Zwang haben viel Jüden die Tauffe angenommen/ aber mit falschen Hertzen.

[*Joh. Wülf. Animadv. in Cap. III. Ther. Jud. R. Zevi p. 208.*] Wir sollen die Jüden nicht zwingen zum Christenthum/ und daß sie unsern JEsum anbeten und ehren/ von welchen wir wissen/ daß sie ihn verspotten und lästern. So wil auch GOTT selbst nicht/ daß man die Leute peinige/ daß sie gläuben/ was sie nicht gläuben/ daß sie lieben/ was sie nicht lieben/ daß sie verstehen/ was sie nicht verstehen.

Daher ist eine solche Menge *Maranen* in Hispanien/ welche auß Furcht grausamer Marter und Todes sich zwar tauffen lassen/ im Hertzen aber Jüden geblieben sind/ welche in ihren Häusern nach den Auffsätzen ihrer Väter leben/ äusserlich aber sich Christen stellen/ und ihrem Gottesdienst beywohnen. Da sie denn GOTT

und Menschen geäffet/ nicht ohne groß Ärgerniß/ Nachtheil/ und Schaden der Christlichen Religion.

Ein Engeländer schreibet also davon: Gleichwol kan nicht verneinet werden/ daß unterschiedliche Jüden sich in diesem Stück einer ärgerlichen Heuchelen gebrauchen. Dergleichen Schlags viel sind/ welche/ wenn sie in die Kundschafft und Gewalt der *Inquisition* gerathen/ sich so bald zu einem Crucifix und Rosenkrantz/ als zu der *Zizith* und *Tephillim* bequemen können. Und bin ich versichert/ daß es mit etlichen Jüden dißfalls so weit kommen/ daß sie geistliche Orden haben angenommen/ und in die Klöster gangen/ doch aber wenn sie an solche Örter kommen/ wo die Jüden geduldet werden/ kein Bedencken getragen/ ihre *Synagogen* zu besuchen.

Dessen haben wir Exempel an zweyen Jüden/ welche/ nachdem sie in Spanien etliche Jahr lang von des *S. Dominici* Orden *Profession* gemacht/ und nach *Legorn* in ihrem Mönchshabit kommen sind/ haben sie so bald die Kappe in eine *Ganephe* verändert/ und sind auß faulen Mönchen schachrende Jüden worden.

Ein ander/ Jüde der mir bekandt/ und bey fünff Jahren zu *Saragoza* in Spanien die Artzney *studiret* hatte/ als er gefraget worden/ wie er mit der *Religion* hätte können zurecht kommen? Gab er mit lachenden Munde diese Antwort: Das seine Bequemung zur *Religion* nur ein Werck seiner Ner- und Musculn gewesen/ und ihm seine *Anatomy* nichts gesagt daß sein Hertz damit zu schaffen gehabt habe.

Jener führete einen Herzog an einen Sabbath-Tage auff einen hohen Thurn/ und sagte/ von dannen möchte er die Jüden/ so zu dem Christum gezwungen/ erkennen/ und von andern Christen leichtlicht unterscheiden: Denn in welchen Häusern er keinen Rauch sehe auffsteigen/ da doch die Jahrs-Zeit/ daß man einheitze/ erfordere/ in denselben wären gewißlich Hebreer/ welche nach Mosis Gebot kein Feur am Sabbat-Tage in ihren Wohnungen machen; welches sich dann auch also befunden.

In Hispanien war ein Jude/ welcher mit Gewalt zum Christlichen Glauben genothiget war/ der aß das gantze Jahr durch ungesäuert Brod/ auff daß ers desto freyer in Ostern essen möchte: Denn er gab für/ daß er keinen Sauerteig vertragen könte. An dem Fest-Tage/ da die Hebreer mit dem Horn blasen/ sind solche gezwungene Christen in Wälder und Hölen gegangen/ und dergleichen gethan. Sie halten heimlich ihre Metzger/ welche das Vieh nach dem Gesetz besichtigen/ das Fett hinwegthun/ und es entädern müssen. Sie haben/ die die Beschneidung in geheim verrichten/ ja etliche thuens selber/ damit sie nicht verrahten/ und zu harter Straffe gezogen werden.

Solches und dergleichen mehr führte *Versorius* ein verständiger Mann dem König *Alphonso* zu Gemüthe/ und sagte: Was hilffts denn/ ô König/ daß man das Tauff-Wasser an die Jüden wendet/ und sie *Petrum* und *Paulum* nennen lässet/ da sie doch halßstarrig auff das Gesetz Mosis bestehen/ und biß in den Todt/ wie *Akiba* und *Tariphon* vertheidigen? Nichts wird damit außgerichtet/ daß man die Jüden

mit Unwillen zu Christen machet/ denn so werden sie nur wider die Christen stoltziren/ grösserer Freyheit sich anmassen/ und die Zölle/ die sie vorhin als Jüden erlegen müssen/ wegern. Kürtzlich/ mein Herr König wolle/ sagt er/ versichert seyn/ *Judaismum morbum esse insanabilem*, daß das Jüdenthum sey wie eine unheilbare Kranckheit.

Darumb sollen alle Mittel in der Bekehrung der Jüden/ die eine Nöthigung scheinen/ doch ohne Zwang seyn/ daß sie nicht gezwungen/ sondern freywillig das Christenthum annehmen/ wie H. *Lutherus* schreibt: Man soll ja einen jeden gläuben lassen/ was er wolle/ gläubt er unrecht/ so hat er gnug Straffe am ewigen Feur in der Hölle/ warumb will man sie denn zeitlich martern/ sofern sie im Glauben irren/ und nicht darneben auffrührisch/ oder sonst der Obrigkeit widerstreben. Mit der Schrifft und GOttes Wort soll man ihnen wehren und widerstreben/ mit Feur wird man wenig außrichten.

Translation

Many Jews accepted baptism out of fear and coercion, but with false hearts.

[Johann Wülfer, "Animadversiones," in ch. 3 of *Therica Judaica* by Rabbi Salamon Zvi, p. 208] We should not force the Jews into Christianity and worshipping and honouring our Jesus, whom we know they mock and blaspheme. So, even God himself does not want people to be tormented so that they believe what they do not believe, that they love what they do not love, that they understand what they do not understand.

That is why there are so many Marranos in Spain who let themselves be baptized out of fear of cruel torture and death, but who have remained Jews in their hearts, who live in their houses according to the rules of their fathers, but outside they are Christians and attend their divine service. They are then mimicking God and people, not without great annoyance, disadvantage, and damage to the Christian religion.

An Englishman writes about it [Lancelot Addison, *The Present State of the Jews* (1675), 30–32]: Similarly, it cannot be denied, that various Jews commit an annoying act of hypocrisy in this issue. Of which sort are many who, once they understand the reach and power of the Inquisition, can just as soon settle for a crucifix and a rosary as for *tzitzit* and *tefillin*. And I am assured that some Jews have gone so far in this that they have entered into Holy Orders, and joined the monasteries, but when they come to such places where the Jews are tolerated, they have no qualms about visiting their synagogue.

And of this we have an example of two Jews, who, having professed the Order of St Dominic in Spain for some years and arriving in Leghorn [Livorno] in their

friar habits, instantly changed their cowl for a *ganephe*, and from idle friars they turned into haggling Jews.

Another Jew with whom I am acquainted, and who for five years had studied medicine in Saragossa in Spain, being asked how he could get on with the religion, made this reply with a laughing mouth: that forcing himself into this religion was only the work of his nerves and muscles, and that his anatomy told him nothing that his heart was to be concerned about.

This man led a duke to a high tower on a Sabbath day, and said that from there he would be able to recognize the Jews who had been forced to Christ and easily distinguish them from other Christians: for in those houses where he sees no smoke rising, even though it was the season when it was necessary to use heating, would certainly be Hebrews, who, according to the commandments of Moses, make no fire in their dwellings on the Sabbath day; which was then also found to be so.

In Spain, there was a Jew who was made to convert to Christianity by force, who ate unleavened bread throughout the whole year so that he might eat all the more freely during Easter: for he pretended that he could not tolerate any leaven. On the feast day, when the Hebrews blow the horn, such Christians by force went into forests and caves and did the same thing. They secretly keep their butchers, who have to inspect the cattle according to the Law, remove the fat, and devein it. They have those who perform circumcision in secret. Indeed, some even do so themselves, so that they are not betrayed and severely punished.

Versorius, a sensible man, brought this and more like it to King Alphonso's attention and said: "What is the use, O King, of applying the baptismal water to the Jews and having them called Peter and Paul, when they obstinately cling to the Law of Moses and, like Akiva and Tarfon, defend it until death? Nothing will be accomplished by turning reluctant Jews into Christians, because then they will only swagger against the Christians, wrest greater freedom, and refuse the tribute that they previously had to pay as Jews. In short," he says, "my Lord King be assured: *Judaismum morbum esse insanabilem*, that Judaism is like an incurable disease."

That is why all the means for converting the Jews which appear to be necessary should be without coercion, so that they are not forced, but voluntarily accept Christianity. As the blessed Luther writes: "One should let everyone believe whatever he wants; if he believes wrong, he will have enough punishment in the eternal fire in hell. Why do you want to torture them in this world if they err in faith and do not even brazenly or otherwise resist the authorities? One should resist and oppose them with Scripture and the Word of God. One will achieve little with fire." [WA 26: 145–46]

Excerpt 5: Tolerating Jews (1)

Source: Bezelius, *Die Herrlichkeit des Christenthums*, under "Historische Zugabe," 230–34 (§ 28).

Text

Man soll dennoch die Jüden dulden.

[*Wagenseil cont. Lipmann. e. R. Salom. Luzzato p. 213.*] Die Jüden rühmen sehr/ wie ihre *Nation*, obwohl durch die Welt zerstreuet/ dennoch sehr mächtig sey. Wie groß die Zahl/ schreibt einer/ kan man nicht eigentlich sagen/ weil wir nicht alle Örter wissen/ da sie wohnen und sich auffhalten. Von den *10.* Stämmen/ welche für der Zerstöhrung deß ersten Tempels von dem Salmanasser gefänglich hinweg geführet/ weiß man noch diese Stunde nichts gewisses/ wiewol der Erdboden nun gnugsam durchwandert und entdecket ist.

Unter dem Perser ist eine grosse Zahl/ und haben gute Gelegenheit/ insonderheit hat ihnen der Türck Unterschleiff gegeben/ nachdem sie auß Hispanien getrieben worden/ daß sie über *100000.* daselbst wohnen.

Zu Constantinopel und Thessalonich ist ihrer mehr als in andern Städten/ und werden gezehlt über *80000.*

in Deutschland findet sich eine grosse Anzahl/ so dem Käyser unterworffen/ aber noch mehr in Pohlen/ Rußland/ und Litthauen/ da sie ihre Academien haben/ und viele Tausend *studiren*, mögen auch ihr eigen Gericht halten in Sachen die bey und unter ihrem Volck fürgehen.

In denen Herrschafften/ die von der Römischen Kirchen abgesondert/ findet man zwar ihrer nicht so viel/ aber doch werden sie in Holland freundlich auffgenommen. Wie ihnen dann in Amsterdam und Roterdam/ wie auch zu Hamburg in Holstein/ als in grossen Handels-Städten Freyheiten gegeben zu wohnen/ und ihren Handel zu treiben.

In Italien werden sie geschützt und in grossen Ehren gehalten/ und schätzt man sie auff *25000.*

In den Königreichen *Marocco* und *Fezza* ist ihrer eine grosse Menge/ und derer/ die besser hinein in *Africa* wohnen/ kan man die Zahl nicht eigentlich wissen.

So nun GOTT der HERR die Jüden duldet/ warumb wolten wir sie nicht dulden und ihrer warten zur Busse und Bekehrung? Es wird erzehlet/ daß der Patriarch Abraham insonderheit sehr Gastfrey gewesen/ daß er sich unglücklich geschätzet/ wenn er einen Tag nicht einen Frembdling auffgenommen und bewirthet [*Vrsin in Arboreto Bibl. p. 2.*] (wie denn auch das *Targum* meldet/ daß er einen Wald fruchtbarer Bäume zu Bersaba gepflantzet habe/ da er einem jeden Frembdling und

Reisenden vergönnet/ hinein zu gehen und zu brechen/ so viel als ihm beliebte; aber mit dem Beding/ daß er den wahren GOTT/ Schöpffer Himmels und der Erden/ von dem alle Gaben kommen/ dafür solte preisen und dancken) Zur Zeit gehet er hinauß auffs Feld/ ob er nicht einen Frembdling antreffen möge/ den er mit sich heim nehme. Da sihet er einen alten Mann/ der von der Reise ermüdet/ sich unter einen Baum geleget hatte/ den redet er freundlich an/ und nöthiget ihn/ daß er zu ihm einkehren wolle. Als nun die Mahlzeit zugerichtet/ und Abraham mit seinen Haußgenossen betet/ da greifft der Alte zu nach der Speise. Abraham erinnert ihn/ daß es sich nicht gebühren wolle/ Speise zu nehmen ohne Gebet und Dancksagung. Aber der Alte spricht/ er sey dergleichen ungewohnt/ denn seine Vor-Eltern ihn solchen GOttes-Dienst nicht gelehret haben. Dessen erschrickt Abraham/ sihet/ daß er mit einem Abgöttischen zuthun hat/ und stösset ihn alsobald zum Hause hinauß. Aber der HErr erschien ihm und sprach: Was machstu Abraham? Solstu also thun? Ich habe diesem Alten/ obwohl er undanckbar gegen mich gewesen/ Leben und Wolthat gegeben über hundert Jahr/ und du magst ihm nicht eine Mahlzeit geben? Du magst ihm nicht einen Augenblick dulden? Da denn Abraham dem Alten nachgeeilet/ ihn wieder zurück geruffen/ ihm auch mit Speise und Unterweisung also zur Hand gegangen/ daß er endlich den GOTT Abrahams erkandt hat.

An welchen wir gantz und gar verzweifeln/ der wird plötzlich bekehret/ und von dem wir grosse Hoffnung gemacht/ der fällt am ersten abe/ und wird der Allerboßhafftigste/ und ist weder unsre Furcht noch unsere Liebe gewiß. Der Mensch weiß kaum was heute ist/ weiß er schon/ was heute ist/ so weiß er doch nicht/ was morgen sein wird. Darumb soll man dulden/ die GOTT duldet/ woferne sie nicht durch unternehmung böser gefährlicher Händel sich unwürdig machen.

Mann soll die Jüden nicht verfolgen/ nicht tödten/ nicht übel *tracti*ren. Man höre was die Schrifft davon saget. David spricht: GOTT erzeigt mir reichlich seine Gnade/ GOTT last mich meine Lust sehen an meinen Feinden. Erwürge sie nicht/ das es mein Volck nicht vergesse. Darumb sind sie in alle Welt zerstreuet/ daß/ indem sie ihre Straffe leiden/ sie zugleich sind *testes nostræ Redemtionis*, Zeugen unsrer Erlösung/ wie abermahl geschrieben stehet: Zustreue sie aber mit deiner Macht/ HErr unser Schild/ und stosse sie hinunter/ im 59. Psalm.

Translation

One should nevertheless tolerate the Jews.

[Johann Christoph Wagenseil, containing Yom-Tov Lippmann and Rabbi Solomon Luzzatto, p. 213] The Jews boast very much about how their nation, although scattered throughout the world, is nevertheless very powerful. How great the number, someone writes, we cannot really say because we do not know all the

places where they live and stay. Nothing certain is known at present about the Ten Tribes who were carried away as prisoners by Shalmaneser during the destruction of the First Temple, although the earth has now been sufficiently explored and discovered.

Among the Persians, there are a large number, and they have good opportunities. In particular, the Turks gave them shelter after they were driven out of Spain, so that over 100,000 of them live there.

There are more of them in Constantinople and Thessalonica than in other cities and they number over 80,000.

There are a large number in Germany who are subject to the Emperor, but even more in Poland, Russia, and Lithuania, where they have their academies and many thousands study; they can also keep their own courts for matters that occur between and among their people.

In those lands that have separated from the Church of Rome, there are actually not many of them, although in Holland they are taken in in a friendly way. Then in Amsterdam and Rotterdam as well as in Hamburg in Holstein and in large trading cities, they are given the freedom to live and pursue their trade.

They are protected in Italy and held in great honour, and there are estimated to be some 25,000.

There are masses of them in the kingdoms of Morocco and Fez, and we cannot actually know how many of them live further beyond in Africa.

So now that the Lord God tolerates the Jews, why will we not tolerate them and wait for their penance and conversion? It is told that the patriarch Abraham in particular was very hospitable, so that he considered himself unhappy if a day passed and he had not received and fed a stranger [Johannes Heinrich Ursinus, *Arboretum Biblicum*, p. 2] (as also the Targum reports: he planted a forest of fruit-bearing trees in Beersheba, and he allowed every stranger and traveller to got here and pick as much as they wanted, but on the condition that they praised and thanked the true God, creator of the heavens and earth, from whom all gifts come.) One time, he went out into the field to see whether he could find a stranger whom he could take home. There he saw an old man who was tired from his journey and had lain down under a tree. He spoke to him in a friendly manner and urged him to call in at his home. When the meal was prepared and Abraham was praying with the rest of his household, the old man reached out for the food. Abraham reminded him that it was not proper to take food without prayer and thanksgiving. But the old man said that he was not used to this sort of thing as his ancestors had not taught him such worship. Abraham was startled by this and realized that he was dealing with an idolater and pushed him out of the house. But the Lord appeared to him and spoke: "What are you doing, Abraham? Should you behave like this? Even though he has been ungrateful to me, I have given this old man life and benefit for over a

hundred years – and you won't give him one meal? You do not want to put up with him for just a moment?" When Abraham had hurried after the old man, called him back again, and helped him with food and guidance, he finally recognized the God of Abraham.

The man, whom we completely despair of, converts suddenly, and for whom we have great hope, quickly falls away and becomes the most evil man and he is certain of neither our fear nor our love. Man hardly knows what today is. If he already knows what today is, then he does not know what tomorrow will be. We should tolerate those whom God tolerates provided that they do not make themselves unworthy by undertaking evil, dangerous activities.

We should not persecute the Jews, not kill them, not treat them badly. Let us hear what the Scriptures say about this. David speaks: "God shows me his mercy in abundance. God lets me see my desire upon my enemies. Strangle them not lest my people forget." Thus, they are scattered throughout the world so that while they suffer their punishment they are at the same time *testes nostrae redemptionis*, witnesses of our redemption, as it is written again: "But scatter them with your power, Lord our shield, and bring them down," in Psalm 59.

Excerpt 6: Tolerating Jews (2)

Source: Bezelius, *Die Herrlichkeit des Christenthums*, under "Historische Zugabe," 234–38 (§ 29).

Text

Wie die verstockten Jüden zu dulden seyn?

Dabey die Frage; Ob man die Jüden mit guten Gewissen an Ort und Enden wieder einnehmen und beherbergen möge/ da sie einmahl außgetrieben und verstossen worden? [*Mengering in Inform. Conscient. Evangel. p. 26.*] Wo die Jüden ihre Herberg und Behausung haben/ lässet man sie nicht unbillich/ wo sie sich anders friedlich/ schiedlich/ und ohne Ärgerniß und Lästerung deß Christlichen Glaubens/ ohne Reitzung und Verführung anderer verhalten und erweisen.

Darumb es dann der Spanischen *Nation* nicht kan gebilliget werden/ daß sie eben zu der Zeit/ da Thessalonich und Constantinopel/ und ein gut theil Grichen Landes von dem Türcken bezwungen/ erobert/ und an den Einwohnern mehrentheils durch jämmerliches niederhauen entblöset worden/ sie in ihren Landen und Provinzen allen Jüden auff gewisse Zeit außzuweichen geboten/ wo sie nicht wolten zu leibeigene[n] Knechten gemachet werden. Daher aus Spanien über die *100000.*

Jüden von Mann und Weibs-Personen gezogen/ die mit sich ein grosses Reichthum und vielerley Künste und Hand-Wercke hinweg geführet/ damit sie dem Türckischen Käyser und Reich sehr lieb und willkommen gewesen/ in dem sie sonderlich die Kunst und Wissenschafft der Geschütze und Artollerey ihnen mit zugebracht: Denn der Türckische Keyser sich ihrer Ankunfft höchlich erfreuet/ und ihnen allenthalben/ wo sie gewolt/ Herberg und Wohnung verstattet und zugelassen/ also/ daß die von Constantinopel kommen/ berichten/ daß noch über *20000*. Jüden zu Constantinopel/ auff den heutigen Tag/ als Bürger und Einwohner gezehlet werden.

Dannoch aber will hergegen nicht im Gewissen rathsam und verantwortlich befunden werden/ wenn man die Jüden/ da sie einmahl von der Obrigkeit außgewiesen und verjaget werden sind/ wieder einnehmen/ und auffs neue sich unter eine Evangelische Gemeine im Lande oder Städten wolle einkommen und flechten lassen.

Wir wollen zwey *Judicia* oder Bedencken und Zeugnisse anhören;

eines ist deß Sel. *Lutheri*, der seine letzte Predigt/ so er zu Eißleben Sontags vor seinem Absterben gethan/ mit einer ernstlichen Vermahnung beschlossen/ das/ da die Jüden sich nicht zu unserm Messia bekehren/ sie die Obrigkeit in ihrem Landen nicht dulden solle/ als offentliche Feinde und Lästerer unsers HErren/ und gemeine Landschäden und Fluche/ darumb Städte und Flecken würden endlich zu Grunde und Boden gehen müssen.

Das ander ist deß Gottseligen Chur-Fürsten zu Sachsen/ Hertzogs *Augusti*, von dem Hr. *D. Selnecker* nachfolgends gedencket; da einsmahls etliche Vorschreibung ankamen/ daß Seine Churfl. Gnaden möchten in ihrem Landen den Jüden ein Ort eingeben/ und der Ort allbereit genennet ward/ da wird mir befohlen/ ich solte mit dem alten Jüden/ Hirsch/ der zugegen/ und die Brieffe gebracht hatte/ reden/ und bey ihm erkundigen/ ob sie auch möchten ihres Irrthums und Blindheit benommen werden. Ich thue es/ berede mich mit den Jüden nach Nothdurfft/ komme wieder/ und sage dem Chur-Fürsten an/ daß ich nicht dafür halte/ daß der Jüde glaube/ daß ein GOtt im Himmel sey/ vielweniger daß Christus GOttes SOhn unser Erlöser sey. Da giebt der fromme Chur-Fürst diese Antwort: Wenn diese und andere Jüden mir auch Geld zuschneieten/ so wolte ich doch sie in meinem Lande/ darinn zuwohnen/ nicht leiden: Denn solt ich die leiden/ die mir meinen HErrn JEsum lästern/ so wäre ich gar treuloß an Christo.

Darumb denn/ was verstockte Jüden sind/ nicht so bloß hin/ sondern mit gewissen und genauen Bedingungen zu dulden sind/ wie angezeiget.

Translation

How are the obdurate Jews to be tolerated?

And the question: Whether we, with a clear conscience, should take the Jews back in and accommodate them in those places from where they were once expelled and cast out? [Arnold Mengering, *Informatorium Conscientiae Evangelicum*, p. 26] Where the Jews have their lodgings and dwellings, they are not treated unreasonably when they otherwise behave and prove themselves to be peaceful and tolerable and without annoyance to and blasphemy of the Christian faith, without the provocation and seduction of others.

That is why we cannot approve of what the Spanish nation did, that when Thessalonica and Constantinople and a good part of the Greek country were defeated and conquered by the Turks and the majority of the inhabitants were stripped bare by pitiful beatings, in their [Spanish] lands and provinces they ordered all Jews to leave by a certain time unless they wanted to be made into serfs. So more than 100,000 Jews, men and women, left Spain; they took with them great wealth and many kinds of arts and handicrafts, so that they would be very dear to and welcomed by the Turkish sultan and empire into which they brought the art and science of guns and artillery in particular. So the Turkish sultan was delighted with their arrival and allowed and permitted them residence and dwellings everywhere they wanted. Thus, those who come from Constantinople report that more than 20,000 Jews can today be counted as citizens and inhabitants in Constantinople.

But on the other hand, it will not be found in one's conscience to be advisable and responsible, if the Jews, having once been expelled and chased out by the authorities, are re-admitted and once again come into and mix with an evangelical community in the country or towns.

We want to hear two judgements or concerns and testimonies:

One is by the blessed Luther, who concluded his last sermon that he gave in Eisleben the Sunday before he died [i.e., 18 February 1546] with a serious admonition: that because the Jews do not convert to our Messiah, the authorities in their countries should not tolerate them as public enemies and blasphemers of our Lord and common spoilers of the land and maledictions for which cities and towns would finally have to perish.

The other is by Prince-elector Augustus, the holy prince-elector of Saxony, memorialized by Dr Nikolaus Selnecker in the following: once, when a number of documents arrived asking his grace, the prince-elector, to give the Jews a place in their land, and the place was already named, I was ordered to talk to the old Jew, Hirsch, who was in attendance and who had brought the letters, and ask him whether they also wanted to be freed from their error and blindness. I did it, talked to the Jews as necessary, came back, and told the prince-elector that I did not think

that the Jew believed there was a God in heaven, much less that Christ the Son of God is our redeemer. Then the pious prince-elector gave this answer: "Even if these and other Jews showered me with money, I would not want to suffer them living in my country, because if I were to put up with those who blaspheme my Lord Jesus, it would be like I had been unfaithful to Christ."

That is why Jews, hardened as they are, are not to be tolerated without further ado but only under certain and precise conditions as indicated.

Excerpt 7: Whether to burn the Talmud

Source: Bezelius, *Die Herrlichkeit des Christenthums*, under "Historische Zugabe," 238–42 (§ 29 [*sic*]).

Text

Ob der *Talmud* zuverbrennen?

Hierüber ist für *178.* Jahren ein hefftiger Streit zwischen dem *Reuchlino* und einem getaufften Jüden/ Johann Pfefferkorn/ entstanden/ [*Sleidan. de Statu Rel. l. 2. p. m. 31.*] darein nachmahls andere Gelehrte mehr mit eingeflochten worden. Die Sache verhält sich also: Es hatte Johann Pfefferkorn offt und viel bey Käyser *Maximilian* angehalten/ daß alle Jüdische Bücher/ sintemahl sie voller Gottes Lästerung und Aberglaubens wären/ und die Jüden hinderten/ daß sie nicht zum Christlichen Glauben kämen/ möchten vertilget/ und ihnen keine Bücher/ ohn allein die Bibel/ solten gestattet werden. Endlich befahl Käyser *Maximilian* dem Ertz.Bischoff von Mäyntz/ daß er etlichen Universitäten/ und Jacob Hochstraten und Johann Reuchlin/ was doch in diesem Fall zu thun/ und ob es unserm Glauben zuträglich/ daß man alle ihre Jüdische Bücher/ ohn allein/ die Bibel/ verbrennete/ zu erwegen und zu beratschlagen Befehl gebe.

Reuchlin schrieb/ was sein Rath und Meinung/ nemlich/ daß der Jüden Bücher dreyerley/ etliche von Historien/ etliche von Artzney/ etliche von ihrem *Talmud*, und diese dennoch nicht alle einerley Gattung. Wiewohl aber viel närrisch und abergläubig Ding darinn geschrieben/ wären sie doch in diesem Fall nütz/ daß sie zu Widerlegung der Jüdischen Irrthümer und Thorheiten sehr wol dieneten.

Da Pfefferkorn solches erfahren/ macht er ein groß Wesen darauß/ ließ ein Buch dawider außgehen/ und zoch den Reuchlin als einen Jüden-Freund und Beschirmer hefftig an/ darauff der Reuchlin mit einer Gegenschrifft antwortete. Er reitzte aber damit viel Universitäten wider sich/ und sonderlich die zu Cöln/ dieselbe war dazumahl die Fürnehmste. Jacob von Hochstraten und Arnold von Tungern/ welcher ein

sonderlich Schmähbuch wider ihn geschrieben/ ja eben dasselbe/ da Pfefferkorn mit umbging/ zu verfechten sich unterstanden/ und das Buch Käyser *Maximiliano* zugeschrieben: Darnach nahmen sie ihn mit Gerichts-Handlung für.

Als es aber nicht gut thun wolte/ *appellirte* Reuchlin an den Römischen Pabst/ dieser übergab den Handel dem Bischoff von Speier. Die zu Cöln aber liessen sich nicht irren/ sondern verdammten des Reuchlins Buch/ und verbrandten es. Solches verdroß den Bischoff von Speier/ und erkandte Reuchlins Buch für rechtschaffen/ dagegen verworffen die zu Pariß das Buch/ daß man es verbrennen/ und der es geschrieben/ zum Wiederruff solte gedrungen werden; [*v. Raynaud. de Bonis & malis libris erotem XIII §. 352, 355.*] Denn der *Talmud* vor Zeiten von den Päbsten billich verdammt/ und von ihren Vorfahrern wäre verbrandt worden. Es ist aber schier ungläublich/ was die *Theologi* zu Cöln mit dieser Sach für Haß und Unglimpf auff sich geladen: Denn alle Gelehrte/ so in Deutschland waren/ liessen allerley schimpfliche Bücher außgehen/ darinne sie den Reuchlin vertheidigten/ und spotteten ihrer auff das lächerlichste/ als ungelährter unverständiger Leute/ die allen Sprachen und guten freyen Künstein feind wären.

[*Gerson in Talmud. c. 18.*] Der getauffte *Gerson* schreibet hievon also: Ob man das gottslästerliche Buch der *Talmud* verbrennen soll oder nicht/ davon hat Johann Reuchling mit Pfefferkorn weitläufftig *disputiret*, ich aber wolte es lieber mit *Reuchlino* als mit Pfefferkorn halten und sagen: Man soll ihn nicht verbrennen. *1.* Dieweil nicht alles böse/ sondern viel guts darinne zu finden ist. *2.* Weil er ein Spiegel deß göttlichen Zorns ist/ wider das Jüdische Volck/ welches also dahin gegeben/ daß/ da es vorhin ein so verständig Volck war/ numehr solche Mährlein und Lügen glaubet. *3.* Weil es keinen Christen schädlich ist/ sintemahl ih[n] niemand lesen noch verstehen kan/ er sey denn von den Jugend auff dazu gehalten. *4.* Weil wir keinen göttlichen Befehl haben/ denselben zu verbrennen/ im Gegentheil aber befielet Paulus die Geister zu prüfen. *5.* Kan man ih[n] auch nicht wol außrotten/ denn wenn schon der Pabst zu Rom/ und alle andere Christliche Könige/ Chur- und Fürsten in allen ihren Landen alle Talmudische Bücher verbrennen liessen/ so würde er doch in Persien/ Türckey/ und andern Landen bleiben/ und würde endlich wieder in diese Lande gebracht werden/ wo nicht offentlich/ doch heimlich. Und würden alsdann die Jüden nur vielmehr darauff bestürtzet seyn (denn Verbot macht Begierde/ daß man vielmehr und eifferiger darnach thut/ als man thäte/ wenn es frey gelassen:)

Auß diesen Ursachen wolt ich lieber wünschen/ daß alle gelehrte Christen den *Talmud* lesen könten/ auff daß sie die Jüden auß ihrem eigenen *Talmud* überzeugen/ und den Apostolischen Catholischen Glauben darauß beweisen und darthun könten/ so würden ohn Zweifel dem HERRN CHRisto mehr Jüden zugeführet werden/ als leyder jetzo geschicht.

Translation

Whether the Talmud is to be burned.

178 years ago, there was a heated argument between Johann Reuchlin and a baptized Jew, Johannes Pfefferkorn. [Johannes Sleidanus, *De statu religionis et rei publicae Carolo V. Caesare commentarii*, vol. 2, middle of p. 31] Later, other scholars were also involved. The matter is as follows: Johannes Pfefferkorn had often asked Emperor Maximilian to destroy all Jewish books as they were full of blasphemy against God and superstition and they prevented the Jews from coming to the Christian faith, and no books bar the Bible alone should be permitted. In the end, Emperor Maximilian ordered the Archbishop of Mainz to give orders to several universities, and Jakob van Hoogstraten, and Johann Reuchlin to consider and deliberate what should be done in this case, and whether it would be beneficial for our faith for all their Jewish books, with the sole exception of the Bible, to be burned.

Reuchlin wrote what his advice and opinion were, namely that the Jews had three kinds of books – some about history, some about medicine, some about their Talmud – and yet these were not all of the same type. Although a lot of foolish and superstitious things are written in them, they would be useful in this case to serve well to refute the Jewish errors and follies.

When Pfefferkorn found out about this, he made a big deal out of it, published a book against it, and viciously attacked Reuchlin as a Jew-friend and protector, to which Reuchlin replied with a refutation. But he provoked many universities against him, and especially the one in Cologne which was the most distinguished at that time. Jakob van Hoogstraten and Arnold von Tongern, who wrote a particularly slanderous book against him, dared to defend the one whom Pfefferkorn was dealing with, and the book was attributed to Emperor Maximilian. Afterwards they took him to court.

But when it did not do well, Reuchlin appealed to the Roman Pope, who handed the matter over to the Bishop of Speyer. Those in Cologne, however, did not let themselves be fooled, but condemned Reuchlin's book and burned it. This annoyed the Bishop of Speyer and he recognized Reuchlin's book as legitimate. On the other hand, those in Paris rejected the book, saying that it should be burned, and whoever wrote it should be urged to recall it, [Theophilus Raynaudus, *Erotemata de malis ac bonis libris*, XIII §§ 352, 355] because the Talmud would have been justly condemned by earlier popes and been burned by their ancestors. But it is completely unbelievable what hatred and disrespect the theologians in Cologne brought upon themselves with this issue, because all the scholars who were then in Germany, had all sorts of opprobrious books published, in which they defended Reuchlin and mocked them in the most ridiculous manner as uneducated, ignorant people who were the enemies of all languages and good liberal arts.

[Christianus Gerson, *Der Jüden Thalmvd fürnembster innhalt, vnd Widerlegung*, ch. 18] The baptized Gerson writes about this: Whether one should burn the blasphemous book of the Talmud or not. Johann Reuchlin and Pfefferkorn discussed this at length, but I would rather stick with Reuchlin than with Pfefferkorn and say: One should not burn it: (1) Because not everything is bad, but a lot of good is to be found in it. (2) Because what is in there is a mirror of divine wrath against the Jewish people, which is spoiled in that way that they had previously been such a sensible people and now only believe such tales and lies. (3) Because it is harmful to no Christians as no one can read or understand it unless encouraged to do so from youth. (4) Because we have no divine command to burn it, on the contrary, Paul commanded the spirits to be tested. (5) We cannot eradicate it because even if the Pope of Rome and all other Christian kings, electors, and princes had all Talmudic books burned in all their countries, it would still exist in Persia, Turkey, and other countries, and it would be end up being brought back to these [Christian] countries, if not publicly, at least secretly. And the Jews would then only be more excited by it (because prohibition creates desire, so that one does it much more eagerly than one would do if it was left free).

For these reasons, I would wish that all learned Christians were able to read the Talmud, so that they could persuade the Jews from their own Talmud, and use it to prove and demonstrate the Apostolic Catholic Faith, which without doubt would lead more Jews to the Lord Christ than has unfortunately happened to date.

Excerpt 8: Usury (1)

Source: Bezelius, *Die Herrlichkeit des Christenthums*, under "Historische Zugabe," 249–51 (§ 29 [*sic*]).

Text

Wucher müste ihnen verboten seyn.

[*Anton. Margar. in Relig. Jud. p. m. 125, 129.*] Ein getauffter Jüde schreibt sehr viel/ und an unterschiedlichen Orten davon/ und vermahnet alle Christliche Obrigkeiten inständig/ den Jüden das Wucher-Handwerck zu legen und ihnen es nicht zuverstatten. Will zu dem/ was schon angeführet/ noch eines und das andere thun. Er schreibet: Wolte GOTT geben/ daß eine Christliche Obrigkeit den Wucher von ihnen nehme/ und daß sie arbeiten müsten/ welche zwey Stücke Ursache sind ihrer Verhärtung/ denn diese zwey Stücke rühmen sie sehr/ und sprechen: An diesen zweyen Stücken haben wir klärlich zu sehen und zu erkennen/ daß wir noch GOttes

außerwehltes Volck seynd/ und er uns nicht gar verlassen hat/ wie die Christen sprechen/ sondern seine Benedeyung bestättiget er noch über uns/ daß uns alle Völcker dienen müssen/ und uns müssig speisen und ernehren/ ja alle Völcker müssen uns für das außerwehlte Volck GOttes bekennen/ und sich für Frembdling/ die nicht GOttes Volck sind/ in dem daß sie von uns entlehnen und Wucher geben. Wenn man aber mit den Jüden handelt nach Inhalt deß Fluchs *Deut. 28*, und vor allen Dingen diese zwey obgemeldte Stücke von ihnen nehme/ so weiß ich/ daß sie in sich selbst gehen würden/ und recht in die Schrifft schauen/ die Augen auffthun/ und den Eckstein aller Propheten recht ansehen/ welchen sie und ihre Väter verworffen haben. Ich versehe mich/ schreibt er abermahl/ wo der Wucher von den müssigen Geitz-Würmern genommen würde/ würden ihrer noch viel zu dem Licht kommen/ von welchen *Esa. 49.* geweissaget hat.

Elias Schadœus erzehlet von einem Jüden/ als derselbe erinnert worden deß langwierigen Elendes/ darinn sie wären/ und daß sie hierauß schliesen solten/ der Messias müste kommen seyn/ daß er/ der Jüde/ habe befohlen auß seinem Keller einen köstlichen Trunck-Weins zuholen/ welchen er jenem in einen schönen Glase fürgesetzt/ und geantwortet: מה תיג בולה Was ist das für ein *Exilium* und Elend? Darauß denn ferner folget (welches doch unbillich ist) daß ein Christ/ wenn er den Jüden schuldig worden ist/ umb desselben Willen *incarceri*ret/ außgepfändet/ und übel gehalten wird (daß mag den Jüden gefallen) also sind die Christen der Jüden Spott/ werden ihre Knechte/ die Würdigkeit deß Christenthums wird *prostitui*ret und leidet Nachtheil/ der Stoltz aber und die *Superstition* deß Jüdischen Volcks wird dadurch bekräfftiget und gestärcket.

Darumb freylich/ so etwas nöthig ist/ dieses ist/ daß den Jüden das Wuchern verboten/ sie hingegen zur Arbeit angewiesen und gehalten werden/ daß sie arbeiten mit ihren Händen/ und ihr eigen Brodt essen.

Translation

Usury must be forbidden them.

[Antonius Margaritha, *Der gantze Jüdisch glaub*, middle of pp. 125, 129] A baptized Jew writes a great deal in different places about this and urgently calls upon all Christian authorities to put a stop to their business of usury and not to allow them to practise it. He wants to add one thing and another to what has already been mentioned. He writes: "If only God were to make it so that a Christian authority took usury from them and forced them to work. These two things are the cause of their hardening because they praise these two things very much and say: 'From these two things, we clearly see and recognize that we are still God's chosen people and that he has not deserted us as the Christians say but still confirms his blessing

over us so that all peoples must serve us and passively feed and nourish us; indeed, all peoples must admit that we are the chosen people of God. And they are foreigners who are not God's people because they borrow from us and pay interest.' But if one deals with the Jews according to the content of the curse in Deuteronomy 28 and above all takes these two aforementioned things from them, then I know that they would turn inwards and look right in the Scriptures, open their eyes, and correctly inspect the cornerstone of all the prophets whom they and their fathers have discarded. I expect," he writes again, "that if usury were taken from the idle stingy worms, then many more of them would come into the light, as Isaiah 49 prophesied."

Elias Schad tells of a Jew who, when he was reminded of the protracted misery in which they [the Jews] found themselves and that they should conclude from this that the Messiah must have come, he, the Jew, ordered a delectable drink of wine be fetched from his cellar, which he placed before him in a beautiful glass and replied: מה תיג בולה "What kind of exile and misery is this?" From this it also follows (which is unjust) that the will of a Christian, if he is indebted to the Jews, is incarcerated, pawned off, and treated badly (this pleases the Jews); so the Christians are the mockery of the Jews, they become their servants, the worthiness of Christianity is prostituted and suffers disadvantage, but the pride and the superstition of the Jewish people are thereby reinforced and strengthened.

Therefore, indeed, if one thing is necessary, it is this: that the Jews are forbidden to practise usury, that they are instructed and made to work, that they work with their hands, and that they eat their own bread.

Excerpt 9: Usury (2)

Source: Bezelius, *Die Herrlichkeit des Christenthums*, under "Historische Zugabe," 271–77 (§ 35).

Text

Man sagt/ die Jüden bleiben nicht beständig/ sie meinen es nicht auffrichtig.

Daß etwas dran sey/ ist nicht allerdings zuläugnen/ die *Maranen* und andere/ die unter dem Christen-Mantel ein Jüdisch Hertz behalten/ ja öffentlich einen Rückfall gethan haben/ sind gnugsam bekandt/ und pflegen die Jüden ingemein zu sagen/ daß noch wol vor der Geburth deß JEsu von Nazareth/ da die Heyden noch Sonn und Mond und andere Sterne anbeteten/ etliche Jüden zu den Heyden gefallen/ darumb daß dieselben Planeten ihre Würckung in den Früchten der Erden haben/

JEsus aber sey ein todter Mensch/ und könne niemand etwas guts thun/ darumb auch jetziger Zeit niemand wegen der Religion von ihnen zu den Christen trete.

Niemand wegen der Religion/ so muß es denn anderer Ursachen halben geschehen/ nemlich/ umb Nutzen willen/ oder auß Furcht/ welches denn beydes keinen Bestand hat. Von dem Letzten habe ich noch dieser Tagen/ als ich zu einer Ergötzung in dem Sitten-Spiegel Herrn *Francisci* laß/ [*Francisci* Sittenspiegel am 1131. Blat] ein Exempel gefunden/ welches ich hie will anführen und erzehlen:

Im Jahr *1618.* am *19. Martij* hat sich zu *S. Jean de Luz* ein seltzamer Handel zugetragen: Es begab sich/ daß etliche Portugiesische Jüdinnen/ aus Furcht/ Leib und Gut zuverlieren/ sich stelleten also wären sie Römisch Catholisch. Derhalben beichteten sie einem Portugiesischen Priester/ Nahmens *Don Antonio*, und empfingen die *Communion*. Dieser Priester aber ward gewahr/ das eine Jüdin/ nachdem sie die Hostie empfangen/ die rechte Hand zum Mund that/ daher gerieth er in Argwohn/ daß sie dieselbe wieder aus dem Mund nehme/ deßwegen er genaue Achtung auff sie gab/ und gewahr wurde/ daß gemeldte Jüdin/ Nahmens Catharina Fernandes/ die Hostie mit ihren Schnupfftuch aus dem Munde that/ und dieselbe in dem Ermel ihres Rocks verbarg. Hierauff fing er überlaut an zu ruffen: Du loses Weib! Was machstu? Wie die Jüdin sahe/ daß ihre Missethat entdecket war/ stellte sie sich/ als ob sie verruckt im Haupt worden/ verhofte hiedurch entschuldigt zu seyn/ und dem Tode zu entrinnen. Aber sie ist gefänglich eingezogen/ und fand das Schnupfftuch sampt der Hostie bey ihr/ darauff kamen etliche Geistliche/ nahmen dieselbige nach ihrer Weise/ und legten sie in eine Pateen.

Des folgenden Tags kam der *General Vicarius* von *Bagonne* zu *S. Jean de Luz* an/ neben dem Königlichen Stadthalter/ diese Jüdin zu *examini*ren. Sie wendete zu ihrer Entschuldigung ein/ sie hätte gehustet/ wodurch ihr die Hoste unversehens aus dem Munde entfallen/ welche sie alsbald in ihr Wischtüchlein auffgefangen/ in Meinung dieselbe mit gelegenheit daheim in ihrer Behausung zu geniessen.

Wie nun der ungehaltene Pöfel sahe/ das der Stadthalter mit dem Hn. von *Sausse* sich lange über dieser Sache beredete/ kam ein Geschrey aus/ die Jüden hätten eine Summe Geldes zusammen geschossen/ und damit den Richter bestochen/ die Jüdin loß zu geben: Wodurch das Volck alsbald bewegt worden/ sie selbst hinzurichten. Sie ward aus den Händen deß Gerichtes genommen/ und in eine leere Schute oder Schiff gesetz/ da man ihr über das Haupt und Arme eine leere Tonne oder Faß stürtzte/ und darauf das Schif mit Hartz/ Leim/ Pech/ Stroh/ dürr Holtz/ und anderer leichtlich brennenden Materie füllete/ alsbald lieffen Männer und Weiber mit Hauffen zu/ zündeten in Gegenwart deß Gerichts das Schif an/ und verbrandten die Jüdin also lebendig/ geboten darauf alle Jüden und Portugiesen/ so sich alda befanden/ angesichts hinweg zu packen/ denn daferne sie deß folgenden Tages sich annoch antreffen liessen/ solten sie ohn alle Gnade gleicher gestalt

verbrandt werden. Wie das die Portugiesische Jüden vernommen/ haben sie sich davon/ und nach Biarnite/ welches eine Meile von *Bayonne* liegt/ hinweg gemacht.

Aber das wäre nicht gut/ daß alle so thäten/ daß alle getaufte Jüden es falsch meinten und wiederumb abfielen. [*D. Müller Judaism. in præf.*] Es haben unterschiedene Christliche Lehrer in ihren Schrifften zusammen getragen/ die Nahmen der Fürnehmsten unter den Jüden/ so das Christenthum angenommen/ und beständig blieben sind. [*Kromeyer in Scrutin. Rel. Disp. IV p. 76. Rumetsch de Conjecturis. ult. temp. p. 88 seq.*] *Nicolaus Liranus*, aus dem Städtlein Lier in Brabrand gebürtig/ *Paulus Burgensis, Petrus Galatinus, Emanuel Tremellius, Antonius Margarita, Isaacus Coloniensis, Paulus weidnerus, Christianus Gerson*, und hat eine gelehrte fleissige Feder schon für *10*. Jahren verheissen/ eine außführliche Verzeichniß der bekehrten beharrenden Jüden herfür zu geben [*Olear. in Abac. Patrol. p. 42.*] (*Conversorum ad Christianam Evangelicamque; fidem Nubem sive Syllogen, fastuosis vanissimorum Apostatarum turbinibus opponendam*, welche sehr nützliche Arbeit ich mit andern verlange/ das sie möge bald heraus kommen/ wenns noch nicht geschehen.

Sehr merckwürdig ists/ was der getaufte Jude *Gerson* von sich schreibet: [*Gerson Talmud. p. m. 1 52.*] Ich wil mit Gedult leiden/ das viel Christen sagen/ ich werde bey meinem Christenthum nicht beständig bleiben/ dieweil sie viel Exempel wissen/ daß sich Jüden aus falschem Hertzen haben tauffen lassen/ und wie das wurmstichige Obst wieder dahin gefallen sind. Daß auch die Cölnische Katze und Mauß propheceye/ es bleibe kein Jüde beym Christenthum beständig/ und was des Dinges mehr seyn mag. Denn auch viel Christen wissen/ daß nicht allein viel von den Leyen beständig geblieben/ und selig worden sind/ sondern daß auch niemahl einer wieder abgefallen/ der etwas *studi*ret gehabt hat/ wie man siehet an *D. Emanuel Tremellio, Johann Isaac*, an *Antonio Margarita*, an *Elchanon Pauli*, und *Paulus weidner*/ welche alle in nächst verflossenen hundert Jahren gelebt haben/ und an vielen andern/ welche Juden gebohren/ und zum Theil noch leben zum Theil aber als fromme Christen gestorben sind.

Aber ich habe sorge/ daß die Leute/ welche immer mit den Worten und Gedancken umbgehen/ und mich damit betrüben/ wenn sie sagen: Er bleibt nicht beständig/ er bleibt nicht beständig: so eine geringe Wurtzel ihres Glaubens haben/ daß sie nicht allein/ wenn eine kleine Verfolgung käme/ abfielen/ sondern daß sie auch nicht ein Huhn/ viel weniger aber ein liebes Kind umb des HErrn Christi willen zusetzen solten/ ja sie solten wol nicht wissen/ wenn sie gefraget würden/ was an Christum glauben heisset.

In Summa/ ich wil und kan alles leiden/ und je mehr werde ich in meinem Hertzen versichert/ das ich bey GOtt in Gnaden/ und dem HErrn Christo/ welcher vielmehr für mich gelitten hat/ etlicher massen gleichförmig worden bin. Sonderlich aber/ weil ich auch weiß/ daß Christus alles in allem ist/ so ist er mir Wancken-

den ein Felß/ mir Nackenden ein Kleid/ mir Hungerigen eine Speise/ mir Irrenden ein Weg/ mir Durstigen ein Tranck/ mir Zagenden ein Trost/ mir Armen ein Schatz/ mir Narren eine Weißheit/ mir Wehrlosen ein Schwerd/ mir Krancken ein Artzt/ und mir Todten ein Leben. Welches des *Gersons* Hertz/ Muth und Sinn/ ich ihnen und allen Jüden wünsche/ die zu uns treten/ durch den Geist unsers HErren JEsu Christi.

Translation

It is said that the Jews do not stay constant; they do not sincerely mean it.

That there is something to this is not to be denied. The Marranos and others, who maintain a Jewish heart under the cloak of Christianity and who have indeed publicly relapsed, are sufficiently well known; and the Jews generally say that still well before the birth of Jesus of Nazareth, while the Gentiles were still worshipping the sun and moon and other stars, a number of Jews fell to the Gentiles, because these very same planets have their effect on the fruits of the earth, but Jesus is a dead man and can do no good for anyone, so no one at this time would come to the Christians because of their religion.

No one because of religion, so it has to be done for other reasons, namely for the sake of benefit or out of fear, neither of which has any validity. I found an example of the latter just a few days ago when I read Mr Francisci's *Mirror of Customs* for amusement [Erasmus Francisci, *Neu-polirter Geschicht-, Kunst- und Sitten-Spiegel ausländischer Völcker* on fol. 1131], which I want to quote and relate here:

On 19 March in the year 1618, a strange affair took place at Saint-Jean-de-Luz: it happened that a number of Portuguese Jews for fear of losing life and property pretended to be Roman Catholics. So, they confessed to a Portuguese priest called Dom António and received communion. But this priest noticed that a Jewess, after she had received the host, put her right hand to her mouth. Therefore, he became suspicious that she was taking it out of her mouth again, which is why he paid close attention to her and noticed that this Jewess, called Catarina Fernandes, took the host out of her mouth with her handkerchief and hid it in the sleeve of her dress. Then he began to shout loudly: "You loose woman! What are you doing?" When the Jewess saw that her misdeed had been discovered, she pretended to have gone mad in her head, hoping to be excused and to escape death. But she was imprisoned, and the handkerchief and host were found on her person. Then several clergymen came, took it as is their custom, and placed it in a shallow dish (*patina*).

The following day the General Vicarius of Bayonne arrived at Saint-Jean-de-Luz, alongside the Royal Governor, to examine this Jewess. As an excuse, she objected that she had coughed and as a result the host had suddenly fallen out of

her mouth, which she immediately caught in her handkerchief, and she intended to take the opportunity to enjoy it at home in her dwelling.

As the indignant mob now saw that the governor was talking to the gentleman from Sausac (António?) about this matter for a long time, there was an outcry. The Jews had got together a sum of money and thus bribed the judge to let the Jewess go, whereby the people were immediately induced to execute her themselves. She was taken out of the hands of the court and placed in an empty barge or ship where an empty cask or barrel was thrown over her head and arms. And then the ship was filled with resin, glue, pitch, straw, dry wood, and other highly inflammable matter. Men and women immediately came running in large numbers and set fire to the ship in the presence of the court and burned the Jewess alive. They commanded all the Jews and Portuguese who were there to pack up and leave for far away, because if they were still present the following day, they would be burned in the same manner without any mercy. When the Portuguese Jews heard this, they made off for Biarritz which is a mile [approx. eight kilometres] from Bayonne.

But it would not be good, if everyone pretended, if all baptized Jews misinterpreted it and fell away again. [Johannes Müller, *Judaism*, in the preface] Various Christian teachers have compiled in their writings the names of the most prominent Jews who accepted Christianity and remained constant. [Hieronymus Kromayer, *Scrutinium religionum tum falsarum tum unice veræ*, IV, p. 76; Johann Christoph Rumetsch, *De Conjecturis ultimi temporis*, p. 88 seq.] Nicolas of Lyre, born in the little town of Lier in Brabrand (!), Paul of Burgos, Pietro Galatino, Emanuel Tremellius, Antonius Margaritha, Isaac of Cologne, Paulus Weidner, Christianus Gerson, and a learned diligent pen already ten years ago promised to produce a list of the converted persistent Jews [Johann Gottfried Olearius, *Abacus Patrologicus*, p. 42] (*Conversorum ad Christianam Evangelicamque; fidem Nubem sive Syllogen, fastuosis vanissimorum Apostatarum turbinibus opponendam*), which very useful work I along with others demand may be published soon, if it has not already happened.

It is very noteworthy what the baptized Jew Gerson writes about himself: [Christianus Gerson, *Der Jüden Thalmvd fürnembster innhalt, vnd Widerlegung*, ch. 18, middle of p. 4 52] "I want to suffer with patience when many Christians say that I will not remain constant in my Christianity, because they know many examples of Jews getting baptized out of wrong hearts and, like the worm-eaten fruit, falling away again. That also the Cologne 'cat and mouse' prophesy that no Jew will remain constant in Christianity and similar things. For many Christians also know that not only many laypeople remained constant and were saved, but that no one who had studied ever fell away again, as can be seen by Emanuel Tremellius, Johann Isaac, in Antonius Margaritha, Elchanon Pauli, and Paulus Weidner, who all lived in centuries past, and by many others who were born Jewish, and some are still alive, but some died as pious Christians.

"But I am concerned when the people who are always dealing with words and thoughts and thereby distress me, say: he will not remain constant, he will not remain constant. They have such a feeble root to their faith, that if a little persecution came along, they would not only fall away, but they would not want a chicken, much less a dear child, to be vexed for the sake of the Lord Christ. Indeed, if they were asked, they would not know what it means to believe in Christ.

"In summary, I will and can suffer everything, and the more I am assured in my heart that I am in the grace of God and in many ways similar to the Lord Christ who suffered so much more for my sake. But especially, because I also know that Christ is everything in everything, so he is a rock to me who falters, a garment for me who is naked, food for me who is hungry, a way for me who is lost, a drink for me who is thirsty, a consolation for me who is unsure, a treasure for me who is poor, wisdom for me who is a fool, a sword for me who is defenceless, a doctor for me who is sick, and a life for me who is dead." I wish you and all Jews, who come to us through the spirit of our Lord Jesus Christ, some of Gerson's heart, courage, and mind.

Appendix 6: Christian Gottlieb Seeligmann, *Jüdischer Ceremonien* (1725)

Source

A Christian Gottlieb Seeligmann, ספר מנהגים של יום טוב וחתנות *Jüdischer Ceremonien Von der Jüden Hochzeiten/ Fest- und Feyer-Tagen Durchs gantze Jahr. Nebst ihrem dabey habenden Aberglauben* (Stockholm: Joh. L. Hornn, 1725)

B Christian Gottlieb Seeligmann, ספר מנחגים של יום טוב וחתנות *Jüdischer Ceremonien Von der Jüden Hochzeiten/ Fest- und Feyer-Tagen Durchs gantze Jahr. Nebst ihrem dabey habenden Aberglauben* (Lund: Ludovig Decreaux, 1737)

https://doi.org/10.1515/9783110986938-008

Text and translation

p. 1 [A1r] ספר מנהגים של יום טוב וחתנות

Jüdischer *CEREMONIEN*

Von der Jüden Hochzeiten/ Fest- und Feyer-Tagen Durchs gantze Jahr; Nebst ihrem dabey habenden Aberglauben/

Zum Dienst der Warheit vorgestellt Von Christian Gottlieb Seeligmann/ Einem *Converso* Jud.

STOCKHOLM, Gedruckt bey *JOH. L. HORRN*, Königl. *Antiq. Archivi* Buchdrucker. 1725. |

7–8 *STOCKHOLM* ... 1725] Gedruckt bey *LUDOVIG DECREAUX Directeur* über die Königl. *Academi*sche Buchdruckerey in LUND. 1737 *B.*

ספר מנהגים של יום טוב וחתנות[1]
About Jewish Ceremonies of the Festivals, Feasts and Days of Celebration of the Jews throughout the Entire Year along with their Associated Superstitions
Presented in the service of truth by Christian Gottlieb Seeligmann,[2] a converted Jew.
Stockholm. Printed by Johan Laurentius Horrn,[3] Royal Antiquarian Archival Book Printer. 1725.

1 Heb.: "A book about traditions of festivals and weddings."
2 Very little is known about Christian Gottlieb Seeligmann. He converted to Christianity in 1712 and published his book on Jewish ceremonies in 1722 (Hamburg and Jena), 1725 (Stockholm), and 1737 (Lund). See Hugo Valentin, *Judarnas historia i Sverige* (Stockholm: Bonniers, 1924), 88–89.
3 Johan Laurentius Horrn (1683–1741), originally from Nuremberg, active as a printer in Stockholm 1717–41.

p. 2 [A1v] עמי עשו

Venerando Ministerio S. & O.

OAnsedt man fast ogärna wille i någon måtto beswära *Vener. Ministerium* uti Stiftet så *obligeras* jag doch för en fattig *Judæo converso* benämbd Christian Gottlieb Seligman, det samma giöra på deß begiäran, efter wår Christendoms plickt för sådana *Neophytis* och *Proselyter*, som ankommma til wår allene rena Christeliga *Religion*; Och såsom man har ett Christeligit hopp om deß beständighet i samma wår saliga lära, så får jag intet underlåta, honom med deß nödträngda hustru och barn, til det bästa hos *Vener. Ministerium recommendera*; Det *Vener. Minist.* af det lofl. Prästerskapet, hwaräst han under resan til *Stockholm* lärer dem anträffa, wille honom och hans hustru och barn af wanlig och berömmelig bemögenhet, med all Christelig wälwillighet bemöta, och sin goda bewågenhet bewisa, hwilken så många och mycket berömbl. mäns, uti wår Evangeliska lära goda wittnesbörder om sin *Conversion* af *Judaismo* til *Christianismum* hafwer, och finnes wara tämmel. grundat uti en oskrymtad Christendom, hwilket wi samptel. genom GUDs obegripel. nåde, hafwa så mycket större orsak at behierta, som wi af en rätt och uppriktig Christens kiärlek, hafwa at noga eftertäncka, af hwad mörcker wi befriade äro, och til hwad Evangeliska lius wi äro försatte, och således en rätt Christelig kärlek och medynksamhet, ei mindre än andra *Religions* Förwanter wärkel. wisa. Hwilken barmhertighet och medyncksamhet emot sådana nödlidande, GUD nådel. lärer anse med ymnigare wälsignelse. Och jag förblifwer altid

Venerandi Ministerii

Lund den 14 Febr. Åhr 1726.

Tienstredebognaste och wälwilligste Tienare.

Jonas Linnerius

Episcopus Scan. & Blek. |

1–26 Fol. A1v is blank in *A*. The text here is from *B*.

עמ״י עש״ו[4]

To the spiritual ministerium[5] of S. and O.

Even though I would rather not trouble the diocese's spiritual ministerium, I am obliged nonetheless on account of a poor Jewish convert called Christian Gottlieb Seeligmann to do so upon his request in accordance with our Christian duty towards such neophytes and proselytes who come to our singly pure Christian religion. And just as one has a Christian hope for their constancy in this our blessed teaching, I cannot neglect to recommend him along with his impoverished wife and child for the best from the spiritual ministerium. The commendable clergy's spiritual ministerium, which he is said to have encountered during his journey to Stockholm, wanted, out of common and glorious power, to receive him and his wife and child with all Christian benevolence and to demonstrate their good attentiveness. So many and very commendable men who are well-versed in our evangelical teaching witnessed his conversion from Judaism to Christianity, which is firmly grounded in an unfeigned Christianity. Through God's unfathomable mercy we all have an even greater reason to heed this. Out of true and sincere Christian love we must carefully ponder from what darkness we have been freed and to what evangelical light we are destined, and thus a true Christian love and compassion, no less than another religion's practitioners really show. God is said to regard such mercy and compassion towards people in such need with more abundant blessing. I remain always yours,

Of the spiritual ministry
Lund, 14 February 1726
Most willing and benevolent servant.
Jonas Linnerius[6]
Bishop of Skåne and Blekinge

4 Heb.: "My help cometh from the Lord, which made heaven and earth" (Psalm 121:2: עֶזְרִי מֵעִם יְהוָה עֹשֵׂה שָׁמַיִם וָאָרֶץ).

5 A spiritual ministerium (Lat.: *Venerandum Ministerium*; Germ.: *Geistliches Ministerium*) is an association of clergy who, among other things, come together to meet the socioeconomic needs of the community.

6 Jonas Petri Linnerius (1653–1734): 1684 professor, 1690 *pastor primarius*, 1714 bishop. See Severin Cawallin, *Lunds stifts herdaminne: efter mestadels otryckta källor*, vol. 1 (Lund: Gleerup, 1854), 129–42 (no. 47).

p. 3 [A2r] JESUM/ Den gecreutzigten und von den Todten wieder auferstandenen einigen Mittler zwischen GOTT und den gefallenen Menschen/ wünsche ich dem geneigtem und wohlmeynenden Leser.

Es sind nunmehro bey 13. Jahr/ da ich durch die unendliche Barmhertzigkeit GOttes aus dem finstern Judenthum errettet/ durch den Dienst zweyer ansehlicher *Membrorum*, eines Hoch-Ehrwürdigen *Ministerii* zu Lübeck/ namentlich *S. T.* Herrn *D.* G. H. Götzen/ Hoch-verordneten *Superintendent*en/ und Herrn *M.* Zacharias Vogel/ nachdem von dem letzten in der Warheit der Christlichen Religion unterrichtet/ durch die heilige Tauffe von jetzt bemeldten Herrn *Superintendent*en/ bey zahl-
p. 4 [A2v] reicher Versammlung in der St. Lorentz-Kirche daselbst dem HErrn | JEsu zugeführet/ und als ein Glied der wahren reinen Evangelisch-Lutherischen Kirche bin angenommen worden.

Ob nun zwar seit der Zeit unter vielen Verfolgungen von meinen vorigen Glaubens-Genossen/ auch sonst bedrängten Umständen als grosser Armuth/ mein mühseliges Leben fortführen/ und von einem Ort zum andern/ als verlassen/ wandern müssen; bis nach Dreßden durch hohe *Recommendation* gekommen/ da endlich ein Hüttlein vor mich und die armen Meinigen gefunden: So preise ich doch GOTT/ der in den allen mein Gemüth in der erkandten Warheit nicht hat lassen wankend werden; sondern mich vielmehr durch alles dieses desto geschickter zu der Nachfolge meines Erlösers/ die da durch viele Trübsahl in das Reich GOttes gehet/ hat machen wollen. Damit nun die Wege GOttes/ die er nach seiner Weißheit mit mir gegangen/ auch andern möchten bekannt/ und mitleidige Hertzen zur milden Beysteuer bewogen werden/ habe diese wenige Blätter durch den Druck *publici*ren wollen. Alles zu dem Ende/ damit das Zeugniß meiner Bekehrung jedermänniglich zum Preiß der Gnade GOttes kund werde; Dann aber auch zu gleicher Zeit mit mir auch andere zum Gebeth/ um Errettung so vieler noch in Finsterniß und Schatten des Todes sitzenden Jüden/ auf das kräfftigste mögen erwecket/ und aufgemuntert werden.

יהוה

Der Jüden Ceremonien/ welche sie bey ihren Hochzeiten vornehmen/ nebst den
p. 5 [A3r] darbey habenden Aberglauben. | SIE glauben zwar/ daß eine jede Ehe von GOtt gestifftet wird/ weilen GOTT der HERR selbsten dem Adam im Paradies die Evam zur Ehe gegeben. Die Rabbinen aber setzen hinzu/ daß so bald der Mensch geboh-

---

4 13. Jahr] 26. Jahr *B.* | **13** Verfolgungen] Vefolgungen *B.* | **16** Dreßden] Cron-reich Schweden *B.* | **26** um] umb *B.*

For the gracious and benevolent reader, I wish Jesus, the indivisible mediator between God and fallen people, who was crucified and rose again from the dead.

It is now 13 years since I was rescued by the infinite mercy of God from sinister Judaism through the service of two respectable members of a highly venerable ministerium in Lübeck, namely the Doctor of Theology, Mr Georg Heinrich Götzen,[7] highly ordained superintendent, and the master Mr Zacharias Vogel.[8] After having been instructed in the truth of the Christian religion by the latter and through the holy baptism of the aforementioned superintendent, I was led to the Lord Jesus at a well-attended meeting in the Church of St Lorenz[9] and have been accepted as a member of the true, pure Evangelical-Lutheran Church.

Indeed, even though I have since then had to continue my toilsome life under many persecutions from my former co-religionists, and also in otherwise oppressed circumstances such as great poverty, and I have had to wander from one place to another like an abandoned person, until I arrived in Dresden by high recommendation where, finally, I found a little hut for me and my dependants, I praise God, who throughout it all did not let my mind waver from the recognized truth, but who rather through all this wanted to make me even more suitable for the discipleship of my redeemer which leads through many tribulations to the kingdom of God. So that the ways of God, which according to his wisdom he walked with me, may also be known to others, and so that compassionate hearts may be moved to pay a small contribution, I wanted to publish these few pages in print. All to the end of making the testimony of my conversion known to every man to the praise of God's grace. But also, at the same time to move others to pray with me for the salvation of so many Jews still sitting in the darkness and shadow of death, that they may be most vigorously awakened and encouraged.

יהוה[10]

The ceremonies of the Jews, which they perform at their weddings, together with the superstitions associated with them. They indeed believe that every marriage is instituted by God, because the Lord God himself gave Eve for marriage to Adam in Paradise. But the rabbis added that as soon as a person is born, it is proclaimed in

7 Georg Heinrich Götzen (1667–1728) was a German evangelical theologian, pastor, and superintendent.

8 Presumably not the famous doctor in Lübeck (1708–72), but some other Zacharias Vogel.

9 The original Church of St Lorenz (Lawrence) in Lübeck, 1661–1899.

10 Heb.: "God."

ren werde/ so werde im Himmel ausgeruffen: זה פלוני יקח ואת פלונית לכתו וגו׳ das ist: dieser Mensch soll diese oder jene zur Ehe bekommen; Da doch in der gantzen heiligen Schrifft nichts davon zu finden ist/ noch weniger jemand im Himmel gewesen und es mit angehöret.

2.) Wann Verlöbniß soll gehalten werden/ nehmen sie die aus ihren Gemeinde bestellten נאמנים oder glaubhafften Leute darzu/ und wann der Kauff geschlossen/ der *Contract* unterschrieben; so nimmt der נאמן oder Beglaubte einen Zippel von seinem Kleide/ und gehet zu denen beyden Verlobten/ daß sie diesen Zippel mit ihren Hände anfassen sollen/ mit diesen Worten: מקבל קנין der kauff sey geschlossen. Darauf so nehmen sie zwey neue Töpffe/ und zerwerffen solche in der Stuben/ wo daß Verlöbniß gehalten wird/ anzuzeigen/ daß so wenig diese Töpffe wieder gantz werden/ so wenig könten die beyden Verlobten geschieden werden. Allein die Erfahrung bestätige vielfältig das Gegentheil.

3.) Von der Zeit der Verlöbniß/ bis zum *Termin* der Hochzeit/ wird dem Bräutigam der Nahme חתן und der Braut der Nahme כלה beygelegt/ und wird ihnen wehrender Zeit über mehr Ehre als sonsten bey allen Zusammenkünfften angethan: Doch aber wird der Bräutigam und die Braut bey Nachts-Zeiten nicht allein gelassen/ damit sie/ ihrer Meynung nach/ von den bösen Geistern nicht angefochten würden. |

p. 6 [A3v] 4.) Wann nun die bestimmte Zeit der Hochzeit herbey/ so beschenket der Bräutigam die Braut nach seinen Vermögen/ welches auch die Braut gleichals thut. An theils Orten ist der Gebrauch/ daß die Braut den Bräutigam einen Tag vor der Hochzeit seine Sterbe-Kleider/ welche in einem seinen leinen Hemde und Kittel/ welchen er über seine Kleider anziehen kan/ und in solchen auch *copuli*ret wird bestehen; die er auch alle Jahr/ am Versöhnungs-Tage in der *Synagoge* an hat/ nebst einer weissen Hauben/ und allen das darzu gehöret/ schicket/ theils daß er sich bey seiner grossen Freude auch der Sterbligkeit erinnern möge; sonderlich aber glauben sie/ daß sie wegen der Zerstöhrung Jerusalem und Verwüstung des Tempels/ keine vollkommene Freude geniesen dürfften/ welches aber eine vergebliche Einbildung.

5.) Einen Tag vor der Hochzeit/ wird eine Mahlzeit vor die unbeweibten und ledigen Jungen Gesellen und Jungfrauen angestelt/ worbey sich der חתן וכלה Bräutigam und die Braut am meisten lustig machen/ mit Tantzen und Springen/

1 וגו׳] וגו *B.* | **9** מקבל קנין] מקב לקנין *B.* | **26** weissen] weisen *B.* | **27** grossen] grosen *B.*

heaven: זה פלוני יקח את פלונית לבתו וגו׳,[11] that is, "This man shall have this or that one in marriage." Yet none of this can be found in any of the Holy Scriptures, much less has anyone been in heaven and heard it.

2) When the betrothal is to be held, they take along the נאמנים[12] or "faithful people" appointed from their community, and when the purchase is concluded and the contract signed, the נאמן[13] or the "trustworthy man" takes a corner of his robe and goes to the two betrotheds so that they are to take hold of this corner with their hands with these words: מקבל קנין,[14] "may the purchase be concluded." Then they take two new pots and smash them in the room where the engagement is being held, to show that just as unlikely as it is that these pots will be whole again, so unlikely is it that the two betrothed couples will be able to be separated. Experience alone would confirm the opposite in many cases.

3) From the time of the betrothal until the date of the wedding, the bridegroom is given the name חתן[15] and the bride the name כלה,[16] and during this time they are given more honour than usual at all gatherings. However, the bridegroom and the bride are not left alone during the night-time, lest they, in their opinion, be attacked by the evil spirits.

4) When now the appointed time of the wedding arrives, the bridegroom gives the bride a gift according to his means, which likewise the bride also does. In some places it is the custom one day before the wedding for the bride to send the groom his death robes, which consist of a linen shirt and robe, which he can put on over his clothes, and he will also be married in such and he will also wear it every year on the Day of Atonement in the synagogue, together with a white head-covering[17] and all that goes with it, [he does so] partly so that he may remember his mortality during his great joy, but in particular they believe that because of the laying waste of Jerusalem and the destruction of the Temple, they should not enjoy perfect joy, which however is a vain illusion.

5) One day before the wedding, a meal is placed before the unmarried and single boys, lads, and lasses, at which the חתן וכלה,[18] groom and bride, have the

11 Heb.: "This one takes the daughter of that one, etc." (cf. Bereishit Rabba 68:4: הַקָּדוֹשׁ בָּרוּךְ הוּא יוֹשֵׁב וּמְזַוֵּג זִוּוּגִים, בִּתּוֹ שֶׁל פְּלוֹנִי לִפְלוֹנִי, אִשְׁתּוֹ שֶׁל פְּלוֹנִי לִפְלוֹנִי, מָמוֹנוֹ שֶׁל פְּלוֹנִי לִפְלוֹנִי [God sits (on the Heavenly Throne) and makes matches: the daughter of this one to that one, the wife (i.e., widow) of this one to that one, the money of this one to that one]).

12 Heb.: "(the) faithful [*masculine plural*]."

13 Heb.: "(the) faithful [*masculine singular*]."

14 Heb.: "(I) receive the property."

15 Heb.: "bridegroom."

16 Heb.: "bride."

17 In other words, a tallit or prayer-shawl.

18 Heb.: "bridegroom and bride."

weil sie nunmehro in einen andern Stand treten/ darbey haben sie den Gebrauch/ daß sie die Braut und den Bräutigam oben am Tisch setzen/ und der neben dem Bräutigam sitzet/ der bringet demselben ein Glaß Wein zu/ darauf giebt ihm der Bräutigam die Hand/ welche dieser nimmt/ und umarmet damit die Braut/ sodann nehmen die beyden den Hut oder breite Hauben/ wie die Juden pflegen auf zu haben/ wann sie in ihrer *Synagoge* sind/ und halten selbige vor ihre beyde Angesichter/ damit sie zusammen reden/ auch nach ihrem Gebrauch einige Liebes-Küsse beybringen können/ gleichwol aber dadurch bey denen Anwesenden keinen bösen Gedancken erwecket werden mögen. Am Hochzeit-Tag wird der Braut frühe p. 7 [A4r] ein Stuhl/ worauf etliche Stücker Betten oder Polster liegen/ mitten in | der Stuben gestellet; auch der Tisch mit Brandtwein oder Lab-Kuchen besetzet. Da kommen erstlich die alten Weiber/ setzen die Braut auf den Stuhl/ und flechten ihr die Haare auf singen ihr allerhand Lieder für/ erinnern sie auch dabey des Ehestandes/ und was sie darinnen zu gewarten hat/ und machen die Braut weinend/ welches so lang dauret/ bis der Rabbiner kommet/ mit einem grossen Gefolg Männern/ der nim*m*t ein SeydenTuch/ welches dazu verordnet/ und bedeckt ihr den Kopff/ daß solches über das Gesichte herunter hängt/ weilen sie dafür halten/ daß/ wann ein Mannes Person die Haare einer Frauen ansiehet/ er in böse Gedancken gerathe/ und das eben so viel/ als wann er eine böse That würcklich mit ihr begangen hätte/ welches sie nennen מבשבה כמעשה רמי Allein wer bedencket/ wie die Haare einer Frau vielmehr einen Eckel erwecken: auch ihre Gestalt weit nicht so annehmlich machen/ als wenn sie sonsten geschmückt oder gezieret ist/ leicht erkennen/ daß dieses vielmehr *Superstition*, als sonst habenden guten Endzweck von ihnen geschiehet.

6.) Sie suchen auch vor allen Dingen die Hochzeit auf eine solche Zeit anzustellen/ da vermuthlich der Braut ihre monatliche Zeit um ist/ und der Bräutigam bey ihr schlafen darf/ jedoch muß sie sich vorher nach ihrem Gesetz reinigen/ und in dem darzu verordneten Kalten-Bad oder מקוה abwaschen. Der Geistlichen Reinigung aber wird mit keinen Wort gedacht.

7.) Die Trauung oder *Copulation* wird gemeiniglich auf öffentlicher Strassen vor der *Synagoge* um Abends-Zeit/ vorgenommen. Es wird erstlich ein Himmel von einer seidenen Decke auf 4. hohe Stangen von etlichen Knäblein gehalten/ | p. 8 [A4v] darunter der Rabbiner/ Vorsinger/ und andere zur *Copulation* gehörige/ dem Bräutigam in seinem Hochzeit und Sterbe-Kleid führen/ stellen ihm zur rechten Hand/ und ruffen bey seiner Ankunfft mit heller Stimme: ברוך הבא d. i. Gesegnet sey der da kommet. Hierauf fänget der Schulsinger an/ und wiederhohlet den Seegen

2 dem] den *B.* | 33 andere] andern *B.* | 35 ברוך הבא] ברור הבא *B.*

greatest fun, with dancing and jumping, as they are now stepping into another status. They have the custom that they seat the bride and groom at the head of the table, and the one sitting next to the groom brings him a glass of wine, then the groom gives him his hand, which he takes and uses to embrace the bride with. Then they [i.e., the bride and groom] both take the hat or wide head-covering which the Jews usually wear when they are in their synagogue, and they hold it in front of their faces so that they can talk together, also as is their custom they can have a few love kisses, but by doing it in this way no wicked thoughts will be awoken among those present. On the wedding day, a chair is placed for the bride in the middle of the room and on it there lie several pieces of bedding and cushions. The table is also set with brandy or gingerbread. First the old women come, seat the bride on the chair and plait her hair, sing all kinds of songs for her, with which they remind her of marriage and what she has to expect in it, and make the bride cry, which lasts until the rabbi arrives with a large entourage of men. He takes a silk cloth, which has been ordered for it, and covers her head so that the cloth hangs down over her face, because they think that if a man looks at a woman's hair, he gets wicked thoughts, and that is just as much as if he had actually committed a wicked act with her, which they call מחשבה כמעשה רעה.[19] But if you think about how a woman's hair actually arouses disgust and how her body is far less agreeable than when it is otherwise adorned or decorated, one can easily see that this is only a superstition and not done by them for a good ultimate purpose.

6) Above all, they try to arrange the wedding at such a time when the bride's monthly time is probably over, and the bridegroom is allowed to sleep with her. However, she must first purify herself according to their law and wash in the cold bath or מקוה[20] prescribed for this. However, not a word is said about spiritual cleansing.

7) The marriage ceremony or *copulatio*[21] is usually performed on the public street in front of the synagogue around evening time. First of all, a canopy of a silk covering is held aloft on four high poles by several little boys, beneath which the rabbi, cantor, and others who are part of the *copulatio* lead the bridegroom in his wedding and death robes. They position him om the right-hand side and call out with a clear voice when he arrives: ברוך הבא,[22] that is, "Blessed be he who comes." Then the synagogue singer begins and repeats the blessing by singing the follow-

19 Heb.: "thought as an evil act."

20 Heb.: "mikvah, ritual bath."

21 Lat.: "marriage ceremony, wedding."

22 Heb.: "Blessed is he who arrives, welcome."

durch einen Gesang mit nachfolgenden Worten: ברוך אלוהינ סימון טוב ומזל טוב ברוך חתן עם הכלה das ist: GOTT Lob zum guten Zeichen und guten Glück/ es soll seyn gesegnet/ der Bräutigam und die Braut. Hierauf bringen die Weiber auch die Braut/ so ihre Hochzeit-Kleider an hat/ und ihr Gesicht mit den seydenen Tuch verdeckt/ führen solche gleichfals unter dem Himmel/ und dreymahl um den Bräutigam herum/ hernach stellen sie sich zu seiner rechten Hand/ darauf nimmet der Rabbiner ein Glaß mit Wein/ und machet den Seegen darüber/ und giebet der Braut und Bräutigam zu trincken/ nach diesem nimmet der Rabbiner den güldenen Trau-Ring/ der keinen Stein hat/ welcher טבעת קדשין genennet wird/ und nimmt des Bräutigams und der Braut beyde Hände und trauet sie/ steckt ihr den Trau-Ring an den Finger der rechten Hand/ und spricht folgende Worte: הרא את מקודשת לי בטבעת קדושין כדת משה וישראל das ist Siehe da/ hiermit bist du mir zu eigen gegeben, vermittelst dieses Trau-Ringes/ nach dem Recht Moses und Israel: Hierauf ruffen alle Anwesende mit lauter Stimme im Hebräischen: זה האות das ist das Zeichen? Dann lieset der Rabbiner mit heller Stimme den Trauschein oder כתובה genannt auf Pergament geschrieben/ worinnen gemeldet ist/ was von beyden Seiten ist zugebracht worden; auch wann der Mann vor ihr sterben solte/ was die Frau haben soll; darnach nimmt er den Trauschein/ und giebt solchen einer Frau die die Braut geführet/ welche den Brief der Braut im Busen stecket.
p. 9 [B1r] Nach diesem wird einem | andern Gelehrten ein Glaß Wein gegeben/ welcher einen Seegen darüber spricht/ und hernach legt man dem Bräutigam ein Glaß unter seinen rechten Fuß/ welches er zertritt/ darauff alle die Anwesende laut schreyen: מזל טוב das ist: gutes Glück. Und damit hat die Trauung ein Ende.

Weiter ist zu *observi*ren, wann die Braut von der Trauung zu Haus geführt wird/ und sie den Bräutigam bey den Zippel des Kleides hält/ so ist sie כשר rein/ und darf wohl bey ihm schlaffen; so sie aber den Bräutigam nicht anrühret und weit von ihm gehet/ so ist sie טריפה unrein.

So bald der Bräutigam und die Braut nach Hause gebracht werden/ so wird ihnen eine gekochte Henne fürgesetzt/ welche sie beyde gantz allein speisen/ haben dabey diesen Aberglauben/ daß sie sich mehren sollen als die Hüner. Es wird Anstalt gemacht/ daß die Hochzeit-Gäste sich bald einfinden/ und die Mahlzeit angehen soll. Bey der Mahlzeit legt der Bräutigam einen *Oration* ab/ ob er schon studiret hat/ wann solche zu Ende/ so stellet sich einer von denen Hochzeit-Ladern

1–2 ברוך ... הכלה] וכלה חתן ברוך טוב טוב סמין אלוהינ ברור לזמו *B.* | **9** טבעת] מבעת *B.* | **12** מקודשת] מקודשת *B.* | בטבעת] בטכעת *B* | קדושין] קרושיז *B* | כדת] בדת *B* | וישראל] נישראל *B.* | **18** giebt] gibt *B* | **19** einer] eine *B.* | **32** Bräutigam] Bräutigem *B.*

ing words: ברוך אלוהינו סימן טוב ומזל טוב ברוך חתן עם הכלה,[23] that is, "God be praised for a good sign and good luck, may the groom and the bride be blessed." Then the women also bring the bride, who is wearing her wedding clothes and has her face covered with the silk cloth. They also lead her beneath the canopy and three times around the bridegroom, after which they position her on his right-hand side. Then the rabbi takes a glass of wine, and makes a blessing over it, and gives it to the bride and groom to drink. After this the rabbi takes the golden wedding ring, that has no stone, which is called טבעת קידשין,[24] and takes both the groom and the bride's hands and marries them. He puts the wedding ring on the finger of her right hand and says the following words: הרי את מקודשת לי בטבעת קדושין כדת משה וישראל,[25] that is "Behold, you are hereby given to me by means of this wedding ring according to the law of Moses and Israel." Then all who are present shout in a loud voice in Hebrew: זה האות,[26] that is, "That is the sign!" Then the rabbi reads the marriage certificate, or the so-called כתובה,[27] written on parchment in a clear voice, in which is announced what has been brought [into the marriage] from both sides, also if her husband were to die before her, what the wife should have. After this he takes the marriage certificate and gives it to a woman who was leading the bride, who puts the bride's letter in her bosom. After this, another scholar is given a glass of wine who makes a blessing over it, and afterwards a glass is placed under the bridegroom's right foot; he crushes it, whereupon all those present shout out loud: מזל טוב,[28] that is, "Good luck!" And that is the end of the wedding.

Furthermore, it can be observed that when the bride is led home from the wedding ceremony and she holds the bridegroom by the corner of his robe, then she is כשר,[29] "clean," and may sleep with him; but if she does not touch the bridegroom and walks at a distance from him, then she is טריפה,[30] "unclean."

As soon as the bridegroom and the bride are brought home, a boiled hen is set before them, which they both dine on alone. They have this superstition about this, that they ought to multiply like chickens. Arrangements are made so that the wedding guests soon arrive, and the meal may begin. During the meal, the bridegroom makes a speech, if he has already studied [i.e., he is learned]. When this is over, one of the masters of ceremony stands on a chair and gives the bridegroom

23 Heb.: "Blessed be Our God, a good sign and fortune; blessed be the bridegroom and bride."
24 Heb.: "A consecration ring."
25 Heb.: "Lo, you are consecrated to me with a ring of consecration in accordance with the law of Moses and Israel."
26 Heb.: "It is the sign."
27 Heb.: "ketubah, marriage contract."
28 Heb.: "congratulations."
29 Heb.: "kosher, ritually clean."
30 Heb.: "treyf, ritually unclean."

auf einen Stuhl/ und giebt dem Bräutigam alle Geschencke/ die die Hochzeit-Gäste geschencket/ welcher es aufschreibet. Wann die Mahlzeit schier zum Ende/ und man das Gebet nach dem Essen verrichten will/ nehmen die Weiber die Braut/ und führen selbige zu Bette/ was sie vor Zeug vornehmen/ achte ich vor unnöthig zu beschreiben. Den andern Morgen kommen die alten Weiber und besichtigen das Braut-Bett/ um zu sehen/ ob auch die Braut ihre Jungferschafft richtig gehabt/ worbey öffters tausenderley Thorheiten auch zum Theil Betrügereyen vorgehen.

So viel ist nöthig gewesen von den *Ceremonien* und Aberglauben der Juden bey ihren Hochzeiten zu erinnern. Nun wollen wir auch sehen/ was die Jüden vor
p. 10 [B1v] Fest- und Feyertage durch | das gantze Jahr haben; auch wie dieselbe von unsern Feste unterschieden; was dieselbe darbey vor *Ceremon*ien/ sowol ausser/ als in ihrer *Synagoge* an selbigen begehen.

Der Jüden-Fest- und Freyer-Tage zehlet man nach der Ordnung/ wie sie in ihren לוח oder Calender stehen. Weilen sie nun ihre Zeit kurtz vor Ostern anrechnen/ wollen wir dieser Ordnung folgen/ und von Ostern gleichfals den Anfang machen.

Das Oster-Fest wird bey den Juden פסח genannt/ von פסח überhuppen/ weil nemlich GOtt der HErr/ da er alle Erstgeburth in Egypten getödtet/ der Israeliten Häuser übergangen/ daher dieses Fest seinen Namen bekommen. Es erinnern sich auch die Juden an diesen Oster-Fest der 210. jährigen Gefangenschafft/ wie sie von dem Könige Pharao mit schwerer Arbeit geplaget/ und an diesem Fest durch Mosen mit starcker Hand aus Egypten erlöset/ und durch grossen Wunder und Zeichen in das gelobte Land durch Josuam sind geführet worden.

Dieses Oster-Fest wird bey denen Juden sehr genau in acht genommen/ daß auch in gantzer 8. Tagen kein Körnlein gesäuert Brod in ihren Häusern darff gefunden werden; sondern allein die ungesäuerten Kuchen/ oder מצות welche sie selbsten mahlen und backen/ mit vielen abergläubischen fabelhafften Ceremonien.

Den Abend vor Ostern durchsuchet ein jeder Haußwirth im gantzen Hause alle Winckel mit einem Licht/ ob vielleicht in einer Ecken gesäuert Brod/ und so er etwas findet/ es sey viel oder wenig/ so verwahret er solches bis auf den andern Morgen/ da wird es auf öffentlicher Strassen mit Feuer verbrannt/ welches aber vor 10. Uhr geschehen muß.

Am Oster-Fest wird einem jeden Haußmann ein ordentlich Bett beym Tisch hingemacht/ und so bald es Nacht ist/ legt der Wirth seine Sterb-Kleider an/ und
p. 11 [B2r] schicket sich zu Tisch/ legt sich | aufs Bett mit unterschiedlichen Ceremonien. Bey Tisch nim*m*t ein jeder ein Glaß Wein/ der gemeiniglich roth ist/ welches sie

3 das] daß *B.* | **13** Freyer-Tage] Feyer-Tage *B.* | **22** Wunder] wnader *B.* | **35** unterschiedlichen] uterschiedlichen *B.*

all the presents that the wedding guests have given, which he writes down. When the meal is coming to an end, and they want to perform their prayers after the meal, the women take the bride and lead her to bed – what things they do, I consider unnecessary to describe. The following morning the old women come and inspect the bridal bed to see whether the bride was also a proper virgin, about which thousands of foolish things and in part even deceptions often occur.

So much has been necessary to be recalled about the Jews' ceremonies and superstitions during their weddings. Now we also want to see what sorts of holidays and feast days the Jews have throughout the year; and also, how these are different from our festivals; how they perform the ceremonies both outside and inside their synagogue during them.

The Jewish holidays and feast days are counted according to the order that they appear in their לוח[31] or "calendar." Because they now count their time from shortly before Easter, we will follow this order and also likewise start with Easter.

The Easter festival is called by the Jews פסח,[32] from פסח[33] "to pass over," because the Lord God, when he was killing all the firstborn in Egypt, passed over the houses of the Israelites, which is how this festival got its name. During this Easter festival, the Jews also remember the 210-year-long captivity, how they were tormented by King Pharaoh with hard labour and on this festival were redeemed by Moses with a strong hand from Egypt, and by great miracles and signs were led into the Promised Land by Joshua.

During this Easter festival, it is very carefully observed by the Jews that not even a grain of leavened bread is to be found in their houses throughout all eight days, but only the unleavened cakes or מצות[34] which they themselves grind and bake with many superstitious, fabulous ceremonies.

The evening before Easter, each head of the household searches all the corners of the whole house with a candle, [to see] whether there is perhaps some leavened bread in a corner; and if he finds some, be it a lot or a little, he keeps it until the next morning when it will be burned in the public street with fire, which must however happen before ten o'clock.

During the Easter festival a proper bed is made for every householder at the table, and as soon as night falls the head of the household puts on his death robes and goes to the table, lies down on the bed with various ceremonies. At the table

31 Heb.: "calendar."
32 Heb.: "Pesach, Passover."
33 Heb.: "pass over, skip."
34 Heb.: "matzot, (pieces of) unleavened bread."

zweymal vor den Essen/ und 2. mal nach dem Essen austrincken/ zum Gedächtniß der Egyptischen Erlösung.

1.) Stellen sie einen grossen Becher oder Glaß mit Wein auf den Tisch/ und sprechen/ es ist Elias sein Becher/ oder כוסשל אליהו hoffen dabey/ daß Elias kommen werde. Da sie endlich sehen/ daß der Elias nicht kommen will: so machen sie die Thür auf/ und ruffen mit heller Stimme שפוך המתדעל הגוימוגו׳: Gieß aus deinen Zorn/ auf die Heyden/ die dich nicht wollen kennen/ und deinen heil: Namen nicht loben/ und stossen auch viel Läster-Wort wieder die Christen aus.

2.) Haben sie den Aberglauben, daß sie die zwey Oster-Nächte von denen bösen Geistern befreyet seyn/ und nennen deßwegen diese Nacht ליל שמורים Nacht der Hütung/ weil sie glauben/ daß sie darinn von denen Geistern behütet: wie sie dann auch die beyden Nächte sich ohne Abend-Gebeth zu Bette legen. Ausser dem machen sie sich viel zu schaffen/ mit allerhand Rabbinischen und Talmudischen Gesetzen/ vergnügen sich mit vergeblicher Hoffnung ihres Tempel-Baues/ und eines noch zukünfftigen *Messiæ*/ da doch wahrhaftig der *Messias* schon längst gekommen/ von welchen alle Propheten einhellig geweissaget haben/ und uns vorstellen als das rechte Oster-Lamm/ welches sich für alle Menschen am Stamme des Creutzes geopffert.

Pfingsten-חג שבעות

Der Jüden Pfingsten betreffend/ so geben sie diesen Fest den Namen Fest der Wachen/ und wird bey den Jüden 2. Tage gefeyert/ auch nennen sie es: יום מתן תורה den Tag der Gebung der Gesetze/ weilen GOtt der HErr an diesem Tage die Zehen
p. 12 [B2v] Gebothe vom Berge Sinai mit Donner und Blitz durch Mosen ge|geben hat; Wir Christen aber feyren solches zum Gedächtniß/ der über die Apostel an selbigen Tage geschehenen Ausgiessung des H. Geistes.

Von der Zerstörung Jerusalems/ und Verwüstnung des Tempels.

Den 9ten *Abh* erinnern sich die Jüden der Zerstöhrung Jerusalems/ und Verwüstung des Tempels/ und halten jährlich diesen Fasttag mit folgenden *Ceremonien*: 1.) Essen sie 9. Tage vorher kein Fleisch/ (es sey dann bey einer Beschneidung) jedoch dürffen alsdann nicht mehr den 10. Personen Fleisch essen. Sie lassen sich auch ihren Bart/ oder Haupt nicht abscheren; auch nicht baden sie in diesen 9. Tagen/ machen auch keine Hochzeiten/ bis sie die Zeit der Zerstörung vorbey ist. Sonderlich haben sie diesen Aberglauben/ daß sie in diesen Tagen mit keinem

4 כוסשל] כוס של *B.* | **6** שפוך ... הגוימוגו׳] שפוך : המתך על הגוים וגו *B.* | **11** darinn] darinnn *B.*
16 geweissaget] geweisaget *B.* | **24** selbigen] selbiben *B.*

everyone takes a glass of wine, which is usually red, which they drink twice before eating and twice after eating to commemorate the Egyptian redemption.

1) They place a large cup or glass of wine on the table and say it is the cup of Elijah or כוס של אליהו[35] with which they hope that Elijah will come. When they finally see that Elijah is not going to come, they open the door and shout in a clear voice: שפוך חמתך על הגויים וגו׳,[36] "Pour out your wrath on the pagans who do not want to know you and praise your holy name," and they also spout many blasphemous words against the Christians.

2) They have the superstition that on the two nights of Easter they are free from the evil spirits, and therefore they call this night ליל שמורים,[37] "night of protection," because they believe that during them, they are protected from the spirits; just as they then also go to bed on the two nights without evening prayer. Apart from that, they keep themselves busy with all kinds of rabbinical and Talmudic laws, enjoy themselves with the futile hope of building their Temple and of a future Messiah. However, the Messiah has long since arrived, about whom all prophets have unanimously prophesied and present to us as the real paschal lamb, who sacrificed himself for all people upon the trunk of the cross.

Pentecost חג שבעות[38]

As regards the Jews' Pentecost, they give this festival the name Feast of the Guards, and it is celebrated by the Jews for two days. They also call it יום מתן תורה,[39] "the day of the giving of the laws," because on this day God the Lord gave the Ten Commandments with thunder and lightning from Mount Sinai through Moses. We Christians, however, celebrate this in remembrance of the outpouring of the Holy Spirit upon the apostles that happened on the same day.

On the destruction of Jerusalem and desolation of the Temple.

On 9 Av the Jews remember the destruction of Jerusalem and the devastation of the Temple, and they observe this day of fasting every year with the following ceremonies: (1) They eat no meat for the nine days beforehand, except for at a circumcision, but even then, no more than the ten people are allowed to eat meat. Nor do they allow their beards or heads to be shaved; nor do they bathe during these nine days; nor do they hold weddings until the time of the destruction is over. In particular they have this superstition, that during these days they are not

35 Heb.: "cup of Elijah."

36 Heb.: "Pour out your wrath on the nations, etc."

37 Heb.: "a waking night, night of watching."

38 Heb.: "Festival of Shavuot."

39 Heb.: "the day of the giving of the Torah."

Christen in Rechts-Sachen etwas vornehmen dürffen/ weilen dieser Monat Israel *fatal*. Des Abends vorher/ ziehen sie ihre Schuhe aus/ und setzen sich auf die Erden/ essen Aschen mit Brodt/ und trauren über der Zerstöhrung Jerusalems. Einige essen Linsen/ weil es eine Trauer-Speise ist/ gehen darauf in ihre *Synagoge* ohne Schuh/ sitzen daselbsten auf der Erden/ singen die Klag-Lieder Jeremiä/ und bleiben nüchtern gantzer 24. Stunden. Den andern Morgen stehen sie auf/ und lauffen ohne Hand-waschen/ und ohne Gebeth in die *Synagoge*, sezten sich nieder auf die Erde/ da lieset der Vorsinger die Klag-Lieder Jeremiä/ und singen allerhand Klag-Lieder von der Zerstöhrung des Trempels und der Stadt Jerusalem. Bey Ausgang der *Synagoge*, gehen sie auf denen Begräbnissen/ und besuchen ihre Eltern und Freunde/ trösten sich hier abermal eines *Messiæ* der noch zukünfftig/ und
p. 13 [B3r] Jeru|salem wieder bauen/ da sie an statt diesen Trauer-Tag ein Tag des Freudens haben würden.

Das Neue Jahr. Welches die Jüden ראש השנה nennen.
An diesem Fest werden unterschiedliche Fabeln und Aberglauben bey den Jüden fürgenommen/ etliche Tage vorher bereiten sie sich darzu mit fasten und bethen/ stehen frühe auf/ und gehen in ihre *Synagoge*, und bitten GOtt um Vergebung der Sünden: Haben aber dabey den lächerlichen Aberglauben/ daß vor einen jeden Menschen im Himmel aufgeschrieben würde/ was ihn das künfftige Jahr begegnen werde/ ob er dieses Jahr leben oder sterben werde. Desgleichen haben sie auch ein Horn/ oder שופר von einem Widder gemacht/ mit dieser Deutung; Daß GOTT soll gedencken an den Widder/ den Abraham an statt Isaacs geschlachtet hat/ und ihnen ihre Sünden vergeben; auch wann der Satan dieses Horn hörete/ so fliehe er davon. Dieser *Roschhaschana* ראש השנה wird bey den Jüden 2. Tage heilig gefeyert/ und mit singen und bethen den halben Tag in ihrer *Synagoge* zugebracht/ und darff keiner so wol Jung als Alt/ was essen/ bis sie das Horn blasen gehöret/ welches auf folgende Art geschiehet: Erstlich machet derjenige/ der das Horn oder *Schophar* bläset/ ein Segen über das Horn/ hernach saget man ihm vor: תקיע שברום תרועה תקיע und bläset bey einen jeden Wort einen andern Schall/ haben auch darbey wieder verschiedene Aberglauben. Nemlich wann das Horn dem/ der es bläset/ keinen rechten Schall giebt/ daß der Satan sich darein gesetzet/ und befürchtet er/ daß er das Jahr sterben müsse. Bey Ausgang aus der *Synagoge*
p. 14 [B3v] wünschen sie: בשנה טובה תכתב das | ist: ich wünsche/ daß du zu einem guten Jahr angeschrieben werdest. Darauf gehen sie nach Hause/ essen und trincken. Haben auch im Gebrauch weisse Kleider anzulegen/ weilen weiß Vergebung der Sünden andeutet. Nachmittag laufft Alt und Jung an den fliessenden Wassern/ und

7 Hand-waschen] Hant-waschen *B.* | *Synagoge*] *Syoagoge B.* | **9** Trempels] Tempels *B.*
20 oder] ode *B.* | **33** טובה] מובה *B.*

allowed to engage in legal matters with any Christian because this month is fatal for Israel. The evening before, they take off their shoes and sit down on the ground, eat ashes with bread, and mourn over the destruction of Jerusalem. Some eat lentils because it is a food of mourning. Then they walk to their synagogue without shoes, sit there on the floor, sing Jeremiah's Lamentations, and remain empty-stomached for the whole 24 hours. The following morning, they get up and run to the synagogue without washing their hands and without prayer, sit down on the floor, and the cantor reads Jeremiah's Lamentations and sings all kinds of lamentations about the destruction of the Temple and of the city of Jerusalem. Upon leaving the synagogue, they go to the graves and visit their parents and friends, here again consoling themselves with a Messiah who is still to come and rebuild Jerusalem as they would have a day of joy instead of this day of sadness.

The New Year which the Jews call ראש השנה[40]
On this festival various fables and superstitions are carried out among the Jews. They prepare many days beforehand by fasting and praying, they get up early and go to their synagogue, and they ask God to forgive their sins. But they have the ridiculous superstition that for every person it is written down in heaven what will happen to him during the coming year, whether he will live or die this year. Likewise, they also have a ram's horn or שופר[41] with this interpretation: That God will remember the ram that Abraham slaughtered in place of Isaac and forgive them their sins; also, if Satan were to hear this horn, he would flee from it. This Rosh Hashanah (ראש השנה) is celebrated by the Jews as holy for two days and they spend half the day singing and praying in their synagogue and no one, young or old, is allowed to eat anything until they have heard the horn blown, which happens in the following way: First the one blowing the horn or shofar makes a blessing over the horn. Then someone says to him: תקיעה שברים תרועה תקיעה[42] and he blows a different sound for each word. Again, they also have different superstitions in connection with this, namely, that when the horn does not give the right sound to the one who is blowing it, Satan is sitting inside it, and he [i.e., the shofar blower] is afraid that he will die that year. Upon leaving the synagogue, they wish each other בשנה טובה תכתב,[43] that is, "I wish that you will be inscribed for a good year." Then they go home, eat and drink. They also have the custom of putting on

40 Heb.: "Rosh Hashanah, New Year."
41 Heb.: "shofar, musical horn made of (ram's) horn."
42 Heb.: "'*tekiah, shevarim, teruah, tekiah*,' types of blasts of the shofar."
43 Heb.: "May you be inscribed for a good year."

schütteln allda ihre Sünden ab/ welche die Fische bekom*m*en sollen/ und sprechen dabey diesen Spruch: תשליך במצולות ים כל חטאתינו וכל חטאות עמך בית ישראל תשליך (במקום) אשר לא יזכרו בהן ולא יפקדו ולא תעלינו על לב לעולם : תתן אמת ליעקב וגו׳ das ist: Du wirst werffen alle unsere Sünde in die Tieffe des Meers/ und alle Sünden deines Volcks des Hauses Israel/ daß sie nicht mehr gedacht werden/ und nicht mehr ins Hertz kommen ewiglich; Du wirst die Treue dem Jacob und die Gnade dem Abraham halten, *etc*. Darauf schütteln sie ihre Kleider ins Wasser/ damit die Sünden sollen zu Grunde fallen/ welches doch ein abscheulicher Aberglauben ist. Wann sie nun meynen/ daß sie die Sünden ins Wasser geworffen/ und die Fische solche bekommen haben/ so kommts doch endlich darzu/ daß wann sie die Fische fangen und essen/ sie ihre eigene Sünden dadurch wieder bekommen müssen/ welches eine lächerliche Fabel/ und bey uns Christen gantz verworffen wird. Wir glauben vielmehr/ das die Sünden nicht so hinweg geworffen werden können/ sondern es wird erst an Seiten des Menschen wahre Reu und Leid über dieselben erfordert/ hernach widerfähret uns Vergebung von GOTT dem Vater durch CHristum JEsum/ welcher für unsere Sünden gelitten und gestorben/ und von Todten wieder auferstanden ist/ sitzet zu der Rechten GOttes/ des allmächtigen Vaters/ von dannen er kommen wird/ zu richten die Lebendigen und die Todten.

p. 15 [B4r] Wir Christen feyren unsern Neu Jahr zwar nur einen Tag/ | und *celebriren* solches mit höchster Freudigkeit; gebrauchen daneben keines Horn-blasen/ den Satan zu vertreiben/ dann Christus JEsus hat den Satan den Kopff zertreten, 1. Buch Mos. 3.

Den 9ten des Monats *Tisri*, das ist einen Tag vor dem Versöhnungs oder Langen-Tag/ bereiten sie sich auf das Versöhnungs-Fest mit Abwaschung der Sünden/ und haben darbey diesen erschrecklichen Aberglauben: Nemlich sie nehmen Hüner oder Hahnen/ sonderlich gern weisse/ und nennen solche כפרות schlagen sie um die Köpffe/ bey einer Mannes-Person den Hahn/ und bey einer Weibes-Person eine Henne/ und sagen bey einem Mann: זה כפרתך זה תמורתך זה חליפתך זה התרנגול ילך למיתה ואתה תלך לחים טובים ושלום Dieser (Hahn) is deine Versöhnung und deine Verwechselung; dieser Hahn soll gehen zum Tode/ und du solst gehen zum Leben und zum Frieden/ und schlagen den Hahn dreymal um den Kopff herum. Zu einer Frau nehmen sie eine Henne/ und verfahren eben also/ als bey der ersten/ sprechen auch diese Worte/ nur daß dieses der Frau angehet.

Gleich darauf/ nach Verrichtung der *Kapparoth* begeben sie sich auf den GOttes-Acker/ und legen sich auf die Gräber ihrer Eltern und Befreunden/ weinen und schreyen/ daß sie bey GOtt vor sie bitten sollen/ darauf gehen sie wieder nach

---

1 und] un *B*. | **5** daß] das *B*. | **7** schütteln] schytteln *B*. | **10** wann] wann wann *B*. **13** Sünden] Sänden *B*. | **16** wieder] wieden *B*. | **22** einen] ein *B*.

white clothes because white signifies the forgiveness of sins. In the afternoon, old and young run to the flowing water and shake out all their sins, which the fish should get, and they say this saying: תשליך במצולות ים כל חטאתינו וכל חטאות עמך בית ישראל תשליך (במקום) אשר לא יזכרו בהן ולא יפקדו ולא תעלינו על לב לעולם : תתן אמת ליעקב וגו׳,[44] that is, "You will throw all our sins into the depths of the sea, and all the sins of your people of the house of Israel, that they will be remembered no more, and no more come into the heart forever. You will keep the faith of Jacob and mercy of Abraham, etc." Then they shake their clothes into the water, so that their sins may perish, which is, however, an abominable superstition. When now they believe that they have thrown the sins into the water and the fish have got them, then it finally comes to the point that when they catch the fish and eat them, they must receive their own sins again which is a ridiculous fable and completely rejected by us Christians. Rather, we believe that sins cannot be thrown away like this but first true remorse and suffering over them on the part of man is required; afterwards we will be forgiven by God the Father through Christ Jesus, who suffered and died for our sins and rose again from the dead, sits at the right hand of God, the Almighty Father, whence he will come to judge the living and the dead.

We Christians celebrate New Year for just one day and we celebrate it with the greatest joy. We do not need any horn blowing to drive out Satan, as Christ Jesus has crushed Satan's head (Genesis 3:15).

The ninth of the month of Tishri, that is one day before the Day of Atonement or the Long Day, they prepare for the Atonement Festival by washing away their sins, and in connection with this they have this terrible superstition: namely, they take chickens or cockerels, preferably white ones in particular, and they call them כפרות.[45] They throw them around the heads – a cock for a man and a hen for a woman – and a man says: זה כפרתך זה תמורתך זה חליפתך זה התרנגול ילך למיתה ואתה תלך לחים טובים ושלוח,[46] "This (cockerel) is your atonement and your substitution; this cockerel shall go to death, and you shall go to life and peace!" And they throw the cockerel three times around their heads. They take a hen for a woman and proceed in exactly the same way as with the first, they also speak these words only that now they refer to the woman.

Immediately afterwards, after performing the kaparot, they go to the cemetery and lie down on the graves of their parents and friends, they cry and scream

44 Heb.: "You will cast all our sins and all the sins of your people, the House of Israel, into the depths of the sea, cast them into a place where they will not be remembered or visited, and will never come to mind. You will perform truth to Jacob, etc." (cf. Micah 7:19–20: וְתַשְׁלִיךְ בִּמְצֻלוֹת יָם כָּל־חַטֹּאותָם: תִּתֵּן אֱמֶת לְיַעֲקֹב).

45 Heb.: "atonements, expiations."

46 Heb.: "This is your atonement, this is your substitute, this is your exchange. This cockerel will go to its death, and you will go to a good life and peace."

Hause/ geben den Armen Allmosen/ und Nachmittag machen die Mannes-Personen *Malkuth* מלקות sie gehen in ihre *Synagoge*, und nehmen einen breiten Gürtel von Leder/ und legt erstlich sich einer auf die Erden auf sein Gesicht/ der andre giebt ihm 40. Schläge mit den Riemen auf den Rücken/ und bey einem jeden Streich/ schlägt der/ so auf der Erden liegt mit seiner Hand an seine Brust/ und bekennet
p. 16 [B4v] seine Sünden; Wann nun einer dem an|dern geschlagen/ so wechseln sie um/ und bekommet der andere der ihm vorhin gestraffet hat/ Schläge/ und sagt eben diese Worte die der erste gesprochen hat.

Hierauf gehen sie wieder nacher Hauß/ und schicken sich/ daß sie bey Sonnenschein das Mahl essen. Mach dem Essen legen sie ihre Sterbe-Kleider an/ und bitten einer dem andern/ wann er ihm etwas zuwider gethan hat/ um Vergebung/ und versöhnen sich also mit ihren Nechsten/ welches sie nennen: מחילה Darauf gehen sie in die *Synagoge*, und zünden grosse Wachs-Lichter/ Seelen-Lichter genennet/ an/ welche 24. Stunden brennen müsten/ damit sie auch sonst viele Tendeleyen vornehmen. Und so bereiten sie sich zum *Iom Kippur*, oder Versöhnungs-Tag.

יום כיפור

Dieses Versöhnungs-Fest ist der 10te Tag in *Tiris*, welcher unter den Jüden vor den grossen Buß-Beth-und Fast-Tag gehalten wird/ mit einen 24. stündigen Fast-Tage/ und casteyen ihre Leiber mit Fasten/ Bethen und Singen/ und meynen/ daß an diesem Tage die Sünden in Himmel versiegelt würden/ und an demselben beschlossen/ was jedem das Jahr über begegnen werde. Bey Ausgang des Versöhnungs-Fest blasen sie einen Schall mit dem Horn/ und sprechen dabey לשנה הבאה בירושרם künfftiges Jahr wollen wir in Jerusalem das Fest halten/ gehen hiemit aus der *Synagoge*/ und verrichten bey Ausgang gleichsam noch ein gutes Werck/ nemlich sie heiligen auch den neuen Monath oder neue Licht mit Huppen und Springen gegen demselben/ und sprechen die nachgesetzten Worte: : בשם שאני רוקד כנגדך ואיני יכול לדעת כך כך לא יוכלו אויבי לגוע בי לרעה : oder gleich wie ich springe gegen dir/ und kan dich nicht anrühren; also sollen mich meine Feinde nicht anrühren können zum Bösen: Den Anfang guter Wercke machen sie an der Laub-Hütten/ da sie etwa nur ein Nagel einschlagen/ und damit sie nur von einen guten Wercke zum andern beflissen sind. Nun lieber Christ/ hie hast du nun gesehen/ was die
p. 17 [C1r] Jüden vor viele *Ceremonien* bey ihren Versohnungs-|Fest gebrauchen/ wie sie ihren Leib mit unnützen Fasten casteyen und peinigen/ und durch diese ihre guten

10 Mach] Nach *B.* | **11** Vergebung] verhebung *B.* | **17** Versöhnungs-Fest] Versöhnunhs-Fest *B.* *Tiris*] *Tisri B.* | **20** und an] an *B.* | **22** הבאה] האבה *B.* | **27** לדעת] לבעת *B.* | כך כך] גך בך *B.* יוכלו אויבי] יובלואויבי *B.* | **33** und[1]] vnd *B.*

that they shall pray to God on their behalf. Then they return home, give alms to the poor, and in the afternoon the men perform malkot מלקות.[47] They go to their synagogue and take a broad leather belt, and the first one lays face-down on the floor, and the other beats him with forty lashes with the belt on his back, and with every blow, the man lying on the floor strikes his breast with his hand and confesses his sins. Now, when the one has beaten the other, they swap over, and the other one who punished him before gets beaten and says the same words that the first one said.

Then they return home and attempt to eat their meal in the sunshine. After eating they put on their death robes and, if one has done something against another, then he asks the other for forgiveness, and they are thus reconciled with their neighbours, which they call this מחילה.[48] Then they go into the synagogue and light large wax candles called soul lights which have to burn for 24 hours, during which they also perform many other frivolities. And this is how they prepare for Yom Kippur or the Day of Atonement.

יום כיפור[49]

This atonement festival is on the tenth day of Tishri, which is held among the Jews as the Great Day of Repentance and Fasting with a 24-hour fasting day and mortification of their bodies with fasting, prayer, and singing. And they believe that on this day their sins will be sealed in heaven, and on the same day it will be decided what will happen to everyone throughout the year. At the end of the atonement festival, they blow a sound with the horn and say: לשנה הבאה בירושלים,[50] "In the coming year we will hold the festival in Jerusalem." With that they leave the synagogue and upon exiting they likewise perform yet another good deed, namely they also sanctify the new month or new light by hopping and leaping towards it, and they say the following words: כשם שאני רוקד כנגדך : ואיני יכול לנגוע בך, כך לא יוכלו אויבי לנגוע בי לרעה,[51] "Just like I jump towards you and cannot touch you, so my enemies shall not be able to touch me with evil." They make a start on good deeds with the tabernacle, in that they hammer in just one nail, and by so doing they are busy from one good deed to the other. Well, dear Christian, you have now seen here what many ceremonies the Jews perform for their atonement festival, how they mortify and torment their bodies with useless fasting, and through these their

47 Mistake for מכות, *makot*, Heb.: "lashes."
48 Heb.: "forgiveness, pardon."
49 Heb.: "Yom Kippur, Day of Atonement."
50 Heb.: "Next year in Jerusalem."
51 Heb.: "Just as I dance towards you and cannot touch you, so my enemies will not be able to touch me with evil."

Wercke meynen ihre Sünden/ so sie durch das gantze Jahr hindurch gethan/ auf einmal loß zu werden. Wann du solches liesest/ so dancke mit mir GOTT/ der und durch sein Wort ein anders lehret/ und JEsum CHristum/ als den einigen Mittler zwischen GOtt und den Menschen/ als das rechte Versöhn-Opffer/ welcher unsere Sünden aufgenommen und eine ewige Erlösung gefunden/ vorstellet; Darum hinweg mit allen äusserlichen *Ceremon*ien und abergläubischen Dingen/ weit besser/ wann man die tröstliche und freudige Worre mit anhören kan: Mein Sohn/ dir sind deine Sünde vergeben. Was hilfft doch den armen Juden ihre *Ceremon*ien/ Casteyen und Fasten/ wann sie der Versicherung der Gnade GOttes/ die da ist in Christo JEsu/ in ihrem Hertzen beraubet seyn.

Von den Jüden Laub-Hütten-Fest/ Welches sie סוכה nennen.
Diese Fest wird bey den Jüden 7. Tage gefeurt/ und bestehet ihr Absehen darinn: Weilen sie zu der Zeit sich ein jeder nach einer warmen Stuben umsiehet/ und darinnen wohnet; so machen sie GOtt zu Ehren ihre Wonungen in der Hütten/ welche ohne ein festes Dach/ und nur mit Laub bedecket ist/ essen und haben ihren Auffenthalt gantzer 7. Tage darinnen/ so daß sie auch nicht ein Mund voll ausser der Hütten essen/ es sey dann wann es regnet/ und die Speise verdürbe/ dann ist ihm erlaubt heraus zu gehen/ sonsten aber nicht; Ja etliche schlaffen auch darinnen. Es darff auch keiner keine Speise geniessen die gantzer 7. Tage der Laub-Hütten/ es sey Jung oder Alt/ sie haben dann erst *Ethrog* und *Lulabh* gesegnet אתרוג ולולב Dieser *Ethrog* und *Lulabh* wird aus Italien gebracht/ und muß gantzer 7. Tage mit Andacht geschüttelt und gesegnet werden. Von selben glauben sie/ daß wann eine Frau schwanger ist/ und beist mit den Zähnen den Stiehl des *Ethrogs*
p. 18 [C1v] ab/ daß sie ohne Schmertzen | das Kind gebähren wird. Den 8. Tag umringen sie ihre *Synagogen*/ damit ist alsdann das Fest zu Ende. Hierauf folget nun der

Hoschanua Rabba הושענה רבה
Dieser Groß-Weyden-Tag ist gleich zu Ende des Laub-Hütten-Fest/ und wird nur den helben Tag gefeyret. Sie hohlen sich von denen Weyden Gesträuch/ machen daraus kleine Gebäude/ den Abend vorher in der Laub-Hütten/ stellen sie ins Wasser bis den andern Morgen. Dann stehen sie frühe auf/ gleich als sie den langen Tag aufgestanden sind/ gehen in die *Synagoge*, verrichten ihr Gebeth/ und zum ende des Gebeths nehmen sie alle Zehen Gebothe aus der Lade des Bundes heraus/ stellen solche auf ihre Cantzel/ und umringen die Cantzel 7. mahl mit dem *Ethrog* und *Lulabh*, und zuletzt stellen sie die Zehen Gebothe wieder in die Lade des Bun-

4 GOtt] GOttt *B.* | **7** Worre] Worte *B.* | **8** doch den armen] doch den armen doch den armen *B.* | **9** GOttes] Ottes *B.* | **15** und[2]] vnd *B.* | **22** Andacht] undacht *B.* | daß] das *B.* | **32** Zehen] Zehn *B.*

good deeds they believe that they are released all at once from their sins that they have committed throughout the year. When you read this, together with me thank God, who teaches something else through his word, and Jesus Christ, who is the only mediator between God and humanity and the true atonement sacrifice, who took our sins upon himself and found eternal redemption. So away with all outward ceremonies and superstitious things! It is far better when one can hear the comforting and joyful words: "My son, your sins are forgiven." Of what help to the Jews are their ceremonies, mortification, and fasting, when they are robbed in their hearts of the assurance of God's grace, which is in Christ Jesus?

About the Jews' Feast of Tabernacles,[52] which they call סוכה[53]

This festival is celebrated by the Jews for seven days, and its purpose consists of this: As each of them is looking for a warm room at that time and lives in it, so they honour God by making their dwellings in the huts that are without a solid roof and only covered with leaves, eating and staying there for the entire seven days, so that they do not eat even a mouthful outside of the huts. If it is raining and the food will spoil, then they are allowed to leave, but not otherwise. Indeed, quite a few even sleep inside. No one is allowed to enjoy any food for the entire seven days of the Tabernacles, be they young or old, unless they have first blessed the *etrog* and *lulav*, אתרוג ולולב.[54] This etrog and lulav are brought from Italy and have to be shaken and blessed with devotion for the entire seven days. About this they believe that when a woman is pregnant and she bites off the stigma [i.e., *pitom*] of the etrog with her teeth, then she will bear the child without any pain. On the eighth day they make a circuit around their synagogue, and that is when the festival is over. This is now followed by:

Hoshana Rabba הושענה רבה[55]

This Great Willow Day is right at the end of the Festival of Tabernacles and is only celebrated for half the day. They take sprigs from the willow trees, make small bundles out of them the evening before in the tabernacles, and put them in the water until the next morning. Then they get up early, exactly as they have for the long day, they go to the synagogue, say their prayers, and at the end of the prayers they take out all Ten Commandments from the ark of the covenant, place them on their pulpit, and make seven circuits around the pulpit with the etrog and lulav, and finally they put the Ten Commandments back into the ark of the covenant.

52 That is temporary shelters, lit. "huts or booths of foliage" (*Laubhütten*).
53 Heb.: "Sukkah."
54 Heb.: "etrog and lulav."
55 Aram.: "Hoshana Rabba."

des/ schlagen die Weyden oder הושענה ab, daß nicht ein Blättlein daran bleibet/ meynen darbey/ daß sie ihre Sünden damit abschlagen und völlig austilgen könten. Am aller *curieuse*sten ist/ daß sie an diesem Tage frühe bey hellem Mondschein aufstehen/ und zwar gantz nackend/ nehmen ein Bett-Laken um ihrem Leib/ und stellen sich damit in Mondschein/ werffen das Bett-Laken von sich/ und breiten sich aus. Wann nun einer seinen Kopff in den Schatten des Monds nicht siehet/ so dencket er/ er sterbe dasselbige Jahr; siehet er aber ein Arm oder ein Bein nicht von seinem Leibe/ so bedeutet es einem von seinen nähesten Befreunden. Da siehest du/ lieber Christ/ was vor ein schrecklicher Aberglauben unter den Jüden vorgehe/ wi sie GOtt versuchen/ und seine Geheimniß wissen wollen: Dafür GOtt dich und mich in Gnaden bewahre.

Schmone Atseres שמנה עצרת
Der 8te Fest-Tag/ nach dem Laub-Hütten/ wird gantz gefeyert/ und an demselben ein sonderlich Gebeth für den Regen gethan/ daß solchen GOtt zur rechten Zeit geben wolle durchs gantze Jahr.

Gesetz-Freude טמחת תורה
Dieses Fest fällt ein den 9ten Tag/ von Anfang des Laub-Hütten-Fest/ daran haben
p. 19 [C2r] sie eine sonderliche Freude mit ihren 10. Gebothen. Sie | bekleiden sie aufs kostbareste/ nehmen sie aus der Laden/ und tantzen damit in ihrer *Synagoge* herum: Machen sich auch mehr als an andern Festen lustig in ihren Häusern/ mit Essen und Trincken. An theils Orten nehmen sie die Bäume von der Hütten/ und zünden Freuden-Feuer an/ und suchen sie den Kindern eine sonderliche Freude mit Obst-Werffen zu machen.

Den 25ten in *Kislea* haben die Jüden *Chanucca*-חנוכה
welches 8. Tage währet/ doch feyren sie solches nur halb/ treiben Handel und Wandel/ und ergötzen sich mit allerhand Spielen. Sie glauben/ daß an diesem Tage den Jüden ein Zeichen oder *Miracul* wiederfahren/ welches sie נס oder Zeichen nennen. Nemlich sie geben vor/ daß als der böse König *Javon*, das H. Oehl/ welches im Tempel unter des Hohenpriesters Pettschafft verwahret zum ewigen Licht/ verunreiniget/ und nicht mehr als nur zu einen Tag zu brennen übrig gehabt/ da es doch 8. Tage hinreichen müssen: So habe GOTT durch ein *Miracul* das Oehl vermehret/ daß es die gehörigen 8. Tage lang gebrannt hätte. Dahero zünden die

4 Bett-Laken] Bet-Laken *B.* | **5** und[2]] vnd *B.* | **13** gefeyert] gefeyrt *B.* | **14** daß] das *B.* **16** טמחת] מטחת *B.* | **20** an] an den *B* | **24** *Kislea*] *Kisleo B.* | **26** diesem] deisem *B.* **28** Nemlich] Nemich *B.* | **32** daß] das *B.*

They beat the [bundles of] willow or הושענה,[56] so that not even a little leaf remains on them. They believe that they thus beat off their sins and can completely eradicate them. The most curious thing is that they get up early that day in the bright moonlight and, completely naked, they wrap a bedsheet around their bodies and stand with it in the moonlight. They throw the sheet off themselves and spread out. If someone does not see his head in the shadow of the moon, he thinks that he will die that same year; but if he does not see an arm or a leg from his body, it means one of his closest friends. There you see, dear Christian, what a terrible superstition circulates among the Jews, how they test God and want to know his secrets: May God keep you and me in mercy from this.

Shmoneh Atzeret שמונה עצרת[57]

The eighth festival day after Tabernacles is celebrated for the whole day, and on the same day a special prayer is said for rain, that God will give it at the right times throughout the year.

Rejoicing of the Law שמחת תורה[58]

This feast falls on the ninth day from the beginning of the Feast of Tabernacles. And on this day they are particularly pleased with their Ten Commandments. They dress them in precious items take them out of the ark, and dance around in their synagogue with them. They have more fun than on other festivals in their houses, with food and drink. In some places, they take the beams from the huts and light bonfires and seek to make the children particularly happy with fruit throwing.

On 25 Kislev the Jews have Hanukkah חנוכה[59]

which lasts for eight days, but they celebrate it only as a half-holiday, engage in trade and commerce, and amuse themselves with all kinds of games. They believe that on this day the Jews experienced a sign or miracle, which they call a נס[60] or "sign." Namely, they allege that when the wicked King Javan defiled the holy oil that was kept in the Temple under the high priest's seal for the eternal lamp, and there was no more left than for one day's burning even though it had to last for eight days, then God increased the oil through a miracle so that it burned for the necessary eight days. Therefore, the Jews also light wax candles or oil lamps for

56 Aram.: "supplication."

57 Heb.: "Shmoneh Atzeret."

58 Heb.: "Simchat Torah."

59 Heb.: "Hanukkah."

60 Heb.: "miracle."

Jüden auch 8. Tage lang Wachs- oder Oehl-Lichter an/ und zwar mit einem absonderlichen Licht/ welches sie שמה nennen/ bis 8. Tage herum sind. Desgleichen auch alle Abend in ihrer *Synagoge* geschiehet/ da grosse Wachs-Lichter auf einer *Menora* מנורה oder Meßingen Leuchter gesteckt werden. Sie thun auch keine Arbeit so lang sie brennen.

Purim פורים Heist im Teutschen Looß.

Kommet her von der *Historia* Hamans/ welcher zu der Zeit des Köhnigs *Ahasverus* alle Jüden ausrotten wolte/ und daher das Looß werffen ließ/ von einen Tag zum andern/ von Monden bis auf den zwölfften Mond/ wie zu lesen im Büchlein Ester 3: 7. Dieses Fest wird gleichfals nur halb gefeyert/ dabey sie diese *Ceremonien* haben. p. 20 [C2v] Erstlich lesen sie in ihrer *Syna|goge* den Abend und den andern Morgen das Büchlein Esther/ welches sie *Megilla* מגילה nennen/ fasten den Tag voher/ weilen die Königin Esther auch den Tag gefastet hat/ dürffen auch nicht essen bis sie die *Megilla* lesen hören. In währenden lesen/ so offt der Vorsinger den Namen Haman nennet/ so fangen die Kinder mit denen bey sich habenden Hämmern grausamlich an zu klopffen/ gleich als wolten sie das Hauß einschlagen. Und wann solches zu Ende/ so beschencken sie sich unter einander mit Gaben/ sonderlich wird den Armen reichlich gegeben/ und sagen dabey: מקוים משלוח מנות איש לרעה das ist: Ich erfülle das Gesetz/ welches gebeut seinem Nechsten Gaben zu senden. Haben auch im Gebrauch/ sich zu verkleiden in *Masquen*, machen allerhand Spiele und Kurtzweil/ und ein jeder hält in seinem Hauß eine herrliche Mahlzeit. Wenn sie sich an diesem Tag bezechen/ daß sie den Unterschied nicht wissen zwischen den Seegen Mardochai/ und den Fluch Haman/ ist doch alles ein gutes Werck.

ארור המן : וברוך מרדכי :

NUn mein geneigter und günstiger Leser! so hast du gesehen was für abscheuliche und erschreckliche Fabeln und Aberglauben unter den Jüden das gantze Jahr im Schwang gehen/ doch habe ich nur das wenigste berühret/ weil es die Gelegenheit nicht leidet/ mig in Weitläufftigkeiten einzulassen. Sey zufrieden mit diesen wenigen/ laß es dir zu einer Warnung dienen/ und bitte GOtt/ daß er dich vor allen Irrthum und Aberglauben bewahren wolle. Ubrigens laß dir meine gehabte gute *Intention* in Liebe gefallen. HERR gib! daß ich und meine Müh/ in lauter Himmels-Seegen blüh/ bis daß ich zu dir reise.

AMEN.

3–4 *Menora*] *Memora B.* | **11** andern] andren *B.* | **17** beschencken] beschenchen *B.* **21** herrliche] herriche *B.* | **22** diesem] deisem *B.* | **25** für] fur *B.* | **28** mig] mich *B.*

eight days with a special light that they call שמש,[61] until the eighth day is over. The same thing happens every evening in their synagogue, because large wax candles are placed in a menorah מנורה[62] or “brass candelabrum.” Nor do they do any work while they burn.

Purim פורים[63] which in German is called *Lose*[64]
This comes from the story of Haman who at the time of King Ahasuerus wanted to exterminate all the Jews, and therefore he had lots cast from one day to next, from month to the twelfth month, as can be read in the book of Esther 3:7. This festival is also only half celebrated during which they have these ceremonies. First, they read in their synagogues in the evening and the following morning the little Book of Esther, which they call *megilah* מגילה.[65] They fast the day before because Queen Esther also fasted on that day, and they may not eat anything until they have heard the *megilah* read aloud. During the reading, whenever the cantor mentions the name Haman, the children begin savagely to bang hammers that they have brought with them as if they wanted to break down the house. And when this is over, they give each other gifts, especially the poor are given plenty, and say: מקוים משלוח מנות איש לרעהו,[66] that is, “I fulfil the law that commands sending one’s neighbour gifts.” They also have the custom to dress up in masks, to play all kinds of games and pastimes, and everyone has a wonderful meal in his house. If they get themselves so drunk on that day that they do not know the difference between Mordecai the blessing and Haman the curse, it is all a good deed.

ארור המן : וברוך מרדכי[67]
Now, my kind and favourable reader! You have seen what abominable and terrible fables and superstitions are current among the Jews all year long, but I have only touched upon the smallest part because the opportunity does not permit me to go on at length. Be content with this small part, let it serve you as a warning, and ask God to protect you from all error and superstition. Moreover, let my good intentions please you in love. Lord, make it so that I and my efforts flourish in sheer heavenly blessings until I travel to you.

Amen.

---

61 Heb.: “helper.”
62 Heb.: “lamp, candelabrum.”
63 Heb.: “Purim, lots.”
64 Germ.: “lots.”
65 Heb.: “megilah, scroll.”
66 Heb.: “Fulfilled is the giving of gifts from one person to another.”
67 Heb.: “Cursed is Haman and blessed is Mordecai.”

Bibliography

Adams, Jonathan. "Hebraiske ord i *Jødernes hemmeligheder* (1516)." *Danske Studier*, 105 (2010): 31–50.

Adams, Jonathan. *Jews in East Norse Literature: A Study in Othering in Medieval Denmark and Sweden*. 2 vols. Religious Minorities in the North: History, Politics, and Culture, vol. 4. Berlin/Boston: De Gruyter, 2022.

Adams, Jonathan. *Lessons in Contempt: Poul Ræff's Translation and Publication in 1516 of Johannes Pfefferkorn's* The Confession of the Jews. Universitets-Jubilæets danske Samfund, vol. 581. Odense: University Press of Southern Denmark, 2013.

Adams, Jonathan, and Cordelia Heß, eds. *The Medieval Roots of Antisemitism: Continuities and Discontinuities from the Middle Ages to the Present Day*. New York/London: Routledge, 2018.

Andrén, Anders. "The *Judensau* in Uppsala." In *Myth, Magic, and Memory in Early Scandinavian Narrative Culture: Studies in Honour of Stephen A. Mitchell*, edited by Jürg Glauser and Pernille Hermann, 351–70. Acta Scandinavia, vol. 11. Turnhout: Brepols, 2021.

Annerstedt, Claes. *Upsala universitets historia*. Vol. 2: *1655–1718 – Senare afdelningen: Universitetets organisation och verksamhet*. Uppsala: Almqvist & Wiksell, 1914.

Annerstedt, Claes. *Upsala universitets historia*. Vol. 3: *1719–1792 – Senare afdelningen: Universitetets organisation och verksamhet*. Uppsala: Almqvist & Wiksell, 1914.

Anton, Carl. *Kurzer Entwurf der Erklärung Jüdischer Gebräuche sowol geistlicher als weltlicher zum Gebrauch akademischer Vorlesungen entworfen*. Helmstadt: s.n., 1751.

Baron, Salo W. "Newer Emphases in Jewish History." *Jewish Social Studies* 25, no. 4 (1963): 235–48.

Baumgarten, Elisheva. *Mothers and Children: Jewish Family Life in Medieval Europe*. Jews, Christians, and Muslims from the Ancient to the Modern World. Princeton and Oxford: Princeton University Press, 2007.

Bell, Dean Phillip, and Stephen G. Burnett, eds. *Jews, Judaism, and the Reformation in Sixteenth-Century Germany*. Leiden: Brill, 2006.

Bengtsson, Herman "Samtida mode eller antisemitism? Demonisering och rasistiska tendenser i medeltidens bildkonst." *Iconographisk post: Nordisk tidskrift för bildtolkning · Nordic Review of Iconography* 3, no. 4 (2016): 4–41.

Berntson, Martin. "Myten om tvångsdöpta turkar i Stockholm under 1600-talet." *Historisk tidskrift* 142, no. 1 (2022): 3–28.

Bezelius, Christophorus. *Die Herrlichkeit des Christenthums/ Welche GOtt/ nach seiner überschwenglichen Barmhertzigkeit und Liebe/ Unter der Vorsorge Sr. Königl. Maytt. zu Schweden/ Zween Jüdischen Männern/ Israel Mandel und Moses Jacob/ Nebst ihren Weibern und Kindern im Jahr Christi 1681. kund gethan hat/ Bey deren Tauffe/ Am Fest-Tage Michaelis geprediget und mit einer Zugabe warhafftiger Begebnissen auch gründlicher Erörterung der Frage; Ob eine allgemeine Bekehrung der Jüden zu hoffen sey?* Stockholm: Heinrich Käyser, [1684].

Blomkvist, Nils, Stefan Brink, and Thomas Lindkvist. "The Kingdom of Sweden." In *Christianization and the Rise of Christian Monarchy: Scandinavia, Central Europe and Rus' c. 900–1200*, edited by Nora Berend, 167–213. New York: Cambridge University Press, 2007.

Bodenschatz, Johann Christoph Georg. *Kirchliche Verfassung der heutigen Juden sonderlich derer in Deutschland in IV. Haupt-Theile abgefasset aus ihren eigenen und anderen Schriften umständlich dargethan und mit 30 sauberen Kupfern erläutert*. 4 vols. Frankfurt [am Main]/Leipzig: Johann Friedrich Becker, 1748–49.

Brilkman, Kajsa. *Undersåten som förstod: Den svenska reformatoriska samtalsordningen och den tidigmoderna integrationsprocessen*. Skellefteå: Artos, 2013.

https://doi.org/10.1515/9783110986938-009

Burnett, Stephen G. "Distorted Mirrors: Antonius Margaritha, Johann Buxtorf and Christian Ethnographies of Jews." *Sixteenth-Century Journal* 25 (1994): 275–87.

Burnett, Stephen G. "Luther's Chief Witness: Anthonius Margaritha's *Der gantz jüdisch glaub* (1530/1531)." In *Revealing the Secrets of the Jews: Johannes Pfefferkorn and Christian Writings about Jewish Life and Literature in Early Modern Europe*, edited by Jonathan Adams and Cordelia Heß, 183–200. Berlin/Boston: De Gruyter, 2017.

Burnett, Stephen G. *From Christian Hebraism to Jewish Studies: Johannes Buxtorf (1564–1629) and Hebrew Learning in the Seventeenth Century*. Leiden: Brill, 1996.

Carben, Victor von. *Dem durchleuchtigsten/ hochbegorenen fursten und herren*. Cologne: [Heinrich Quentell Erben], 1508/09.

Carben, Victor von. *Opus aureum ac nouum et a doctis vivis diu exspectatum*. Cologne: Heinrich von Neuss, 1508.

Carlebach, Elisheva. "Attribution of Secrecy and Perceptions of Jewry." *Jewish Social Studies* 2, no. 3 (1996): 115–36.

Carlebach, Elisheva. *Divided Souls: Converts from Judaism in Germany, 1500–1750*. New Haven/London: Yale University Press, 2001.

Carlebach, Elisheva. *Palaces of Time: Jewish Calendar and Culture in Early Modern Europe*. Cambridge, MA: Harvard University Press, 2011.

Carlsson, Carl Henrik. *Judarnas historia i Sverige*. Stockholm: Natur & Kultur, 2021.

Castro Lusitani, Benedicti à. *Serenissimæ ac Potentissime Principis ac Dominæ Dn. Christinæ, Suecrum, Gothorum, Vandalorumque Reginæ, &c. Medici Monomachia sive certamen medicum: Quô verus in febre synocho putrida cum cruris inflammatione medendi usus per venæ sectionem in brachio demonstratur, præposterus autem ejus abusus per sanguinis missionem in pede, tanquam perniciosus improbatur*. Hamburg: Jacobus Rebenlinus, 1647.

Cawallin, Severin. *Lunds stifts herdaminne: efter mestadels otryckta källor*. Vol. 1. Lund: Gleerup, 1854.

Christian, Magnus. *Tractätgen von denen Jüdischen Fabeln und Aberglauben, So sie haben von ihrer Kranckheit an, bis zum Tode, Begräbniß und Trauer, Was sie dabey vor Ceremonien und Aberglauben brauchen Und Wie dieser Aberglauben widerleget wird; Bestehend in Achtezehan Puncten Aberglauben, Und eben so viel Widerlegungen oder Gegentheilen*. S.l.: s.n., 1718.

Cohen, Jeremy. "Traditional Prejudice and Religious Reform: The Theological and Historical Foundations of Luther's Anti-Judaism." In *Anti-Semitism in Times of Crisis*, edited by Sander L. Gilman and Steven T. Katz, 81–102. New York: New York University Press, 1991.

Coudert, Allison P., and Jeffrey S. Shoulson, eds. *Hebraica Veritas? Christian Hebraists and the Study of Judaism in Early Modern Europe*. Philadelphia: University of Pennsylvania Press, 2004.

Deutsch, Gotthard, and Henry Malter. "Prossnitz, Löbele (Prosṭiẓ)." *The Jewish Encyclopedia*. Vol. 10, edited by Isidore Singer et al., 225b. New York: Funk & Wagnalls, 1901–06.

Deutsch, Yaacov. "Polemical Ethnographies: Descriptions of Yom Kippur in the Writings of Christian Hebraists and Jewish Converts to Christianity in Early Modern Europe." In *Hebraica Veritas? Christian Hebraists and the Study of Judaism in Early Modern Europe*, edited by Alison Coudert and Jeffrey S. Shoulson, 202–33. Philadelphia: University of Pennsylvania, 2004.

Deutsch, Yaacov. *Judaism in Christian Eyes: Ethnographic Descriptions of Jews and Judaism in Early Modern Europe*. Translated from the Hebrew [(2004) יהדות בעניים נוצרים] by Avi Aronsky. New York: Oxford University Press, 2012.

Diemling, Maria. "Anthonius Margaritha on the 'Whole Jewish Faith': A Sixteenth-Century Convert from Judaism and his Depiction of the Jewish Religion." In *Jews, Judaism, and the Reformation in Sixteenth-Century Germany*, edited by Dean Phillip Bell and Stephen G. Burnett, 303–33. Leiden: Brill, 2006.

Diemling, Maria. "'As the Jews Like to Eat Garlick': Garlic in Christian–Jewish Polemical Discourse in Early Modern Germany." In *Food and Judaism*, edited by Leonard J. Greenspoon, Ronald A. Simkins, and Gerald Shapiro, 215–34. A Special Issue of Studies in Jewish Civilization, vol. 15. Omaha, NE: Creighton University Press, 2005.

Diemling, Maria. *"Christliche Ethnographien" über Juden und Judentum in der Frühen Neuzeit: Die Konvertiten Victor von Carben und Anthonius Margaritha und ihre Darstellung jüdischen Lebens und jüdischer Religion*. University of Vienna, Diss. Phil., 1999.

Dreves, Lebrecht. *Geschichte der katholischen Gemeinden zu Hamburg und Altona: Ein Beitrag zur Geschichte der nordischen Missionen*. Schaffhausen: Verlag der Huter'schen Buchhandlung, 1850.

Elyada, Aya. "Protestant Scholars and Yiddish Studies in Early Modern Europe." *Past and Present* 203 (2009): 69–98.

Engel, David. "Away from a Definition of Antisemitism: An Essay on the Semantics of Historical Description." In *Rethinking European Jewish History*, edited by Jeremy Cohen and Moshe Rosman, 30–53. Liverpool: Liverpool University Press, 2008.

Eskhult, Josef. "Andreas Norrelius' Latin Translation of Johan Kemper's Hebrew Commentary on Matthew." Uppsala University, PhD thesis, 2008.

Eskhult, Mats. "'Rabbi' Johan Kempers skrifttolkning – en maktpåliggande frihet." In *Ordets makt och tankens frihet: Om språket som maktfaktor*, edited by Rut Boström Andersson, 159–67. Uppsala: Studentbokhandeln, 1999.

Eskhult, Mats. "Svensk stormakt och levande hebreiska: exemplet Joh. Kemper." In *Den nordiska mosaiken: Språk- och kulturmöten i gammal tid och våra dagar*, edited by Rut Boström Andersson, 97–103. Uppsala: Studentbokhandeln, 1997.

Ettinger, Shmuel. "The Beginnings of the Change in Attitude of European Society towards the Jews." *Scripta Hierosolymitana* 7 (1961): 193–217.

Even-Shemuel, Yehuda. מדרשי גאולה. פרקי האפוקליפסה היהודית מחתימת התלמוד הבבלי ועד ראשית האלף השישי [*Midrashei Geula: Chapters of the Jewish Apocalypse Dating from the Completion of the Babylonian Talmud until the Sixth Millennium*]. Jerusalem: Mosad Bialiḳ, 1953/54.

Fabre-Vassas, Claudine. *The Singular Beast: Jews, Christians, and the Pig*. Translated from the French [*La bête singulière: Les juifs, les chrétiens et les cochons*] by Carl Volk. European Perspectives: A Series in Social Thought and Cultural Criticism. New York: Columbia University Press, 1997.

Faierstain, Morris M. (ed.). *Jewish Mystical Books: Book of Visions and Book of Secrets*, preface by Moshe Idel. The Classics of Western Spirituality. New York: Paulist Press, 1999.

Feuchtwanger-Sarig, Naomi. "Synagoga Veritas? Johannes Pfefferkorn and his Synagogue Descriptions in the *buchlijn der iuden beicht*." In *Revealing the Secrets of the Jews: Johannes Pfefferkorn and Christian Writings about Jewish Life and Literature in Early Modern Europe*, edited by Jonathan Adams and Cordelia Heß, 97–119. Berlin/Boston: De Gruyter, 2017.

Frey, Winfried. "'Der Juden Spiegel'. Johannes Pfefferkorn und die Volksfrömmigkeit," in *Volksreligion im hohen und späten Mittelalter*, edited by Peter Dinzelbacher and Dieter R. Bauer, 177–93. Paderborn: Schöningh, 1990.

Fürst, Julius. *Bibliotheca Judaica*. Vol. 3. Leipzig: Wilhelm Engelmann, 1863.

Gow, Andrew Colin. *The Red Jews: Antisemitism in an Apocalyptic Age 1200–1600*. Leiden: Brill, 1995.

Graf, Johannes, ed. *Judæus Conversus: Christlich-jüdische Konvertitenautobiographien des 18. Jahrhunderts*. Frankfurt am Main: Peter Lang, 1997.

Guthertz, Johann Friedrich. *Beschreibung der Jüdischen Ceremonien und Gebräuche der heutigen Juden, daß sie dabey Gottes Gebot hindansetzen, und die Aufsätze ihrer Väter weit höher achten*. Brieg: Tramp, 1747.

Guthertz, Johann Friedrich, and Christian Gottlieb Hamburger. *Beschreibung derer Ceremonien und*

Gebräuche der heutigen Juden: daß sie dabey Gottes Gebot hindansetzen, und die Aufsätze ihrer Väter weit höher achten in einem kurzen Auszuge nach der Wahrheit vorgestellet. Frankfurt [am Main]/Leipzig: s.n., 1755.

Hammarström, Per. "I sällskap med judar: Association, assimilation och konversion i Stockholm 1809–1838." In *Nationen så in i Norden: En festskrift till Torkel Jansson*, edited by Urban Claesson, Henrik Edgren, Bo G. Hall, and Lars M. Andersson, 157–68. Skellefteå : Artos & Norma bokförlag, 2013.

Hammarström, Per. "Israels omvändelse som jordens fulländning: Antijudiskhet och antisemitism i Missionstidning för Israel 1874–1885." In *Makt, myter och historiebruk : Historiska problem i belysning*, edited by Stefan Dalin, 123–42. Skrifter i Humaniora vid Mittuniversitetet. Sundsvall: Mittuniversitetet, 2014.

Hammarström, Per. "Judiska konvertiter till kristendomen i Stockholm 1775–1870." *Historisk tidskrift* 140, no. 1 (2020): 31–65.

Hammarström, Per. "Luthersk kyrkotidning vs. Sanningsökaren: 'Judefrågan' i kristen offentlig debatt i Sverige under 1870- och 1880-talen." In *Moderniteten som framgång och tragedi: En vänbok till Lars M. Andersson om ett föränderligt 1900-tal*, edited by Mattias Hessérus, Karin Kvist Geverts, Pontus Rudberg, and Malin Thor Tureby, 239–48. Lund: Nordic Academic Press, 2021.

Hammarström, Per. "Omvändelseberättelser, judemission och svensk lågkyrklighet runt sekelskiftet 1900." In *Från legofolk till stadsfolk: Festskrift till Börje Harnesk*, edited by Erik Nydahl and Magnus Perlestam, 137–53. Skrifter från Institutionen för Humaniora. Härnösand: Institutionen för Humaniora, 2012.

Hellström, Gunnar. *Stockholms stads herdaminne från reformationen intill tillkomsten av Stockholms stift: Biografisk matrikel*. Stockholm: Stockholms kommunalförvaltning, 1951.

Heß, Cordelia. "The Medieval Roots of Antisemitism in Sweden: Old Swedish and Latin Manuscript Traditions." *Nordisk judaistik · Scandinavian Jewish Studies* 34.1 (2023): 6–22.

Hodgen, Margaret T. *Early Anthropology in the Sixteenth and Seventeenth Centuries*. Philadelphia: University of Pennsylvania Press, 1964.

Holm, Erika. "Bilden av hat." *Judiska krönika* 65, no. 4 (1997): 16–18.

Holm, Gösta. *Epoker och prosastilar: Några linjer och punkter i den svenska prosans stilhistoria*. Lundastudier i nordisk språkvetenskap, ser. A, vol. 17. Lund: Studentlitteratur, 1970.

Hsia, Ronnie Po-Chia. "Christian Ethnographies of Jews in Early Modern Europe." In *The Expulsion of the Jews: 1492 and After*, edited by Raymond B. Waddington and A. H. Williamson, 223–35. New York: Garland, 1994.

Isaksson, Bo, Mats Eskhult, and Gail Ramsay, eds. *The Professorship of Semitic Languages at Uppsala University 400 Years: Jubilee Volume from a Symposium Held at the University Hall, 21–23 September 2005*. Studia Semitica Upsaliensia, vol. 24. Uppsala: Acta Universitatis Upsaliensis, 2007.

Israel, Jonathan I. *European Jewry in the Age of Mercantilism, 1550–1750*. 2nd edn. Oxford: Clarendon Press, 1989.

Jacobs, Neil G. *Yiddish: A Linguistic Introduction*. Cambridge: Cambridge University Press, 2005.

Jellinek, Adolph. *Bet ha-Midrasch: Sammlung kleiner Midraschim und vermischter Abhandlungen aus der älteren jüdischen Literatur*. Leipzig: F. Nies, 1853–77.

Joëlsson, Nathanaël. *Judiska lagstiftningen, eller Gamla testamentets stadgar, jämte de talmudiska tilläggningar och ceremonier, hwilka af hwarje jude iakttagas*. Vol. 1, no. 1. Stockholm: Kumblinska, 1801.

Kaufmann, Thomas. "Luther and the Jews." In *Jews, Judaism, and the Reformation in Sixteenth-Century Germany*, edited by Dean Phillip Bell and Stephen G. Burnett, 69–104. Leiden: Brill, 2006.

Kaufmann, Thomas. *Luther's Jews: A Journey into Anti-Semitism*. Oxford: Oxford University Press, 2017.

Kessler, Edward. *Bound by the Bible: Jews, Christians and the Sacrifice of Isaac*. Cambridge: Cambridge University Press, 2004.

Kirchner, Paul Christian. *Jüdisches Ceremoniel, D. i. Allerhand Jüdische Gebräuche, Welche Die Juden in und ausser dem Tempel, bey allen und jeden Fest-Tagen, im Gebeth, in Opffern, in Bedeutungen, in Copulation, in Auslösung der Erstlinge, im Sterben und Begräbnissen, in Erbschafften, in Essen und Trincken und dergleichen mehr pflegen in acht zu nehmen*. Erfurt: Weinmann, 1717.

Kirn, Hans-Martin. *Das Bild vom Juden im Deutschland des frühen 16: Jahrhunderts. Dargestellt an den Schriften Johannes Pfefferkorns*. Texts and Studies in Medieval and Early Modern Judaism, vol. 3. Tübingen: J. C. B. Mohr [Paul Siebeck], 1989.

Klemming, Gustaf Edvard, and Johan Gabriel Nordin. *Svensk boktryckeri-historia 1483–1883 med inledande allmän öfversigt*. Stockholm: P. A. Norstedt & söner, 1883–84.

le Roi, Johann F. A. de. *Die evangelische Christenheit und die Juden in der Zeit der Herrschaft christlicher Lebensanschauungen unter den Völkern*. Vol. 1: *Von der Reformation zur Mitte des 18. Jahrhunderts*. Karlsruhe/Leipzig: H. Reuther, 1884.

Levine, Lee I. *The Ancient Synagogue: The First Thousand Years*. New Haven: Yale University Press, 2000.

Lewien, Johann Christoph. *Ein Tractätlein von denen jüdischen Fabeln und Aberglauben so sie haben von ihrer Geburth an biss zur Beschneidung und Kirch-Gang, was sie dabey vor Ceremonien und Aberglauben, gebrauchen und wie diese Aberglauben wiederleget werden: bestehend in fünff Puncten Aberglauben und eben so viel Wiederlegungen und Gegentheile*. S.l.: s.n., 1722.

Lindberg, Bo S. *Inte vid helt sunda vätskor: Gustav Vasa och hans söner ur ett medicinhistoriskt perspektiv*. Uppsala: Uppsala universitet · Medicinhistoriska museet, 2017.

Ljungberg, Johannes. "Det respekterade samvetet och den riskabla samvetsfriheten: Perspektiv från det tidiga 1700-talets riksdagsdebatter och statliga utredningar." In *Samvete i Sverige: Om frihet och lydnad från medeltiden till idag*, edited by Linde Lindkvist and Johannes Ljungberg, 77–100. Lund: Nordic Academic Press, 2021.

Luther, Martin. *Om judarna och deras lögner*. Gothenburg: Ernst Hansson, 1934.

Luther, Martin. *Om judarna och deras lögner*. Stockholm: Svea rike, 1943.

Majern, Christoph Paul. *מינהגים. Das ist derer heutigen Jüden Ceremonien, und Gebräuche*. Wittenberg: Johann Wilken, 1678.

Maler, Bertil. "Drottning Kristina, Abraham Teixeira, Daniel de Prado och greve Bernardino de Rebelledo." *Nordisk judaistik · Scandinavian Jewish Studies* 2, no. 1 (1977): 22–26.

Marcus, Ivan G. *The Jewish Life Cycle: Rites of Passage from Biblical to Modern Times*. Seattle: University of Washington Press, 2004.

Marcus, Moses. *The Ceremonies of the Present Jews*. London: J. Roberts, 1728.

Margaritha, Anthonius. *Der gantz Jüdisch glaub mit sampt ainer gründtlichen vnd warhafften anzaygunge/ Aller Satzungen [...] Mit schönen vnd gegründten Argumenten wyder jren Glauben. Durch Anthonium Margaritham Hebrayschen Leser der Löblichen Statt Augspurg/ beschriben vnd an tag gegeben*. Augsburg: Steiner, Heinrich von Augsburg, 1530.

Martin, Ellen. *Die deutschen Schriften des Johannes Pfefferkorn: Zum Problem des Judenhasses und der Intoleranz in der Zeit der Vorreformation*. Göppingen: Kümmerle, 1994.

Mears, Abraham [Gamliel Ben Pedahzur]. *The Book of Religion, Ceremonies and Prayers of the Jews: In their Synagogues and Families on All Occasions*. London: J. Wilcox, 1738.

Michman, Dan. "Anti-semit-ism: When and Why was the Term Coined and Embraced and is it Still Useful?" Keynote lecture for the conference *Global Perspectives of Antisemitism*, Bar Ilan University, 12 June 2023/23 Sivan 5783.

Morosini, Giulio. *דרך אמונה. Via della fede mostrata a'gli ebrei*. Rome: Sacra Cong. de Prop. Fide, 1683.

Munck af Rosenschöld, Viktoria. *Främlingsbilder: Om judar och judendom i medeltida danskt och svenskt kalkmåleri*. Master's dissertation, Lunds universitet, 2007.

Nilsén, Anna. *Program och funktion i senmedeltida kalkmåleri: kyrkmålningar i Mälarlandskapen och Finland 1400–1534*. Stockholm: Kungl. Vitterhets Historie och Antikvitets Akademien, 1986.

Nirenberg, David. *Anti-Judaism: The Western Tradition*. New York: W. W. Norton, 2013.

Noack, Thomas. "Die Bibelübersetzungen von Swedenborg und Tafel." *Offene Tore Jahrbuch* (2014): 131–87.

Nyman, Magnus. *Press mot friheten: opinionsbildning i de svenska tidningarna och åsiktsbrytningar om minoriteter 1772–1786*. Uppsala University, PhD thesis, 1988.

Oberman, Heiko A. *The Roots of Anti-Semitism in the Age of Renaissance and Reformation*. Translated from the German [*Wurzeln des Antisemitismus: Christenangst und Judenplage im Zeitalter von Humanismus und Reformation*] by James I. Porter. Philadelphia: Fortress Press, 1984.

Osten-Sacken, Peter von der. *Martin Luther und die Juden: Neu untersucht anhand von Anton Margarithas "Der gantz Jüdisch glaub" (1530/31)*. Stuttgart: Kohlhammer, 2002.

Pamp, Bengt. *Svensk språk- och stilhistoria*. Lund: Gleerup, 1971.

Petri, Olaus. *Samlade skrifter af Olavus Petri*, edited by Bengt Hesselman, 4 vols. Uppsala: Sveriges kristliga studentrörelse, 1914–17.

Pfefferkorn, Johannes. *Der Joeden Spiegel*. Cologne: Johannes Landen, 1507.

Pfefferkorn, Johannes. *Nouiter in lucem data: iudeorum secreta*. Translated from the Latin [*Libellus de Judaica Confessione*] by Poul Ræff. Copenhagen: Poul Ræff, 1516.

Picart, Bernard. *Cérémonies et coutumes religieuses de tous les peuples du monde*. 7 vols. Amsterdam: Bernard, 1723–37.

Pollack, Herman. *Jewish Folkways in Germanic Lands (1648–1806): Studies in Aspects of Jewish Life*. Cambridge, MA: The M.I.T. Press, 1971.

Reich, Wilhelm Friedrich. *Tractätgen von denen Jüdischen Fabeln und Aberglauben, So sie haben von ihrer Kranckheit an, bis zum Tode, Begräbniß und Trauer, Was sie dabey vor Ceremonien und Aberglauben brauchen Und Wie dieser Aberglauben widerleget wird; Bestehen in Achtezehn Puncten Anberglauben, und so viel Widerlegungen oder Gegentheilen*. Gotha: s.n., 1717.

Reich, Wilhelm Friedrich. *Das andere Tractätlein von denen Jüdischen Fabeln und Aberglauben, So sie haben von ihrer Geburt an/ bis zur Beschneidung und Kirchgang, Was sie dabey vor Ceremonien und Aberglauben brauchen, Und Wie dieser Abergleuben widerlegt wird; Bestehend in fünff Puncten Aberglauben, Und eben so viel Widerlegungen oder Gegentheile*. Gotha: s.n., 1719.

Rubin, Noga. "*Sefer Lev Tov*, Prague 1620: The First Edition of the Book?" *Zutot: Perspectives on Jewish Culture* 5, no. 1 (2008): 121–27.

Schoeps, Hans-Joachim. "'Rabbi' Johan Kemper in Uppsala: Ein Beitrag zur Geschichte und Theologie der Sabbatianer." *Kyrkohistorisk tidskrift* 45 (1945): 146–77.

Schreckenberg, Heinz. *Die Juden in der Kunst Europas: Ein historischer Bildatlas*. Göttingen: Vandenhoeck & Ruprecht, 1996.

Seeligmann, Christian Gottlieb. ספר מנהגים של יום טוב וחתנות *Jüdischer Ceremonien Von der Jüden Hochzeiten/ Fest- und Feyer-Tagen Durchs gantze Jahr. Nebst ihrem dabey habenden Aberglauben/ Zum Dienst der Warheit vorgestellt*. Jena: Ritter, 1722 / Hamburg: Rose, 1722 / Stockholm: Johan Laurentius Horrn, 1725 / Lund: Ludovig Decreaux, 1737.

Seeligmann, Christian Gottlieb. *Ein Tractätlein von denen jüdischen Fabeln, und Aberglauben, so sie haben, von ihrer Geburth an, bis zur Beschneidung und Kirchen-Gang, was sie dabey vor Ceremonien gebrauchen, und wie diese Aberglauben widerleget werden; bestehend in: fünff Puncten Aberglauben, und eben so viel Wiederlegungen und Gegentheile, aufgesetzt*. Lund: Ludovig Decreaux, 1740.

Seidman, Naomi. *Faithful Renderings: Jewish-Christian Differences and the Politics of Translation*. Chicago: University of Chicago Press, 2006.
Selig, Gottfried. *Der Jude, eine Wochenschrift*. 9 vols. Leipzig, 1768–72.
Selig, Gottfried. *Der Jude, oder Altes und Neues Judenthum*. 3 vols. Leipzig: Rumpf, 1781–87.
Shachar, Isaiah. *The Judensau: A Medieval Anti-Jewish Motif and its History*. Warburg Institute Surveys, vol. 5. London: Warburg Institute, 1974.
Svanberg, Ingvar, and Mattias Tydén. *Tusen år av invandring: en svensk kulturhistoria*. Stockholm: Gidlund, 1992.
Tissard, François. *De Judeorum ritibus compendium*. Paris: Egidius Gourmontius [Gilles de Gourmont], 1508.
Trachtenberg, Joshua. *Jewish Magic and Superstitions: A Study in Folk Religion*. Foreword by Moshe Idel. Rev. edn. Philadelphia: University of Pennsylvania Press, 2004.
Trachtenberg, Joshua. *The Devil and the Jews: The Medieval Conception of the Jew and its Relation to Modern Anti-Semitism*. Rev. edn. Philadelphia: The Jewish Publication Society, 1993.
Valentin, Hugo. *Judarna i Sverige*. Stockholm: Bonniers, 1964.
Valentin, Hugo. *Judarnas historia i Sverige*. Stockholm: Bonniers, 1924.
Valentin, Hugo. *Urkunder till judarnas historia i Sverige*. Stockholm: Bonniers, 1924.
Vogt, Judith. *Jødens ukristelige image: et studie i katolsk billedmageri*. Copenhagen: C. A. Reitzel, 1996.
Voß, Rebecca. *Disputed Messiahs: Jewish and Christian Messianism in the Ashkenazic World during the Reformation*. Translated from the German [*Umstrittene Erlöser: Politik, Ideologie und jüdisch-christlicher Messianismus in Deutschland, 1500–1600*] by John Crutchfield. Detroit: Wayne State University Press, 2021.
Weisberg, Chana. *Expecting Miracles: Finding Meaning and Spirituality in Pregnancy through Judaism*. Jerusalem: Urim Publications, 2004.
Westrin, Theodor. "Anteckningar om Karl XII:s orientaliska kreditorer." *Historisk tidskrift* (1900): 1–56.
Wiedl, Birgit. "Laughing at the Beast: The *Judensau*: Anti-Jewish Propaganda and Humor from the Middle Ages." In *Laughter in the Middle Ages and Early Modern Times: Epistomology of a Fundamental Human Behavior, its Meaning, and Consequences*, edited by Albrecht Classen, 325–64. Fundamentals of Medieval and Early Modern Culture, vol. 5. Berlin/Boston: De Gruyter, 2010.
Willig, Carl Gottlieb. *Ein Tractätlein, von den jüdischen Fabeln und Aberglauben, so sie haben von ihrer Geburth an, biss zur Beschneidung und Kirchen-Gang, was sie dabey vor Ceremonien und Aberglauben, gebrauchen, und wie diese Aberglauben wiederlegt werden,bestehend: in fünff Puncten Aberglauben, und eben so viel Wiederlegungen und Gegentheile aufgesetzet*. Stockholm: s.n., 1736.
Wolf, Johann Christoph. *Bibliotheca Hebræa*. Vol. 4. Hamburg: Widow of Theodor Christoph Felginer, 1733.
Yuval, Israel Jacob. *Two Nations in Your Womb: Perceptions of Jews and Christians in Late Antiquity and the Middle Ages*. Translated from the Hebrew [שני גויים בבטנך: יהודים ונוצרים - דימויים הדדיים] by Barbara Harshav and Jonathan Chipman. Berkeley: University of California Press, 2006.
Xavier, Franciscus. *Tractatus de fabulis et superstitione Judaeorum inde a nativitate usque ad circumcisionem. Darin wird die Blutbeschuldigung gegen die Juden widerlegt*. Hamburg: s.n., 1719.
Xavier, Franciscus. *Über die abergläubischen Gebräuche der Juden in der Zeit von dem Sterben bis zum Begraben*. Hamburg: s.n., 1720.
Zunz, Leopold. "Heißt Raschi Jarchi?" *Israelitische Annalen* (1839): 328, 335.
Zunz, Leopold. *Gesammelte Schriften*. Berlin: Louis Gerschel Verlag, 1875.

Index

Biblical references

https://doi.org/10.1515/9783110986938-010

People, places, and terms